LIVERPOOL MISS

Helen Forrester was born in Hoylake, Cheshire, the eldest of seven children, and Liverpool was her home for many years until she married. She has now lived in Canada, in Edmonton, Alberta, for nearly thirty years.

The other two volumes of her autobiography, *Twopence to Cross the Mersey* and *By the Waters of Liverpool*, and her novels, *Liverpool Daisy* and *Three Women of Liverpool*, are also available in Fontana. Her most recent book is *Lime Street at Two*, the fourth volume of her autobiography.

HELEN FORRESTER

Liverpool Miss

FONTANA/COLLINS

First published by The Bodley Head Ltd 1979
First issued in Fontana Paperbacks 1982
Thirteenth impression January 1986

Made and printed in Great Britain by
William Collins Sons & Co. Ltd, Glasgow

To my family and my friends
who helped me to remember

Chapter one

It had begun to rain and I was shivering, as I manoeuvered the squeaking Chariot over the road to the corner of Castle Street. Avril was red in the face with rage. She stormed at me because I would not take her out of the pram and let her walk amid the busy lunch-time crowd. At the other end of the pram, beneath the leaking hood, Baby Edward grizzled miserably for the same reason.

Since the October day was too cold for us to walk in the park, I had brought them into the city, thinking that it would be more sheltered and that we could amuse ourselves looking in the shop windows. And now we had wandered into the business district.

Pretty secretaries, rushing back from lunch, and smart businessmen, carrying umbrellas and brief cases, glanced impatiently at the intruding pram with two grubby urchins in noisy protest. It belonged away in the slums, like the tatterdemalion who pushed it.

I did not care. I was resigned to people staring at my long, wind-chapped, bare legs, at my toes sticking through a pair of old plimsolls, at an outgrown gym slip worn without a blouse, a ragged cardigan covering part of my nakedness.

Through the increasing rain, I pushed the pram

dreamily amongst them. In my mind I was not walking in black, depressing Liverpool; I was in the countryside and then in the fine, old southern town from which I had been unceremoniously plucked two years before. It was market day, and Father and I were looking at the horses brought in for sale. As we moved about, the ploughmen, the shepherds and the farmers would touch their forelocks to the distinguished-looking gentleman, strolling around with a little daughter in the uniform of a good private school.

'*Echo! Liverpool Echo.* Read all about it!' shouted a man in a cloth cap, thrusting a paper towards the hurrying throng. I blinked, and hurriedly swerved to avoid him.

Would we always have to stay in Liverpool, I wondered depressedly. Would we always be cold and hungry?

'Oh, shut up, Avril,' I scolded crossly, and stopped the pram while I tucked an old overcoat round Baby Edward's knees and then pushed the edges of it up over her lap. 'Look, love. See up there – on the top of the town hall. There's Minerva. She's looking at you.'

Avril turned her woebegone face upwards towards the dome I had pointed out.

'See,' I said. 'She's smiling at you. Hasn't she got a lovely golden face? But I think she's got smuts on her nose, just like you.' I touched Avril's damp, little nose with a playful finger, and she sniffed and stopped crying.

Baby Edward could not see what I had pointed out; but, when I touched his nose and laughed at him, he saw hope of a game and tried to reach forward to touch my hooked nose. Tiny fingers grasped at my horn-rimmed glasses. I backed away hastily before they fell off.

Laughing at each other, we continued along the street.

Many people thought it was Britannia who sat looking down at Liverpool, but Father had told me it was Minerva, the Goddess of Wisdom, Invention and Handicrafts. He assured me that she also took care of dramatic poets and actors.

There were plenty of craftsmen in Liverpool of whom she might have been proud, even some actors and a poet or two, but most of them queued at the Labour Exchanges, their abilities unused. They stood idly round the dock gates, where ships lay in every stage of decay. They hung around outside the gaily lit public houses. Her sailors, skilled men, sat hungry in their cold kitchens, while their despairing wives nagged and their children went barefoot.

Amongst the defeated men in the queues at the Labour Exchange, Father had stood for over two years. Ruined by the Depression and, in part, by his own extravagances, he had brought us back to his native city in the hope of finding work. But, in the Liverpool wet, he had seemed like a lost butterfly, with wings beaten useless by the rain. He had watched, helpless, as Mother struggled, without medical aid, to recuperate from a major operation and a mental breakdown. Though the wartime marriage had not been a happy one, her degeneration into a haggard virago must have broken his heart.

To look at his seven children was almost too much for him. We were a hungry, ragged and increasingly unruly crew, disoriented by our parents' disasters, seven small sparrows with our beaks open, loudly demanding to be fed.

Because Mother was at first so ill, I suddenly had thrust upon me, as the eldest child, the task of caring for her and for my brothers and sisters. The Public Assistance Committee gave Father forty-three shillings a week, out of which we paid twenty-seven shillings a week for three unheated attic rooms. The remaining sixteen shillings had to cover every need of nine people; and for a time it seemed certain that Baby Edward would die for lack of milk, and I often looked with terror at our empty food shelf.

Recently, a little hope had entered our lives. Father had obtained a small clerical job with the Liverpool Corporation. He earned only a few shillings more than the Public Assistance allowance and the extra money was swallowed up by his expenses. But it was a new beginning for him.

About the same time, we obtained a bug-ridden terrace house at a few shillings less rent than our rooms. I no longer had to face the irate complaints of the tenants in the rooms beneath us, about the noise the children made. The bugs bit unmercifully and they made a horrible smell, but the children did not complain.

I had high hopes, when Father started work, that I would be allowed to go to school and then to work, and that Mother would become the housekeeper. But Mother had obtained part-time employment as a demonstrator in various department stores, and she announced that she would be continuing this work.

'Why can't you stay at home, like other mothers do?' I implored.

'The doctor said I should work – remember?'

'Yes. But that was when you were convalescent. He wanted you to walk about in the fresh air to get strong again. But you are quite well now.'

'Oh, don't be stupid, Helen. Stop arguing. We need the money.'

'But must I always stay at home, Mummy? I'm over fourteen now. I should be at work – like other girls are. Couldn't we find someone to help out at home?'

'Really, Helen. Be sensible. How could we afford to *pay* anyone?'

We did need the money, it was true, and we never paid anybody we could avoid paying but I had all the adolescent's doubts about my elders, and I distrusted Mother's motives. There had never been much love between us. I had always been taken care of by servants; in fact, Mother had never had to take complete care of any of her children. I sensed angrily that she found it easier to go out to work than to stay at home and face the care of seven, noisy children. I found coping with six brothers and sisters, who daily became less disciplined, very hard indeed.

So, as I walked through the rain along Castle Street and absent-mindedly played with Baby Edward, and diverted Avril's attention to Minerva and then to a warehouse cat stalking solemnly across the street, I was bitterly unhappy.

We had to stop, while a desk was carried across the pavement from a furniture van into an office building; and I looked again up at Minerva.

She seemed almost to float in the misty rain, and I wondered suddenly if something more than a statue was really there, some hidden power of ancient gods that we do not understand, and I said impulsively, 'Hey, Minerva. Help *me* – please.'

The big man in a sacking apron, who was supervising the transfer of the desk, turned round and asked, not unkindly, 'Wot yer say, luv?'

I blushed with embarrassment. I must be going mad with all the strain. I'm crazy.

'Nothing,' I said hastily. 'I was just amusing the baby.'

'Oh, aye,' he replied, smiling down at Edward, while the desk disappeared through a fine oak doorway. 'You can get by now, luv.'

Chapter two

I was not quite twelve when we came first came to Liverpool, and my parents were able to keep me at home because the Liverpool Education Committee did not know of my existence. I had come from another town and did not appear in any of their records. Six weeks before my fourteenth birthday my presence in Liverpool was reported by my sister, Fiona's, school teacher. And much to my parents' annoyance, I had to attend school for those six weeks.

Now I was over fourteen, my parents had no further legal obligations in respect of my education. So, at home I stayed, simmering with all the fury of a caged cat.

I had had an aunt, a spinster, kept at home all her life to be company to my grandmother, who lived on the other side of the River Mersey. This aunt seemed to have no real life of her own, and I dreaded being like her, at the beck and call of my relations, a useful unpaid servant, without the rights of a servant. She was such a shadow of a person that I never ever thought that she might help me.

I raged to myself that I was always the last to be provided with food and clothing. I did not even think about the lack of pocket money or other small pleasures – they were beyond my ken.

In our hard-pressed family, shoes and clothing

were given first to those who had to look neat for work, and then to those who went to school. I could always manage because I did not have to go out, I was told sharply.

As housekeeper, I had to apportion the food. I fed Baby Edward first, then Avril, who was nearly five, then the two little boys, Brian and Tony. After them, frail, lovely Fiona and cheery Alan. I would then serve Father, who never complained about the small amount on his plate. What was left was shared between Mother and me. Sometimes there were no vegetables left for us, and frequently no meat, so we had a slice of bread each, with margarine, washed down with tea lacking both sugar and milk.

Mother still looked so dreadfully haggard that I would sometimes say, with a lump in my throat, that I was not hungry and would press the last remaining bits of meat and vegetable upon her. All my life I had been afraid of her tremendous temper, but such fear had long been overridden by a greater fear that she might die.

In response to my frequent complaints at not being allowed to go to work, Mother often said absently, 'Later on, you will marry. Staying at home is good practice for it.'

But I had always been assured by Mother and the servants that Fiona had the necessary beauty to be married; and I – well, I did have brains.

'You can't help your looks,' our nanny, Edith, used to say, as she scrubbed my face. 'Maybe your yellow complexion is from being ill so much. It might improve as you get older.' She used to seize a brush and scrape back my straight, mousy hair into a confining ribbon bow on the top of my head; but she spent ages curling Fiona's soft waves into ringlets.

'Why do you have to be so disobedient? You're nothing but a little vixen, you are. Nobody's going to marry a faggot like you when you grow up,' she would shout exasperatedly. 'Get those muddy shoes off, before I clout you.'

In a desperate effort to save myself from spinsterhood, I learned to obey a raised voice like a circus dog. But it did not do me much good. I was still sallow and plain, sickly and irritable.

After Father found a job, I fought a great battle with my parents for permission to attend night school three evenings a week. It became the single joy of my life. There was order and purpose in the musty, badly-lit classrooms with their double wooden desks in which, for most classes, sat more than forty pupils. The bare board floors, the faded green paint and chipped varnish were much more pleasant and clean than my home.

For the first two winters of my attendance, nobody would sit by me, because I was so blatantly dirty and I stank. Only the teachers spoke to me. In some subjects I was so behind that I needed dedicated helpers. And the teachers gave me that help.

The bookkeeping teacher taught me the simple arithmetic which I had forgotten through long absence from school. The English teachers gave me essays to write, in addition to the business letters they demanded from their other pupils. They drew my attention to poems and to essays I should read. Later,

I took German and French, and again the teacher drummed additional grammar into me, and introduced me to the translated works of foreign authors. Shorthand, a possible gateway to employment, was largely a matter of practice, and I practised zealously.

I dreamed of becoming the treasured secretary of some great man of affairs, like Sir Montague Norman, the Governor of the Bank of England, to whom I had once been introduced. He had given the silent, small girl by Father's side a new shilling, and I had curled up in an agony of shyness and refused to say thank you, much to Father's embarrassment. But, of course, when I became a secretary, I would always be ready with the correct, polite remark and flawlessly typed letters ready to be signed.

During the day, as I walked little Edward in the squeaky Chariot and, particularly after my more trying charge, Avril, had joined her brothers and sister at school, I read books balanced on the pram's raincover. I discovered Trevelyan's histories and read all those that the library had. The librarian suggested histories of other countries, so I read, not only the histories of France and Germany, but those of China and Japan, of the United States and of the countries of South America.

The heroines of some of the Victorian novels I read studied philosophy in their spare time, so I plodded through the works of several German philosophers far too difficult for me.

'Don't know what they are talking about,' I told Edward crossly.

I found a book by Sigmund Freud and decided

that he did not understand females at all. And what was it that people were supposed to be repressing all the time? Men behaved like men and women behaved like women. How could they behave any other way other than by being natural?

I tied myself up in mental knots, considering Freud, and never associated his work with the strange spasms and longings in my own maturing body. To my mind, Freud did not seem to do so well at interpreting dreams as Joseph in the Bible did.

Beneath this rabid desire for an education, for knowledge, simmered a mixture of fear and rage: I felt my parents did not really care what happened to me, as long as I continued to serve them.

Chapter three

Despite our big family, I suffered great loneliness. When Father was not too tired he would sometimes talk to me about his wartime experiences in Russia or we would discuss eighteenth-century France, of which he had a considerable knowledge. Mother ordered; she did not discuss. Without pen, ink, paper or stamps, I could not write to the school friends I had left behind in my earlier life. In fact, at first my parents refused obdurately to allow me to write.

'Why not?' I demanded crossly.

'Because it costs money, and there may be some creditors who still want to trace your Father.'

They also forbade me to write to my grandmother, Father's mother, with whom I had always spent several months of each year. Grandma, Father said, had been most unreasonable and he had quarrelled with her. I suspected that she had finally grown tired of the scandals of the gay life my parents had led before the Depression, and then of helping to pay their debts.

When I went to the local shops, I saw only older, married women, or children sent on messages, and, to me, some of the girls who lived in neighbouring streets seemed hardly human. On Saturdays and Sundays they went about in twos and threes, dressed in cheap finery. They gawked and giggled and shrieked at the gangling youths hanging uneasily about the street corners. Because their labour was very cheap, these girls had work in stores and factories. Once they were sixteen years old they usually joined their unemployed brothers.

Sometimes, when I passed a group of them as I pushed Edward along in the Chariot, they stared and laughed at me behind their hands. Garbed in the tattered remnants of my school uniform, occasionally with no knickers under the short skirt, I had to walk very uprightly lest a bare bottom be revealed to them. Once or twice they shouted at the idling boys to inquire which of them had 'caught' me. It was a long time before I realised that it was generally assumed that Edward was my illegitimate child. When I did discover it, I cried with mortification, because I knew that to have a baby out of wedlock was very wicked.

I was very vague about the origins of babies. I did not think about it very much. Dimly, uncertainly, I imagined that they came from the same place as foals and lambs and calves did. But I had never actually seen a birth and how this could be was beyond my imagining. I never equated men with stallions, rams or bulls. But, to be respectable, a child had to have a visible father or a substitute, like a gravestone, to account for his absence – that I knew. Once, when I was small, Mother dismissed our parlourmaid without a moment's notice, and I knew from the maids' gossip that she was expecting a baby – and she was not married.

Occasionally, when Edith was angry she would hiss savage remarks about my parents' lack of feeling, and quote this incident as an example of it. The housemaid left us shortly afterwards, in protest, according to Edith. Edith herself stayed with us until we left the district, because she was engaged to a young farmer nearby; and I clung to her as a mother substitute. She was a plump, comfortable country girl with rosy cheeks and fluffy, long brown hair, and was downright in her speech. I never doubted anything she said.

I had only two close contacts to assuage this sense of isolation. One was a very old interpreter, who sometimes sat in Princes Park to sun himself. We talked a lot about the Middle East and about other languages, as I sat and supervised the children's play. One day he was missing from his usual seat and never came again. I presumed he had died and had gone to join his wife and two sons. The boys had been killed in the war and he grieved for them.

The other friend was a Spanish woman named Cristina. She and her husband, Alonzo, lived in the basement of the house next door to that in which we had originally rented an attic. Her children were all grown up and had left home. She was extraordinarily kind to Edward and me, and it was she who had given us the Chariot in which I wheeled Edward and Avril around.

In my position as surrogate mother, I had neither time nor opportunity to play. As the children became rougher and, in order to survive, became more like the other boys and girls in the district, the gulf widened between us and there seemed to be no close communication. Even Alan, so close to me in age, was to me a child; I did not worry him with details of our empty pantry.

Because I did not have a shopping bag, the greengrocer used to wrap up potatoes and other vegetables in newspaper for me, and when I arrived home I used to read these papers. There were descriptions of local tennis tournaments amongst young people, and stories of balls and receptions. I would stand dreaming with the muddy paper in my hands, imagining myself scampering about a tennis court delivering serves that raised cheers from the onlookers; or I would think how lovely it would be to skim around a ballroom in a billowing net dress. And how good it would be to go to the theatre again. In me were the stirrings of womanhood, though I did not understand them, and I had an instinctive desire to be clean, to be prettily dressed, to hide as much as possible the ugliness which I had been assured was mine.

When I thought about it, I became so afraid of the friendless, empty future, that sometimes my legs would begin to give under me, and I would have to stop walking and cling to the pram handle until the sense of blind panic passed.

Chapter four

Mother worked on short contracts in the bigger city department stores. She demonstrated new products, like kitchen gadgets, or was engaged specially to sell slow-moving goods that might deteriorate if kept in stock too long. She slowly gained a good reputation, and stores would pass her from one to another, to get rid of piles of baby baths in unpopular colours, baby clothes that threatened to harbour moths, cameras and photographic supplies left over from the summer season, and the newest wringer washers and gas stoves.

She became an excellent saleswoman, and it used to amuse me to carry Edward into a shop and watch her demonstrate the use of a gadget. It fascinated me to observe how she could beguile housewives into impulsive purchases.

One day, Avril and I stood at a discreet distance behind her in a baby-wear department. I held Edward in my arms and, though he must have known he was watching his mother, he placidly sucked his thumb and did not call out. She was selling violently pink rubber baths.

She tenderly picked up a rubber doll and plunged it into imaginary water, talking all the time, first to the doll as if it were a baby and then to her audience, who, quite amused, slowly gathered round her. She dried the doll and dusted it with baby powder and put on its nappy. Young mothers and obviously expectant mothers were her targets, and they soon found themselves hooked into friendly conversation. Mother seemed to be able to make them feel that their baby was her only interest in life; and if they already had a baby bath, she would skilfully pass them to one of the shop assistants, whose battle for a sale of baby clothes was, of course, already half won.

Before Father went bankrupt, she had for years been a member of Operatic and Dramatic Societies, and she knew enough of stagecraft to use her voice and manner to the best effect. She was never paid enough for her ability.

She looked very attractive, despite her thinness, in a black dress and black shoes purchased from a second-hand shop. I used to cut her hair for her with Father's cut-throat razor and then curl it each morning with a pair of curling tongs, bought for a penny from the pawnbroker's oddments table set up outside his shop.

Of course, I never approached her while she was working; and Avril understood that she must be quiet and tiptoe away at an appropriate moment. I doubt if she noticed that we were there, because she never mentioned seeing us.

Avril's and my great enemies were the shopwalkers. Sometimes when we were cold, we would go into a big shop and skulk around the different departments until we became warm again. And then the shopwalker would pounce.

Shopwalkers always looked very imposing. They were usually elderly gentlemen dressed in stiff, white, Victorian wing collars and black suits. They perambulated stiffly up and down the aisles of the shops, hands clasped behind their backs. They glared ferociously at the young girls and boys who served behind the counters. Then, with a slight bow, they would lend a courteous ear to customer inquiries, the whispered remarks almost drowned by the loud rings of the containers, holding payments or change, shooting along wires above their heads on their way from the counter to the cash office.

I never argued with shopwalkers.

'What do you want?' they would snarl.

'I'm just looking,' I would say loftily, exactly as I had heard people round me say.

The usual reply was, 'You can look in the windows.'

Then they would stride crossly to the nearest door and fling it open, and Edward, Avril and I would slink out like lost puppies.

One October day, we went into a shop in which Mother was working, to get warm. Mother was selling photograph albums. Her voice penetrated clearly through the murmur of shoppers as she extolled the advantages of having an album for each particular type of photograph. Avril, Edward and I settled down to watch.

I had not been feeling well for two days. My back ached, as did my head. I had got very wet in a rain storm earlier in the week, and I shrugged off the low level discomfort as being due to this. As I watched, however, the pain in my back began to feel as if an iron belt had been suddenly clasped round my waist. Pains shot down the sides of my stomach.

I gasped to Avril that we had to go home quickly, and dragged her back to the pram, parked in the shop doorway. She protested in a loud whine as I plunked her into the pram with Edward. Panting with pain, I began the long ascent up Renshaw Street, Hardman Street and Leece Street.

The pain came in ever increasing waves. Sweat beaded my forehead and I leaned on the pram handle for support, as I almost ran for home.

In St Catherine's Street, opposite the Women's Hospital, I stopped to lean against a brick wall as a particularly agonising pain ripped down the side of my stomach. Though I stared at the hospital with glazed eyes, it did not occur to me to seek succour there. To a child, in those days, hospitals were usually where old people went to die. Fiona had once gone to hospital and her lurid tales of her experiences had been enough to frighten all of the children. So the hospital was just another impersonal red brick building to stumble past on my way home.

Avril was whining and snatching at the twig with which Edward was playing. Mercifully, they both seemed unaware that anything was wrong.

I ran the pram up to the front step of our house, and tugged at the string sticking through the letter-box. The string pulled back the lock, the door swung open and I almost threw first Edward and then Avril into the narrow hall.

The pain was again surging in my stomach.

Frightened to death, I slammed the front door,

snatched up Edward and carried him through to our back yard, leaving an angry Avril howling in the hall. Perhaps if I went to the lavatory I would feel better.

I left the lavatory door ajar, so that I could watch Edward, while I snatched down my knickers.

The torn, grey garment was covered with blood.

I thought I would faint with sheer terror.

Was it appendicitis?

Again the waves of pain. I dropped down on to the seat, clasping my stomach. When the pain eased slightly, I hitched up the soaked knickers and took Edward back into the house. I had to lie down.

Avril was sitting on an upturned paint can, nursing a stray cat which had wandered in a day or two before. She had been crying and when she saw me, she let out a fresh bellow. Normally, I would have comforted her, but this time I dumped Edward unceremoniously down beside her.

'Watch Edward,' I ordered.

Where should I lie?

My bed upstairs was a door set on four bricks and I could lie on it. But Edward might follow me up the stairs and then fall down again.

Better to go into the nicely furnished front room, a place I normally did not enter because Edward was usually with me – and he always had grubby hands and was not yet reliably watertight.

Edward did follow me in, and I hastily gave him the new, unused bronze fire irons to play with. A resentful Avril stayed with the cat.

My parents, with their usual blithe inconsequence, had furnished the front room very well on the hire purchase system, regardless of the fact that the children still slept three to a bed under a motley collection of old coats and bits of blanket; and I did not even have a bed.

I was thankful enough that day, however, to curl up on the green leatherette settee. In the foetal position the pain lessened, though during the next surge I fainted.

I sobbed to myself and prayed that Mother would come home soon. Then the scarifying spasms retreated slightly and I fell into a doze.

Father shook me gently to awaken me and asked anxiously, 'Are you all right, dear? You look very white.'

My stomach and back were tight knots of pain, increasing and decreasing like waves on a seashore. I was also shivering with cold from the unheated room. I hardly dared to move, as I whimpered out the story of the torment I was enduring.

'My underneaths are bleeding, Daddy. Do you think I've got appendicitis?'

Bent over me, he listened. Then his eyes began to twinkle, his lips to twitch. A loud guffaw burst from him.

I was horrified at such a reaction to my story.

'Daddy!' I reproached him, and then broke into a moan as the pain increased.

Father straightened up and, still smiling, let out a slow sigh of relief.

'Didn't your mother explain this to you?'

'What?'

'This – this bleeding?'

'No. Was she expecting it?' I was totally bewildered, and I sobbed as the pain hit new heights.

'Well, of course. She must have been. You're a girl.'

'Of course, I'm a girl,' I gasped. 'What difference does that make? Daddy, could you get the doctor? The pain's getting worse.' I was deeply upset at his laconic attitude.

He hesitated for a moment. Then he said, 'You just stay where you are for the moment, until Mother comes home. Fiona's making the tea. I'll ask her to bring you a cup. She peeked in here and thought you were sleeping, so she has laid the table for you and cut the bread and butter. I will make the fire in the kitchen for the children.' His voice was kind.

With eyes screwed tight to help me bear the raging pain, I put my head down again on the inhospitable green leatherette. I heard him open the door, pause a moment and then say, 'Don't be afraid, old lady. This is nothing to be frightened about. You don't need a doctor.'

I did not answer him, because I did not believe him. I could not understand how anyone could be in such pain and not need a doctor. 'Mummy, come soon,' I sobbed. Cold, indifferent Mother seemed to be the key to it all.

The door clicked again and I opened my eyes. Fiona entered, carefully balancing a coarse china cup on a saucer which did not match. Despite her care, the tea slopped as she put the cup and saucer into my hand. She looked at me anxiously from beneath a roughly cut fringe of nut brown hair.

'Daddy said to drink the tea while it is very hot. What's the matter, Helen? You look awful.'

I was shaking so much that, as I raised myself a little, I slopped the tea on to the new settee. 'I don't know, Fi,' I answered, as I tried to sip the scalding liquid. 'Daddy says it's nothing – but, oh, Fi, I've got such a terrible pain in my back and tummy – and I'm bleeding underneath.'

Fiona's pink cheeks blenched. 'Bleeding?'

I nodded affirmatively. The tea was comforting and I drank it eagerly, though it was hot enough to burn my tongue.

'Oh, Helen!' she whispered.

'Daddy said to stay here till Mummy came. Can you manage?'

'Yes, of course. Daddy's making the fire and Alan is fetching the coal for him. You rest. Mummy will come soon.' She was trying hard not to panic herself.

'Where's Edward?' I asked.

'He's in the kitchen. He's fine.'

I could feel a warm trickle between my thighs and I took deep breaths to avoid screaming in fright.

'Go and have your own tea,' I told her in a strained whisper, and she went, stopping at the door to look back at me with fearful violet-blue eyes.

'Don't be afraid, Fi,' I panted and tried to muster a smile for her sake. 'I'll be all right.'

She smiled back with sudden relief and shut the door quietly after her.

I was sure, as I sank back on to the settee, that I was on my death bed. And Father did not care!

Chapter five

Mother sat down on the green leatherette easy chair opposite to me, and took off her hat. She looked tired and irritable.

'Oh, Mummy,' I wailed. 'I've got such a terrible pain – and I'm bleeding.'

'Oh, stop crying, Helen,' Mother snapped wearily. 'There's nothing the matter with you. This is what I told you about years ago. All girls bleed every month.'

I looked at her with wide-eyed horror, while I pressed my hands into my raging stomach. 'I don't remember your telling me.'

'Of course, I did – when you were about nine.'

If she had told me, the information must have been given so obliquely that it did not then register on my childish mind.

My teeth were chattering, as I asked incredulously, 'Every month – and pain like this?'

'Of course not. It doesn't hurt at all. You have just worked yourself into a panic, and that has caused the pain. It will go away quite soon. We'll try to get some aspirins, before it is due next time.'

Mother smoothed her hair, ruffled from her hat, and got up briskly. 'I'll put a kettle on and when it is boiled, you can come into the kitchen to wash yourself. I'll get a piece of cloth and show you how to keep yourself dry.'

'Will it be like this ever again?' I asked between dry sobs.

'I doubt it, if you don't have hysterics.'

Twenty minutes later, I was seated by the kitchen fire, washed and tidied, drinking another cup of hot tea. The heat from the fire helped and gradually the pain receded, as Mother had promised.

The boys stared at me because they had been told that I had had hysterics over a perfectly normal tummy ache; and they went away, Alan to night school, Brian and Tony to play bus on the stairs.

It had been a terrifying promotion to womanhood. I felt humiliated and stupid, and blamed myself for my pain. I had been aware of changes in my body, but I was so undernourished that the changes were slight and they had come slowly enough not to scare me.

Three weeks later, I collapsed with pain in night school. The English teacher made me swallow two aspirins, told me I would be all right in an hour and sent me home. Mother said the same thing and sent me up to bed, where I groaned and moaned my way through the next eight hours or so. In the early hours of the morning I fell asleep, exhausted.

From month to month the pain persisted, and Mother became more concerned. She bought dried mint and made a tea for me to drink at the onset of the first ache. It did not help. Cristina, my Spanish friend, recommended a thick paste made with ginger spice and hot water, to be licked off a spoon. Trustingly I downed this horrible concoction, but the pain continued. Cristina laughed, and said all the pain would cease either on marriage or after having a baby.

I knew I was too bad-tempered and too plain to hope for marriage; and I was certain in my mind that, however babies came, I was not going to have one outside marriage. So I smiled dimly at her and did not reply.

All the well-meaning adults in my life assured me that menstruation was just part of growing up and that some girls had more difficulty with it than others did. Nobody suggested that I should see a doctor. Since doctors cost money, and I rarely thought of acquiring anything that required payment, it did not occur to me either.

For a week or two, I would forget the pain in the bustle of caring for the children's endless needs, and running off to night school through misty streets, where strange, shadowy women lurked; and then apprehension would begin to creep over me. I would ask Mother for some of her aspirins and store them behind the alarm clock on the kitchen mantelpiece. I learned that heat was comforting and when I saw a pile of new bricks lying on a building site, I begged two cracked ones from the bricklayer and brought them home. I heated them in the oven beside the kitchen fire, and when the onslaught began I wrapped them in newspaper and lay on the green leatherette settee, clutching them close to me. Edward began to think it was a new game and wanted a brick for himself. He thought it was a great joke to cuddle up close with the bricks between us. Since he must often have been cold, the heat was probably comforting to him, too.

One freezing winter day, I fainted in the butcher's

shop. When I came round I was in an easy chair beside a fire, in the living quarters behind his little shop. His wife was forcing brandy down my throat. She must have succeeded in getting me to swallow quite a lot, because the pain did dull slightly and I felt exhilarated and yet sleepy. Edward had been propped in a matching chair on the other side of the fireplace. White rivulets down either grubby cheek marked the passage of tears. He had, however, a cheering ring of red jam round his mouth and in one hand was holding the crumbling remains of a tart.

The tiny, stuffy room was packed with furniture, and the blaze in the hearth glanced off a gilded china shepherdess on a shining sideboard opposite to me. It danced off the glass dome covering a pair of stuffed birds and made the glasses of my hostess flash.

The butcher's wife was a tiny woman dressed in the greyish, washed-out skirt, blouse and cardigan which seemed to be the uniform of women in Liverpool. Wisps of hair had escaped from her bun and draggled round a careworn face.

'Are ye feeling better?' she asked.

'Yes, thank you,' I said. I blinked at her rather hazy face through spectacles that had slipped down my nose. 'In fact, I feel fine.'

'Aye, that's good brandy, that is. You gave me husband a real fright when you keeled over.'

'I am sorry. I get a pain each month,' I faltered shyly.

She smiled. 'Oh, that was it, was it? Oh, aye. Brandy was the best thing to give you then. Does a lot for a woman at such times.'

'It seems to,' I said blithely.

Then I remembered the children's lunch, yet to be made. 'I must go home,' I said hastily. 'My brothers and sisters will be coming from school.'

'Think you'll be all right? You only live down the road, don't you?'

'Yes.'

I got to my feet. They did not feel very certain as to where the floor was; but I managed to stagger over to Edward and to pick him up. He put his arms round my neck, and sent a shower of pastry crumbs over the threadbare carpet.

Reeling slightly, I again thanked the butcher's wife. She laughed.

'It's nothing. Aye, brandy's gone to your head, hasn't it?'

'It has,' I giggled. 'But the pain is less.' I wanted to kiss her, but decided I could not aim straight. So I said effusively, 'Thank you very, very much,' and staggered, still giggling, through the lace-draped door to the shop, which she held open for me. She smiled broadly at me, as I passed.

Though sometimes the pain would rise above the effects of the brandy, and I had to stop walking and grip the handle of the old pram until the wave passed over, I hummed most of the way home. I was merrily drunk for the first time.

I rolled round the icy living room and the kitchen as I boiled and thickened the minced meat I had bought; it was as well that it was ground, otherwise it would have been unchewable. I peeled the potatoes and boiled them to a mush, before the penny in the gas meter ran out and the gas stove refused to deliver any more heat. I spread clean newspaper on the table, and laid it. Seated on a wooden chair, I waited, at first happily, for the children to come in. But as the effects of the brandy began to seep out, the chill of the dirty, comfortless room began to invade – and the pain was once more paramount.

Edward, too, was chilled and hungry and began to whimper. I took him up on my knee and wrapped us both in the old coat I used to cover him in the pram. It smelled of urine and long use. We warmed each other a little. He sucked his thumb and dozed, while I wept silently on to his scurfy little head.

I wished I had some more brandy or anything else which would stop the grinding misery within me. As I waited, I saw suddenly the expression of pain which frequently lay on my father's face – and in a burst of warm understanding I realised why he needed to drink sometimes. The burden of bereavement from the loss of most of his friends, in a war which, though it seemed a long time ago to me, was probably still quite close to him. The terror of the long, threatening winters he had spent in tiny block houses or in peasants' huts during the Russian campaign, while the Revolution surged around the tiny force, so that one did not know who was friend and who was foe—what must it have done to a delicate refined man unused to any hardship? And then to lose his fortune, his occupation, his home? He sometimes told us stories of his experiences both during the war and after it, and he made us laugh. But if one analysed those stories, they were filled with horrors.

Poor Father. I laid my head against Baby Edward's and wept not only for my own suffering, but for my father's distress as well.

Getting drunk can leave one very low afterwards, I discovered.

Chapter six

There was a silent conspiracy between Father, Mother and me, to keep from the other children as many of our troubles as possible.

We had as many creditors in Liverpool as Father had had in wealthier days. Now, instead of the tailor, the dressmaker, the grocer and wine merchant, I faced the owner of the local tobacco and newspaper shop trying to collect for the cigarettes he had supplied, the club man demanding the weekly payment for cheques issued to my parents by finance companies, for purchase of clothing at specific shops; the agent of our aristocratic landlord threatening to throw us into the street; the heavy-jowled hire purchase man growling threats to repossess our well-chosen sitting-room furniture.

Ominous clouds of danger seemed to encompass me and sometimes, after getting rid of a desperate bullying man, I would lean against the inside of the front door and cry with pure fright.

In our other life in another world, I had often heard Mother say to the parlourmaid that she was not at home to anybody, and she thus evaded personal confrontation with creditors, whose bills and threatening letters lay in the wickerwork wastepaper basket.

Here in Liverpool I had to answer the door myself. No frilly-aproned, sniggering parlourmaid stood between me and outraged men whose own livelihood was precarious. Occasionally, when I felt defeated, I would prevail on Fiona to answer the heavy bangs on the front door. She looked much younger than her age and had an expression of angelic innocence. She would say with convincing firmness, 'Everybody is out except me.'

The creditor would leave, grumbling under his breath, to mount his bicycle parked at the pavement's edge. They never shouted at her, as they did at me.

I was never given a fixed sum from which to do the housekeeping. A shilling or two was slung on to the kitchen table with instructions to buy a list of groceries for which the money was almost invariably inadequate. Consequently, Edward and I tramped for miles to save a halfpenny on a loaf of bread, or to go to a shop which would cut a twopenny, half-pound pack of margarine into quarter pounds, so that we could buy one. Stores which did this kind of splitting up of goods could, with patience, make a lot more than those which did not. A sixpenny one-pound pot of jam, sold by the ounce at a penny an ounce, assured an excellent profit. Such shops were filled with black-shawled, unwashed women and skinny, barefoot children.

We had two lots of wages coming into the house; yet no housekeeping priorities were ever established. Mother sometimes made long lists of proposed expenditures and debt repayments, but they always ended up being tossed into the fireplace. Creditors who shouted the loudest and threatened most got paid eventually; those that did not received nothing.

Cajoling credit out of shopkeepers who respected an Oxford accent was reduced to a fine art by my parents.

I can remember one pay day Mother coming triumphantly home with a box of cream cakes, when we lacked meat, milk, shoes and soap. The children, of course, thought the cakes were wonderful, and I began dimly to understand why our rough, largely Irish, neighbours spent so outrageously on weddings and funerals, cinemas and drink, whenever they got the chance. Life seemed so hopeless that they snatched at any treat, as if they had only the present and there was no future.

There was, however, a number of families nearby with less money than we had, but whose kitchen grate always seemed to have a fire in it, though it might be of slowly collected driftwood rather than of coal. Their children, friends of Fiona, Brian and Tony, were neat and clean; they ate regularly, though I cannot remember a single fat child amongst them. Their mothers obviously mended and washed frequently and could often be seen sweeping the dust out of their front doors, across the pavement and into the gutter. I often heard the sharp snap of rugs being shaken in the back yards, and saw them kneeling on the front pavement as they scrubbed and donkey-stoned their single front step. Some of them even scrubbed the pavement itself as far as the street. The menfolk were usually craftsmen or seamen, skilled with their hands. Some of them, for a couple of shillings, rented a small allotment garden from the City. These gardens were often close to railway embankments or at the edge of the city, and good crops of fruit and vegetables were raised on them during the otherwise empty summer days.

Neither of my parents had been trained to manage money. Grandpa died when Father was six. Father was sent to an excellent public school when he was ten, a school famous for the Shakespearean plays its boys enacted. He acquired a deep understanding of French and English history, and his mathematical abilities were of university level. But nobody taught him how to keep a budget or to manage a family.

Mother was equally ill-prepared for life. She was an orphan, brought up in a convent. She learned how to embroider fine altar cloths and copes; she acquired a smattering of French and other social graces, and a great love of reading. She had a fine singing voice and she learned to sing very well, though not to professional level – that would have been vulgar. The nuns who taught her hammered in the need for virtue in women, but not the basic knowledge which would make a good housewife. Since all their charges were segregated from the opposite sex, except for the skirted priests, the girls appeared to have had a wild curiosity about men and to have forgotten their lessons on virtue. Some of the girls went home to a normal family life during their holidays. But Mother's guardian was a bachelor, so she stayed at school, to spend summer holidays taking walks with the nuns and other homeless girls, and Christmases and Easters largely in church.

Unlike most of her contemporaries, Mother had had some business experience. Her guardian was the owner of a string of libraries, and when Mother became fifteen he removed her from the convent and taught her his own business. A few years later, he married. Mother was jealous of the new wife and she ran away to North Wales, where she found a post as librarian. There, she met my father during the First World War and married him.

Now we were all suffering dreadfully as a result of their frivolous, irresponsible life after the war. Even hunger, cold, sickness and pain failed to teach them to manage any better.

Poor diet produces rotting teeth, and all of us at times had to endure severe toothache. To alleviate this, we painted the offending tooth with a pennyworth of oil of cloves. Though this did sometimes ease the pain, it did not stop the tooth from deteriorating further. Then abscesses formed. Brian and Avril often sat weeping, while I applied hot poultices to their faces until the abscesses swelled and burst. Father already had false teeth when we arrived in Liverpool. But Mother's excellent teeth began to loosen from gum disease. When one became too loose, she would wiggle it with her tongue until she could pull it out with her fingers. This must have hurt her and, of course, the gaps in her mouth did not improve her looks, which must have hurt even more. Mouths full of poor teeth were, however, very common in Liverpool, and it was not unusual, particularly in respect of women, to have lost all one's teeth by the age of twenty-five.

During the second winter of attendance at night school, I found I could not see very well. I had lost some sight and my glasses needed to be replaced.

I had also grown, so that the frames were too small for me and my already plain face was made to look even more out of proportion.

A further affliction was an annoying disease called pink eye. At different times all the family caught it. It is an acute inflammation of the eye which causes a heavy discharge, so that the eyes are sealed tight during sleep and in the daytime are flushed a sickly pink. The chemist sold me tiny packets of boracic acid which we made into a solution with hot water, and it helped when we bathed our eyes with it.

But my eyes were always sore, from too much reading through wrong glasses in a bad light. Frequently we lacked pennies to push into the gas meter for the light in the living room, so I read by candlelight or, if we had no candles, I would do my homework leaning against a lamp post, to take advantage of its dim rays. The streets were lit by gas in those days, and the lamplighter would dash on his bicycle from one cast-iron lamp post to the next to pull the chain that lit the lamp. In the early part of the night school term, it was frequently warm enough for me to do my homework in the park, sitting on a bench watching the children, or there was sometimes sufficient daylight to enable me to do it at home. But the deep winter was a time to be dreaded.

I came to my studies hopelessly tired, and always hungry. The quiet order of the school, however, helped my mind to focus; and I made such a violent effort that at the end of the first year I was awarded a very small scholarship to cover the cost of books and fees for the following year. At the end of the second year, if I passed the examinations, I was to move on to a Senior Evening Institute. There the cost of books would be greater; and I had moments of panic while I waited for the results of the examinations, wondering what I would do if I did not win a scholarship this time. And even worse, what would be my fate if I failed the examination itself? My only hope would be gone.

With the exception of Baby Edward, who was still too young, the children had been sent to a local church school as soon as they reached the proper age. They attended with reasonable regularity. If I was ill, Fiona was kept at home to help, but the boys never were. I resented this blatant discrimination. Why, I often argued, was so little attention given to Fiona's and my future? A lot of anxious talk went on about careers – never jobs – for the boys. Could not girls have careers? My parents thought such remarks were funny, and they laughed. Girls got married, they said.

At night school, the other girls were talking hopefully of getting jobs as shorthand typists or as bookkeepers, and some of them were already at work in shops and offices. They did not seem to be counting on having a husband to keep them, and yet they were all much prettier than me.

I used to watch them as they filed into class, usually dressed in hand-knitted jumpers and dark skirts, rayon stockings and high-heeled court shoes. Their hair was always neatly cut and sometimes Marcel waved. They used powder and lipstick generously and some of them, I noted wistfully, had necklaces, bracelets or rings.

I knew that unless a miracle occurred, I would never manage to look as nice as they did. What chance would I have of employment, even if my parents allowed me to apply for jobs? Just to get rid of the vermin on me would be a heavy task for a Fairy Godmother.

Chapter seven

At best, the years between the ages of fourteen and seventeen are not very balanced ones. Children tend to query and test the prevailing social mores, even when they have been blessed with a stable, comfortable life. Like a window pane through which a stone had been thrown, our family's life had splintered in every direction, leaving a gaping hole. Almost nothing that I had been taught as a child by Edith or by Grandma seemed to have any relevance in slums where fighting and drunkenness were everyday occurrences, where women stood in dark corners with men, fumbling with each other in a manner I was sure was wrong, though I had no inkling of what they were actually doing; a place where theft was considered smart and children openly showed the goods they had shoplifted; where hunchbacks and cripples of every kind got along as best they could with very little medical care; where language was so full of obscenity that for a long time I did not understand the meaning.

Even in my parents' light-hearted group, ideas had been discussed, theories of existence expounded, the war knowledgeably refought in the light of history. The availability of music, paintings and fine architecture had been taken for granted. Dress, deportment, manners, education, politics, were all taken seriously.

The comparison was so hopeless that I sometimes

laughed. But beneath the laughter, I seethed with suppressed rage and apprehension that even if the rest of the family managed to crawl out of their present sorry state, I would be left behind.

Like water held behind a dam shaken by an earthquake, this anger burst through my natural diffidence, one wet February afternoon, when a plainly dressed lady called at our home. Her hair was hidden by a navy blue coif, such as our Nanny used to wear; and her glasses were perched on a nose reddened by the chilly weather. She wore no makeup, and her navy blue mackintosh reached down to ankles covered in grey woollen stockings. Her black shoes, flat and frumpy, shone despite the rain. I did not recognise my fairy godmother.

When I opened the door a fraction, afraid of yet another creditor, she blinked at me in a friendly way and asked if Mother was at home.

'No,' I said cautiously, shifting Edward in my arm so that he could peep round the door, too, without my dropping him.

'And you are – ?'

'I'm Helen,' I said. 'Mother will be at home this evening, if you would like to call again then.'

The wind drove a patter of rain down the street and I heard the click of the front door of the next house as it was opened; the unemployed man next door liked to lean against his own door jamb and listen to my battles with creditors. He would stand and laugh as if he were watching a variety show, and then when it was over, would spit on to our doorstep and go indoors again.

Our visitor's eyes flickered towards the other door. Then she said, 'I wonder if I might come in for a moment. I am sure I can explain to you what I have come about.'

Reluctantly, I opened the door wider so that she could step into the muddy hallway. I heard the next door snap shut.

I ushered her into our front room. She paused on the threshold and looked round the room in obvious surprise, as she took off her gloves. The comparison between Edward's and my threadbare appearance and the pleasantly furnished room must have struck her immediately. The bugs in the walls gave it an unpleasant smell, but in the hope that they had not yet penetrated the pristine easy chairs, I invited her to sit down.

She sat down gingerly on the edge of one of the chairs, while I stood in front of her holding Edward. I did not want to put him down because his feet were bare and very cold.

She said she had come from the church to which the children's school was attached, and I nodded, though it seemed to me to be remarkable; during the two and a half years that the children had been attending the school no one from the church had called on us, and we, being so shabby, had never attempted to attend it. In fact, I had forgotten that the church existed.

Edward sucked his thumb and laid his head in the curve of my neck, so that throughout the conversation I could hear the placid slush-slush of his little tongue.

The visitor said in a bright, brittle voice that she had heard from Brian's and Tony's teachers that their singing voices were good enough for them to sing in the church choir. She had come to inquire if my parents and the boys would be agreeable to this. She knew that Mother worked part-time and she had hoped to catch her at home.

It was never possible for me to forecast what reaction my parents might have to any new situation, so I thanked her cautiously and said that Mother would be home at five o'clock.

She smiled gently up at me, but she did not get up to leave. Instead, she sighed and looked at Edward's blue bare feet.

There was an uneasy silence, and then she said in a much softer voice, 'Did you attend our school?'

'No.'

'Or the church? Have you been confirmed?'

I cleared my throat nervously and replied again, 'No.' Then, since my replies seemed abrupt, I added, 'I go to night school. I'm in Second Year Commerce.'

'Where did you go to school?'

Her face was so kind and her interest seemed genuine, so I told her about my four years in a variety of private schools up and down the country, and said rather sadly, 'I didn't learn very much. I think, if Grandma had not taught me to read and my aunt to write, I would be illiterate.'

Very slowly, while I rocked a sleepy Edward in my arms, she drew out of me the story of my struggle to go to night school, the fact that I had no clothing to speak of and the other children very little. And with a catch of self-pity in my voice, I finished up, 'There doesn't seem to be much hope for anything better for me, unless I can be free to go to work. But there is nobody to look after little Edward, if I do go.'

'But things seem to be getting better,' she comforted me. 'This room is very nicely furnished.'

'I'd rather Edward had some shoes and socks,' I retorted suddenly. 'And you should see the other rooms.'

The dam burst. 'Come and see,' I almost ordered her, and strode to the open door. 'Come and have a look.'

Without a word, her face very serious now, she got up and followed me.

Up the stairs she trudged after me, to the icy, fetid bedrooms, to inspect three iron beds with thin, old-fashioned felt mattresses on them, the urine stains uncovered by any sheet. I had tidied up the bits of blanket and old coats which we used to cover us, and some of the pillows had grubby, white pillow-cases on them.

She looked, aghast, at the door on which I slept. It was balanced on four bricks, one at each corner, and had wads of old newspaper piled on it, instead of a mattress, with a grey piece of sheeting to tuck over them. There was no other furniture, and, of course, there was no bathroom.

In a passion, I swept her downstairs again, to look at the living room, with its bare deal table, assorted straight chairs and upturned paint cans helping out as seats. The only sign of comfort was an old, wooden rocking chair and a very ancient, greasy-looking easy chair, in which was curled a stray cat which Brian had earlier brought in from the rain. On the tiled floor lay a piece of coconut matting, filled with dust. In the old-fashioned iron fireplace I had laid the fire, ready for the children's return home.

The kitchen looked quite large because there was so little in it. A small table flanked the gas stove, and there was a built-in soapstone sink in one corner. The opposite corner was taken up by a brick copper, with a tiny fireplace under it, for boiling washing. Our single bucket stood under the sink; our only wash basin caught the steady drip from the house's cold water tap.

Long lines of shelves ran down one side of the kitchen. They held a motley assortment of rough, white dishes and cups, two saucepans and a dripping tin. A kettle sat on the gas stove beside a tin teapot. A small wooden table held our bits of food, a packet of tea and a blue-bagged pound of sugar, some margarine in a saucer and a new loaf.

I was shivering with cold and with emotion, and my visitor turned pitying, gentle eyes upon me. 'Don't you have a fire?' she asked. They were the first words she had spoken during our lightning tour.

'Edward and I manage during the day. I light the fire for the children coming home at lunch time, and then I re-light it for tea time.'

I realised, as I said this, that Edward and I were just as vulnerable to cold as the others were, but we remained in the frigid house while everyone else spent the day in warm buildings. No wonder my joints hurt when I moved. No wonder Edward sometimes cried because of the cold.

'Where do you keep your food?' she asked.

'On the table here,' I said. 'I buy it every day.'

She bit her lips, as she pondered over the bread and margarine, and I said a little defensively, 'Avril or Tony will fetch a pint of milk from the dairy when they come in.'

Edward had gone to sleep, so I led the way back into the living room and laid him down in the easy chair, after pushing off the cat. He stirred, but slept on, his tiny legs spread-eagled. 'I'll get something to cover him,' I told the lady, and flashed up the stairs to get a coat.

When I came back she was still standing where I had left her, and I hastily tucked Edward up before I turned again to face her. My hysterical outburst had spent itself and I felt exhausted and ashamed.

'I'm sorry,' I said, 'I should not have bothered you with all this. And I'm sorry it is not very clean – but I have nothing but a broom and cold water with which to clean – it's just impossible.'

She seemed wrapped in thought, almost as if she had not heard me. Then she smiled at me and very sweetly. 'I'm glad you did show me,' she said reassuringly. 'I can understand better the struggle you are having. Don't be discouraged – things have a way of getting better.'

I tried to smile back. I did not believe her.

'I'll come again this evening to see your mother,' she continued, a briskness in her voice.

As I let her out of the house, she turned again to me. 'Now remember. No getting discouraged.'

I nodded, then she smiled and went out into the

rain; her coif was wet before I had closed the door.

She came, as promised, and then again and again. She was a deaconess, and mother seemed to like her because she was a gentle, cultivated woman. First Brian and, later, Tony joined the choir, their white surplices saving them from the embarrassment of their shabby clothes. Later on, Tony became an altar boy, and the faith he acquired whilst kneeling in the richly decorated sanctuary never left him. He has always been an active member of the Church of England. The experience must also have helped mischievous, highly-strung Brian because, if nothing else, he learned music by many of the great composers in a bright and beautiful church. Both boys were allowed to retain the one shilling and eightpence per month paid to them for their services.

Apparently, the deaconess did not tell Mother of her tour of our house. She did, however, become an earnest advocate on my behalf. Not all fairy godmothers carry wands.

Chapter eight

Father sometimes bought a *Liverpool Echo* to read on the tram while coming home from work. A day or two later, before using the newspaper to start the fire, I would read it, as I knelt on the coconut matting in front of the big, black, living-room fireplace.

I loved news of Royalty. Love of the royal family is still quite strong, but in those days, particularly amongst women, it was close to a passion. All our princes were officially handsome, and the courtship of Princess Marina of Greece by Prince George, Duke of Kent, was a romance about which many a girl like myself dreamed wistfully. I followed developments from day to day with eager anticipation.

I also began to read the advertisements, including the ones offering jobs. Once or twice I stole a piece of Mother's notepaper and wrote replies. I was not a very good writer but I had been taught in night school how to formulate a letter of application, which was a help. I said I had been privately educated. This was true and absolved me from having to say how few years I had been in school. It also accounted for my not having matriculated, because some girls in private schools did not attempt matriculation; they went on to finishing schools in France or Switzerland. I imagined my childhood friend, Joan, was currently attending such a school.

I told the advertisers that my appearance was neat, which was far from true, and that I was honest and hardworking and was attending evening school. With the letters wrapped in a piece of newspaper to keep them clean, I then wheeled Edward down the long hill to Victoria Street in the centre of the town and hopefully slipped the letters in the box provided by the *Liverpool Echo* for replies.

Nothing happened.

Then one day I received a reply, in handwriting far worse than my own, from a sweet shop near St Luke's Church. They wanted an assistant and asked me to come to see them the following day, a Saturday. I was dazzled at the prospect.

I hummed all day, as I waited for the evening and the return of my parents. The children found me unusually cheerful at midday, as I gave them their main meal, a half-pound of stewed, minced beef between the six of them, and mashed, boiled potatoes. They had tea to drink. Because they had a little meat, the food was an improvement over their fare during the first two years of our sojourn in Liverpool. It was also easier for me to cook it. An old gas stove was already in the house when we rented it and it worked, as long as I had the necessary penny to put in the meter. In the apartment we had first rented, I had had to cook on a bedroom fireplace, on a fire frequently kept going with scraps of rubbish culled from the streets.

Mother and Father ate their lunches in cafes or took a sandwich with them. My lunch was boiled potato. This, with the occasional addition of carrots, onions or cabbage, was my staple meal for a number of years, and it is doubtful if my parents fared much better.

Lack of nourishing food added to my parents' irritation. Mother had always had an uncontrollable temper, terrifying to maids, children and shell-shocked husband alike, and these towering tantrums reached almost insane levels during the years in which we suffered so much poverty. So I approached my parents on the subject of the letter with the care of a cat stalking a mouse.

To no purpose.

Father, at times, seemed to live in a never-never land of illusion. He looked at me over his gold-rimmed spectacles, while he sipped a last cup of tea, and said firmly that I could not be spared to go to work at present. Who would look after Edward and the children's dinner if I were absent? Perhaps, later on, he added cheerfully, I could be sent to a teachers' training college and become a school mistress. But a shop assistant? Never! That would be absurd.

I almost laughed at him. 'Which training college would consider a girl with only four years of schooling?'

His reply was drowned out by Mother's musical contralto saying firmly, 'Your place is at home, Helen. It's the most sensible arrangement. In a few years you will marry and by then Edward will be old enough to look after himself.'

I was aghast. 'But you've always said – everybody's always said – that I am so plain. How can I get married if I'm so ugly? I'll be stuck here for ever.' I began to cry, with hot, angry sobs.

I knew I looked terrible. I had seen myself once in a shop mirror. There was no greater ragamuffin in all Liverpool than me. So when Father and Mother suddenly started to talk about my getting married, I became almost hysterical. I had read fairy tales where princes materialised from all kinds of unexpected places – but the princesses were always beautiful. No prince was going to come riding by to collect a sinful, ugly hoyden like me. I had shed many bitter tears already over this fact, so successfully hammered into me by a thoughtless mother and impatient servants. I classed myself with cripples who could hope only for attractive souls, appealing to God alone.

In a paroxysm of rage all the frustration came pouring out. I raved helplessly at them, and they raved back.

I was ungrateful, thoughtless, utterly selfish. Father and Mother worked all day to maintain the family. The least I could do was to keep house. And, anyway, no matter what happened, I could not become a shop assistant. It was beneath our station.

Beside myself with fury, I ranted that Mother was working in shops. Why could not I?

The boys, with long-suffering looks, went out to play with their friends. Avril burst into tears and howled nearly as loudly as me. At such times she would go so red that even her scalp under the fine golden hair and thick scurf would flush, and she would look as if she might at any moment drop dead from apoplexy.

Fiona snatched up her ancient doll and fled upstairs.

It was night school time, but still the argument raged. Finally, I could think of no more reasons why I should go to work and I sat on a paint can, buried my face in my hands and wept uncontrollably.

Mother angrily seized some of the dishes off the table and took them into the kitchen. Father folded up the newspaper into a neat small square, a habit he had. Suddenly the room was quiet, except for miserable sobs from Avril, sitting on the floor in a corner, sturdy small legs spread in front of her. Occasionally, she would kick the tiles with her heels, as if to emphasise her misery. My own sobs were almost silent; I had long ago learned to cry without drawing attention to myself.

Mother returned from the kitchen and Father said rather carefully to her, 'Perhaps if Helen went to this shop for the interview and saw how much work a place like that would expect from her, she might realise that she is better off at home. Small places like that usually squeeze the very life blood out of their people.' He ran one finger along the newspaper's folds to neaten it, while I looked up quickly at Mother.

I swallowed a sob. Here was a tiny opening. I was sure I could do any amount of work. I conveniently ignored the fact that my physical condition was so poor that quite small exertions could make me dizzy, and each month I had to face a day of almost unbearable pain.

Between sniffs, I begged Mother in watery, meek tones, to let me do as Father suggested.

Mother had wearied herself with her tirade. She sat down suddenly and was quiet. Then she said resignedly that she had no work for the next day, so she supposed she might as well take me to see the shop. Fiona could look after Edward, since the following day was Saturday.

I had not considered that Mother might accompany me, and I had expected to have to face the interview alone. This had worried me, because I had no idea how one should behave or what one should say in such a situation, particularly as I did not want to give any indication of the kind of life we led. I felt instinctively that I would stand a better chance of getting work if it appeared that I came from a stable working class or lower middle class home, with less well-born parents than I had. What kind of an impact on a small businessman would Mother have, a lady who spoke 'with ollies in her mouth?'

I sighed, but made no objection to her coming. I said instead, 'I'd have to make myself look respectable, somehow.'

I looked at Mother hopefully. She was still dressed in her black business frock, though she had taken off her shoes and stockings and wore father's old bedroom slippers on her feet. Her face looked haggard under her make-up and her hair, which I had waved the night before, was ruffled and untidy.

Mother returned my look. 'Yes, you would,' she replied, so sharply that it sounded like an implied threat and made me jump apprehensively.

I was as tall as Mother, though with a much slighter frame, and after surveying me for a moment, she said I could borrow the dress she was wearing. Since it would be Saturday the following day, I could also borrow Fiona's black woollen stockings and black, flat-heeled shoes; Fiona was not consulted, and was very grumpy when she discovered what had been agreed. 'You'll tread them out,' she complained, 'Your feet are too big.'

'I'll be very careful,' I promised, as I recklessly washed my hair and then the rest of me in a quart of hot water in the tin basin, and used up the last sliver of soap we possessed. There would be a row with the boys in the morning about the lack of soap, but it could be endured.

I borrowed from Mother the only pair of scissors we had. She carried them in her handbag, so that they could not be misused, but even so, they were blunt and the nails on my right hand had to be finished off by biting them. Toenails were always left to grow until they broke off, and sometimes they looked like cruel, yellow claws before they finally cracked off.

The scissors were too small to cut hair, so I combed my unkempt locks with the family comb, also normally carried in Mother's handbag, and hoped it would stay off my face until the interview was over. When I received some wages, I promised myself, I would ask Mother if I could buy some hair clips.

Even after these efforts, I must have looked very odd in a black dress too long and too looose for me and without an overcoat, though it was late February and the weather was damp and chilly.

Full of hope, though shivering with cold, I trotted along beside Mother through the misty morning, past the Rialto Cinema and Dance Hall with its tawdry posters, and the dim outline of the cathedral, to the sweetshop.

It was a very little shop, in a shabby block of other small shops and offices. Its window, however, sparkled with polishing despite the overcast day. Through the gleaming glass I could dimly see rows of large bottles of sweets and in front of them an arrangement of chocolate boxes, all of them free of dust. Beneath the window, a sign in faded gold lettering advertised Fry's Chocolate.

Mother, who had not spoken to me during the walk, paused in front of the shop and frowned. Then she swung open the glass-paned door and stalked in. I followed her, my heart going pit-a-pat, in unison with the click of Fiona's shoes on the highly polished, though worn, linoleum within.

An old-fashioned bell hung on a spring attached to the door was still tinkling softly when a stout, middle-aged woman with a beaming smile on her round face emerged through a lace-draped door leading to an inner room.

'Yes, luv?' she inquired cheerfully.

'I understand that you wrote to my daughter about a post in your shop?' Mother's voice was perfectly civil, but the word 'post' instead of 'job' sounded sarcastic.

The smile was swept from the woman's face. She looked us both up and down uncertainly, while I agonised over what Mother might say next.

'Helen?' the woman asked, running a stubby finger along her lower lip.

'Helen Forrester,' replied Mother icily.

'Ah did.' The voice had all the inflections of a born Liverpudlian. She looked past Mother, at me standing forlornly behind her. Her thoughtful expression cleared, and she smiled slightly at me. I smiled shyly back.

I felt her kindness like an aura round her and sensed that I would enjoy being with her, even if she did expect a lot of work from me.

'Have you ever worked before, luv?' she asked me, running fingers on which a wedding ring gleamed through hair which was improbably golden.

I nodded negatively. Then cleared my throat and said, 'Only at home.'

'What work would Helen be expected to do?' asked Mother, her clear voice cutting between the woman and me like a yacht in a fast wind. She had also the grace of a yacht in the wind; but the sweet-shop owner was obviously finding her more trying than graceful and answered uncertainly, 'Well, now, I hadn't exactly thought. I need a bit o' help, that's all. 'Course she'd have to wash the floor and polish it, like, every day. And clean the window and dust the stock. And when I knowed her a bit she could probably help me with serving, like. I get proper busy at weekends – and in summer the ice cream trade brings in a lot o' kids, and you have to have eyes in the back o' your head or they'll steal the pants off you.'

Mother sniffed at this unseemly mention of underwear, and then nodded.

'And what would the salary be?'

I groaned inwardly. I was sure that in a little shop like this one earned wages not a salary.

The beginning of a smile twitched at the woman's lips, but she answered Mother gravely.

'Well, I'd start her on five shillings, and if she was any good I'd raise it.'

Even in those days, five shillings was not much. The woman seemed to realise this, because she added, 'And o' course, she can eat as many sweets as she likes. But no taking any out of the shop.'

I could imagine that this was not as generous as it sounded. After a week of eating too many sweets, the desire for them would be killed and few people would want them any more.

Mother inquired stiffly, 'And how many hours a week would she work for that?'

'Well, I open up at half past seven in the morning to catch the morning trade, you understand. And I close up at nine in the evening.' She paused a moment and then said, 'But I wouldn't need her after about seven o'clock. Me husband's home by then, and he helps me after he's had his tea. And I close Wednesday afternoons, so she'd have the afternoon off after she'd tidied up, like. Me husband helps me Sundays, too, so I wouldn't want her then either.'

I wanted the job so badly that I did not care how many hours I worked, how often I scrubbed the floor. The shop seemed so lovely and warm, after our house, and I sensed that in a rough way the woman would be kind to me. I tried to will the woman to agree to take me.

A little boy burst through the shop door, leaving the bell tinging madly after him. He pushed past us and leaned against the corner of the counter.

'Ah coom for me Dad's ciggies,' he announced, turning a pinched, grubby face up towards the sweet-shop owner.

'Have you got the money?'

'Oh, aye. He wants ten Woodbines.' A small hand was unclenched to show four large copper pennies.

The cigarettes were handed over and the pennies dropped into the wooden till.

'Now don't be smoking them yourself,' admonished the woman, with a laugh.

The boy grinned at her and bounced back to the door, his bare feet thudding. As he went through the door, he turned and gestured as if he were smoking.

'Aye, you little gint!' she said.

The interruption had given Mother time to make a rapid calculation. As the woman turned back to her, she said sharply, 'There is a law about how many hours a minor can work – and, incidentally a law about selling cigarettes to minors. I am sure that over sixty hours a week – at less than a penny an hour – are far more hours than are allowed.'

The woman shrugged huffily; her eyes narrowed, giving her a cunning expression.

'I'm sure I don't know about that,' she replied tartly. 'If she doesn't want the job she doesn't have to take it. There's others as will be grateful for it.' She sniffed, and looked at me disparagingly. 'Anyway, I wouldn't take her. The sores on her face would put the customers off. I got to have a clean looking girl.'

I looked at her appalled, hurt to the quick. In front of our broken piece of mirror, I had carefully squeezed each pimple on my face, so that the acne was temporarily reduced to raised red blotches with a fresh, golden scab on each. I had no make-up to cover the results. But I had hoped that I looked clean.

Mother's face flooded with angry colour. For a moment she looked like Avril in a tantrum. She cast a scornful glance at the shopkeeper, who stared back at her with her chin thrust upwards, quite unabashed.

'Good afternoon,' Mother snapped, as she swung round and opened the street door. The little bell tinkled crossly at being so forcibly disturbed.

'Helen, this way.'

It was an order, and I slouched out through the doorway, closely followed by my wrathful mother.

Chapter nine

Mother scolded sibilantly all the way home, and blamed me for wasting her time. I was too crushed and disappointed to respond.

Back I went to the kitchen and little Edward, who trotted patiently by my side, while I fumed miserably. In saner moments, I acknowledged that Mother had saved me from savage exploitation. But her motives in doing so were, to me, suspect. And as the years went by I felt that my increasing efficiency at home was daily making more certain that I stay there. Probably a few pennies of pocket money or a modicum of praise would have done much to soothe me. But everything I did was taken for granted. Failures were bitingly criticized. There was no one to turn to for consolation, except, occasionally, to Fiona.

And yet I yearned to love my parents and be loved in return, to have with them the tender relationship I had had with Grandma during the long months I had frequently spent with her during my childhood. But Grandma had vanished with the rest of my friends. In my innocence, I did not understand that my parents' fast and extravagant life in the post World War years had alienated every relation they had. Father's widowed mother – the last to desert them – had left her son to learn the hard way the teachings she had failed to inculcate in him when young. She probably had no conception of the depth of our sufferings.

There is no doubt that Mother never forgave her friends for deserting her after Father went bankrupt; it was as if she declared a silent, ruthless war against her own class. The depth of her bitterness was immeasurable.

I remembered well the doll-like creatures who used to frequent our drawing room and dining room. In short, beige georgette dresses, their Marcel-waved hair covered by deep cloche hats, they teetered on high heels in and out of our old home in considerable numbers. Afternoon tea or dinner were served by a parlour maid in black and white uniform. Sometimes well-tailored young men, who also had time to waste, came to drink a cocktail or have a cup of tea.

Several times, a man vanished from the usual circle. One of the ladies would say, between puffs on a cigarette held in a long holder, 'Gas, dahling – his lungs couldn't stand it,' or 'He was loaded with shrapnel – a piece moved round to his heart. Too utterly devastating.'

I was allowed to attend the tea parties. Edith would dress me in my best frock, usually shantung silk, long white socks and brown lace-up shoes, and I would sit and nibble a piece of cake and watch the prettily dressed visitors. I soon learned that most of the men were unemployed, ex-army officers; they usually had some private means left them by more enterprising forefathers, but as prices rose their money shrank. They had no special qualifications and sought jobs as car salesmen or vacuum cleaner salesmen. One of them regularly allowed me to reach up and touch the silver plate the doctors had implanted to replace the top of his skull; another had an artificial leg which creaked when he walked. Father himself had trouble with his hands, which had been frost-bitten during his service in Russia. He also got chest pains, forerunners of the heart attacks to come.

So, perhaps my parents' friends, bereaved, disillusioned, wounded in a war of frightful, unnecessary suffering, had so many troubles of their own that they were unable to help one of their number who had failed largely through his own inadequacies.

I was born after the war, so it was only history to me. Had I realised, when I got so cross with my parents' ineptitude, how close it still was to them, how they had already gone through the shock of seeing the kind of life they understood crumble, I would have been much more compassionate.

One windy March evening, when the children's need of clothing seemed particularly dire, Mother decided to write to some of her old acquaintances to ask for second-hand clothing. After all, she said bitterly to Father, the most she could lose was a three-halfpenny stamp, since she appeared to have lost any friendship there was.

When the children had gone to bed, she sat at one end of the living-room table and wrote three letters, while I sat at the other end and did my homework.

Three days later, a scented letter dropped through our letter box. As far as I could remember, it was the first letter, other than a bill, which we had received since coming to Liverpool.

Opening it was a ceremony, carried out under the eager eyes of the entire family.

'It's from Katie,' said Mother, naming a gay, childless married friend, as she slit the envelope with the kitchen knife.

It contained a single sheet of notepaper wrapped round a five pound note. Katie was sorry about us and sent the enclosed with love. Mother had found a technique for adding to our income.

Until she had exhausted every possible person she could think of, Mother wrote at least one begging letter a week. She rarely got money out of the same person twice. But she had had an enormous circle of acquaintances, and when she ran out of these she wrote to the parents of the children's friends and also moving letters to their teachers. After that, she wrote to people whose names she had picked out of library reference books.

She learned to write eloquently of the children's woes and her own efforts to find work. She did not mention Father in letters to strangers, perhaps to give the impression, without actually saying so, that she was widowed. She frequently passed her efforts over to me to read – one of the few times when she took me into her confidence. I had never heard of confidence tricksters and I read them admiringly, believing them to be a perfectly honourable way of earning money. After all, Grandma had always said that charity was a great virtue, and we were certainly in need.

There were many professional begging letter writers in Liverpool at that time. Earnest gentlemen sat in their tiny bed-sitting rooms and wrote passionate appeals for help to any monied person who came to their attention. They invented whole families of starving children, aged parents in need of shoes, wives dying of tuberculosis, and so on. And they made a steady living at it. In contrast, Mother could say honestly that her children were in dreadful need, even if bad management was part of the cause of it.

Some well-to-do people, including Royalty, who were bedevilled by begging letter writers, would send the letters to a charitable organisation in the city, with the request that they investigate the need; it was remarkable how generous people were when the need was found to be genuine. I do not recollect, however, anyone coming to investigate us as a result of one of Mother's letters.

Thanks to the kindness of many people unknown to me, a few comforts began to trickle into the house, amongst them a second-hand iron bed for me. The spring was hollowed out like a hammock and it was a number of years before I acquired a mattress. I shared it for a while with Edward, but it represented my first personal gain at home since we had arrived in Liverpool. It was at least another five years before I got proper blankets and sheets for it; and lying chilled to the marrow through endless winter nights was one of the greater hardships for all the children.

Sometimes parcels of clothing or bedding arrived in response to the letters. Clothing for the younger children was almost invariably given to them and it helped to keep them tidy for school. Sometimes there was clothing which fitted Mother; men's clothing was rarely sent, perhaps because of the difficulty of fitting.

The bedding was usually bundled up with some of the clothing, ready for pawning.

Seared by disappointment, I would take the cloth-wrapped parcel to the crowded pawnbroker's shop with its three golden balls hanging in front of it, and, after much good-natured haggling with the pawnbroker, I would receive four or five shillings, and a ticket so that I could later redeem the parcel.

The parcel was whisked away from the high, black counter and thrown up a chute to the pawnbroker's assistant in the store room above. After a year, if the goods had not been redeemed or interest paid on the loan, the parcel would be torn open and the contents sold. So many goods were for sale that the pawnbroker's was an excellent place to buy almost anything, from clothing and boots to an engagement ring or a bedspread or a concertina; and there were always women wrapped in shawls or in long, draggling men's overcoats, picking through the merchandise on the bargain tables set out in front of the store on fine days.

The money raised from the pawnbroker might be used for a little extra food or, more frequently, to pacify a creditor who had threatened court procedure. Cigarettes were almost always one of the first things bought with it, and sometimes Mother would go to the cinema. She often remarked angrily that if Father could afford a drink, she could afford a cinema seat.

The local newspaper-shop proprietor, after a fierce row with me because Father owed him a whole pound for cigarettes, obtained a Court Order against us. This meant that the bill had to be paid by regular instalments set by the Court, on threat of the bailiffs selling us up if we failed to pay. This added enormously to my fears, because I had stood and watched while whole houses of furniture were sold by the bailiffs for a few shillings to settle a ridiculously small debt. Mother once bought for sixpence a superb hand-made rocking chair when there were no other bids for it.

I never knew where my parents might run up another bill or who might pounce on me, as the hapless housekeeper who had to answer the door. I had always been afraid of people who shouted, and I would stand shivering with my shoulder against the inside of the door, while someone hammered and shouted on the outside.

Once or twice I considered running away, but in those days there was no support from welfare organisations for such a runaway. And who would employ someone like me?

I once threatened to go to Grandma, but my Father said grimly that she would probably turn me away, that I should be thankful for what I had. Things would get better one of these days.

Grandma had become a loving, distant dream to me, and I was shocked beyond measure at the idea that she no longer cared. Yet I believed what Father said.

Chapter ten

Spring had come at last. The trees lining Princes Avenue were stickily in bud; the privet hedges behind the low, confining front walls of the houses were already bursting into leaf, and the sparrows and pigeons were a-bustle with the need to mate.

I wheeled Edward down Parliament Street to the small Carnegie library in Windsor Street. A playful wind flipped dust and pieces of paper round its railings, against which women leaned, shopping bags on arm, to gossip in the pale sunshine. The soot-covered library was a handsome little building with high, arched windows which made it pleasantly light inside. Its battered books passed through my hands at the rate of about half a dozen a week and helped me to forget hunger, cold and humiliation. The librarians knew me and sometimes recommended a new book which had come in. In those days, librarians seemed to be great readers and both Father and I enjoyed discussions with them about books we had read.

I parked the Chariot close to the iron railings at the front. Edward was a patient child who would sit and watch the passers-by while I hastened to find something new to read.

As usual, I went directly to the section devoted to travel books. A new travel book was a great treat to me, I learned all I know of geography from them. I would carefully follow on the maps in the books journeys through countries as diverse as Tibet and Bermuda, examining myopically photographs which ranged from very fuzzy to very clear. I was always annoyed when there was no map in the book because I did not have an atlas, and poor photography was also a great disappointment. Later, more affluent generations would travel by hitchhiking the routes my fingers traced so longingly on maps.

I pushed my straggling hair back behind my ears and took off my faulty glasses to peer closer at the shelves; sometimes I could see better without the glasses than I could with them.

'Helen Forrester, isn't it?' inquired a voice from behind me.

I turned slowly, surprised that anyone should know me by name.

It was the deaconess from the church, to whom in a rage I had shown our house. It was no wonder that I had not recognised her voice. During our previous encounter, she had said so little while I had said so much. I blushed at the memory of my unpardonable outburst.

I murmured shyly that I was Helen. She looked very sweet in her coif and frumpy clothes.

'I was about to come to see you,' she announced unexpectedly. Then she glanced round the book-lined room. 'Perhaps we could talk here, though. Let's go over there.' She took my elbow and guided me into a corner of the Fiction section.

'I wanted to ask you, my dear, if you would like a

job as a telephonist. A charity I know of needs a girl, and I immediately thought of you, because you have such a pleasant voice.'

I gaped at her, struck dumb by the unexpectedness of the offer. Then I gasped, 'Oh, yes.'

She smiled at me, and continued, 'The salary is not much – about twelve and sixpence a week. Would you like me to arrange an interview for you?'

Twelve shillings and sixpence a week seemed a huge sum to me. All the wonderful things it would buy danced before me, mixed with a terrible apprehension that I would not get the job because I was so dirty and had no clothes except the grubby, ragged collection I was wearing.

The deaconess was talking. 'I thought I would ask you first, before speaking to your mother.'

At the mention of Mother, I remembered the sweet shop episode.

'My parents will never agree to it,' I said hopelessly. 'I have to look after Edward.'

'I've already thought of that,' she responded eagerly. 'Alice Davis lives a few doors away from you. She has an invalid mother who cannot be left alone and she badly needs to earn a few shillings. I am sure she would take care of Edward during the day – and she wouldn't charge much.'

A fairy godmother in a blue coif! A true fairy godmother. A wave of gratitude surged through me, but I did not know how to express it. 'Would she, really – would she do it?' I whispered.

'I'm sure she would, if I ask her.'

I was acquainted with Alice. She belonged to the

Salvation Army. I said 'good morning' to her most Sundays, as she strode along the street pushing her mother's wheelchair down to the Citadel. Her mother would be bundled up in rough grey blankets, regardless of whether it was winter or summer; and Alice wore a navyblue uniform, with a matching Victorian bonnet trimmed with a red ribbon proclaiming 'Salvation Army' across the front. Her sturdy legs were clad in sensible black stockings and the shine on her black shoes equalled that on the shoes of our local police constable. Her cheerful face shone like her shoes. Occasionally, the Salvation Army band played at the end of our street, and Alice would rush down to them, clutching her cymbals, ready to join in while they were so close to her home. Alice was rough, but Edward would be safe with her.

Please, Lord, please let it happen, I prayed silently. Aloud, I said, 'Thank you very, very much. I would love the job if you think I can do it.'

She smiled. 'Of course you can do it. Shall I call on Mrs Forrester tonight? You might like to talk to both your father and your mother first.'

'I will,' I said, though I had no real hope. Perhaps, however, with an advocate like this respectable lady, just perhaps, they could be persuaded.

'I'll come this evening, then?'

'Yes, please,' I mumbled.

In a daze, I wheeled Edward home, pushing the pram unseeingly through the usual crowds of black, white and yellow men idling at the corners. Some of them murmured resentfully as the pram brushed carelessly past them.

How on earth was I to approach Mother and Father about this offer? I worried. A chance of freedom at last, a tiny flame of hope in a very bleak world.

The whole routine of the family would have to be altered. Alan and Fiona would have to shoulder some of my work. And Alice would have to be paid. Some clothes would have to be redeemed from the pawnbroker – or obtained from somewhere else. Where would Mother find the money?

At home, I poked up the fire and began to make toast for the children's tea, while I thought once again of running away. Could I live on twelve shillings and sixpence? Boys sometimes ran away to the south, where there was more work than in financially ruined Liverpool. Occasionally, girls did, too. I had, however, read in the newspaper about the flourishing white slave traffic into which girls were sold. I was not clear what happened to white slaves, except that they were kept in bondage and abused by ruthless men until they died. I imagined them being misused like American black slaves, and I had no wish to die a dramatic death like Uncle Tom in *Uncle Tom's Cabin.* I had wept over this tragedy as a small girl and did not wish for a similar fate.

I did some careful arithmetic. A small, unheated housekeeping room could be found for about seven shillings and sixpence a week; food, say, four shillings, firing in winter would take the other shilling, leaving nothing for clothing. I did not consider that I might need tram fares – I had been walking, now, for the past three years all over south

Liverpool; make-up was beyond my experience, and pocket money an idle dream, anyway.

The children drifted in for tea and I dealt with their squabbles and their hunger as best I could.

Father and Mother returned from work soon after the children. Inside five minutes, they were quarrelling violently. I cannot remember what triggered the trouble. It did not matter, because the underlying animosity smouldered all the time and needed very little to make it flare up. As usual, they drew each child into the argument in an effort to make them take sides, and this frequently reduced Avril and Brian to hysterics as they agonised between the parents. Fiona and Alan were old enough to retreat to friends' homes if they got desperate enough, but poor Avril, Tony and Brian had no such refuges. Tony usually managed to stay a little calmer, though he was always upset, and Edward just stuck firmly in whichever lap he happened to be cradled when hostilities broke out.

Even when I was very small, I wondered why my parents stayed together. I knew a girl whose mother was divorced, and I quite envied her. But I had been fortunate in having Edith to take care of me and there were the long absences from home when I stayed with Grandma. In their conversations about the people they knew, they taught me that not all families were riven by warfare. Now, as the fight raged over the tea table, I wished passionately I could run to Grandma for help.

Alan had piled into the fight with some furious, rude remark and was sharply slapped by his father.

He shot out of the kitchen door into the back yard, raging nearly as incoherently as Father was.

Fiona wept helplessly, her head on the table. Brian and Tony stonily munched their toast, their movements nervous and uncoordinated; they did not answer the passionate appeals of Mother and Father to take their side. Avril stood behind Mother's chair, holding on to it and shaking it, as she shouted hopelessly, 'Stop, everybody. Why can't you stop?'

Neither protagonist would give way.

I was silent with despair. I hardly heard the words hurled around me or addressed to me. What was I going to do when the church lady arrived? Mother seized a cup and saucer from the table and hurled them into a corner. Through her screams of rage, I heard a knock on the front door.

The other children had also heard the sharp rat-tat. When they instinctively turned their heads towards the front of the house, Mother stopped in mid-scream.

'What was that?' asked Father, his lips turned back in a snarl.

'Someone is at the door,' I said, too much in anguish to move.

'Well, get a move on, girl. Answer it. Say we are not at home.'

Reluctantly I obeyed, feet dragging. I shut the living-room door behind me.

As I turned the lock on the front door, I wished, for the first time, that it was only a creditor. The moment I swung back the door, she was in the muddy hall and pulling off her gloves, as the wind gusted behind her.

'It's quite cold this evening,' the deaconess said cheerfully. 'Well, have you asked them, my dear?'

'I haven't had an opportunity yet,' I apologised.

Her smile faded, and she sighed. 'Never mind. I'll ask for you.'

'They said they are not at home tonight.'

From behind the closed door came the sound of renewed strife, though the level seemed more subdued. The interruption had broken the continuity of the argument. The lady laughed and looked at me conspiratorially. The living room was suddenly quiet. The feminine chuckle must have penetrated to the family.

The deaconess tucked her gloves into her handbag and said briskly, 'I imagine your mother would be at home to me. We know each other well enough to call occasionally without warning, don't we?'

I tried to smile at her as I heard the living-room door open behind me. 'Will you come into the front room?' I asked hastily. 'I'll inquire if they are at home.' These were phrases I had often heard May, our parlourmaid, use, and they came automatically to mind in such a difficult situation.

I opened the door to the front room and ushered the blue-clad lady into it, just as Avril stumped out of the other room, her eyes tearful, her mouth surrounded by black toast crumbs. She marched into the sitting room after the visitor, and stood staring at her.

I heard the deaconess speaking softly to the frightened little girl, as nervously I announced our visitor to Mother and Father. Both parents were standing motionless, like alerted hares, as they tried to judge who the visitor was.

Mother, her face and neck still red from combat, pushed past me and went into the front room. Father gave a great sigh and flopped into a chair. His hands were trembling as they always did when he was upset.

Fiona had ceased to weep and gazed up at me with great pansy eyes still dewdropped. Brian and Tony asked Father's permission to leave the table.

'Yes,' he said peevishly.

They scrambled down from their chairs and I heard the back door slam, as they went out to play in the last of the evening light.

Father turned back to me. He gestured with his head towards the front room. 'What does she want?' he asked. I think he was always nervous that his wife had done something outrageous which he did not know about.

I knelt down on one knee and began to pick up the bits of cup and saucer that Mother had shattered. Through my draggling hair, I hesitantly answered him.

'She has come about me.'

He sat up straight and looked at me. 'About you? What have you done?'

I stood up and faced him. 'I haven't done anything. She's got a job for me. And she's keen that I should take it.'

'What nonsense!' He sniffed, and then added angrily, 'I wish she would mind her own business.'

'She means well, Daddy.'

'She should hie her back to her nunnery and stay there. She has no right to interfere with my family.' He thumped the arm of his chair. 'She has no right to put ideas into your head.'

I stood irresolutely before him, the broken dishes in my hand. I wanted to put my arms round him and beg him to intercede for me. When I was small and he was not too busy, we had been able to talk to each other. But this ease between us had got lost in the maelstrom of trouble which had engulfed us. So I hesitated, and the opportunity was lost.

'Where is the newspaper?' he demanded irritably.

I put down the broken china and picked up the paper from the floor, where it had been thrown down during the quarrel. He shook out the pages and vanished behind them.

Chapter eleven

Washing greasy dishes in cold water without soap is not easy. The grease impregnates the hands and forms an oily ring round the basin. I had two saucepans left over from lunchtime to wash, and their exteriors were covered with soot from the fire. To save the gas, I had put the pans on the living-room fire to finish the cooking of the children's midday dinner. Now the soot floated revoltingly amid the grease. I did not dare to put a kettle of water on the fire as I was afraid of irritating Father further by pushing past him. I let the water from the single cold water tap cascade into our tin wash basin to sweep out some of the soot, and stood gazing at the backs of my hands in the light of the candle I had just lit.

My hands were small and well-formed. The skin was ingrained with dirt and round the quicks the nails were almost black. The nail tips were long and uneven and filled with grime. Sometimes I tried to clean my nails with a sliver of wood, but without plenty of soap it was a hopeless task. I remembered the scathing remark of the sweet-shop lady, and, with a stomach clenched with apprehension, I realised that to make myself thoroughly clean and neat for work would be very difficult.

In a painfully sweet voice, Mother suddenly called me from the front room, and I was jolted back from depressing contemplation to frightening reality.

I wiped my hands on the family's solitary towel which hung on a hook on the back door. The towel was nearly black from use by nine people and it invariably stank. I added a streak of soot to it.

Father had joined Mother and the deaconess, Miss Ferguson, in the front room, and was perched uncomfortably on the edge of one of the easy chairs. I could feel the blood draining from my face; and, as I gave Miss Ferguson a nervous smile, I wanted to faint.

'Miss Ferguson insists on hearing from you personally that you do not want to go to work,' announced Mother frigidly, and Miss Ferguson shifted uncomfortably around in her chair. 'I understand she spoke to you in the library this afternoon.'

'Yes, she did,' I whispered, in answer to the second statement.

Miss Ferguson took a large breath, as if the effort to speak was going to be too much for her. Then she turned her worried-looking face towards me, and said very carefully, 'I have been trying to persuade Mr and Mrs Forrester that it would be greatly to your advantage if you could go to work and be trained for some worthy occupation, and that it would be possible for them to spare you from the house to do this. I tentatively made an appointment for you for tomorrow afternoon at three o'clock.'

Father made a wry face, and I had the feeling he wished he was a hundred miles away.

Mother interjected, 'Helen will not be keeping the appointment, I am sure.'

Undeterred, Miss Ferguson pressed on. 'I have assured your mother that you will be working with nice women, all from good families, and I am sure you will be well trained.' She turned to Father and said very earnestly, 'She would be quite safe there,' as if any other place of work was probably a cesspool of immorality.

Father was embarrassed. 'I don't doubt it,' he muttered, and looked across at Mother.

I looked down at my hands resting on the back of the easy chair, and burst into tears. It was easy to see that my parents were boiling with suppressed anger at the intrepid little deaconess's foray into our affairs. They would raise hell when she was gone. I put my head down on my hands and cried until the tears ran through the fingers on to the shiny green leatherette of the chair.

Avril, who had been sitting on a matching poof, sucking her thumb and watching the proceedings very quietly, suddenly started to cry as well, and was immediately whisked into the hall and the door shut on her. I could hear her wailing in the dark.

'Don't cry, Helen,' said Father ineffectually.

Mother turned to Miss Ferguson, as she shut the door after Avril.

'Helen is obviously very upset, Miss Ferguson. Perhaps we should discuss the matter with her and let you know in a day or two what has been decided.'

I was not just upset; I was nearly out of my mind with despair. But the tears came with such tremendous force that I could do nothing to stop Miss

Ferguson being quickly, though politely, eased out of the house.

When I heard the latch on the front door click shut, I flung myself wildly on to the settee and continued to sob. What was the use of a day or two, when the appointment was for tomorrow?

It was fortunate that Father and Mother had already exhausted themselves with one quarrel that evening, and Mother, therefore, contented herself with ordering me to control myself, while Father asked how they could talk to me when I was making such a racket.

I made a violent effort, sat up and dried my face with the backs of my hands.

Mother looked so terribly exhausted, when finally I lifted my eyes to look at her, that I felt an overwhelming guilt and said, 'I'm sorry, I really am.'

Mother had been dreadfully ill just before we arrived in Liverpool. She had had no real care since then, so that she was soon drained of strength. I truly did not want to add to her hardships; yet I could not bear my present miseries much longer.

'Have you been talking to Miss Ferguson or to the Fathers at the church, behind our backs, Helen?' asked Mother. There was an implied threat in the question. Family affairs, we had been taught from infancy, were not discussed with servants or outsiders. Childish revelations, whenever discovered, had been dealt with by a sharp spanking or, sometimes, caning.

I was too upset to care or remember about Miss Ferguson's tour of our house, so I said indignantly that I had not. I took off my glasses and wiped them down the front of my gym slip, while I tried to think how my going to work could be managed.

'You know, Daddy,' I said, approaching the weaker partner, 'the salary offered is quite good. It would mean three salaries coming into the house.'

'Alice Davis wants ten shillings a week to look after Edward,' interrupted Mother. 'And there are still the other children's needs.'

'Surely if everybody helped, we could manage between us. It wouldn't hurt Fiona and Alan to help – they are quite big now.'

Mother dismissed Fiona and Alan with a gesture.

'On Sundays I could clean the house, and, if Fiona and Alan could make the tea, I could put Edward and Avril to bed when I came in.'

'It is not very practical,' Father said. 'Someone has to be at home to make the children's lunch.'

My temper was rising, that incorrigible devil which dwelt within me. I fought it by praying each night that I would manage to keep calm until prayers the following night, and so often I failed. I made tremendous efforts to control it, not realising that insufferable people and unbearable circumstances could make a saint angry.

I stood up and flounced towards the door.

'I am going for the interview, whether you like it or not. I may never get such a chance again. I must take it.'

'Helen, you forget yourself,' exploded Father.

'Oh, no I do not. For once, I am remembering myself.'

'Helen!'

Mother's voice came in behind him. There was more than a little malice in her tone, as she said, 'You have no suitable clothing, anyway.'

'I'll borrow some,' I replied recklessly.

'Helen! That would not do at all.' Father sounded genuinely shocked.

'It's no worse than borrowing money,' I retorted, and his face whitened. I had hit home most cruelly. Savagely satisfied, I fled from the room and back to the sooty saucepans.

Chapter twelve

I peeped over the railings surrounding the area. The curtains had not yet been drawn over the barred windows of my dear Spanish lady's basement living room. In the soft light of her oil lamp, I could see her sitting in an easy chair on one side of the fireplace, with a pile of crochet work on her lap. Her handsome, black-eyed husband, Alonzo Gomez, sat opposite her on another easy chair. He was reading the newspaper, while a large black cat crouched on his shoulder, its lemon-shaped eyes glowing in the light. The remains of their evening meal still lay on a nearby table.

I opened the iron gate and ran down the winding iron steps of the area, knocked at the plank door under the main entrance steps of the house and, after waiting a moment, walked in.

I was engulfed by skinny brown arms and a flood of mixed Spanish and English words of welcome. Alonzo put down his paper as I entered their living room.

'Come, come,' he said, gesturing towards the blazing fire with one hand, while he smoothed his handlebar moustache with the other. He got up and bowed me to his chair.

Suddenly, I was in a different world.

Despite the general squalor, there were many

people like Cristina Gomez who created real homes out of attic crannies or damp basements in once fashionable houses. There was never much money, though Alonzo Gomez worked as a carter for a fruit merchant in the city and the couple's children were now grown up and had moved away; and yet the old kitchen had an air of cosiness, as if affection was exuded from the walls with the damp. The few pieces of well-worn furniture, the primitive cooking utensils hanging by the fireplace, the stone floor covered in the centre by a piece of coconut matting, all were clean and well cared for. Alonzo was known to have an explosive temper, but the explosions seemed to be rare, and at other times there was a lot of good-natured banter and teasing, when they laughed like children.

Cristina Gomez had a good collection of clothing. She had once told me that whenever her husband earned overtime money or won on the horses, he would spend the money on clothes for one or the other of them. And now I needed to borrow a whole outfit.

All Cristina's clothes were black, even her petticoats, but that would not matter. Black was the uniform of work. It was usually worn by shop assistants and by many office workers.

After I had been cuddled and installed in Alonzo's chair, while he sat on a straight-backed one, an orange was sliced and put on a saucer and a cup of strong, black coffee set before me on a brown-painted orange box. The health of all the family was inquired after by Cristina, and Mother's poor health sighed over with much rolling of eyes and shrugging of shoulders.

At the mention of Mother's health, my determination faltered. If I went to work, her load would inevitably be increased. Then, as Alonzo told a funny story about a cart horse which loved to steal apples from displays outside the Fruit Exchange, I realised that, on average, Mother did not earn much more than I would get, that if she stayed at home to look after the family, we would be very little poorer. And my resolve hardened.

Cristina asked me how I was faring at night school, and this gave me a chance to talk about my own troubles and the reason for my visit, to borrow a dress, shoes and stockings, if she would be kind enough to lend them to me.

'Certain, certain, you can have anything.' She paused and looked uneasily at her husband. 'I would not wish to anger your good Mother, though.'

'She need never know where I got the clothes from,' I assured her. 'I only need them for one afternoon. I'll think of another way of getting clothes for the job itself.' I had already thought of a possible source from which to obtain at least a dress, but not quickly enough for the interview.

Though Cristina might have qualms about offending my parents, her swaggering gallant of a husband had none. I think he had always resented my parents' supercilious attitude towards their neighbours and his pride had been hurt.

'Give them to her,' he ordered his wife, with such

a lordly gesture that the cat was disturbed from his shoulder and did a quick leap to the floor.

Cristina's eyebrows went up expressively and she shrugged. She got up from her chair, flicked her black shawl up round her shoulders, and said kindly to me, 'All right, my little one. Let us see what we can find.'

I bounced out of my chair, suddenly gay, and followed her. She had lent me old shoes on one or two earlier occasions, when she had observed that my running shoes were soaking wet; and long ago her gift of the Chariot had saved me the heavy task of carrying Edward everywhere when he was too young to walk.

Half an hour later, I glided through our back door, through the deserted kitchen and down the steps to the coal cellar, where I stowed away a brown paper bag containing shoes and stockings. On the inside of the cellar door, I hung a coat hanger which held a black dress with matching jacket shrouded in a piece of discarded curtaining.

'Who is there?' Father's voice came sharply from the living room.

'It's only me, Daddy.'

I opened the door and went in. The gaslight had been lit. The mantle was broken and the flame hissed and flickered over the comfortless room. The fire was out. Upstairs, I could hear the boys fighting in their bedroom. Presumably, Fiona, Avril and little Edward were asleep, since there seemed no sound from them.

'Where have you been?' Father's voice was freezing.

'To see Mrs Gomez. Where's Mummy?'

'She has gone down to Granby Street to buy a pair of stockings.' He flicked over a page of his book impatiently. 'You know I don't like you mixing with local people.'

I hung my head, but did not reply.

'If you have no homework to do, you had better go to bed.'

'Yes, Daddy.' I wondered if I should give him his usual good-night kiss, but he did not look up from his book, so I crept by him and went forlornly up to bed. I knew I had hurt him beyond forgiveness, and perhaps he really did not know how to cope with me.

Chapter thirteen

In the usual rush to get everybody off to school and themselves off to work, my parents had no time to discuss Miss Ferguson's visit with me. Mother gave me a shilling, as usual, to buy food, and two extra pennies to put in the gas meter. Father asked me to wash his second shirt ready for the next day, and suddenly Edward and I had the house to ourselves.

Greatly daring, I borrowed a large pair of scissors from a crippled Jewish lady who lived across the road. I was acquainted with her, because on cold winter Saturdays, Brian lit her fire for her and went over occasionally to make it up, since her religion demanded that she do no work on that day.

I stood in front of our piece of mirror in the kitchen window and hacked off the greasy rat's tails of hair until I was left with a short bob. I wished I had the family comb, but Mother had taken it to work with her. Then I attacked my nails, which were not very easy to cut with such big scissors, but finally they were snipped down to the flesh and that got rid of much of the dirt under them as well. Hair and body were then washed with a kettle of boiling water and a rag. I combed my hair with my fingers and smoothed it with the dirty towel.

My hands still looked awful. Then I remembered an old beauty trick of Grandma's. Feeling as if I was robbing Edward of a breakfast, I took a small pinch of oatmeal, damped the hands again and rubbed the oatmeal in hard. The hands emerged looking clean and much whiter than usual.

I put on the new pair of black woollen stockings which Cristina had lent me and found they would stay up fairly well if I twisted a piece of coal very tightly into the top of each.

How did one behave at an interview? I worried. What did one say? During the past three and a half years I had been practically cut off from all social contact. At an age when most middle-class girls would be being taught social graces by their school mistresses and their mothers, I had been walking the streets of Liverpool in rags, pushing a baby in a pram. Sometimes I was afraid I would forget how to speak properly. Only at night school did I ever get a chance to express myself. The lack of mental stimulation, the ever present lack of food, and the lack of fun and young friends had played havoc with an already shy personality – and I knew it.

As I scuttled round the shops in Granby Street with Edward in tow, and bought bread and potatoes and margarine, I silently said the General Confession and then the Lord's Prayer, turning towards the only help I knew. God received a rather wild collection of prayers that morning.

This mental exercise reminded me of Father's question as to whether I had approached the Anglican Fathers at the church about a job. The pressure Miss Ferguson had put on my parents *was* more than might normally have been expected. Perhaps Miss Ferguson had, after her tour of our house, consulted the priests. None of them had come to see us; but they had hooked Brian and Tony into the choir, so they knew we were High Anglicans. The idea that they might be trying to help me filled my romantic teenage heart with a kind of joy and lifted me for a while out of my wretchedness.

I fed the children when they came in for dinner and then dragged Fiona into the kitchen and confided to her the story of the job. Would she look after Edward for me, while I went for the interview?

'What if Mummy finds out?' she quavered, her eyes wide with misgiving.

'Oh, Fi, just take Avril to school and then slip back here. I'll be back ages before the boys or Mummy and Daddy come. They'll never know.'

'I'm scared, Helen. Teacher may be cross, too.'

'Look, I'll take all the blame. You can say I bullied you into it. They'll believe that. They'll blame me anyway.'

'Helen!'

She was very frightened and yet I had to have a baby-sitter for a couple of hours.

'Please, Fi, darling. Please.'

She shifted around unhappily and finally agreed.

While she took Avril to school, I put on the dress and the little jacket and then, as I squeezed a large acne spot on my chin and anxiously examined two more at the side of my nose, I agonised that she might not return. I peered anxiously at myself in the broken mirror. Behind the outgrown glasses my eyes were red with strain or pink eye. A further black rim round them from lack of food and rest did not add to my looks. I sighed, and ran to the window of the sitting room to see if Fiona was coming.

I had nearly given up hope, when she suddenly rounded the corner and dawdled down the street towards our house.

The walk down the hill to town was more painful than I had expected. The borrowed shoes pressed on the ragingly painful chilblains on my heels and toes. The wind blew the carefully arranged hair all over the place, and emphasised the need of a hat and a comb. Some of the euphoria which had sustained me evaporated, and was replaced by plain fear of the unknown.

To add to that, I had defied Father and Mother and I feared that I might be punished by God for it. He had said, Honour thy Father and thy Mother, and I presumed He meant what He said.

The closer I got to the city centre the more I quailed. And yet some stubborn instinct kept me going.

Without a watch, I did not know whether I was late or early and I hurried into the office building, which I had passed many times with Edward in the pram. It was a tall, Victorian structure with high, narrow windows looking out on a very busy side street.

The main floor was occupied by a tea-blending firm, and this confused me for a moment. A jolly, little woman with a steaming bowl of tea in her hand came to my rescue and directed me up the stone stairs.

I climbed and climbed. Half way up I had to stop.

Though I walked a lot in the fresh air, I was wasted from lack of food. A middle-aged lady in a green overall ran past me down the stairs without so much as a glance. A fat Irish woman in a black shawl and skirt panted her way upwards, muttering to herself. She gave me a sly grin as she passed.

Up I went again, and finally found the door mentioned by the lady with the tea bowl. I knocked and cautiously entered.

It was a big, ill-lit room with dusty yellow walls. There were several large tables, piled with files and papers, at which people sat engrossed in their work. In one corner stood a small table with a telephone on it. Behind the telephone stood a large wooden box with rows of knobs along its front. For a second, I imagined myself seated before the telephone transacting all kinds of important business.

At the back of the room stood rows of deep bookcases filled with files, and several girls in blue overalls were running about with stacks of brown folders in their arms. The only man in the room was a dark, saturnine person in a formal business suit, who sat at a large table writing in a big book. Two well-coiffured, smartly dressed ladies sat at the same table writing busily.

The gentleman looked up at my entrance.

'Yes?' he snapped.

Quivering with fright, I explained humbly over the bent heads of his lady helpers that I had come for an interview with the Secretary.

He sniffed, and gestured towards a young lady sitting before a typewriter. She smiled at me, took my name and made me sit down on a wooden chair with my back to the room.

While the typist knocked and went into an inner room, I thankfully regained my breath and tried surreptitiously to ease the agony of my feet inside the borrowed shoes.

When the typist returned to usher me into the inner room, I was sure I would faint with fright. However, she smiled very kindly at me, so I shuffled unhappily into the furnace.

At first I could not see anybody in the big, gloomy room. Then I realised that a woman, a tiny person, was seated at the desk by the window. I stood quaking just inside the door, after closing it silently behind me, until she looked up and took notice of me. She was plain to the point of ugliness, with greying hair combed neatly to her head. She had, however, a tremendous aura of authority, like all the ferocious head mistresses who had had me in their care rolled up into one powerful, scarifying personality.

While she examined me in the poor light from the overcast day, I stood with hands clenched together in front of me, awaiting the verdict.

Her voice when she spoke was cool and sibilant.

'You may sit down.'

Too scared to look at her again, I sat down on the edge of the chair by her desk. In answer to her questions, I said, 'Yes, madam,' or 'No, madam,' exactly as servants had done when addressed by Mother. I volunteered no information for which she did not explicitly ask. She had a file in front of her and occasionally she would flick over the papers in it with a long thin finger. It was apparent that she knew something of our family, and I presumed that Miss Ferguson had told her about us.

Finally, she said, without looking up, 'You may commence work next Monday. The hours are from nine to five-thirty on week days and nine until twelve-thirty on Saturdays. Two overalls will be provided for you to wear in the office and you will be expected to keep them clean. The salary is twelve shillings and sixpence a week.' She paused, and then said, after some consideration, 'The salary is payable monthly. However, in view of your family's circumstances I will arrange for you to be paid weekly.'

'Thank you, madam,' I said weakly. I'd got it! A real job!

'Report to Mr Ellis on Monday – in the outer office.'

'Yes, madam.'

I hesitated, uncertain whether I was dismissed or not. Part of me was mentally singing a Te Deum, part of me was so scared that for a moment or two I could not have moved.

'You may go now.' The voice was cold and disinterested, as if the mind behind it was already giving attention to other matters.

'Thank you very much, madam,' I said to a head already turned away from me.

But she had opened a Minute Book and was immersed in reading it, so I crept shakily to the door and went quietly out into the hustle of the general office.

I said, 'Thank you,' to the pretty typist, as I passed

her and she nodded back cheerfully, her fingers keeping up a constant tattoo on the typewriter before her.

Nobody else took any notice of me, so I slipped away, down the long staircases, like a warehouse cat. For a moment I shivered in the great pseudo-Gothic doorway, and then plunged into the crowd which thronged the pavement.

A blister had formed on top of a chilblain on my heel and it hurt sharply as I climbed the long hill towards home. The wind was so strong that it pushed and tousled me as if it had human hands. Fear of what lay ahead at home stole through me and sapped the strength from me; fear also that I would not be able to please my new employer. She had such a fearsome presence that I quailed at the memory of her.

She had asked me a number of questions, but she had not asked me the most important one. Had I any experience of using a telephone?

I had never spoken on a telephone, never even held a receiver in my hand. What it sounded like, how it worked, were both mysteries to me. The closest I had ever been to a phone was when I had occasionally stepped into a public phone box to press the 'B' button, to see if I could retrieve twopence forgotten by a caller who had failed to get his connection.

Chapter fourteen

It was nearly half past four when I hurried silently through the back door, slipping Cristina's jacket off as I ran.

The living-room door was slightly ajar, and I could hear the hurly-burly of the children at tea. Bless Fiona for making the tea!

In the cellar's cold blackness, smelling of coal and long departed cats, I carefully removed the borrowed dress, shoes and stockings, and pushed the latter back into the brown paper bag I had left down there. Naked, except for a torn pair of knickers, I ran up the stone steps and hung the precious dress and jacket on the inside of the cellar door. I hoped frantically that there was no coal dust on them.

Standing on the top step I slipped on my hopelessly short gym slip and a grey cardigan long since abandoned by Mother. Back in the kitchen, I stuffed my tortured feet into battered gym shoes; and I was back in character.

In the living room, Brian, Tony and Avril had left the table, and Brian was laying down the rules of a new game he had invented. The stairs would be a train, he would be the driver and the others the passengers. Without even looking at me, they ran into the hall, and I could hear them squabbling on the stairs about the details of the game and who would fall out first.

Edward was chewing a crust at the table, and I ruffled his hair playfully as I walked round him and sat down at the table opposite Fiona and Alan.

'How did you get on?' asked Alan. He nodded his blond head towards Fiona, and added, 'Fi told me.'

I told them of my success and they were jubilant. In spite of the family row the previous night Alan said he thought Mother and Father would relent. 'You've got to start some time,' he said firmly. 'It's only fair.'

It sounded as if he had given the matter some thought, and Fiona was equally enthusiastic, though it is doubtful if the poor, suppressed child ever really thought deeply about anything, other than what was happening to her at any given moment. Only when she unexpectedly burst into floods of tears did one know that deep inside the beautiful, doll-like creature was a human being who suffered dreadfully.

I had a misbegotten hope that my parents would be too tired to wage another battle. It was my mistake; they were never too tired to fight each other or lash out at me.

After they had eaten the scanty meal I had kept for them from the midday meal served to the children, and Mother was about to go upstairs to take off her work dress, I said in a carefully controlled voice that I would like to speak to them about Miss Ferguson's offer of a job.

They both looked at me with cold suspicion.

When I told them about the interview, they were

outraged. I was standing quite close to Father and he was so furious that he jumped up and struck me across the head. This stalled the hysterics I could feel rising inside me. They seemed more incensed about my disobedience than by the actual interview, and they took turns ranting about my general insubordination and lack of respect for their wishes.

I was myself very fatigued and was therefore quieter than usual, so that, unfueled, their fury began to trail off. Summoning up as much courage as I could muster, I announced that either I should be allowed to go to work or I would run away.

'What nonsense!' shouted Father. 'The police would bring you back, my girl. You are not even fifteen yet.'

I was frightened by his mention of the police, but I answered steadily, 'Not if I went to Grandma. If she lets my cousin work, she would let me go, too.'

Fortunately, they did not remember that I had no money for the ferry I would have to take to get to Grandma, and my threat sobered them.

Father laughed, and then said in a sad, dead voice, 'You would certainly not be welcome.'

Mother said savagely, 'The whole idea is absurd. You are needed at home.' She began to move towards the hall. 'Besides I could not possibly find the clothes for you. It's hard enough to keep myself dressed suitably.'

'I know, Mummy,' I replied quietly. 'And I've never ever asked you for clothes.' Then I added eagerly, 'But I have thought how I could get something to wear. If you would write to Mrs Fox, my friend Joan's mother, I think she would send me some. Joan and I were always much the same size – and she has wardrobes full of clothes.'

Mother tossed her head. 'I seem to remember your meeting Mrs Fox and her precious daughter in the town some time back, and that you told me they cut you dead.'

'They did, Mummy,' I agreed miserably. 'But when I thought about it some more, I think I understood how they felt. If they had stopped in Bold Street to speak to a ragamuffin like me, a crowd would have gathered. People would have thought I had stolen something off them or was begging.' I gave a shivery sigh. 'They did the right thing.'

'Humph,' said Mother, her hand on the knob of the hall door.

'I don't think you have ever written to Mrs Fox,' I went on persuasively. 'She's really very kind and generous.'

Father was looking me up and down, as if he had never seen my clothing before. He said suddenly, 'Helen needs clothes very badly by the look of her. That gym slip is hardly decent. It doesn't cover her properly.' He turned to Mother. 'Try to wheedle some clothes for her out of that Fox woman. She has more money than sense. It wouldn't hurt her to help her daughter's friend. I am sure Helen would feel much better if she had some decent garments.'

Perhaps he thought that, placated by some new clothes, I would be more amenable to being the family drudge.

'She might send some money, too,' I suggested.

Mother looked again at Father. He gave her the smallest affirmative nod.

'Very well,' said Mother coldly. 'I will write. We both need clothes.' Then in another burst of sudden anger, she turned to me. 'This doesn't mean that I have agreed to your going to work. I will not hear of it. You can't be spared.'

I ground my teeth, as I swallowed the angry retort I longed to make. Seething inwardly, I replied, 'Yes, Mother.'

The letter was written there and then, while Father watched; and the next few days were filled with anxiety. Creditors were visibly astonished when the front door was whipped open at their first knock, as I joyfully anticipated the coming of the postman. I listened sullenly to their upbraidings and then promised to tell Father all they threatened.

On the fourth day, the postal van arrived with two very large parcels. They were addressed to me, not to Mother.

I tore them open and went through the contents with wonderment. The dear woman had thought of everything; underwear, skirt, two blouses, shoes, gloves, overcoat, even a small, rather tired-looking handbag and a plain tam o'shanter for my head. There was a short letter wishing me well and mentioning that Joan was at a finishing school in Switzerland.

For a few moments, I touched and fondled the garments as if they were specially beloved possessions. I tried on the crumpled coat, a blouse and the skirt. They fitted reasonably well, though they were a little loose. I took them off reluctantly and folded everything into a pile. All the garments were so clean and sweet smelling, a gift from a world of bathrooms with soap and hot water, efficient laundries, and houses kept sparkling clean by maids armed with the newly-fashionable vacuum cleaner, tins of polish and bottles of disinfectant and liquid soap. As I stroked the little fur collar on the coat, I felt an overwhelming sadness, the sadness of someone bereaved who has come to terms with that bereavement but still at times mourns the loss.

I pulled myself together and picked up the string. Untangled, it would be strong enough to make a clothes-line across the kitchen on which to dry the children's clothes on wet days.

Gathering up the heap of clothes with the brown paper underneath them, I took them upstairs and laid them on Edward's and my bed. I hoped that the cleanliness of the clothing would deter the bugs from crawling on to them. When, later on, the fire would be lit for the children's homecoming I would heat our single flat iron and press the garments ready for Monday.

I dreaded the fighting yet before me; and I knew, from experience, that unless I was particularly adamant the parcel's contents would end up at the pawnbroker's.

Chapter fifteen

Edward and I went for our afternoon walk. It was raining slightly, so he rode in the Chariot and I put the ancient pram's hood up to protect him from the wet. Though the frame protruded through the rents in the cover, it still sheltered him fairly well. The rain slowly soaked my cardigan. I was used to it and did not care.

Our street was a straight line of terrace houses, once respectable working-class homes. Now the inhabitants were very mixed; and my father and a fireman who lived further down the street were the only two men in regular employment. Many of the homes had more than one family in them and were dirty and neglected. A few were very well kept; mended curtains arranged neatly on either side of the front window, with an aspidistra in a pottery bowl filling up the middle space, the window sill highly polished and the front step whitened.

Our beige curtains, as yet unpaid for, looked tidy behind windowpanes which I had washed with hot water and newspaper pads. Our front step, however, was littered with dried orange peel and cigarette ends flung there by our next door neighbours, whose front door abutted ours. They also spat on our step, as they sat on their own doorstep and smoked and read comic books. We never spoke to the man and wife and toddler who lived there. They would stare at us when we passed them, as if we were beings from another planet, and I suspect that they made ribald jokes at our stuffiness.

We walked the length of the long street, crossed Kingsley Road, which still had some shabby gentility about it, and continued on to Lodge Lane, where we spent a little while shop gazing, and I taught Edward the names of some of the household utensils exhibited in a chandlery shop.

The April clouds rolled away and the sun came out to make the rain-washed streets glitter with sudden cleanliness. When we neared home again, Edward said he wanted to walk. The pavement was no longer very wet, so I set him down on it and he ran ahead of me. I had made him a pair of bootees out of an old felt hat. They were stitched with wool from an unravelled sweater, and between two felt soles I had put a double layer of cardboard. I hoped the damp would not penetrate to his tiny feet.

Alice Davis was leaning against the doorjamb of her home as we came near, and she called to the small boy. He stopped and gave her one of his winning smiles. She stepped into the street and squatted down in front of him to talk baby talk to him. Then she ran back into the house and returned with a plain biscuit for him, which he snatched gladly out of her hand.

Though Alice was only about twenty-five years old, her face was lined and her smile practically toothless. She wore her black hair screwed into an unbecoming bun at the back of her head. Her blue-grey eyes were merry as she gently teased Edward.

I stopped to thank her for the biscuit and made Edward say, 'Thank you.'

'That's nothing,' she replied. Then she went on, 'That Mrs Ferguson come to see me about Edward. I said I'd take him. Did you get the job?' Her voice had the thick nasal accent of the born Liverpudlian.

'Yes,' I responded dully. 'I'm supposed to start on Monday.'

'Well, aren't you?' She looked me over disparagingly, and burst out, 'You're lucky, you are, to get a job.'

I nodded agreement. 'I know I am.' Then I thought suddenly that there is nothing like a *fait accompli*, so I said boldly, 'If you will look after Edward, I can start.'

'Oh, aye. I said I would. He's a little dear, he is.'

'I could pay you the ten shillings every Saturday afternoon when I come home from work. I think I would be paid on Fridays, but I am not certain. So I'll promise to bring it every Saturday.'

'Isn't that your Mam's business?'

I hesitated. I could not say that I doubted if Mother would pay regularly, so I said, 'We'll settle it between us. I'll bring Edward down every morning before I go to work, and Fiona can collect him when she gets back from school.'

Alice threw back her head and laughed. 'First few days you could bring him. After that he'll run up and down by himself, won't you, luv?' She bent down and chucked Edward under the chin. He swallowed the last of the biscuit and giggled and twisted away from her. ' 'Tis only a few doors away,' she added.

'If you think he'll be all right,' I said anxiously.

'Sure, he will. I'll see our door is open for him. And he can have a bit to eat with us at dinner time.'

"Thank you, Alice. I'm very grateful to you. See you on Monday morning – about eight o'clock.'

Alice bent down again and picked up Edward and nuzzled her face into his, laughing all the time. 'Yes. We'll have a proper nice time together.'

And with great relief I felt that she was right.

*

Clean out the grate, make the fire, lay clean newspaper on the table, cut the bread, make the tea, all with a stomach tight with apprehension. Would I ever know what it was like not to be frightened?

It was worse than I had expected.

Firstly, I had opened the parcel. Did I not realise that letters and parcels were opened by parents, regardless of how they were addressed? Furthermore, I had ironed the garments, thus accepting them without parental permission.

I had no right to speak to Alice. I had no right to say that I would begin work on Monday. Parents decided such a thing and they had decided that I should stay at home. It seemed to me that I had no rights at all, only a formidable list of obligations.

Cornered, terrified rats turn and attack. Some human beings, however, have less courage, and I was ready to give in, when help came suddenly from an unexpected quarter.

Fiona said in a quivering voice, 'I can make the tea and take care of Edward and Avril till you come home,

Mummy. And I can help to put them to bed. I could even do the shopping if you gave me a list.'

It must have cost her dearly to speak up on my behalf. It came as a surprise to me that she should love me enough to do so. I gave love but I did not expect anything in return. I had always protected her as much as I could from hunger and cold and jeering local boys and girls, helped her with her homework because she had great difficulty in learning, and frankly admired her because she had such a sweet temperament. And now, on my behalf, the gentle creature was laying herself open to our parents' bitter censure. I was moved beyond words and was still gaping at her, when Alan put down his toast and said, 'I don't mind giving a hand as well.'

Alan and I had always got along very well, once I had recovered from the infant jealousy which his birth had engendered; and I was grateful for his intercession. Mother loved her sons and would listen to him.

Alan was saying stoutly that all girls went to work now. A lady from the employment exchange had come to the school to counsel them about work, and she had interviewed the girls as well as the boys. So it must be so.

Though Father was still trembling with rage, I could see he was listening to Alan's remarks. Mother started to cry and say that she could not manage, and I felt dreadful, because the ultimate responsibility for all of us rested on her shoulders. She was not idle after returning from work; she would rest for a little while and then spend some time with Edward and

Avril. While I was at night school, she would check the children's clothes after they had gone to bed and sometimes did part of the washing and ironing. She was not in the best of health, and her tears racked me.

Fiona and Alan were, however, arguing in a soothing way that the family was big enough and each of them old enough to make it possible for me to be spared.

Father got up suddenly and swung out of the room. I saw him take his trilby hat off the hall peg and clap it down on his head. Without a word, he lifted the latch of the front door and went out into the ill-lit street. I knew from experience that when he came back he would smell of beer and would be amiably jocular with all of us.

As he went, Mother blew her nose quickly, and then shouted after him, 'You can't face anything, can you? Must you always waste money on drink?'

He did not reply. Shell-shocked, war weary, he had been ill enough himself to draw a full army pension for several years after serving in Russia. Probably his nerves screamed for sedation, and his comfortless home and unruly family made the pain unbearable.

Fiona got up and put her arms round Mother's neck. 'Don't cry, Mummy. If Helen goes to work, she's so clever she'll soon earn lots and lots. And then you will be able to stay at home and not have to work any more.'

Fiona's and Alan's advocacy gave me a little courage again. I was so terribly unhappy myself that I felt I could not go on as I had been doing; something had to give. Unlike Fiona, I was quite sure that the last thing Mother wanted was to be at home with her family all day; yet my needs deserved consideration, too.

'Let us try, Mummy,' I begged. 'I should get more money after a little while and it would help.'

But Mother was still flaming with wrath. She pushed Fiona away, bounced out of her chair and shook her finger at me. 'You are talking rubbish. You are disobedient and ungrateful. You haven't even matriculated. You are unskilled in anything.'

I fired up immediately, 'And whose fault is that?'

Mother nearly choked. She slapped me across the face. 'I never heard such impudence,' she screamed.

I backed away from her, snatched up my night school books from the mantelpiece, and tried not to scream back, as I said, 'I don't care. I'm going to work on Monday. Otherwise, I am going to Granny's – so you won't have my help anyway.'

Mother had been a very beautiful woman. Convulsed with rage, she looked like an infuriated witch, and I was terrified.

'Go!' she yelled at me. 'All right. Go to work! You will soon discover that the world is a very cruel place and you will long to be at home again. Get out of my sight.'

By this time all the children were bellowing like frightened cows. Fiona and Avril clung to Mother, crying, 'Don't, Mummy, don't.' Brian, Tony and Edward were all in noisy tears. Only Alan sat tearless; he yelled, 'I don't know why everybody had to make such a row!'

I backed through the door. Then turned and followed Father into the night.

Mother did not need to tell me that the world outside was a cruel place. I knew that already. But faintly, faintly on the horizon it had its rays of hope.

Chapter sixteen

'Mr Ellis,' I whispered shyly, 'I am the new telephone girl.'

Four other girls in the room paused in their work to stare at me, while Mr Ellis put down his pen carefully on his desk and looked up at me. He frowned at what he saw.

'Humph. You are?' He took out his handkerchief and held it to his nose. I heard a girl giggle.

I lowered my eyes. I knew I looked awful. Joan's skirt and blouse hung on me. My rough-cut hair could have served as a mop. Both feet throbbed with the pain of blisters rubbed on tender chilblains, and I was biting my lips as I endured the misery of it. Over me lay the smell of poverty, of a body poorly washed, clothes unaired, foul breath and fatigue.

The man before me was thin and dark-visaged, with the same air of nervous tension as Father had. He called to a girl sitting in front of the telephone switchboard.

'Miss Finch, show t' girl what to do.'

He gestured towards the switchboard with his pen, as he picked it up, so I silently went over to Miss Finch. While I stood awkwardly beside her, I could see out of the corner of my eye, two other girls sniggering behind their hands as they watched.

Miss Finch answered the telephone in a thick

Liverpool accent. In between calls, without preamble, she explained to me that people wishing to apply to the Charity for help entered through the basement, where there was a waiting room. A girl took their names and telephoned them up to the room we were in. The switchboard operator wrote them down and handed the slips of paper to the filing clerks. The applicant's file, if any, was then sent down to the Interviewing Floor directly below us, where there was another waiting room.

The applicant was then sent upstairs, past the Tea Blending Company on the main floor, to be united with his file. At this point, a senior staff member inquired what he had come about, and he was then seated in the second waiting room. He was finally interviewed in a side room. It was a long, slow process for the applicants.

Miss Finch was a black-haired, rosy-cheeked girl, who seemed to resent me very much. She told me she was the office girl and was filling in on the switchboard until I could take over. I presumed that she had not won promotion to the job of telephonist because of her bad accent.

'Names beginning A to J go to Dorothy Evans; K to Z to Phyllis over there.' She got up and handed me the phone. 'You take the next call from the basement.'

Gingerly, I lifted the receiver to my ear, while Miss Finch moved the appropriate switches. A garbled rattle came through the receiver. I could not interpret it. In a panic, I handed the instrument back to Miss Finch, who hastily jotted down a name on her pad.

'What's the matter?' she asked impatiently, as she handed me the slip. 'Give this to Phyllis Barker.' When I hesitated uncertainly, she hissed, 'Over there. Be quick.'

Phyllis snatched the slip out of my hand, quickly jumped up and vanished down her aisle of files. Her high-heeled patent leather shoes flashed, as she moved.

'How do you answer the phone and deliver the names to the filing clerks at the same time?' I whispered to Miss Finch.

Miss Finch made a wry face. 'You run,' she whispered back. 'Everybody runs.'

She was right. The filing clerks, the telephonists, the disembodied voice in the basement, the whimpering nervous girl who served in the Cash Department next door, Miss Finch herself as she made tea and delivered letters, all ran. Like convicts, at the double, they scuttled upstairs and downstairs, scurrying in and out of offices to look for files or deliver messages, running, running, running. Sometimes, I almost expected them to take wing, like one does in nightmares. They were not allowed to use the lift, because the charity was short of money and it was necessary to keep the electricity bill to a minimum.

Miss Finch left me to manage the telephone alone for a few minutes. She had to sort some letters into a round for hand delivery and did this at another table. In seconds, the awesome Presence who had interviewed me and had given me the job, shuffled out of her room, to inquire of Miss Danson, her secretary, why she had found herself speaking to her own basement when she wanted to speak to the Public Assistance Committee two miles away.

Miss Danson murmured about the new girl just starting and eased her back into her room, while Mr Ellis barked at both Miss Finch and me to be more careful.

It was a dreadful morning, during which I managed to create telephonic chaos. I could hardly hear what was said. I had no idea of the names of the other staff or where they were to be found. I had no list of commonly required outside numbers and had to look each of them up in the telephone book. And, quickly enough, I realised from Miss Finch's manner that she did not feel it was in her interest to help me to make a success of the job.

I was left alone, while Miss Finch went to make the office's morning tea, and I called almost tearfully to Phyllis to come to help me sort the switchboard out.

'Not Phyllis, Miss Forrester,' roared Mr Ellis, behind me, 'Miss Barker, if you please.' He paused, while I sat paralysed with fright, and then said, 'Can't you speak quieter? I can't stand that la-dee-da accent.'

'Yes, sir,' I whispered, as Phyllis Barker kindly came to my aid.

I realised suddenly that, except for Mr Ellis, everyone in the room whispered. And nobody laughed. Not one girl, except Miss Barker, had even smiled at me yet. The constant tattoo of the typewriter of the Presence's secretary, the buzz of the telephone switchboard, the flutter of paper and the steady hiss of whispers made up the noises in the room.

Miss Finch told me my lunch hour would be from

one-thirty to two-thirty, and the morning seemed endless. She dumped a cup of tea in front of me with a biscuit tucked in the saucer, and I ate and drank eagerly. In a quiet moment Miss Barker found me a list of commonly-used telephone numbers and I tried to master it. The names and figures danced in front of me. I needed badly a list of the names of the staff and their numbers on the switchboard, so that I could connect incoming calls to the correct extension; and when Miss Finch returned to assist me, I asked her for this.

She shrugged and said I did not need a list. I would soon learn the names. In the meantime, outraged voices on every extension phone sibilantly rebuked me. It was a nightmare.

At twelve o'clock, the basement waiting room closed and there were no more names to write down and deliver to the filing clerks. This gave me more time to deal with other calls and contemplate more quietly the hateful, buzzing board.

Just before lunch time, a thin waif of a girl wearing large horn-rimmed glasses came out of a door on the other side of the room.

With an apprehensive glance at Mr Ellis, she crept over to me and said in an almost inaudible voice, 'The Cashier would like to see you during your lunch hour.' She sniffed, and I saw that she had been crying. Her nose was red and her eyes heavy with tears. It looked as if she had been in even more trouble than I had.

'The Cash Department is over there,' she added, pointing to the room from which she had come.

I smiled up at her. 'Thanks. I'll come.'

She managed a glimmer of a smile back and then fled across the room and through the door she had pointed out to me.

Fear of what lay in wait in the Cash Department was added to my fear of the telephone.

*

I knocked at the Cash Department door and a female voice snapped, 'Come in.'

I entered. The room was partly divided by a frosted glass screen and at first appeared to be empty. I paused.

'Well?' snapped the same voice again, from behind the glass screen.

I approached cautiously.

Behind the screen, at a littered desk, sat a small, grey-haired woman. She looked at me almost belligerently. 'What do you want?'

'You sent for me, Madam. I am Helen Forrester.'

'Hmm.' She looked me up and down, and her nose wrinkled in distaste.

She turned round and took two folded blue garments from a shelf behind her. These she almost threw into my arms.

'Your overalls. You will wear them at all times in the office and will keep them clean.'

'Yes, madam.'

'You will be paid on Friday afternoons. Such a nuisance to have to pay a single member of the staff on a weekly basis. What is your full name and address? And age?'

I told her.

'Very well. You can go.' She turned back to her desk, and I tiptoed out, past two empty desks where presumably the weepy girl and another person worked.

The general office was empty, except for an elderly lady in a pretty grey dress who was manning the telephone. She nodded to me as I went out.

I went up to the cloakroom on the top floor of the building. This had been shown to me when I arrived, by a hurrying lady in a green overall whom I had met on the stairs. I laid the two blue overalls on the floor under the hook where I had hung my coat, and wondered what to do. There was nobody about and the silence seemed unearthly. I began to cry, my head pressed against my coat.

I had no money to buy lunch, and there had been no bread left after breakfast to bring with me. Both parents had left me severely alone, to get myself ready for work and Edward ready to go to Alice's. Feeling like a pariah, I had taken the cheerful little boy to his new friend's and he had stayed with her without a murmur, and then I had walked to work.

There was no doubt in my mind that my parents were united in their attitude that I should find going to work so difficult that I would eventually be thankful to return to housekeeping.

At the memory of their stony faces, I felt suddenly weak. I moved to the wash basin and clung to it, as my legs began to give under me. Wild colours flashed before my eyes and I felt myself sinking into oblivion. I knew from experience that I rarely passed out completely, so I clung to the wash basin until the world stopped swimming about.

I cupped my hand under the cold tap and drank some water, slurping it up and splashing my face. Greatly daring, I decided to have a wash. My face was soaped as it had never been soaped in the past three years. I rinsed and rinsed in gorgeous hot water, then dried myself on the spotlessly clean roller towel.

The light was poor, but in the mirror I could see green eyes with black rings round them, peering out of a face dead white, except where it was blotched with acne. Short eyelashes hardly showed on the reddened eyelids. Smooth eyebrows looked very black below a rough fringe of brown hair. I grinned ruefully at myself. The teeth thus exposed looked good – the cavities at the back did not show.

The wash had done me good and, as nobody disturbed me, I washed my glasses, dried them on the towel and put them on. The face in the mirror came into sharper focus, and I could see again how defeatingly plain I was. How I longed for a perfectly straight nose, like Fiona's, instead of the high-bridged, haughty-looking Forrester nose.

Without a watch I did not know the time. Meanwhile, I needed to sit down, and there was no chair in the cloakroom.

Hesitantly, I looked along the line of blue overalls hung neatly on their owners' hooks, and saw beyond them a door leading off the cloakroom.

Very quietly, I approached the door and opened it.

I was in a small passage. To my left, an open door revealed a neat kitchenette. It had a big window and was bright with light. Another closed door faced me. When I turned its handle, it gave a sharp click.

'Hello. Come in,' said a soft feminine voice very cheerfully.

Chapter seventeen

Embarrassed that I had disturbed someone, I swung the door wide and stood dithering on the threshold of a small room that seemed packed with furniture bathed in dazzling sunlight. Light from a skylight poured down onto the burnished brown head of a thin woman, about twenty-five years of age, who was seated facing me behind one of the three typists' desks crowding the room. She had an open paperback in one hand and was eating a sandwich. As she looked up at me from her book, her long, narrow face radiated good humour. She had a beautiful pink and white skin, delicately accentuated by good make-up, and light, almost catlike brown eyes gazed at me through very large horn-rimmed glasses.

'Hello, come in,' she said, as she put her book down on top of her typewriter. 'What brings you here? You must be the new telephonist.'

'Yes,' I replied. 'I am sorry to intrude. I was looking for somewhere to sit down.'

'Oh, take Miss Short's chair for a while. She won't mind.' She pointed to a swivel chair by another typist's desk. 'Like a sandwich?'

'Thank you.'

I willed myself not to snatch from the proffered square of greaseproof paper. Carefully, I took the tiny triangle and made myself eat it in several delicate, polite bites, when I really longed to bolt it down. It was a cucumber sandwich and reminded me poignantly of long ago afternoon teas. The other girl ate the two remaining sandwiches and tossed the empty wrapping into the wastepaper basket. She insisted on my sharing a small piece of fruit cake with her.

I smiled at her, as I ate the cake, and asked, 'Are you somebody's secretary?'

'No.' She laughed. 'I'm just one of the also-rans. I do any typing jobs they want.'

'Could I ask your name?' I queried. 'I don't know the names of any of the staff, except some of the filing clerks, and it is terribly difficult when answering the phone.'

'Well, I'm Miriam Enns. And Miss Short and Miss Brown work up here. Miss Short is the Head Typist. Then Miss Danson in the Filing Department is the secretary to Miss MacAdam, who runs the place. You probably saw her when you applied for the job.'

'I did.' Then I added, without thinking, 'The Presence.'

'The what?' Miriam chuckled delightedly. 'That's lovely.'

I blushed, and smiled nervously. Then I said, 'Well, she seemed like a Presence.'

'You are right. She's a great lady and she works very hard, though she is so frail.' She swung round on her chair, took a piece of paper out of her stationery stand and put it into her typewriter. 'I'll make you a list of the staff – it won't take a minute. I don't know the numbers of their phones on the switchboard, but I can tell you which floor they are on.'

She rattled away on the machine, while I sat quietly watching her. She seemed to me the nicest person I had met for a very long time, and as I watched her long, slender fingers flash over the keyboard, a new emotion welled up in me, a great desire to give and receive friendship.

'That Ellis man should have seen that you got a list like this,' she said irritably, as she whipped the paper from the roller and handed it to me.

'Thanks,' I said happily, as I carefully folded the paper up. 'Is he the only man on the staff?'

'No, there is one more. But I think Ellis finds it hard in a sea of women.'

I did not venture a comment. I was a bit afraid of Mr Ellis, who did not approve of la-dee-da accents.

'Have you got an overall yet?' asked Miriam. She took a packet of cigarettes out of her own blue overall pocket, struck a match from a box on her desk and lit up.

'Yes.'

'Better put it on. We lowly types wear blue ones. Senior staff – the social workers – wear green ones.'

I nodded agreement.

There was the sound of the cloakroom door being opened and slammed, and running feet.

Miriam glanced at her wrist watch. 'It's twenty-five past,' she said. 'Better put on your overall and go downstairs – or Ellis will be after your blood.'

I jumped up. I felt a lot better.

'Thank you for your help,' I said warmly, looking down at the pixie face of my new friend.

Miriam had the same type of wide, red-lipped

mouth as Fiona had, and she smiled broadly up at me. 'When you get desperate, come up here,' she advised. Her smile became a yawn and she took off her glasses and rubbed her merry, brown eyes with her knuckles.

'I'd love to,' I assured her enthusiastically.

'Shut the door as you go out. Miss Short doesn't like it left open.'

Obediently I closed the door after me. I paused in the passage outside, my hand still on the door knob, feeling again the warm friendliness of the girl in the typing room. For the first time since arriving in Liverpool, I had talked with someone fairly young, who spoke as I did and treated me as an equal.

Chapter eighteen

The aim of the organisation in which I found myself was to make the poor aware of the many charities available to help them; to counsel; to provide a little legal aid given voluntarily by a few city lawyers; and to disburse, in the most constructive way, funds donated to the organisation itself. The senior staff provided a friendly ear for sorrows to be poured into, and sympathetic visitors to the sick and other housebound people; they tried also to aid the elderly and the many despairing mothers who, under impossible circumstances, struggled to make ends meet. Though they were not well paid, all the staff had shining neatly combed hair, clear skins and well-fed bodies. Their clothes were fresh looking and everything matched, as was the fashion. I was thankful to be shrouded in an overall.

Filled with dismay at my lack of knowledge, not only of the telephone, but of the myriad of social nuances, the courtesies, of this new world, I struggled on to the end of the day. The other girls, with a hasty 'good-night' ran for their trams, and I trudged slowly home, head bent against a blustery wind. A cup of tea brought to me during the afternoon had reduced the pangs of hunger, but I felt very weak. Night school would begin at seven o'clock, and I wondered how I would manage to get there in time.

I badly needed food, warmth, and a little comforting encouragement that tomorrow I would do better.

When I slowly opened the door of the living room, I saw that Father was seated in the old easy chair, deep in a book. I wondered why he was not reading in the front room, but decided it was probably too cold for him in there. Alan, his blond cowlick swinging over his forehead, was seated on a small upturned oil drum by the fire. His head was bent over an exercise book while he did his homework.

Brian, Tony and Avril were sailing an imaginary ship across the floor. Brian was shouting to his bosun, Tony, 'Ahoy there, Bill. Belay there.' And then to Avril, he called, 'Hard astarboard, you lazy landlubber.' And Avril laboriously turned a huge, imaginary wheel. They were so absorbed in the game that they did not reply when I said, 'Hello, children.'

'Hello, Daddy. Hello, Alan.'

They both looked up from their occupations and nodded acknowledgment in a vague, guarded way, then went back to their reading. Only Baby Edward, who was whining steadily, toddled towards me, to put his arms round my legs. I picked him up and hugged him, in an effort to assuage the terrible sense of emptiness within me, and carried him into the kitchen from which came the clatter of dishes.

Fiona was filling the sooty, tin kettle from the tap, and she half-turned and smiled at me timorously in the flickering light of the candle on the draining board. Beside her, Mother was emptying teacups into the soapstone sink. She said, 'Oh, you've come. have you? You *are* late.'

I stroked the back of Edward's scurfy head, as I answered, 'It took a long time to walk home.'

I looked uneasily at both of them. I sensed that something had gone wrong. I could almost smell it. And it was my fault. I could see it in Mother's stiffened back and frozen look as she swung round to the back door, teapot in hand, to empty the leaves down the outside drain.

'Down?' requested Edward, and very slowly I slid him on to the worn tiles, my eyes on Fiona, in the hope that she would give me a hint while Mother's back was turned. Her eyebrows went up and she gave an almost imperceptible shrug. She seemed scared, and turned hastily back to the kettle, which was running over with water.

Mother clicked her tongue when she saw the overflow.

'Fiona, you stupid girl. Empty some of it out. Put the lid on and then put it on the fire.'

Obediently, Fiona did this and then slid past me into the living room, to put the kettle on to heat. Edward toddled after her, and I could hear him saying to Brian, 'Me, too. I want to play.'

I was left to face Mother.

'You had better get yourself something to eat,' she said frigidly.

I had begun to tremble. It started in my legs and worked its way up, until all of me seemed to be shaking. Was nobody interested in what had happened to me? Surely, normal curiosity would have brought a question or two. Whatever had happened in my absence must indeed have been terrible to blot out all remembrance that this had been my first day at work. I waited for the blow to fall, as I whispered, 'Yes. I am very hungry.'

I turned to the deal kitchen table upon which lay half a loaf of bread and a very misused-looking pat of margarine sitting on its wrapping paper. 'Can I make some tea?'

'Yes,' replied Mother. 'The milk is still on the table. That's all the bread we've got.' She went swiftly into the living room and I heard her go through to the front hall.

I closed my eyes, as if by shutting out the world, I might persuade the trembling to cease. I wanted to seize the spongy piece of white bread, tear it apart and stuff it in my mouth and gobble it down. I could have eaten the margarine in big, revolting chunks. But Mother's words had gone into me like a sharp hat pin. What she had really said was, 'You should not eat anything. If you do, the children will not have any breakfast.'

But I had to eat. So I took up the knife and very carefully, because my hands were so unsteady, I cut a slice off the loaf and put some margarine on it. Despite a throat tight with misery, I ate it, standing there, staring down at the grey surface of the table.

When I went into the living room to ask Fiona for some water from her kettle in order to make a cup of tea, she was standing aimlessly watching the game of ships. I touched her shoulder. She jumped and turned towards me, her expression unaccountably defensive as if she expected to be struck. I saw that she had been crying.

At my request, she took the singing kettle off the fire and brought it into the ill-lit kitchen.

I asked in a low voice, as I put a pinch of tea into a cup and poured water on to it. 'What's up, Fi? What has happened?'

She looked suddenly as if she would burst into tears again, and my trembling increased. Her usually red lips looked almost bloodless and she pushed her straight brown hair back from her face with hands that shook. She whispered dismally, 'Oh, Helen. I did a terrible thing. Mother and Father are furious. And they're awfully cross with you, too, for not being here . . .'

In my opinion, Fiona never did anything wrong, so probably it was my fault. As she started to cry, I quickly reviewed the family. Everybody seemed well; nobody appeared to have been hurt.

Fiona was nearly as tall as me, and I put my arm round her lanky frame. 'What is it, Fi?' I asked, through chattering teeth. But she just put her head on my shoulder and cried harder, long, slow sobs, silent like mine usually were, but sobs that seemed to be wrenched out of the innermost depths of her. My own despair was forgotten in the new fear of what had happened to upset her so much.

'What is it, Fi?' I implored again

She gave a huge snuffle and began to mutter into my ear.

'Well, some men came with a big van – and they hammered on the front door until I simply had to answer. And they said they had come to collect the furniture because we were behind in our payments.

And both Mummy and Daddy are so angry because I let them in and they took it.' She lifted her face towards mine, and then said desperately, 'But I couldn't help it, Helen. They were so big – and one of them put his foot in the door so that I couldn't slam it shut. I was so scared, Helen.' And she began another flood of tears.

'They really took it away?'

'Yes. The front room is empty.'

I began to chuckle quietly, so as not to draw Daddy's attention.

'It's nothing to laugh about, Helen,' Fiona whispered forcefully. 'It was terrible.'

'There, now, Fi. Don't cry. Don't you see? We don't have to pay for it any more. That is five more shillings a week in the house. It's glorious. Think, five shillings will buy at least twenty more loaves a week. That's two loaves a week each. Cheer up, love.'

Fiona wiped her eyes with the back of her hand.

'Oh, no,' she said harshly, her voice heavy with sarcasm. 'No such luck. Father says we have to go on paying, whether we have the furniture or not. It's in the agreement.'

My trembling ceased entirely at this sudden revelation. I looked at her unbelievingly.

'Pay for what we haven't got? What nonsense.'

In my innocence, I knew nothing of hire purchase agreements or how they were abused by some companies doing business in the city. Many, many people were caught up in this vicious system, and many of them paid for years, because they either failed to read the small print in the agreements they signed or they did not understand the jargon in which they were couched. There were, of course, many reputable companies who stood by the spirit as well as the letter of their agreements. But my parents had apparently fallen victim to the blandishments of some salesman who was, perhaps, himself desperate for the commission he would get on the sale.

'We do, Helen. We have to pay.'

I looked wildly round me, for someone or something on which to vent my frustration.

'Where was Alan when all this happened?' I asked savagely. 'Couldn't he have helped you keep the door shut?'

'He wasn't home from school. It wasn't his fault. I left Avril with him and ran on ahead. I wanted to have the tea ready for you when you came home.' She looked piteously at me and sobbed again.

'Never mind, Fi, dear. You did your very best. Don't cry any more. I have to go to night school. And I must get Edward and Avril off to bed.'

I patted her on the shoulder, took a large breath and strode into the living room. 'Bybyes time, darling,' I said to Edward, and with a laugh swept him up off the imaginary ship. A few minutes later, I forcibly dragged Avril away from the game to have her face, hands and knees hastily wiped before popping her into bed. Brian and Tony began to quarrel as to who should be thrown overboard to the sharks. Father told them irritably to get ready for bed, and Alan asked equally irritably if he would ever be allowed to do his homework in peace.

I had brought my books down from the bedroom

after hearing recalcitrant Avril's prayers, and now I picked them up and ran out through the back door. Fiona was washing her face under the tap and I shouted goodbye to her as I went by.

Two quiet, orderly hours in school restored me.

Chapter nineteen

The next morning, a few minutes after I arrived, breathless and hungry, the Presence sent for me. I was still very upset from the bitter recriminations of my parents, which had burst forth from both of them as they rushed between living room and kitchen getting themselves washed and dressed for work. Mother had gone out the previous evening to the pawnbroker and had pawned all the clothes which Mrs Fox had sent, except what I was wearing, and this had added to my distress. It was a very miserable and frightened young girl who crept into the Presence's office, and stood humbly waiting for her to speak.

She looked up from her desk and in a few crisp, sharp words she dismissed me for inefficiency. She gave me a week's notice.

My small world, my new hopes, shattered round me. It was as if they fell like tinkling glass from a broken window, leaving me naked to a winter wind.

As I stood dumbly staring at her without any idea of what I should do, she turned the pages of a file on the desk in front of her. Gradually my eyes focused on her long, shrivelled fingers and following the line of them, I saw that the file was marked 'Forrester', in large capital letters.

In the silence, the significance of the file slowly dawned upon me. At some point, my parents must have applied to my employers for help. And a file on our family must have been sitting on the shelves in the outer office, available for all the girls to read. I felt so mortified at the idea of a social worker's report on our poverty-stricken home being read by the other girls, that I wondered how I would manage to face them during the week's notice the Presence had just served on me.

She was speaking again. 'Miss Finch will be promoted to telephonist. I am prepared to give you another chance as office girl in her place. Her salary is ten shillings a week.'

Reprieve! I snapped up the offer.

Ten shillings would pay Alice. And people got rises in pay, didn't they? Perhaps I would, if I could last out long enough.

She lifted the telephone receiver. 'I will speak to Mr Ellis. Report to him.' She gave me a grim, small smile of dismissal, and I crept out of the room. Her manner was cool and distant, and yet I felt that, amid the many worries of her day, she had tried to help me.

I did not look at any of the other girls, as with eyes downcast I went over to Mr Ellis's desk and stood by him, waiting to be noticed. He was saying, 'Yes, yes. I understand,' down the telephone. Finally he hung up the telephone receiver, and swivelled round towards me.

'That's a proper mess now, isn't it?' he barked.

I hung my head and said nothing.

While I waited, crestfallen, he reorganised his staff, so that Miss Finch could spend the day showing me what to do. Then I was borne off by a naturally triumphant Miss Finch to hurry into our outdoor clothes again.

All letters addressed to destinations within approximately one mile of the office were delivered by hand, as were urgent ones to more distant addresses. One of the sights of the city was the vast number of small office boys and girls trotting about, delivering letters. Their wages were cheaper than the cost of postage.

I knew the city well and soon sorted the letters into a round, and Miss Finch and I set out together. In and out of lawyers' offices, shipping offices and shops we tramped. There was even a letter for the Liverpool Playhouse, which we excitedly delivered at the stage door, hoping against hope that we might catch a glimpse of one of the actors. But we were disappointed. A joking, cheerful doorman took the missive from us.

Mary warned me that the lift men in some of the buildings were not to be trusted, and several times she insisted that we walked up the stairs, once as far as the sixth floor.

I did not understand the import of her warning until the next day, when I did the round on my own. Two men pawed me, while with one hand they pulled the rope that carried the lift upwards. I shrank into the far corner where I could not be reached. This did not deter one of them who, with a grin, stopped the lift at a deserted top floor and pinned me into the corner.

Instinctively I screamed at the top of my voice, and pushed away the exploring hands with all the force I could command. The letters scattered over the floor of the lift. I was panic-stricken, though I could not have said what I was frightened of.

When I shrieked the man let go of me. He turned and angrily flung open the iron gates, and told me to get out and walk. He picked up the letters and threw them after me, as I shot past him onto the landing. I snatched up the letters and scampered down the staircase to the floor I needed. I was sickened, as he slowly followed me down in the lift whispering obscenities which I had previously only come across scribbled on the walls of public lavatories and had never quite understood. His leering face, seen through the iron gates as I passed them on my way down, haunted my nightmares for several days.

This was the first time that anyone had made a sexual advance to me, and, since I did not really understand what the threat to me was, I was filled with nameless terrors for a long time, and learned to run upstairs like a rabbit. Practically all the novels I read ended with a first kiss and I imagined that a happy marriage was a life of gentle tenderness. That there was a physical side to it was unknown to me. I had washed my brothers often enough to know that there was a difference between boys and girls, and Edith had always washed us and dressed us in front of each other, so it all seemed perfectly natural, as did the fact that elm trees and oak trees had different types of leaves.

I had once watched a bull amongst a herd of cows and understood from the cowman that they were making calves. I vaguely understood that babies were carried in their mothers' stomachs, because some of my brothers and sisters had been born at home; and I had picked up from scurrying maids a little of what was happening, but how the baby got there was unknown to me and I presumed that its beginning was spontaneous, though I gave it surprisingly little thought. I knew I was too plain for marriage so would not be having any babies anyway.

During the past two years, while I had been developing into a woman, I had been entirely cut off from the speculative gossip of young girls. Mother had not seen fit to explain anything to me or to warn me of any danger to myself. Yet I sensed now a real physical danger and I gave a wide berth to all liftmen and commissionaires.

When Miss Finch and I returned to the office, we dashed up the stairs to the kitchen to make the morning tea. A tray was spread for the Presence, kettles were filled and cups and saucers were assembled on other trays. A box of biscuits was opened and a biscuit put on every saucer.

While Miss Finch delivered tea to the Presence and to the people working on the same floor as the Filing Department, I ran down the innumerable stone stairs to the basement, carefully balancing in one hand a cup of tea for Miss Lester, who took the names of the clients when they first entered.

The stench in the badly-ventilated cellar room was appalling, as I handed the cup of tea to the blue-clad girl seated at a tiny table facing the clients. She thanked me, while about twenty pairs of eyes watched silently. I paused by the table, expecting Miss Lester to make some light remark or other. Gossiping, however, was a major sin in the eyes of Mr Ellis, so she said nothing.

I looked out over the clients and they stared back at me. There were fat women in black shawls, black skirts and white aprons. They were Liverpool Irish, I knew. Once or twice, while sitting in the park watching the children play, I had spoken to such women shyly about their children, and found them kind and responsive. Some of them still had the high colour of country women, but most of them looked white and drained of strength.

There were also a few women in coats and hats, shabby and grey. A number of men in stained working clothes sat quietly, with their cloth caps held neatly on their laps. One or two children fidgeted fretfully on the wooden benches or sat on the coconut matting which covered the stone floor. Low watt bulbs cast a poor light over the well-ordered crowd.

Perhaps it was their quietness, their resignation to the long wait for attention, which was most depressing. They seemed people who had lost all hope, and my heart went out to them. I understood why they smelled, the exhaustion which made them so very quiet. The organisation, I guesssd correctly, had not enough money to enable them to offer their clients a cup of tea. Thoughtfully I stole back up the stairs to the kitchen.

'You were a long time,' complained Miss Finch impatiently. 'Take this tray down to the first floor. Give each of the interviewers a cup – and don't forget the volunteer at the centre table.'

I took the heavy tray of filled cups and carried it

carefully down to the first floor. Balancing it on one hand, I pushed the landing door to open it. A youth as thin as a broomstick held it open for me as I passed through. I saw his face light up at the sight of the tea tray, and I felt dreadful because I could not give him a cup.

It was another waiting room which smelled equally badly and was equally gloomy. There was only one light hanging above a centre table round which a screen had been set. A well-dressed lady sat at the table, a neat row of files before her. At the side of the table on a wooden chair sat an ancient bundle of bones hunched under a thick blanket shawl. Her tiny face, dark from lack of washing, peered anxiously out from the shawl, like a mouse peeping out of its hole. Little hands clutching the shawl across her breast were equally mouselike. She watched me put a cup of tea down by the voluntary worker, and I felt for a second the old woman's clemmed stomach, the agony of the smell of the tea.

A number of small rooms ran off this waiting room. These were the interviewing rooms, where in reasonable privacy the clients could at last whisper out their difficulties. It seemed to me sometimes that the whole place ran on whispers, as if it were a scared place where one dared not speak in a normal voice for fear the gods might be disturbed.

I took a cup of tea to each lady in a green overall in the interviewing rooms. In every room was an old-fashioned roll-top desk with a number of baskets of files at the back of them. The baskets were marked 'Visit' or 'Letter' or 'In Hand' or 'Filing'. The clients were seated on wooden chairs at the side of the desk, and they hardly paused in their recitals to the interviewer as I brought in the tea. In one room, Dorothy Evans was riffling through the file baskets, looking for a missing file. The interview was continuing despite Dorothy's presence, and I soon learned, like her, to be quiet and unobtrusive in such a situation and never to say anything except, 'Excuse me.'

When my tray was empty, I scurried up to the kitchen on the top floor. Miss Finch was filling another cup.

'Take this down to Miss Dane – her office is next to the Cash Department.'

Miss Dane, I discovered, was the Assistant Presence. Since she was not quite so weighed down by responsibility as the Presence herself, she had time to stop her perusal of a mountain of correspondence, to ask me if I was the new office girl.

In case it was not obvious, I said, 'Yes, madam, I am.'

She was a pretty, dark-haired woman, and she smiled sweetly at me, as she said, 'I hope you will be happy here,' as if she really meant it.

'Thank you, madam,' I replied warmly, and became her devoted slave.

Tea having been served, Miss Finch and I leaned thankfully against the kitchen counters and had tea ourselves. At that time, Mary Finch was sixteen years old, a year and a half older than me, and this seemed a big gap to bridge, so our conversation was desultory.

After a few awkward minutes, we did another run up and down stairs to collect the dirty cups, and then washed them up. Our overalls still showed wet splashes from our washing up, when we again presented ourselves to Mr Ellis.

'The index cards are ready for filing,' he said. 'Get on with it.'

We obediently sorted the cards into alphabetical order and filed them. Then we took another trip to the basement waiting room to relieve Miss Lester, while she fled upstairs to the cloakroom.

Two new girls to look at caused the clients to rustle in their seats and murmur to each other behind shielding hands. There were no magazines for them to read, so their boredom must have been intense.

Miss Finch sat down at the table and I stood by her and looked around me. One wall was shelved and was packed with fat, dusty envelopes set upright.

'They're old files,' explained Miss Finch. 'If you can't find a file upstairs, it may be down here.' And as if to justify her words, the phone rang and she was requested to check if a certain file was on the shelves.

It was. And to save Miss Barker, K to Z , coming down for it, I was sent hurrying upwards with the grubby envelope. The staircases were rapidly beginning to feel like Mount Everest to me, they were so long and steep.

When I returned, a woman in a faded cotton frock and grey cardigan was standing in front of Mary. She was holding a baby and her stomach was already swollen with another child. Mary wrote down her name and address, and handed the slip to me.

'You phone it up,' she said lazily.

I took the slip as if it might bite me and reluctantly

went to the little cubbyhole where the phone was. Slowly, I lifted the receiver.

Immediately came the soft hello of the volunteer temporarily manning the switchboard.

I gave the name carefully, spelling it out to make sure that it was correctly recorded.

'Thank you,' said the voice from the switchboard very clearly.

I hung up the receiver on its hook and stood looking triumphantly at the phone. I had managed to use the instrument and I could hear on it. Joyfully I went back to Miss Finch. Perhaps, one day, I would be able to manage the switchboard.

Chapter twenty

After our visit to the basement waiting room, Miss Finch and I spent an hour sorting and filing index cards under Mr Ellis's eagle eye.

As her fingers flew along the drawers of cards, Miss Finch explained to me in a whisper that at half past eleven we had to go to a famous cake shop and restaurant to collect a sandwich lunch for a Committee, which would meet in the Committee Room on the top floor during the lunch hour. We had also to make coffee for the members, and lay the table.

The walk to the restaurant was not very far, but after all the stairs I had climbed in the course of the morning, it seemed a long way. Still, the fresh air blowing off the river and the bustle of the city were welcome. In this district there was little hint of the frightful effects of the Depression upon Liverpool; just an occasionally empty shop, and a larger number of offices to rent than usual. The businessmen hurrying up and down the street were well dressed, and no unemployed men hung about the street corners.

The lunch was not quite ready, so we waited unobtrusively in a corner of the cake shop and watched the fashionable crowd passing through to the restaurant at the rear. Ladies in flowered or feathered hats with veils drooping over their eyes were greeted by men in immaculate, dark suits, their neatly rolled umbrellas hooked over one arm, black felt hats held in their hands, as they ushered the ladies into the dreamland beyond. I remembered when Mother had been just such a lady meeting one of her men friends in a restaurant for lunch. She sometimes took me with her, as a sop to propriety, I presume.

My eyes wandered to the display counters. Behind the glass there was a wonderful collection of cakes, chocolate éclairs, *babas au rhum* topped with cream, *petits fours* in delicate pink, white or mauve icing, French sandwiches oozing with raspberry jam and cream and smothered in icing sugar. There was a fruit cake with at least an inch of marzipan resting on its top. It was flanked by chocolate swiss rolls, and my mouth watered. It all seemed part of a dream of long ago.

'Here, take this,' ordered Mary Finch.

She thrust a large confectioner's box into my hands and balanced another on top of it, while she turned to pay the shop assistant with money given her by the cashier.

'Be careful,' Mary warned, as we struggled through the lunch-time crowds. 'We'll get into trouble if the cakes are squashed.'

In the kitchen, we set out on plates the pretty cakes and the tiny rolls filled with different meats and wisps of mustard and cress. Then we laid the long, narrow table and made a pot of coffee, wrapping up the latter in tea towels to keep it warm.

With a last glance at the inviting table, Mary Finch hustled me out and down one floor to the silent lift.

'Committee members are allowed to use the lift,' she explained. 'You'd better know how to run it.'

I was dreadfully hungry and this announcement threw me into immediate panic. I foresaw another débâcle, like that of the switchboard.

Mary showed me how to start and stop the lift, and then said, 'Now, you try.'

Gingerly I closed the gates at the main floor, pressed the handle and, with a sense of shock, found that instead of going up we had descended to the basement waiting room. The astonished clients – they were, according to Mary, always to be referred to as clients – had seen all those preceding them sent up to the Interviewing Floor by the stairs and they were obviously surprised at this sudden arrival of a lift.

'Stupid,' hissed my teacher, who must herself have been both tired and hungry. 'Turn the handle the other way.'

I did so, and we shot upwards, passing a bewildered gentleman in a bowler hat standing on the ground floor.

We were at the top again and the lift automatically clanked to a stop. The door of the Filing Department opposite flew open. The Presence's typist, her face forbidding, asked, 'Why are you running the lift? The Secretary wishes to know.'

Trouble again. I opened my mouth like a cod fish, but it was Miss Finch who answered smartly, 'I'm teaching the new girl how to run it, ready for the Committee.'

'I see.' The typist returned to her desk.

'Phew!' exclaimed Mary. 'The old geezer's got the

ears of a cat. Now run the lift down, and stop at every floor. Try to get it level.'

We sailed straight down to the basement again, and I whispered to Mary, 'Caves, catacombs and coal mines, bargain floor.'

Mary started to giggle.

The man in the bowler hat must have decided to walk up the stairs, because the main floor, opposite the tea merchant's door, was deserted.

'Graveyards, grizzlies, golliwogs, gamps, goats, tea shop, main floor,' I announced gravely.

Mary laughed, and waited expectantly for the next floor.

'Overalls, olive oil, ostriches, offal, first floor,' I said, in the same sing-song voice of a department store lift girl.

'Secretaries, sausages, soap, Somalis, shoes, Simnel cakes.' I flung open the gate at the second floor, stepped out and bowed to Miss Finch as if she were an honoured customer and I a shop walker.

But Miss Finch looked past me, her face immobile. I whirled round. The Assistant Presence was watching me, her eyes twinkling with amusement.

Horrified, I waited for the guillotine to fall. But she was laughing, as she wagged an admonishing finger. 'The Committee will be arriving. I saw Mr Thompson walking up just now.'

'I'm sorry, Miss Dane,' said Mary, and with silent grimaces to each other we descended to the ground floor, while Miss Dane walked up to the Committee Room on the top floor which was not served by the lift.

There was a sound of running feet in the hall, and

a young man carrying a brief case almost flung himself into the lift. He was breathtakingly handsome, and his immaculate white shirt showed up a regimental tie to perfection. Before I could close the gates, he was joined by two white-haired ladies wafting a soft perfume with them. They greeted each other; and, after peeping out to see if anyone else was coming, I carefully closed the gates. The three passengers turned towards the gates and waited in silence as we travelled upwards, like a small congregation listening to a priest reciting the Creed.

At the top, I positioned the lift with a series of sharp little ups and downs, and then let the passengers out. None of them had said anything to either Miss Finch or me. The ladies loosened their furs and walked slowly up the remaining flight of stairs, while Miss Finch and I, like little marionettes, ran the lift up and down, ferrying other Committee members. Later, I learned that many of these people were members of old Liverpool families famous for their charities through several generations. They were all concerned by the sad state of their native city, and they gave generously of both time and money in an effort to help their suffering fellow citizens.

As I watched them from under lowered lids, it sometimes felt odd to me that my grandmother and grandfather had probably wined and dined with these people or their parents, had done business with them, had attended balls and concerts with them; and, there I was, so hungry that I could have eaten all the lunch waiting upstairs, running a lift for them as if I was part of the machinery.

Chapter twenty-one

I had been tired at the end of the first day of work, but by the end of the second day it seemed as if every muscle had its own particular ache. My imagination boggled at the thought of how many stairs had been climbed, how many miles walked. Even Miss Finch, who was a strong, well-fed girl, looked worn out; and I had done the same amount as she had on less food than a prisoner of war could hope for. As I trailed home, I realised that on the following day I would have to do the same work without Miss Finch's help.

At the end of the day one of the duties of the office girl, I discovered, was to collect any remaining outgoing letters from their various signatories, put them into their envelopes and take them to the nearby General Post Office and drop them in the letter box. There was always a flurry on the part of the stenographers to bring down last minute letters for signature by the Presence.

The Presence was a very hard-pressed woman and was frequently in the middle of phone calls or interviews, when the letters arrived. The stenographers laid the letters on her desk, thankfully put on their hats and coats and went home. The little office girl stood outside the office and waited for the letters to be brought out by the Presence's secretary, who was a volunteer; and on some evenings she waited and she waited.

The office clock would tick remorselessly on towards Edward's and Avril's bedtime and the hour of night school. My stomach would tighten with fear of Mother's temper if I was not there to help. And night school teachers could be very sarcastic if one was late for class.

Finally, the letters would be brought out. The pretty secretary would help me put them into their envelopes. Those to be delivered by hand were put on one side. With a smile of relief, the secretary would hand me the ones to be posted; and I would run down the stairs, across the busy streets, and dutifully drop them into the post office's mighty maw.

At home at last, I took off my hat and coat and hung them on a peg in the hall. There was no night school on that second day of work. But there was homework to do, English essays to write, arithmetic problems to solve, shorthand to practise. Then there were the beds, left from the morning, waiting to be made, dishes to wash up, Edward and Avril to wash and put to bed, clothes to be washed or sponged and pressed, all the thousand and one tasks of a large family. I sighed as I entered the living room.

The room looked different.

Everybody was present, except Fiona and Avril whom I could see through the window. They were skipping in the back yard.

The window!

It was shining clean and the grubby net curtain which usually covered it had been washed.

I glanced around. The big, old-fashioned iron grate with its side oven shone with blacking. The battered wooden chairs had been polished till all the nicks and chips in them appeared covered. The up-turned paint drums had been scoured. The mantel-piece, usually littered with bills and replies to Mother's begging letters, was dusted and tidied, the papers neatly stacked under a well-washed stone; and the alarm clock ticked merrily in the dead centre; it seemed to be sticking out its chest with pride at its pristine green paint and its twinkling glass. The worn linoleum on the floor was speckless and the piece of coconut matting in the centre had obviously received a good beating.

Mother was sitting by the fire. She had changed her work dress for a shapeless, grubby cotton frock and her bare feet were thrust into a pair of old carpet slippers. The varicose veins on her legs showed in sickening knots, and her face was lined with fatigue. She had started to darn the boys' socks ready for them to put on again in the morning, and she was frowning heavily as she pushed the big needle in and out. She looked up as I entered.

'Goodness, Mum,' I exclaimed, as I looked round admiringly. 'You have been busy. The room looks lovely.'

'Humph.' She looked down at her darning again.

I eased around the *Liverpool Echo* and gave Father a cautious peck on the cheek, in the hope that I was forgiven for going to work. And then I leaned over and gave Mother an equally careful kiss. But Mother, for once, did not seem angry with me. She said, 'Hello, dear,' rather absently and went on darning.

I picked up Edward and gave him a hug. He

laughed at me as I put him down, and then scrambled away under the table, where, judging from the dialogue, Brian and Tony had established a castle. Their imaginations were so fertile that they were able to create a whole strange world out of almost nothing, and it probably saved them in some degree from the effects of the savage reality of our life.

Mother said very mildly. 'There is some dinner in the oven for you, dear.'

Alan looked up from his book, and said, 'Hello. It's sausages.' He sounded cheerful and his red-rimmed, bright blue eyes were, as usual, friendly in their expression.

I grinned at him, and then I looked back at Mother. Sometimes I was more afraid of her when she was being kind than I was when she was not. Carefully, I moved round the back of her and opened the heavy oven door. Two sausages sat on a plate accompanied by a good tablespoonful of dried up cabbage and a whole potato. I whipped the hot plate over to the table, found a knife and fork and thankfully sat down to eat. From time to time, I took a peep at Mother's clouded face.

'The dinner's nice,' I said appreciatively. This brought no response, so I added, 'You must have worked awfully hard today, Mum.' I looked again round the room and wondered where she had got the soap, the polish and the blacking from. There had never been any money for such things while I had been keeping house. The floor must have been scrubbed with a scrubbing brush, which we did not possess, before it could be shined as it had been.

Father rose, picked the teapot off the hob and brought it to me. He looked down at me with an odd expression on his face – as if he were trying to warn me. 'Here you are, old girl,' he said kindly, as he put the pot down on the table. 'Have some tea.'

What had I said that I should not have said?

'Thanks, Daddy.'

Mother stabbed a sock to death. 'I have not been working here,' she announced icily. 'I have been in Lewis's all day, demonstrating automatic toasters.'

Alan did not look up from his book, but the eyelid furthest from Mother went down in a clear, slow wink.

'That must have been interesting,' I said firmly, as I poured a cup of well-boiled tea. 'I've never seen an automatic toaster.'

'I hope I never see another,' said Mother with feeling. Then her rage burst out of her. 'Alice – that Alice – had the temerity to walk into this house this morning, without permission, and clean this room. She actually let herself in. It's outrageous!' Mother rolled up a pair of socks and flung them into the fruit punnet we used as a sewing box.

'Alice cleaned it?' I exclaimed.

'She did and I am furious.'

'She did a marvellous job,' I said, with honest admiration.

Mother's chin quivered and her thin chest heaved, as she seized another sock and thrust her hand into it.

'I will decide when my house needs cleaning. I will not have a peasant walking in and out of here, as if she owned the place.'

I was so tired, and I thought how marvellous it would be to come home every day to a clean, tidy house, so I said pacifically, 'You know, Mummy, if she did not charge very much, it might be worth getting her to do it regularly. It would save us both.'

'She didn't charge anything,' interjected Alan. 'When she brought Edward home, she said it gave her something to do while her mother was having a nap and that Edward liked being in his own house.'

'What nonsense!' Mother said angrily.

'Where did she get the blacking from? And the polish?' I inquired, as I scraped my plate.

Alan laughed. 'She brought her own.'

Mother caught her breath and I looked quickly across at her. She was biting her lower lip and a tear ran down her face. Suddenly I understood her humiliation, and instinctively I jumped up and went over to her. I put my arm round her shaking shoulders.

'Try not to cry, Mummy,' I urged. 'Everybody knows you have been ill and she probably thought she was being kind and helpful. I know that people round here help each other a lot. They always seem to know where help is needed, because they gossip so much.'

Mother nearly choked. 'I don't want them gossiping about me,' she shouted. 'When I want help I will pay for it.'

Father had been watching the scene over his newspaper, and now he said exasperatedly, 'You should not be upset. The girl meant well. She's not going to do it again, I am sure.'

'She certainly will not,' snapped Mother. 'As you observed, I settled that point once and for all.'

I felt as if Mother had stabbed me with her darning needle. 'Don't let it be so, O Lord. Please!' I almost whispered aloud.

But it *had* happened. Alice had been dismissed as firmly as I had been the previous day. And I had yet to tell my parents about my dismissal and reinstatement.

'What about Edward?' I asked, trying to keep calm.

'Oh, you will have to stay at home. This idea of going to work is ridiculous. See what an upset it has caused to all of us. And you are worn out.'

I *was* worn out. Mother so rarely looked at me unless I had done something wrong, that I was surprised that she had noticed. But the gulf opening in front of me was so abhorrent to me that I gained a fresh surge of strength. And I fought back as if defeat would mean certain hanging in the morning.

Every member of the family joined in the battle. Mother had hysterics, Father roared, Edward howled. Avril, stretched to her full thirty inches of height, shook her finger at us all and demanded in frantic tones that we stop. Alan took my part with reckless abandon. Fiona wept and screwed her piece of skipping rope into knots as she swore she was not going to stay at home, as I suggested. From the castle under the table, the sounds of knights preparing to go out to slay a dragon ceased and two scared faces peeped out.

'Who is going to see that the boys don't get into trouble?' Mother asked dramatically, as they emerged.

'I will,' shouted Alan.

'They're big enough to look after themselves,' I screamed, most unfairly.

Brian and Tony began to bellow as they, poor innocents, suddenly became the focus of the quarrel. They must have felt that they were being abandoned by all of us.

Sometimes, in those difficult days, I identified myself with an alley cat which I had once seen engulfed in a football crowd racing down a train platform from a football special. Slipping, sliding, slithering in and out amongst the hob-nailed boots, fearing all the time that small paws would be crushed, wispy tail agonisedly trodden on; expecting any moment to feel a steel toe in the ribs flinging it over the platform edge into dark, unknown depths of misery; finding, for a second, shelter by a pile of luggage in which to lick quickly at bruised sides; only to be caught up again in the ruthless rush; looking madly for a wall up which to race or a kindly hand to sweep it up and tuck it inside a shirt, away from the terrible boots.

This time I thought that Minerva had forgotten her stepchild.

The abuse was largely verbal but the threat of physical punishment was always there. The elder children had when young all felt the weight of a cane and sound spankings with a hand; and occasionally both Father and Mother would strike out quite hard at one or the other of us. I do not think it occurred to any of us, even Alan who was growing quite tall, to strike back.

I would not yield. Mother said she would go to see the Presence and would demand my dismissal. The organisation had not, after all, purchased me, she said acidly.

Suddenly I remembered the Presence's words about a week's notice. Presumably, on my side, a week's notice would also have to be given before I could leave. I announced this triumphantly as fact.

'What rubbish,' shrieked Mother. She was thrashing round the small room like a tiger, and the children moved mechanically to get out of her way as she advanced on each one of them.

Father, who was still sitting in his chair, as if it offered a modicum of safety, the newspaper crumpled in his clenched fists, said in a more normal voice, 'She is correct. Either we pay a week's salary to them or she must work the week.'

Fiona wailed loudly, 'I don't want to stay at home.'

'You'll have to,' I said mercilessly. 'Fi, you'll have to. I have done my bit. You must take a turn. It's only till Edward is big enough to go to school.'

'I won't,' she screamed. She flung her skipping rope to the floor. 'No.'

'No,' Mother flashed at me. 'Oh, no. You are not going to push your responsibilities on to poor Fiona. She is much too frail, poor darling.'

Chapter twenty-two

The need to give notice saved me.

Fiona was ordered to stay at home with Edward for the following two days. Mother's contract with the toaster manufacturer expired on Thursday night; she would start a new contract at another store the following Tuesday. This, I argued, would give her time to arrange some fresh care for Edward.

Poor little Edward. Poor Fiona, red-faced and deeply resentful. Mother actually smiled, however, when I presented her with my total earning for the week, less fourpence for contributions to National Health and Unemployment Insurance and another penny contributed to a hospital fund. She hardly heard me when I explained that the following week, I would be earning only an office girl's pay.

In the office, I ran so hard and whispered so softly that my appointment was confirmed, despite my gauche manners and poor grooming.

A few weeks later, the other girls asked me to accompany them to the cinema. Bashfully, I refused, owning up that I did not have the money. They looked at me askance and did not ask me again for a number of years; perhaps they thought I did not like them.

Night school came to an end and I passed the examinations. This gave me more time to help Mother at home. The office staff, in turn, went away for two weeks' holiday to the mountains or the seaside. They usually went with their parents and came back with breathtaking stories of the boys they had met. They giggled behind the stacks of files until Mr Ellis roared at them to return to their work. He seemed to be the only person who spoke above a thin whisper.

I had no adventures to share with the girls. I was not entitled to a holiday that year, and my world of screaming family rows, of creditors, of pawnbrokers, of the lack of the most basic human needs, seemed to be so divorced from the experience of the staff, that there was no common ground. I was obsessed with the need to survive, with simple worries, like how to squeeze a pair of rayon stockings out of Mother, or even darning silk with which to mend the ones I wore. I was totally dependent upon the whims of Mother. She seemed to take it for granted that anything I earned was hers, and this idea stayed with her throughout my working life. Girls did not need money for expenses; boys did.

One day, the Presence told me sharply to tidy up my hair. It was pay day and, in despair, I took out of my nine shillings and sevenpence a single bright shilling. A comb cost twopence, some hairclips a penny. Ninepence would buy a good, stout pair of rayon stockings.

Mother was so infuriated that she tried to snatch Joan's old handbag off me in order to extract the shilling, but I whisked it under me and sat on it and, tearfully, refused to move.

Father came home and walked into the middle of

the scene, and I appealed to him, because sometimes he did seem to regard me as a human being, even if I was a girl. Without any hesitation, he said I should keep the shilling, and have one each week, so I thankfully fled with my handbag to the kitchen and left my parents to fight it out.

The weekly shilling was usually spent on second-hand articles of clothing. But I soon learned not to leave any pieces of clothing at home unless they were wet from washing, because they would be immediately pawned; stockings or gloves would be used by Mother herself or given to Fiona. On days when there was nothing to take for my lunch, I would buy a penny bread roll from Lunt's bakery near the office.

An overwhelming ambition in those days was to be able to afford from Lunt's a roll packed with cheese. These cost twopence, however, and I had to content myself with buying them for other members of the staff or just looking longingly at them through the bakery's steamy window.

And so I struggled blindly on from day to day. The trees in Princes Park, where on Saturday afternoons I took Edward to play, turned yellow and carpeted a neat circle of grass beneath them with curled-up leaves. Wet days became more frequent, and I delivered the letters each morning in shoes that became quickly sodden; the cardboard put into them to block up the holes disintegrated, and tender bare soles were exposed to the pavement. I caught so many colds that the days when I was without one became ones of rejoicing. Liverpool air is always damp and, in those days, was filled with black particles from a myriad of chimneys, so that nasal catarrh and bronchitis were endemic and gave rise to the famous, snuffly Liverpool accent. Like many of the population I blew my nose through my fingers on to the pavement, and kept my single handkerchief for neat dabs at my nose in the office.

Alan reached the age of fourteen in November and left school shortly afterwards. I was plunged into bitter and unfair jealousy, as I watched him set out for his first job as office boy in a new suit bought for the occasion from Marks & Spencers. In his pocket he carried a bit of lunch wrapped in an old margarine paper and a penny for the tram, so that he would not have to climb the long hill home. He was given pocket money as a matter of course, so my battle evidently helped him. He was intelligent and quick-witted and very articulate. He had snatched the job from dozens of other applicants and deserved all the help my parents could give him.

The life of an office boy was very hard. In a tall, gloomy, Victorian building, he worked from eight-thirty in the morning until six o'clock at night and until one o'clock on Saturdays, for a wage of seven shillings and sixpence a week. Office boys were commonly hit when they made mistakes or if they dared to answer their seniors back, and the tight-lipped bookkeeper who taught him how to keep accounts was very heavy handed. He was still far from being fully developed and, like me, was painfully thin. Since he spoke 'with an olly in his mouth', he had been in many fights at school – it is not only sparrows who attempt to destroy those different from themselves – and sometimes, in the absence of the bookkeeper at lunch, a general fight would break out amongst the young men in the office. Though he fought back fairly skilfully, I can remember seeing bruises across his buttocks where he had been beaten with an old-fashioned rounded ruler.

Attached to the church was a troop of Boy Scouts and Alan had joined this. Although we were certainly not the poorest family in the parish, the Scoutmaster must have found it impossible to obtain money from my parents for a uniform for him, and, therefore, provided him with one. He once went away to camp with them and returned looking strong and rosy and very freckled, but the fair skin soon became white again and the beguiling freckles faded, to be replaced by acne in its worst forms. Great boils covered his face and neck. A cheerful expression helped to compensate for this affliction. His tousled cowlick was neatly slicked back with the aid of brilliantine and the black pocket comb tucked into his jacket pocket. His pale skin gained a slight ruddiness as, like me, he ran through the streets of Liverpool, in and out of horse and motor traffic, delivering letters and messages.

Like me, Alan suffered from the lack of a raincoat and from inadequate footwear. Liverpool shares with Ireland not only Irish inhabitants but Irish weather. When it is not actually raining, there is still a misty dampness which seems to penetrate one's bones. Older people always seem to be complaining about 'me rheumatism' or 'me arthritics' and say that they 'hurt something wicked' on wet days.

Alan, Brian and Tony all played cricket in the street, often with a beer bottle as a wicket and a piece of board as a bat. Alan had had the advantage, when quite a small boy, of playing the game in better circumstances. A couple of professionals had taken an amused interest in the little eager beaver who haunted their practice ground and had coached him. This acquired ability had led him into the school team. One of his older colleagues at work gave him his old cricket bat and pads, and this enhanced his chances of playing with other teams after he left school. He got a lot of pleasure from these games.

He also went to night school. He always says he learned a lot there. But he did not stay in the system very long, and he probably learned much more in the Auxiliary Air Force, which he joined a few years later.

I rejoiced in his good beginning in the business world. Because my parents kept pressing me to stay at home again and be the unpaid housekeeper, I was most unchristianly envious of the interest and encouragement lavished on him by both Mother and Father. I cried for hours through freezing winter nights, and prayed frequently and earnestly for strength to keep my temper. I was convinced that most of my misery was caused by lack of self-control over envy and bad temper. It was a long time before I realised that there is a limit to anybody's self-control; and that the only sin I had committed was to be born to my Mother at a time when she would otherwise have divorced my Father. She could never forgive me for it.

Chapter twenty-three

As autumn merged into winter the children began to look forward to Christmas, having been reminded of its coming by Brian and Tony's extra choir practices. For years, Fiona and I secreted all kinds of bits of wool, old socks and cotton scraps, and out of them we manufactured gifts for the family. Golliwogs and rabbits emerged from the socks, hand-hemmed handkerchiefs, handkerchief cases, pin cushions and hair tidies, prettily covered boxes and pyjama cases were made from the cotton scraps. I once made Fiona a doll's bed out of a shoebox; it was complete with little blankets and a bedspread, and she joyfully put her tattered doll into it. The doll was her only treasure from our old home. It was dreadfully dirty, and its papier mâché feet and hands were nearly worn out; but its glass eyes still opened and closed and it still had some hair.

Another time, I made a horse and cart for Edward. The horse was made out of corks found in the street. It had wobbly legs made out of slivers of firewood. The cart, which was a carton from a box of matches, had high wheels made from the tiny lids of ointment tins, also found in the street gutters. Though it was not a very robust toy he played with it for several days before it fell to bits.

From their choir money, Brian and Tony bought

little gifts for everybody. One of my most treasured possessions is a pottery black cat given me by Tony and, until recently, I had a tiny pottery donkey with a red pincushion on its back, bought for me by Brian. When, after forty-five years, I recently smashed the donkey I stood over the scattered bits and cried. Both these treasures travelled half way round the world with me. Another treasure is a crocheted red and yellow egg cosy made for me by Avril in one of her earliest sewing classes. Sometimes I take it out and think of the small, determined little girl stabbing away with a crochet hook too big for her fingers.

Alan's shilling a week was strictly for pocket money, so he bought us all kinds of delightful gifts, like bottles of perfume and talcum powder from Woolworth's.

My parents always tried to make Christmas pleasant for the younger children. Only the first two Christmases in Liverpool were without any real effort at celebration, and for both of those we enjoyed one of the Christmas boxes of food distributed to the poor of Liverpool during the festive season.

For two Christmases after I began work, a mysterious stranger telegraphed us five pounds. We never discovered who sent it but it provided a dinner and a stocking full of small gifts for the little ones.

Alan and I, like all working people, had two days' holiday. Such was his exhaustion that on any holiday Alan slept until midday. For Fiona and me, however, there was never such a luxury. Boys needed rest; girls could manage without. Brian and Tony had to be got up and given their breakfast in time for them to sing at the Christmas services. Edward, like most little boys, was awake at sun-up, as was Father. On Sundays and holidays, Mother stayed late in bed and Avril slept late, too. Holidays for me were not a time for relaxation, and I was always thankful to escape back to work. At work, people occasionally said, 'Thank you.'

In February, the cold and the lack of food caught up with me, and I fell ill. I staggered round the spinning office, dumbly terrified that if I said I was ill I would be dimissed, as girls in shops sometimes were. There was the further fear that if I had to stay at home, Mother would find means of keeping me there. She looked after Edward on days when she had no work; occasionally Fiona would be kept at home to mind him, and on other days he was handed round to various neighbouring women to be watched for a few hours. The problem was solved when he reached the age of four and could run along to school with Avril. Nothing seemed to disturb him much. He was used to a large family and seemed to add any strangers to that family. He was obedient and had a tranquillity which the rest of us lacked. Perhaps he realised that, despite the fights which raged over his head, he was never attacked and we all loved him very much.

Though the gulf between Mother and me had, since infancy, appeared to me to be unbridgeable, she had recently begun to talk idly to me as if I were a woman. Only the surface of her mind seemed to be engaged in the conversation; somewhere deep underneath lay the real woman, with true passions and motives. But it was better than nothing. Despite this small break, I still dreaded that she would again pass over her family responsibilities to me. So that in overwhelming fear I fumbled about the office making tea, sorting index cards, going out to deliver letters, while Mr Ellis ranted that I was more than usually slow and stupid. My chest hurt and my throat hurt and I ached all over as I sought to please him. On the second day, like an Edwardian heroine, I collapsed quietly into a chair.

Everybody was concerned and kind. Smelling salts were thrust under my nose, tea was made; and, when I could get up, Mary was instructed to escort me to the tram. I was not very clear about what was happening and was shivering, as Mary bundled me into the vehicle.

I sat down by a workman in torn work clothes, and took out my last penny from Joan's handbag. I dropped it, and it rattled away down towards the front of the vehicle. The workman looked up from his *Echo*, while I sat aghast, feeling that even if I could find the coin under the feet of all the other passengers, I would collapse if I bent over to retrieve it.

The middle-aged workman next to me was staring, as the skinny conductor, rattling his money bag as warning, came down the aisle to collect the fares. I sat silent, waiting to be thrown off at the next stop because I did not have the fare.

The man folded up his paper and proffered a sixpence to the conductor. 'Two woons, lad,' he said.

The conductor punched two tickets, handed them to him, and wandered on down the aisle. The man handed one of the tickets to me. ‘ ’ere ya, luv,’ he said, his rough red face beaming.

My voice seemed to come from far away, as I said, ‘Thank you. Thank you very much. You are most kind.’

‘Aye, that’s all right, luv.’

He looked down at his folded paper and I looked down at the stubby fingers holding it; they were scarred from many cuts about the knuckles and the nails were broken to the quick. The memory of them and of their wonderfully perceptive owner stayed with me through the illness that followed.

Contributions to National Health Insurance entitled workers to the services of a doctor. When my parents came home and found me shivering in my bed, they sent for the general practitioner with whom I had registered my name.

He came marching into the smelly, bug-ridden bedroom, went straight to the window and flung it open, waited for a moment and then closed it partially. In the light of a candle held by Mother, he examined me and diagnosed influenza and tonsillitis. The tonsillitis had caused an ear infection. He ordered that more covering than the single blanket and old overcoat on my bed be put over me, a fire be made in the bedroom, the window kept slightly open. He painted my throat with tannic acid, put drops in my ears and ordered aspirin to alleviate the influenza. He was a handsome man with a very white skin and a large black moustache. He was exceedingly kind to me over the three weeks of my illness, coming in daily to paint my throat, and assumed an almost Godlike character in my romantic mind.

He also ordered a light diet of milk, eggs and orange juice. This seemed to be out of the question. But Mother did make bread and milk for me, and for the rest I had Oxo cubes dissolved in hot water, toast and tea. When there was enough coal, a fire was made for me by Father, but most of the time we were too short of fuel, despite the fact that my kind employer continued to send my wages by mail and Mother cashed the postal orders.

For days I lay in my cold bed watching the sleet and rain of February through the dusty, finger-marked window, too exhausted by fever and pain to think. The children were used to my retiring temporarily to bed with bouts of tonsillitis and rarely came to see me except at bedtime. Edward had been moved from my bed in case of infection and shared my parents' bed; but as soon as the fever had departed Mother used me as a baby-sitter for him, which meant I dared not sleep during the day.

Once I could walk about the house, I asked the doctor to certify me as fit. I told him that if I was away much longer, I might lose my job. This was such a common reason for going back to work before one was fit, that he signed the certificate. I washed and ironed my blouse and panties, mended my stockings and the next day reported to work.

It seemed as if the staircases had grown longer in my absence and the distances I had to walk to deliver letters seemed to have expanded to infinity. Several times I had to lean against a wall until bouts of faintness passed.

It took such a very long time to walk home that

Father became anxious and set out to meet me. We came face to face beside the Philharmonic Hall, where he had paused to glance at the tattered black and white posters announcing their concerts.

His cheap navy blue suit shone at the elbows and seat, and it hung on him. He looked cold and forlorn without a raincoat, and his thin, lined face showed anxiety, as he hastened towards me.

'Where have you been?' he inquired, as he took my elbow and turned towards home. 'We have been worried about you.'

'I had to wait for the letters to be signed before I posted them,' I muttered, my breath coming in short gasps after the effort of climbing the hill.

'You should have taken the tram home,' Father said. 'You're not fit to walk.'

'I didn't have any money,' I wailed suddenly, all the misery of years bursting from me in one long, subdued howl.

'Good God! I thought it was arranged that you should have a shilling a week for pocket money and fares.' He stopped and looked into my woebegone face.

'Mother didn't have any of my wages left, when I asked her this morning,' I sobbed.

He clicked his tongue in annoyance. 'Dear Lord!' he exclaimed in exasperation.

This was the first time for many years that Father and I had been together without any other member of the family present, and it was as if he came out of his usual absent state and really looked at me. The sight seemed to have some impact.

I continued to wail softly as we inched our way along dark Myrtle Street and turned into Catherine Street, while he supported me by the elbow.

My sobs receded and I turned towards him. His large, high-bridged nose was scarlet from acne roseola, the rest of the skin an unhealthy yellow. His shirt and collar had reached an off-white colour from too much washing with too little soap, and his trousers badly needed pressing. His expression was so sad that I nearly burst into tears again. When he was not absorbed in a book or quarrelling with Mother, he could be quite light-hearted and very witty, but now I was again reminded of a butterfly caught in a rainstorm. With horrid clarity, I saw, not a vague, exasperating figure called Father, but a defeated man; and for a moment I walked with him through the morass of despair into which he had fallen. There seemed nothing left of the cheerful young man, described to me by Grandma, who had gone off to war, despite his short-sightedness, and ended up in the forests of Russia. My first memories of him had been of a voice screaming with terror in the night. He suffered scarifying nightmares of his war experiences while he tried to re-establish himself in a post war world, which was fed up with returning soldiers and their needs. He was a cultivated man, clever in his way, but now he worked as a clerk for the city, earning more than he handed over to Mother, but still very little. With the rest of the family, he suffered very much from the lack of intellectual companionship as well as lack of food and comfort.

As we slowly made our way along Catherine Street,

we began to feel comfortable together, like walking wounded helping each other along. Though we did not talk much, because I was too exhausted, a feeling of understanding began to grow between us.

Before we entered the house, Father took a sixpence from his waistcoat pocket and pressed it into my hand.

'Come home on the tram every day,' he ordered.

I stared down at the tiny silver coin, too tired even to thank him, and then nodded agreement and slipped the coin into my handbag.

He pulled the string hanging from the letterbox and released the latch of the front door. He swung the door open and stepped back on to the pavement with a little bow, to allow me to pass in first. Poignantly, that polite gesture brought home to me, more than anything else, how different he was from the men who lived round us. Little Avril once expressed a similar idea. She said, 'I love Daddy. He is so gentle and he is the only man in the street who wears a collar.'

Chapter twenty-four

I soon gained strength again and, through long days, slid silently between the patient, smelly clients, carrying cups of tea or files or messages. Sometimes I felt like advising the quietly courteous interviewers that our funds would do as much good if they were simply scattered in the back streets and left for the inhabitants to pick up. In large areas of Liverpool there was barely an inhabitant who was not in distress. Workless, half-starved, they were packed into deteriorating houses lacking proper toilets or running water. They were often shiftless and stupid, many spent their money on drink and some on drugs, but their need was blatantly manifest to anyone who cared to walk down the long treeless streets and through the narrow courts. Born and bred in such shocking conditions, who could blame them for seeking at every opportunity the garish warmth of the public houses on almost every corner?

It was pathetic to watch the clients doing their best not to use coarse language before the gently-bred ladies of our organisation. Their usually loud voices were lowered to the whispers of the confessional, as they hesitantly chose words that would please, not offend. They never laughed.

In fact, nobody laughed, except the shorthand typists in their isolated nest on the top floor. It was not an environment calculated to raise the spirits of a sad and sick fifteen-year old.

Grandma had, however, taught me to read out of the Bible, and I believed firmly in miracles. I had also not yet totally lost my belief in fairies, particularly Robin Goodfellow, a wicked sprite who sometimes snatched cups from my careless fingers and smashed them on the floor or who lost my pencils and dropped the hairpins out of my hair.

When the Presence sent for me one sunny May morning, therefore, I was expecting to be upbraided for the breakage of a cup and saucer, Robin Goodfellow having been rather busy the previous day. Instead, she performed a miracle.

I stood humbly before her desk, blue overall crumpled and splashed, greasy hair untidily knotted into a bun at the nape of my neck. Fortunately, she was too busy to look up at me.

She had a letter in her hand and she announced, as she read it, that I was entitled to two weeks' holiday that summer and had been granted a free holiday in a place called Kent's Bank. Mr Ellis would tell me when I could go, and a train ticket would be sent to me by the charity concerned. It did not strike me at the time that she might have asked me if I would like to go. I was ordered to depart for Kent's Bank on a date to be arranged.

Beside myself with excitement, I thanked her and fled back upstairs to the kitchen, where I stood quivering in front of the sink. A holiday! An undreamed of luxury. A miracle.

Later, I cautiously inquired of one of the filing

clerks if she knew where Kent's Bank was. She looked derisively at me for a moment and then sniggered. That little choking laugh told me that a recipient of charity was contemptible, and that she knew why I asked.

'It's on Morecambe Bay,' she said, and turned superciliously back to her file sorting.

Terribly hurt, I slunk back to the kitchen.

*

As I ate potatoes and cabbage and gravy, saved for me from the hot meal Mother had made at tea time, I told her about the holiday.

'It's all free, Mummy. Even the train ticket. Except I think I would simply have to have a nightgown and some walking shoes – if you could get them, Mummy.'

'I can't afford them,' said Mother simply. She was sitting in the easy chair, Edward on her lap, and smoking a cigarette.

'It is time you provided things like that for yourself, now that you are at work.' She took a slow pull at the cigarette and exhaled the smoke through her nostrils. 'You must have had a rise in salary since you started. You have been working for over a year now.'

Startled, I blinked at her. I had hardly given a thought to pay increases. I had concentrated solely on retaining my job.

'No, Mummy. I've never had a rise – only a reduction the first week. I'm still the office girl.'

Mother's eyebrows rose. 'That's absurd. You must have had an increase.'

'Honestly, Mummy. I haven't. I would have told you if I had.'

Her lips twisted and she stared hostilely at me. It was clear that she did not believe me.

My throat constricted. Then I said stiffly, 'I don't cheat, Mummy.'

'They don't have money to give increases,' interjected Father, looking up from his book, laid on the table in front of him beside a half-drunk cup of tea. 'Helen should go. She still doesn't look well. Perhaps we could get a one pound cheque to buy the things she needs. Try. See what you can do.'

While they argued and Mother fretted about the peremptoriness of the Presence, who had obviously not considered that my help might be needed at home, I rescued Avril from a fight on the front pavement and put her and Edward to bed. Avril always wanted to be included in the boys' games; and this time they had not allowed her to join in a game of marbles and she was in a howling tantrum over it. She transferred some of her furious frustration to me, as I hauled her into bed and told her in true sisterly fashion to shut up.

It was a further miracle which found me standing on the doorstep of a fine stone mansion in Kent's Bank run as a guest house by an organisation which used its profits to provide free holidays for the less fortunate. The June sun warmed my back and the clear, sharp smell of the sea wafted round me. In my hand I held a brown paper bag containing a clean blouse and panties, a nightgown and a toothbrush. On my feet I wore a second-hand pair of boy's shoes.

Fiona had volunteered the loan of her raincoat which was a little short on me, but made me look quite neat. All the children had been delighted that I was to go on a holiday, though it was clear from their wistful faces that they wished they could come, too.

In answer to my timorous knock, a middle-aged man, swarthy and black-haired, ushered me in and up a fine, well-carpeted staircase, to a large bedroom containing six single beds.

'You are the first arrival, so choose whichever bed you like,' he said with a cheerful grin. 'You can put your toilet things on the dressing-table there and clothes in the wardrobe.' He gestured towards two enormous pieces of shining Edwardian furniture.

'I'd enjoy being by the window,' I replied shyly, pointing to the furthest bed which stood close to a tall light window draped in white net curtains. Through the window I could see pine trees waving in the breeze and a dazzling glimpse of the sea.

'Fine,' he said. 'Come downstairs to the lounge and have some tea, as soon as you are ready.'

I smiled my thanks and he went away.

Feeling very nervous, I put the paper bag in the wardrobe, and then like a cat in a new place I walked round the room, examining the peerless white pillows on the beds, looking down at the highly polished linoleum on the floor, and finally stopping to wash my hands in a tiny basin in a corner. I combed my hair and redid my bun in front of the spotted dressing table mirror, and then cautiously opened the bedroom door and ventured downstairs.

The lounge was full of chattering men and women,

who all seemed much older than me, and I hesitated in the doorway while the scene came into clearer focus.

An elderly gentleman was sitting on a settee directly opposite the doorway. When he looked up from his teacup and saw me, he smiled, and evidently realised that I was feeling very shy. He motioned me to come over and sit by him, which I did, perching nervously on the edge of the settee.

He had a large, grey moustache and heavy black eyebrows under which bright blue eyes twinkled merrily. He took a pipe out of his mouth and said, 'Just arrived?' I nodded, and he put down his teacup. 'I'll get you some tea. Do you take milk and sugar?'

I assented with another shy nod, and he went to the tea table and returned with tea and three biscuits. He pulled a small table forward and set the cup in front of me.

'There we are,' he announced. His voice was deep, with a pleasant Welsh sing-song to it. He sat down beside me and took up his own cup again. He had put his pipe away in the pocket of his finely cut tweed jacket.

'My name is Emrys Hughes,' he said. 'And that's my brother, Gwyn, over there.' He gestured towards the mantelpiece against which leaned a tall, thin man, also grey-haired, talking to a lady in a green dress. 'What's your name?'

I told him, and, while I sipped my tea, he asked where I came from and whether I was still at school. Each question came out in such a breezy, cheerful manner that I was soon relaxed and laughing with him. He told me that he and his brother owned two big drapery shops in North Wales, that he himself had had a heart attack at the beginning of the year, so he had come to Kent's Bank for a holiday. He had prevailed upon his bachelor brother to come with him, and they had left the businesses to the tender mercies of managers.

The teacups were removed, and still we gossiped. For the first time for many years, I was among people who knew nothing about me and judged me by what they saw. Gwyn brought the lady in green over to us. She proved to be a school teacher, who had already been at Kent's Bank for a week. Emrys looked at a heavy gold pocket watch which he took out of his top pocket, suggested that we all go for a stroll in the grounds and then eat dinner at the same table. So, much to the amusement of the older people, I spent a happy half hour running about among the trees, trying to get close to one of the many squirrels, and arrived at the dinner table glowing with the fresh air and the happy anticipation of an adequate meal.

The staff who served the meal seemed to be accustomed to very hungry people, and I ate my way through three plates of meat and vegetables and two of pudding. Emrys, who had to keep his weight down, he said, leaned back in his chair and watched me speculatively, while Gwyn and Margaret, the school teacher, chipped me about how such a small person could find room for so much food.

Having lived so much with Grandma, I felt quite at home with older people. I lost my nervousness completely, my usual gauche manners gave way to the good conduct instilled in me as a child, and I felt so happy I thought I would explode. Emrys had a way of sitting quietly and giving complete and careful attention to what was said to him. He would run his tobacco-stained fingers through his thick, grey hair, worn rather longer than was then the fashion, and smile, and comment or argue carefully on any subject discussed with me, as if I was an adult whose ideas were important to him. I was unused to anyone giving me their full attention and if I had been less innocent, I might have been troubled at such affability. But as I responded to his good-humoured teasing I knew only a great gaiety and lightness of heart. A liveliness I did not know I had began to emerge.

The first two days of the holiday were taken up with long, organised walks in the countryside, broken in the middle by a picnic lunch. The guests were divided into two groups, those who could take very long walks and those who preferred easier ones. Since both Emrys and I had been ill, we chose the easier walks and Gwyn and his school teacher came along with us.

I now shared the bedroom with five mill girls from Rochdale. All of them had been ill and said frankly that they, too, were enjoying free holidays. They all had several changes of clothing and enough money to buy tickets for the bus trips, later in the week, and to purchase endless sweets and ice cream cones from the village shop. They ignored me, and kept up a raucous conversation amongst themselves. Though I had often heard foul language in the streets of Liverpool,

I had never lived with people who used it, and I was frequently shocked and sickened by them. They also came on the easy walks, but fortunately stayed within their own group.

I danced along beside Emrys, through forest glades dappled with sunshine or along the sides of fields waving silvery green with growing oats. Occasionally, Gwyn would make us stop, while Emrys sat down to rest. He carried a piece of macintosh in his pocket and when a convenient wall or bench did not present itself, he spread the macintosh on the ground and sat on that. While he regained his breath, I would cast around, picking wild flowers or small sprays of fresh green foliage, which one of the staff would put in a vase on the dining table for me. Emrys did not know the names of many of the plants, but I had learned their names from Edith and was able to identify them for him.

Though I had handed to Mother three weeks' salary paid in advance, she had not seen fit to give me any money. I had only a few pennies in my purse, because I had spent most of the three weekly shillings on stockings. This made it impossible for me to buy tickets for the coach tour arranged for the third day.

Emrys and Gwyn had not yet come down to breakfast, so I ate the meal rather soberly in the company of Margaret and another middle-aged lady. Margaret was herself convalescing after a dose of influenza and we compared our respective illnesses and then talked about books.

'See you later,' she said gaily, and I nodded. I went

up to the empty bedroom and wondered how to employ the day. I heard the arrival of the motor coach and the bustle of departure, as I sat with a copy of Lytton's *Last Days of Pompeii* in my lap. I had already read the story twice and this seemed to hold true of all the books in the lounge downstairs. Finally, I tossed it aside. I would have a bath. I had tried several times since my arrival to do this, but the bathroom had invariably been occupied. Today, however, all the other guests had gone out so I could take my time about it.

The bath was a huge, Victorian tub, left over from the time when the house had been a private home. I turned on its great brass taps and let the water thunder in until it was quite deep. There was a large, used tablet of soap in a wire basket stretched across the bath. Quickly I stripped off and stepped in.

This was the first bath I had had for four years and the water rippling across my stomach felt odd. I looked down at long, slender legs wavering beneath the water, at a stomach which stuck out too much like that of a hungry child, at surprisingly prominent young breasts, at arms so thin they looked like sticks. The skin was a dull yellow, almost bronze in places. I had not looked at myself properly since I was a child, in that long ago world which we had left so precipitously. As I soaked in the hot water, I remembered how Father had told his biggest creditor to sell up his house and its contents, and how he had walked out of it, allowing us to take nothing with us, except the clothing we were wearing and a blanket to cover his sick wife and newest child. He knew nothing of his rights to clothes and bedding, to the minima of existence. With this one quixotic gesture, he had deprived the family of all that even the most hopeless debtor was legally entitled to. His last money had been spent on train tickets to Liverpool, his home city, which did not want him.

I kneeled up in the water, dipped my head in and then soaped it thoroughly. Three times the brown locks were soaped and rinsed. Then the thin body was soaped until it looked like a snowman. The water was covered with grey soap suds.

Like a dripping muskrat, I climbed out, emptied the bath and began to refill it.

The door burst open and a young, male member of the staff rushed in, pulling off his apron as he came. He was well into the huge bathroom, before he realised that I was standing there naked, one hand on the brass tap.

He stopped, his startled face registering shock. Then he blushed hotly.

'I say, I am sorry!' he exclaimed, and turned and fled.

I was so used to being intruded upon by my brothers in a house where all washing had to be done in the kitchen that I was undisturbed. But I did for a moment wonder why he should be so flabbergasted. A girl in her skin was nothing special as far as I could see.

I repeated the scrubbing and, when I finally emerged from the bathroom, hair wrapped in a towel like a turban, I was scarlet from head to heel.

I drew back the net curtains and sat down by the

window to dry my hair in the breeze. Such quietness enfolded me as I had not known before. Leisurely I combed the wet hair over my shoulders, and watched the sun glancing on the sea. I could smell the salt and, closer to hand, the pine trees in the garden. For the first time for years I had nothing to do. It was as if every nerve slowly loosened and relaxed. Three nights of deep, warm sleep and two days of stacks of food had helped to heal both mind and body.

I sat on the hard bedroom chair for a long time, the two rows of carelessly made beds behind me, the fine view framed by the window in front of me. My mind was empty. There was no past, no nagging family, nothing. No future, except the happy anticipation of welcoming Emrys Hughes and the other kindly guests when they returned, and then eating and eating and eating.

A train arriving at the nearby station roused me. I got up and went to the spotty mirror to arrange my hair in a bun again.

I peered short-sightedly at the image in the mirror and was surprised at what I saw. The hair, usually so straight because of its greasy coating, now waved softly down each side of the thin cheeks; its mousy brown carrying in it a rich red burnish. Surprised, I coaxed it into deeper waves.

From under smooth black brows, large green eyes, no longer bloodshot, stared sadly back at me. A few lumpy spots marred a complexion which was surprisingly white. I smiled cautiously at myself. The teeth were not straight and were tinged with yellow. I had scrubbed them well but I had no toothpaste.

With newly awakened vanity, I decided I had a nice smile. I wondered if make-up would cover the spots, and then sighed because there was no money for such luxuries. Telling myself to stop playing Narcissus, I put my hair up, taking care, however, not to draw it back too tightly and spoil the waves.

Lunch was not served in the holiday home to guests, so I went without. It was probably as well, as it gave an over-taxed digestive system time to recuperate. I spent the rest of the day washing my spare blouse and panties and ironing them dry with an iron borrowed from the kitchen. Then I went for a long walk.

The lanes had all the bright greenery of June, but last year's leaves lay sodden at the bottom of puddles formed by overnight rain. They reminded me of winter.

I dreaded the winter. Another year of cold, sopping wet feet, of piercing wind, of long stone staircases to be climbed, of shivering in a freezing bed. Another winter, too, of incredible loneliness.

Fiona is growing up, I comforted myself. She will be company. Yet instinct told me that Fiona would never really communicate with me; she was too crushed, too determined never to be caught out of character, as a passive, pliable, inoffensive, obliging person, guaranteed not to answer back. The steel which I felt lay deep within her would be used for her own self-defence. She would crouch behind it, hiding any real feeling lest someone take offence. Just as I had been cast as a maiden aunt, she had been cast by my parents as a lovely girl who would make a good marriage which would help to raise the family again to its former stature. And yet, sometimes, I thought that Fiona might surprise my parents more than I ever could. As with the rest of the children, I could give Fiona love, but she was incapable of giving me friendship.

After my walk I tidied my windblown hair and then went down to the lounge. There was a number of women's magazines in a magazine rack and I curled up on a settee with these in excited anticipation.

Except for *Peg's Paper* which Edith had allowed me to read when I was small, I had not seen any women's magazines, and I soon was engrossed in enthralling stories in which the heroine was always blonde and invariably won the hero over the machinations of a dark sultry villainess. The kisses were passionate.

Chapter twenty-five

The bus disgorging a noisy crowd of returning guests put an end to my quiet day. I reluctantly uncurled myself from the settee and put down the magazine I had been reading. Emrys came puffing into the lounge, grey raincoat flying behind him, pipe aglow like a watchman's stove. He was followed more slowly by his brother, Gwyn.

'Why didn't you come?' he asked. 'We missed you, didn't we Gwyn?'

Gwyn smiled kindly down at me. 'Yes, we did,' he assured me.

I went pink with embarrassment, and said, 'I thought I'd have a quiet day. Did you enjoy the trip?'

'I'd have enjoyed it a lot more if you had been there,' Emrys replied roundly, and playfully pinched my cheek.

Now I was blushing at the compliment. He evidently saw it, as he struggled out of his coat, and laughed.

'Well, I've made sure you come on the other trips. Gwyn and I have bought tickets for all of 'em for you. Now you *have* to come.' He gusted with laughter, and Gwyn chuckled and said, 'Well, we hope you will.'

'That's immensely kind of you both,' I told them, laughing myself, because I could not help it.

While Gwyn helped Margaret off with her coat,

Emrys stood in front of me, sturdy legs apart, while he struck matches to relight his pipe. He had told me that he was not supposed to smoke, but he could not give it up. As he gossiped about the lakes they had seen, I wondered what he would think if he saw my poverty-stricken home. Both brothers were obviously prosperous; both had gone to the prayer meeting held in the lounge each evening and both had joined earnestly in the prayers that were offered; kindness and thoughtfulness in small things was obvious in every move they made. They were very different from anybody I had ever met before. I could well imagine them behind their drapery shop counters, cheerfully and patiently dispensing everything from two pennyworth of buttons to forty yards of damask for curtains.

As the fortnight progressed, my friendship with Emrys deepened. I began to feel a real affection for the man, but such was my innocence that I never considered what he might be feeling. He was so much older than me.

Once, when he held my hand during a bus trip, some of the ladies saw it. They teased me and said I had made a conquest. This embarrassed me, because I felt that anybody could see I was incapable of conquering any man; I was too plain.

He never overstepped the bounds of propriety, however, and I never felt frightened with him. A couple of days before the holiday was due to end, he wrote out his home address for me, and said he hoped I would come to see him.

'My wife died three years ago,' he said simply.

'Gwyn and I keep house together in a flat over one of the shops. But my sister lives nearby, and you could stay with her.'

I doubted in my mind that I would ever manage to travel as far as North Wales, but the idea gave me much pleasure, and I said with genuine enthusiasm, 'I would love that.'

He looked at me very soberly for a moment, and then said, 'Would you?'

I nodded.

He grinned at me. 'Then we'll arrange it.'

On the last day of the holiday, we all went to see Cartmel Priory, and were ambling round the old church, behind our guide, when Emrys stopped suddenly and began to gasp for breath. He clutched his chest and turned and stumbled into a pew to sit down. The rest of the party had moved on ahead a little.

I leaned over the side of the pew and put my arm round his shoulder. 'What is it, Emrys?' But I knew what it was. I had seen it happen to Father when he was a young man. 'I'll get Gwyn. Just keep sitting.'

I ran over to Gwyn, and whispered to him. He spun round, at the same time taking a small bottle out of his jacket pocket. He fumbled in his top pocket as he ran back and produced a worn, tin spoon.

He pushed into the pew, and asked me to support Emrys's head, while he poured out a colourless liquid and forced it into the gasping man's mouth. Some dribbled down Emrys's chin, but most went in. Then, after he had put the cork back into the bottle, he stuck it down on a pew shelf, while he rolled up his raincoat and made a pillow.

We laid Emrys along the pew seat, while the other guests, suddenly aware that something was wrong, came thronging anxiously over to us.

Slowly, Emrys's face lost some of its agony, the breathing became more normal. I crouched in the narrow space beside him and chafed his hands anxiously. Someone lent a coat to put over him. The verger was asked to telephone the guest house and arrange for a doctor to be called.

Emrys's eyes had been tight closed, but as he relaxed he opened them and looked at me. 'Helen.'

As soon as he felt he could bear to be moved, two men in the party made a seat with crossed hands and carried him into the bus and laid him down on the back seat. Gwyn cradled his head, and I knelt by him and held him, so that he did not fall off. He lay quietly.

The bus driver manoeuvred the bus very carefully over the narrow lanes, and as soon as we reached the guest house, two of the staff came running out with a wooden chair with arms. Emrys was lifted from the bus into the chair, despite mild protests that he thought he could walk. He was not a heavy man and the two young men made short work of carrying him up the stairs and into his room. He was closely followed by a doctor carrying a black bag and by his anxious brother. I stood forlornly at the bottom of the stairs, and then reluctantly went to my room to wash before dinner.

Everybody in the dining room seemed to be talking about the fatal heart attacks they had witnessed, and I was very cast down, though Margaret did her best to cheer me up.

Gwyn did not come down to the meal, so when we had finished Margaret and I went into the hall and, after a moment's uncertainty on Margaret's part, went to the office to inquire if they had news.

We were told that while we were at dinner an ambulance had come and Mr Hughes and his brother had gone to a hospital in a nearby town. Margaret and I looked at each other, and then in silent consent went to the prayer meeting.

I did not sleep much. I was filled with a strange emotion such as I had not experienced before, a fear of the loss of a loved one.

The next morning, before breakfast, I plucked up enough courage to go myself to the office to inquire if they had news of Emrys. They had not, but the manager allowed me to use the telephone to inquire from the hospital how he was.

Mr Hughes was resting comfortably, I was told primly. He was not yet allowed visitors.

At breakfast I passed this information to Margaret. Despite my depression, I ate a huge breakfast and while still at table, said good-bye to Margaret, because she had to leave immediately in order to catch her train home. I went up to the bedroom and silently put my few belongings back into their paper bag, while the turmoil of the packing being done by the five mill girls went on around me. There was a strong smell of dirty washing and violet perfume, and I was glad to escape.

I said good-bye to the staff and to several other guests, and caught the train back to Liverpool and to reality.

Chapter twenty-six

The family were quite pleased to see me back and asked many questions, which I answered frankly. I told Mother about the Hughes brothers, and she made a little grimace with her mouth, and asked, 'They didn't touch you, did they?'

'Emrys held my hand,' I said.

She laughed in a deprecating way, and I was unaccountably incensed.

'They were very good to me,' I said defensively, and retreated to wash the dishes before I was provoked into saying more.

Such an excellent holiday gave me a lot more strength, and I formed the ambition of learning to type. The evening schools did not give courses in typing; my shorthand speed was rapidly increasing, but without a concomitant skill in typing, it was not much use to me.

I went to see Miriam in the attic. She very willingly allowed me to use her typewriter in the lunch hours and showed me how to manipulate the machine. She saved wastepaper so that I could use the back of it for practising. The three typists crammed into the little room took turns in instructing me how to set out letters, agendas and minutes. The head typist also showed me how to use the big Gestetner duplicating machine with its huge tubes of very black, very sticky ink.

Emrys was constantly in my mind and I daily hoped for a letter to say he was well again. But there was none. I told myself that I was such a small, unimportant person that perhaps I had been only someone to amuse him while he recuperated from his earlier heart attack. But I would see him again in my mind's eye, teasing, talking, laughing with me, and thus reassure myself that we had been really good companions and a true friendship had been formed.

At the end of the month, I plucked up courage, took a piece of copy paper from Miriam's store and, one lunch hour, wrote to the address he had given me, to inquire how he was.

Again, I began to watch for a letter, but still there was nothing. My new-found strength began to fade under the constant pressure of work at home, work at the office, work at night school, and the everlasting hunger. I fell into a quiet depression and found it hard to concentrate on my studies.

One hot sultry August day, when I arrived home to find the family, as usual, just finishing their evening meal, I was greeted by Mother with the information that my friend had died. She said it not unkindly, as she tossed an open letter across the table to me.

I slowly turned back into the hall and hung up my hat and coat. I did not want to touch the letter; I did not want to have the shocking news confirmed. I stood panting in the hall trying not to cry. People did not die; they got better from heart attacks, didn't they?

Mother was saying, 'Have a look at your letter.'

Reluctantly I picked it up. First I looked at the signature. Gwyn Hughes.

It began, 'Dear little Helen' and for a second I was tripping along beside a rushing river, and Emrys was saying, 'Be careful, little Helen. Don't fall in.'

Gwyn apologised for not writing to me earlier, but he had had so much to do that it was only now that he was able to attend to his personal correspondence.

Emrys had recovered sufficiently from his heart attack for the hospital doctor to say that he could make the journey back to Wales in a private car, if they broke the journey frequently enough for him to rest. At the moment of leaving the hospital, he had been stricken by another massive attack which had taken his life. His body had been taken home and had been buried beside those of his wife and his son, who had died when he was twelve.

Gwyn was sorry to have to send me such bad news. My companionship had been a great pleasure to both of them, and Emrys had been determined not to let the friendship lapse. He was going to write to me as soon as he returned to Wales.

With quivering hands, I put the letter back in the envelope. I was too shaken to complain about the letter's being opened. All I wanted to do was to go to bed and rest, shut myself out of life for a while.

Brian and Tony, those great companions, were staring at me uneasily. Probably death frightened them, too.

I smiled wryly at them. 'He was quite old,' I reassured them. 'It was natural.'

'I'm sorry,' said Father. 'They sound like very nice people. Very kind.'

I put the letter in my handbag. 'I will write to thank him,' I said.

'You should,' said Mother. 'Come and have your tea, dear.'

Fiona silently gave up her chair to me, and Alan passed over the bread and margarine. Mother brought me a small plate of lettuce and cold meat. For the first time that I could remember, I was aware of an aura of kindly sympathy throughout the family. Very slowly, in a dazed way I began to eat.

Chapter twenty-seven

I knew Emrys Hughes for only two weeks, but he left me a legacy which changed my whole life. He taught me that I was worthy of love and respect. He revealed to me that, given normal circumstances, I could be a cheerful, merry companion. He gave me self-respect, a belief in myself. This change in attitude did not reveal itself immediately because I was locked into circumstances beyond my control. But it was there, tucked away in the back of my mind to give me strength of purpose when the time came.

The raunchy cotton mill girls had also done something for me. I had not at first understood their conversation, because I did not know the words they used, but constant repetition soon made their meanings clear. They talked of nothing but sex, and their lurid discussions soon knitted together for me much that I knew subconsciously before. Then the reading of a great number of files and observation of the prostitutes in the streets greatly added to my understanding. One is supposed to be shaken by such revelations, but it all seemed quite normal to me and I accepted it without being disturbed. Perhaps because I was so starved, I had almost no feelings myself. My days were choked with work that had to be done, giving little time for contemplation of anything other than the next essay to be written, the next cup of tea to be provided.

I did not think of sex in connection with Emrys Hughes. He was a dear person, very careful of me, and I gave him the same kind of affection that I gave my grandmother, uninhibited and unthinking. Only years later, in the ripeness of womanhood, I realised that he might well have fallen for an innocent slip of a girl. He would not have been the first man to love someone thirty years younger than himself. But that last fortnight of his life was not wasted. It enriched mine immeasurably.

*

One of the more understanding ladies dressed in green overalls was a psychologist, a Mrs Croft, and, unlike the others, she would sometimes talk to me when I took her in a cup of tea at a time when she had no client with her. She knew that I attended night school and was learning shorthand. She asked me if I could teach another girl this subject.

The girl lived too far from the city to attend evening school. She could, however, take a lesson immediately upon finishing work and before going home. I could use Mrs Croft's husband's office as a place to give the lesson, and could charge about one shilling and sixpence each time.

So once a week, on an evening when there was no night school, I went to Mr Croft's office for an hour and gave a lesson to a languid, uninterested girl a little older than myself, while the cleaning staff mopped and dusted round us.

Probably because I was not a very good teacher, the girl quickly lost interest. But I earned enough money to enable me to put an advertisement in the *Liverpool Echo*, and acquire another pupil. A boy of about sixteen, suffering from epilepsy, asked to be taught at home. He was a very different kind of person, eager and enthusiastic. He practised assiduously and, by the time his parents moved with him to a milder climate, he was writing steadily at forty words per minute.

My parents approved of this tutoring, though Mother grumbled because I would not be available to help until late in the evening. I said that I proposed to keep the one shilling and sixpence a week that I was earning, towards buying lunches and some clothes.

At first, Mother frequently borrowed what I made, by riffling through my handbag and taking the money out. She never considered it necessary to pay it back. Finally, I made a stout little cotton bag to hold the precious pennies, and hung it round my neck by a piece of string. Once a week, I went to Woolworth's cafeteria at lunch time and bought a threepenny bowl of excellent soup and a roll. It was a treat to look forward to.

Before I thought of keeping my teaching money in a bag round my neck, and had managed to accumulate a few shillings, the shoes I had worn on holiday got to a point where there was so little sole left that I could not keep the pieces of cardboard from falling out. Finding shoes for all the children must have been a nightmare for Mother, and the best she could do for me was to give me her summer sandals which still had a little wear in them.

I woke up one morning to a black city suddenly made into a wonderland by an early fall of snow. I spent my last penny on a tram to work, but still my feet were sopping wet and freezing before I arrived at the office.

I sat down in the office kitchen, took off the sandals and wiped them with the floor cloth. Then I rubbed the stockinged toes with the same cloth.

The letters for hand delivery that morning were fortunately all for nearby offices, and I was just about to set out with them when the Cashier sent for me.

This forbidding lady always frightened me and she was not in the best of moods. She had a letter to be delivered to the Dental Hospital about a mile and a quarter away. It was still snowing, so I asked if I might take the tram.

'No,' she snapped. 'We haven't any money to waste on tram fares.'

By the time the local letters had been delivered, the snow was nearly up to my ankles and I was in real pain. Before setting out for the long trudge up the hill to the Dental Hospital, I sat down on an office stairway, took off the sandals and knocked the snow out of them, then brushed off the ice clinging to the stockings. I was weeping, and I wondered if I took the letter back to the office and refused to deliver it, I would be dismissed.

I decided that I probably would lose the job, and I dreaded this more than anything else. So up the hill I went through almost deserted streets, delivered the letter, and came down again at a stumbling run, crying all the way with pain in my feet. I envied Alan the new pair of shoes that had recently been bought for him. But he also got his feet wet that day.

Back at the office, I stripped off shoes and stockings filled a sink with water and, teetering on one toe, plunged each foot in turn into the hot water. Then I tried to dry them on the roller towel, an impossible feat. So I left a trail of water leading to the kitchen, while I went to dry them on the floor cloth.

As I put on the wet stockings again, I began to laugh shakily at the idea of the Presence surprising me with one foot caught in a roller towel. She was kind enough that, had she known about it, she would probably have been very upset at my being sent so far in such bad weather.

I was still shivering as I ran to make the tea and then fled up and down the eternal stone steps to deliver it, but probably the exercise helped to restore the circulation. I was left with only a very bad cold.

That lunch time, Miriam offered to lend me a portable typewriter for a week, so that I could practise at home. She was a member of the Communist Party and did all she could to attract other members. Another of the stenographers was an equally ardent member of the Roman Catholic Church and also keen on converts. So between the two of them, I received a lot of attention. Life was such a struggle for me, however, that I had neither time nor strength to consider their arguments and remained totally uncommitted.

The loan of the typewriter was most kindly meant

and I wanted to hug Miriam in gratitude. She brought it to the office the next day and I took it home, with some scrap paper, and put it in the empty front room. The children all wanted to try it, but I told them it had to be taken special care of because it was on loan. I joyfully practised far into the night, much to the irritation of Father, who could not sleep because of the steady tapping. I was myself always short of sleep, because I did my homework in the early mornings before the family got up, or late at night after they had gone to bed, provided that there was a penny to put in the gas meter to obtain light, or a stump of candle.

When I had finished my long practice, I returned the typewriter to the safety of the front room, put a penny from my handbag into the gas meter ready for the morning and crept up to bed. I was filled with hope that a good typing speed would help me to get a better job.

Chapter twenty-eight

The following evening I had to go to night school, so I was too busy to practise on the typewriter. On the third evening, I hurried through my work and then ran into the empty front room to fetch the machine.

There was no typewriter.

Perplexed, I looked in a built-in cupboard by the fireplace, but it held only the gas meter.

Mystified, I went back into the living room, where Mother was sitting by the fire reading the newspaper. Edward and Avril were playing on the coconut matting, squabbling over a few cigarette cards they had found.

'Mummy, did you move the typewriter from the front room?'

Mother looked up with studied casualness, and I knew instinctively that something was wrong.

'Yes, I did,' she said carefully.

'Well, where did you put it?' I asked impatiently. 'I want to practise.'

'It is not here.' Her cultivated voice was without expression.

The fearful apprehension in which I spent most of my life suddenly reached swamping proportions.

'Mother! What have you done with it? You haven't sold it, have you?'

'No.' She was looking at me with a kind of lazy indifference. I felt as if she had me impaled on a pin and that in the back of her mind she was enjoying the situation. My childish belief that parents always did the best they could for their offspring had long since vanished, and I was very frightened.

'Mother,' I whispered. 'What *have* you done with it? Are you teasing me – joking?'

'I never joke,' said Mother, and I realised that that was true.

She got up from her chair with a slow graceful movement, walked past me and into the hall. Through the open door, I watched her leisurely put on her hat and then her coat.

'Where is it, Mother?'

'In pawn.'

'Oh, my God! For how much?'

'Three pounds.'

I gasped. 'But I've got to return it in a couple of days!'

'Oh, don't worry. I'll get it out in due course.' She turned towards the front door.

'By Friday?'

'Oh, I doubt that.'

'Oh, Mummy!'

'Don't be so melodramatic,' she fumed irritably, as she opened the front door. 'You must make an excuse to keep it another week. It's time Avril and Edward were put to bed.'

The cold was thick in my head and my throat was so sore and constricted that I could hardly ask the next question.

'What shall I do if Miriam says she needs the machine?'

She snapped back angrily, 'That's your headache. You should be able to manage something like that.'

I stared speechlessly at her as she stepped out on to the pavement slamming the front door after her. All the horrors that could possibly befall me if the machine was not returned flew through my head. Accusations of theft, of court proceedings, loss of my job. I could tell Father, but what could he do? He had no money to speak of.

There was no one to help me. I wished that the dirty, linoleumed floor would open up and swallow me, so that I did not have to face poor Miriam.

My terror was so great that it blotted out everything else. I failed to hear instructions given to me in the office, and was constantly in trouble for forgetting small errands which the filing clerks pressed upon me. I forgot to take a voluntary worker a cup of tea. I accidentally put a 'By Hand' letter into the post box; the firm it was addressed to telephoned to complain about having to pay the postage. I carried a big tea tray carelessly through a doorway and knocked the spouts off two teapots. I stood, appalled, while tea gushed all over the floor, and the Cashier ranted that I would have to pay for new teapots. I nearly laughed at her. At night school, I sat at my desk and saw and heard nothing. The essays and assignments set me remained undone.

'Whatever is the matter, Helen?' each teacher, in turn, demanded testily.

Miriam reluctantly agreed to allow me to keep the typewriter for another week.

At home, I moved like a zombie through the usual routine of baby-sitting, shopping, cooking, cleaning, washing, ironing. The children were used to my being quiet, except when embroiled in a fight with my parents or a rare spate with Alan or Fiona, so I doubt if they noticed much change. Father lived in his dream world, went most evenings to the library and on Saturday and Sunday went out for a drink with a colleague. I saw no point in asking Father's help; it would spark another family row. Only Mother knew, and she made no reply when I pestered her to redeem the machine.

I had never considered that children might love their mothers. I always feared mine.

I think that sometimes, when I was little, Mother felt guilty at pushing me on to Grandma or to Edith, and it was then that she would send for me. She would listen to my reading or give me a sweet and ask me about school. But she did not really hear me when I replied, and I would thankfully rush back to Edith or close my eyes and look forward to the next visit to Grandma's house.

At the end of the second week, Miriam said she needed the typewriter. Her rich brown crown of shining hair swung round her pixielike face, as she looked up at me with such a friendly grin that I wanted to cry.

'I'll bring it in on Monday,' I promised, my voice strained with the cold and sheer terror.

At home, Father was out, and I had a fearsome row

with Mother to no purpose, and retired to bed crying hysterically.

On Tuesday, Miriam, her expression a little puzzled, inquired again.

I apologised for forgetting to bring the machine in the rush of getting to work. On Thursday and Friday, I muttered the same apologies. She just nodded and looked curiously and unsmilingly at me. Undoubtedly, she had begun to worry about her prized possession.

I was saved from having to face her on Saturday morning. One Saturday each month was free, and I stayed at home and did the washing.

Dressed in an old cotton frock, I was carefully washing my work skirt in the kitchen sink, when there was a polite rap on the iron door knocker.

Mother was cutting bread and margarine for tea, so, with hands still dripping, I went into the empty front room and peeped through the piece of net curtaining we had pinned across the windows.

Standing on the pavement looking up at the decrepit brick house was Miriam.

I flitted back to the kitchen.

'Mother!' I whispered in a panic. 'It's Miriam! She must have come for the typewriter. What am I going to do?'

Mother looked up from her bread cutting, knife poised in mid-air.

'Don't answer the door,' she said simply.

'But she must have come all the way over from the north end of town specially.'

'I said, "don't answer".'

I wrung my hands, as I hissed back, 'But, Mummy. . .'

She was implacable. 'Don't answer.'

I was panting with fright and stared at her helplessly for a minute. Then I said angrily in a normal voice, 'I *will* answer. I can't bear it any more. I will tell her exactly what has happened.' My voice rose in hysteria. 'I just can't endure it any longer.'

Fiona, the only other person at home, came in from the lavatory in the back yard. She stared at us in scared apprehension.

Miriam rapped again, louder. I started for the living room through which I would have to pass to reach the front passage.

'Oh, no, my lady.' Mother dropped her knife, swiftly slammed the door and put her foot against it. She glared at me. 'How dare you?'

I stopped. I wanted to strike her to make her move, but it was so alien to me that I could not.

In a fever of fear, I shouted, 'I will tell them in the office on Monday and then they will know you stole it.'

Mother went white. 'You would not dare to tell such a lie,' she retorted, as the knocker sounded once again.

But I did not care what happened, as long as the intolerable burden was removed from me, and I replied determinedly. 'It is not a lie and I certainly would dare.'

'All right. I will speak to Miriam. You remain here.' She was bristling with anger.

She opened the living room door and marched through to the front of the house.

I clung to the kitchen table, hardly able to stand, while the sound of the front door opening and then Mother's delicate voice echoed through the house.

Mother and Miriam had not met before, so Miriam first explained who she was and then asked politely if she could have the machine back, because she had some work to do on it. Mother said enthusiastically how delighted she was to meet her and how grateful she was for her kindness to me. I closed my eyes and prayed, wondering what she would say next.

The well-bred voice was explaining that she herself had ventured to use the machine yesterday. Unfortunately, one of the letters had fallen off and needed soldering on again, so she had taken it up to town to have it repaired.

'Oh, dear,' exclaimed Miriam. 'Where did you take it?'

'Um, you know that place on Dale Street? I took it there. They said it would be ready on Tuesday.'

Miriam sounded very relieved, as she replied, 'Oh, that's not too bad. I could pick it up myself.'

Mother's voice chimed in with measured charm. 'Oh, I won't hear of it. I must pay for it. I will arrange for Helen to bring it into the office on Wednesday. I am so sorry that up to now she has been so delinquent about returning it. I will make sure that this time she does not forget.'

There was a mumble of polite, friendly argument, then good-byes were said, and the front door was softly closed.

I was so shaken that I wanted to vomit.

'What was that about?' asked Fiona, as she took her skipping rope off a hook on the back door.

I did not reply for a moment, and then I said wearily, 'It's so complicated, Fi, I can't explain it. But everything is O.K. now.'

Chapter twenty-nine

Mother had barely shut the front door, when the string on the latch was pulled and the door again swung open. Brian and Tony came bursting in from playing football in the street. They were excited because it had begun to snow heavily, and they thought that later on they might be able to make a snowman. They were followed almost immediately by Avril and Baby Edward, who had toddled down to Granby Street together, to buy a pint of milk; the milkman had refused to deliver any more until his bill was paid. Giggling together triumphantly, they handed me the bottle.

Since the children were there, Mother said nothing to me, but, as she picked up the bread knife again, her contemptuous look spoke volumes. Feeling wretched, I returned to the sink full of washing.

As I was hanging the garments over a piece of string strung across the kitchen, Father and Alan came through the back door, laughing and shaking the snow off themselves.

I must tell Daddy, I thought. I simply have to. But not now, because of the children. Mother will turn on me, the minute I open my mouth. But three pounds is a huge sum to raise. How does Mother imagine she is going to do it?

Mother was very quiet during tea. By silent

consent nothing was said about Miriam before the children.

I had to give a shorthand lesson that evening, so immediately after tea I prepared a protesting Edward for bed. I borrowed Fiona's macintosh from her to put over my cotton dress, because my skirt was not dry and my own very light macintosh was neither windproof nor waterproof. I would have to talk to Daddy in the morning. With a quick glance at the clock, I snatched up my shorthand books and ran to catch a tram outside the Rialto Cinema. To reach my pupil's home, it was necessary to take a tram to the Pier Head and another one out again to his district. There was no question of being able to walk the distance in a reasonable time.

The snow was coming down in great fleecy flakes and my feet were soaked before I reached the end of our street. The bright lights of the cinema seemed to be floating amid the flakes, and a drift was forming across its curved front steps. The clumsy trams looked like glittering ghosts as they churned their way slowly along Catherine Street. Few people were about, and for a second I considered turning back. But I needed money so badly that when my tram arrived, I swung on to it without hesitation.

'Lousy night,' remarked the conductor as I tendered the fare.

At the Pier Head, the wind was driving the snow in whirling sweeps across the stone sets, almost obliterating the Royal Liver Building and the squat Cunard Building. The Church of our Lady and St Nicholas was lost amid the white downpour. As if from nowhere, the sounds of the fog horns and the harsh bells to guide the ferry boats came floating round my head. One or two shadowy people scurried past me.

Surrounding the tram superintendent was a tight knot of drivers and conductors, red ears sticking out from navy blue caps and glowing cigarettes drooping from their mouths. They were arguing about stopping the service. I was shivering, and clutched the macintosh collar round my neck to stop the snow trickling down inside, as I waited for their decision. The wind from the river seemed to penetrate my bones.

The superintendent vanished in search of the telephone.

I blew my nose on a square of newspaper, then shoved my bare hands into my mac pockets in an effort to keep them from freezing. The heavy flakes clung to my hair and I brushed a rosette of snow off my bun. The drivers and conductors climbed back into their respective trams to get out of the wind. I did not dare to follow one of them for fear I missed my own tram, which had not yet arrived.

Long before I saw the tram I needed, I could hear the driver pinging its bell with one foot, as he edged the great vehicle slowly round the curve of Mann Island. Between the sharp pings of the bell came the sound of the slap of the river water around the floating dock behind me, the sound of the Mersey which lay between Grandma and me. For a moment, I felt like chancing my tram fares on a ferry fare instead and running away to her.

'Don't be a fool,' I told myself sharply. 'You haven't got the fare for the bus on the other side – and an eight mile walk in this storm is impossible.'

The supervisor, bustling with importance, came towards the newly arrived tram. The driver stepped down to meet him; he did not want to take the tram out again. The supervisor irately pointed out that on his return journey he normally picked up men coming off a night shift in an outlying factory. After some argument, the driver reluctantly climbed on to his platform, and I thankfully clambered into the back, shaking myself like a collie dog. I sat down on the wooden bench which ran the whole length of the car, bent over and lifted an almost solid crown of snow from the top of my head. It splashed all over the ridged floor as I dropped it. The interior of the vehicle was comfortingly warm, but I continued to shiver and my feet were bitterly cold. I was the only outgoing passenger and I stared glumly at the empty bench opposite, until the conductor came to collect my fare.

The driver slammed open the intervening door, letting in a great gust of snow-laden air. He shouted down the length of the car to the conductor that they would be lucky if they saw their beds that night. He was not going to be responsible if the bloody tram got stuck; he'd told the bastard back there that they would never make it up the hill. These remarks did not cheer me up. The tram was already far behind schedule and I would be very late for the lesson.

At Pembroke Place the points of the track were solid with ice and did not yield to the driver's poking at them with a metal bar. The conductor climbed down and a committee of two was held over them. Then, shaking themselves free of snow, they climbed back in again. The driver eased the brake off and let the tram roll slowly backwards down the hill for a few yards. Then he took the line up London Road. We were off the proper route, but not so far that I would not be able to run to my pupil's house.

As we crawled along, the thin, underclad conductor came into the body of the tram and closed the back door. He sat in the far corner from me, silently smoking cigarette after cigarette.

I was heavy with the cold which I had caught nearly three weeks earlier and had failed to shake off. As the chill from my waiting at the Pier Head wore off, I gradually began to feel stiflingly hot, and I almost envied the driver out in the wind. My head ached abominably and I laid it against the cold windowpane and closed my eyes. I suffered greatly from headaches, partly, I think, from eye strain, so another one was nothing to worry about.

After what seemed an interminable time of grinding noise as the tram laboured onwards, I was jerked awake. The tram had stopped. The lights were still on and the motor was throbbing.

The driver pushed open his door and came in, puffing and blowing, his face nearly purple between his peaked cap and great muffler. The conductor looked up.

The driver addressed me.

'Can't go no further, Miss,' he announced.

'God spare us,' exclaimed the conductor, and

threw his cigarette butt angrily on to the floor. 'Where are we?' he asked.

I picked up my wet shorthand books from beside me, as the driver replied, 'West Derby Road, near Green Lane. I thought I could work my way round, like, to me proper route. But I couldn't turn at Shiel Road like I hoped. Had no luck at all. And now there's two abandoned trams on the track ahead of us. I can't see no sign of drivers or conductors.'

West Derby Road! I was miles from where I should have been and at least three miles from home. I looked in alarm at the two men discussing what they should do. They seemed to be fuzzy round the edges. I got up from the seat. My legs wobbled, and I sat down again quickly. I was suddenly afraid of the bitter cold outside.

The driver said, 'We'd better all get home as best we can. If I can find a phone box on the way, I'll phone the boss to say where the tram is.' He took off his big scarf, as he spoke, and shook a shining cascade of snow off it. 'Could try taking the bloody thing in in the morning, when I'll be able to see better.'

Trams can be driven from either end. They do not have to be turned, so I asked, 'Couldn't you drive it back again to the Pier Head?'

'What for, luv? There's nothing there but wind and water.'

The conductor peered ineffectually through a bit of window he had rubbed clear of steam. 'Snow's so deep, we'd probably stick anyway. Best get home, like you say.'

I nodded and the pain jabbed through my head. How was I to find my way through a maze of narrow streets, snow-choked and deserted? Yet there seemed nothing else to do. Once the driver turned off the power, the tram would quickly become very cold indeed.

'Do you know how I can get to the Rialto Cinema?' I asked.

They looked at me appalled. 'Eee, you do have a way to go,' exclaimed the driver.

Again, a committee of two was formed. The driver lived in Holt Road, the conductor in Old Swan, which in normal circumstances was no great walk from where we were stranded. The conductor decided to leave us. He turned up his overcoat collar, said 'Ta-ra, well,' very dolefully, cautiously stepped down into the street and plodded away into the night.

The driver, sighing heavily, decided to drive the tram back along the route he had come to the nearest point to his home street or until the vehicle stalled. This would help me, too, and he said he could direct me home from where he lived. He floundered outside again and succeeded with difficulty in reversing the trolley on the overhead wires, and then heaved himself into the rear of the tram to drive it.

He left the communicating door slightly ajar, so that he could talk to me and I moved up to the end of the bench closest to it. We sailed slowly down the same side of the street up which we had travelled. I hoped we would not hit another vehicle which might be coming towards us. There seemed, however, to be no other thing moving in the city, and our tram finally refused to go any further after reaching Shiel Road.

The driver slammed the vehicle's doors shut, and took my arm. Together we struggled on foot along Shiel Road, while the wind blew the snow into our faces, down our necks and up our coat sleeves. The driver had boots, an overcoat, a cap, a scarf and gloves. I had on a cotton dress, a macintosh and a second-hand pair of walking shoes which I had bought from the pawnbroker for two shillings. My head and hands were bare, and rayon stockings did not offer much protection. I was also very thin, with no proper layer of fat to hclp ward off the cold. I regretted bitterly ever having set out.

By the time we found the driver's brick, terrace house, with his wife peeping anxiously through the tiny bay window, the wind had eased and the snow was thinning.

His wife invited me in to rest and shelter for a while, but my mind seemed to be fogged up and all I could think about was the desperate need to get home and into bed. Stupidly, I said that the snow was easing and I could manage to walk home.

She nodded doubtfully at me, as her husband stamped about behind her in the narrow hallway, and she closed the door slowly as I moved away.

Durning Road to Tunnel Road, from dim gas lamp to dim gas lamp, alternately freezing and perspiring, I struggled on, through totally deserted streets. This was not a district of private cars, but here and there a van or truck had been abandoned and snowdrifts were rising round them. Each window sill I passed had a neat traycloth of snow on it, each doorstep its unbroken drift.

I was beginning to think that I would have to knock at the nearest door and ask for shelter, when I suddenly found myself at the junction of Upper Parliament Street and Smithdown Road. And through the unearthly silence, came unexpectedly the distant rumble of a tram. I looked quickly down Smithdown Road from where the sound seemed to come. I saw the electricity spit and its reflection flash across the snow as its trolley crossed a wire. I half stumbled, half ran towards it.

The driver – there was no conductor – was astonished to have a passenger suddenly emerge from the storm. He stopped, and let me on through the front of the tram.

'Eh, Miss. You must be frozen. Where you tryin' to get to?'

'The Rialto,' I gasped, as I felt down my chest and eased out my little money bag, to get a penny from it. A pain like a knife wound was shooting through my back and my throat was swelling in its old threatening manner.

'Eh, you don't have to pay t' fare,' he said, through the slightly ajar front door, near which I had thankfully taken a seat. 'I'm trying to get that far for me own sake. I got a flat in Catherine. But I reckon points will be frozen, so I won't be able to turn.' He jerked his head to indicate the way he had come, and added, 'It was bloody awful back there. I let me conductor off by his house.'

I nodded dumbly. In the warmth of the tram, my head was whirling as the snowflakes had been, and all I could think about was home.

The snow had stopped when, about fifteen minutes later, I pulled the string on our door latch and stumbled in, into my father's arms.

Chapter thirty

I have a dim remembrance of Father rolling off my stockings in front of the fire and putting my feet into a basin of luke-warm water, to restore the circulation; of Mother holding a cup of scalding hot tea to my lips, and of being surprised at the anxiety in her pale blue eyes. Then I was in bed with Edward's hot water bottle pressed to my back and Father was cursing as he tried to make a fire in the bedroom fireplace.

Faces came and went in the candlelight. Or was it sunlight? Medicine was forced down my throat, a poultice applied to my back. Fiona helped to hold me on a chamberpot placed on the bed. Once it seemed to me that Edith was there and I called out to her, but she faded away. I dreamed that Minerva came down from her seat on the top of the town hall and shook her spear at me for being so foolish. Then there was a great nightmare during which I was arguing with the pawnbroker about the return of the typewriter. I kept shouting at him that he must give it to me because it was stolen property. I had long spasms of coughing, when all of me seemed wracked with aches and pains. I was dreadfully hot and kept throwing off the bed-clothes, but they were always tucked round me again.

Then, quite suddenly, I was shivering in the light of the pale Liverpool sun coming through the bedroom window. My feet were sticking out from under the coverings, and I pulled them up close to me. The movement sent a shooting pain through them. A cold hot water bottle lay at my side and I tried to push it away, but somehow my hands would not obey so I lay still.

After a little while, I opened my eyes again and turned my head. A small fire was smouldering in the grate, and, in the double bed on the other side of the room lay Brian. He was tucked up tightly in a pile of bedding and coats. His hair stuck up like the hairs of a shaving brush and the face beneath was yellow with two bright red spots on the cheekbones.

I tried to ask him what had happened, but when I moved, such a pain shot through my head from both ears, and my throat seemed so swollen, that I barely got the first word out.

He seemed to understand, and one small, chilblained hand crept out of his covering and he pointed to his throat. He managed a wry little smile.

Mother came slowly in. Her feet dragged, as she came over to me. Without make-up and without her hair combed, she looked faded and pinched. She must have been exhausted, after having two invalids to care for, particularly since I would normally have taken a lot of the load from her.

She saw with obvious relief that I was awake. To allay the pain, I lay perfectly still while she put her hand on my forehead to check the temperature.

'How are you feeling?'

I tried to smile. 'Ears hurt – and throat and legs,' I croaked. 'Brian?'

Mother nodded. 'He has quinsy, poor boy. He is going into hospital this afternoon, to have it cut.' The lines on her face deepened. Brian was one of her favourite children.

'Where is he going?'

'The Ear, Nose and Throat Hospital.'

Very carefully, I turned my face towards the other bed. Despite his illness, Brian's eyes crinkled up cheerfully at me.

For a long time, I lay looking at the cracked, grey ceiling, trying not to weep with weakness and pain, because crying only constricted the already painfully tight throat. Mother brought both Brian and me a cup of tea and supported us in turn as we drank.

The doctor came in the afternoon and dispatched Brian, still stoically cheerful, in an ambulance to the hospital. Then he turned to me.

'I was beginning to think I'd have to send you in, too,' he said, as he probed round my neck with his fingers.

I smiled weakly. 'What have I had?'

'You've had a nasty attack of bronchitis – in fact, it is still with you – but I think you will mend now. You also managed a bad dose of 'flu. And now we have to tackle your throat and ears.'

I nodded, while he took a camel hair brush out of his bag and a bottle of tannic acid, so that he could paint my throat. After he had done that, he put drops in both ears. He was very gentle, his handsome young face filled with concern. Afterwards, I learned that he did not charge for his visits to Brian, since he was already in the house to see me. Brian's hospital stay would be covered by charitable contributions to the hospital, he told Mother. He came every day, twice, to paint my throat and check my ears.

All I could eat for a while was a cup of Oxo with bread mashed into it or a cup of tea, but I slept a lot.

Two days after my delirium left me, I remembered Miriam's typewriter. I lay sobbing quietly for hours in great fear about it, while Mother did an afternoon stint in a department store.

Father was home first. I had heard Fiona come in, followed by the other children, but she was making the tea, judging by the sounds that floated up the stairs, and had not come to see me. Father came straight upstairs and still had his hat in his hand as he sat down on the bed, careful not to shake me.

'Well, how's my girl?'

'Not bad,' I whispered.

He patted my hand, and I asked him eagerly, 'Daddy, do you know about the typewriter?'

He looked grim, as he said that he did.

'Were you able to get it back? Has Miriam got it?' It seemed as if my whole life hung on the answer.

He gave a little snort, with a hint of laughter in it. 'Yes, dear. She has.'

'Thank God,' I muttered. 'Thank God.' The burden was off me.

He sat staring sombrely at the empty fireplace – we had run out of coal. After a minute, I asked huskily how he had done it.

'Well, your Mother had applied for a five pound cheque to buy some clothes for the boys – and the finance company granted it. So we bought everything we could on it and pawned the lot. And we didn't pay the rent, so that made enough. Your Mother took the machine into the office – and I understand that Miriam was very nice to her.' He sighed heavily, and then said, 'Don't worry any more. You should have told me immediately it happened. I doubt if I would have known about it at all, if you had not shouted your head off over it while you were in delirium.' He looked down at me and laughed suddenly. 'There was quite a rumpus.'

I could imagine the row there must have been between Mother and him, and I grinned back at him.

'And I was out of it all,' I chuckled. My throat hurt and I stopped suddenly. 'It's a dreadful load of debt.'

'Nothing new,' he said, with the same sort of optimism that Alan sometimes displayed. 'You are not to worry. Just get well.'

'How long have I been ill?' I asked.

'Eight days.'

'When can I get up?'

'It will be some time yet.'

I laughed again, this time a little more carefully. 'Fiona still has to hold me on the chamberpot – so I suppose it will be a while.' Then I began to cough and to wince with pain in my chest and head. The smoke from his cigarette had got into my throat.

One day, the doctor asked Mother to refrain from smoking in the bedroom. She was very offended and railed against him as soon as he had gone. He had also lectured her on the necessity for getting some weight back on to both Brian's and my wasted bodies. He ordered cream, butter, potatoes, fresh vegetables, liver and eggs – and rest, lots of rest and fresh air for both of us.

Mother listened, and bowed her head politely from time to time, as he urged her quite passionately to stuff us with food. But when she had quietly closed the front door on him and had returned to the bedroom to give me a dose of cough mixture, she first fumed about his rudeness in asking her not to smoke, and then said crossly, 'And where does he think I will get the money from for cream?'

Tears of weakness forced themselves through crunched up eyelids, as I lay back on the pillow. I remembered the slice of bread for breakfast, the lack of lunch until I had managed to buy myself a bowl of soup or a roll and butter, the tiny plate of dinner kept from the hot meal Mother made either at lunch time or teatime, according to her work schedule. She did not eat much herself, but I was still growing; my needs were at least as great as Fiona's. I thought of Alan, able to go to the cinema on the strength of his pocket money, of the lunch he carried each day, of his new shoes and his tram fares. Why could not I have had the same?

And the answer seemed obvious. Because you are a girl old enough to be more useful at home than at work; a girl, moreover, whose very existence was resented from the day of her birth.

People, least of all parents, do not analyse their attitudes to children; and I am sure Father and Mother saw me only as a recalcitrant, disobedient offspring who had to be brought to heel. Their lives had been ruined and they were too exhausted to think their children's problems through. Mother used quantities of aspirin to sedate herself and Father, when he got the chance, vanished off for a drink. And they both smoked incessantly. They had neither time nor inclination to give sober, careful thought to what was happening to me.

Mother did, however, begin to bring me plenty of bread and margarine and big bowls of porridge with a little sugar and milk. But a great lassitude enveloped me. After a few mouthfuls, the throat seemed choked and I could not eat any more. Frequent small helpings were difficult for her to arrange because she worked a half-day on most week days, and she was herself tired to death.

Fiona helped me to use the chamberpot and she and Mother washed me. At first I accepted these attentions with about as much response as a rag doll would give. Then, as I grew a little stronger, the wells of gratitude were loosed and I would thank them effusively for every service, however small.

I began to worry that such a long absence would mean dismissal from my job. And how long would it take me to get strong enough to face those awful stone stairs and heavy trays again? And my night school work would be weeks behind.

I asked Fiona to bring me my text books and I lay with them on the bedclothes, too weak, too tired to lift them up and read them. When Mother went to the library, she very kindly brought me a pile of novels and these were the first books that I read, as I grew a little stronger and was able to sit up.

As the fear that I might die receded, Mother began to get impatient with my slow recovery. She was weary, weary beyond words, after coping with Brian's and my sickness, her own periodic jobs and all the tasks that I normally did. Fiona had been pressed into service, but Fiona was as good as Mahatma Gandhi at practising passive resistance; she had no intention of inheriting my domestic shoes. She learned quickly that trade union habit of working to rule. And who could be angry with such a gentle, helpless, blue-eyed beauty? None of us could.

When Brian returned from hospital, and, after a week's convalescence at home, was allowed to return to school, Mother seemed to feel that I should automatically have recovered as well.

I was unable to oblige, though our patient doctor had managed to bring down the inflammation in my throat, and the abscesses in my ears had burst and were healing. I was also able to sit on a chair, though I found a hard wooden one difficult to sit on because I had no fat on my buttocks.

Christmas was nearly upon us, though I had given no thought to preparing gifts and my parents had not mentioned it, when Fiona brought a letter up to me. Though the letter was addressed to me, it had been opened. It was from the Presence.

The Presence announced that she was very concerned that I had been so ill, and she would call to see me at three o'clock in two days' time.

The thought of such an important visitor as my employer coming into our bedroom threw me into a panic. What would she think of the stuffy, dirtiness of it, of the lack of bedspreads, even enough blankets? How would she regard a room furnished only with two beds, a candlestick, a wooden chair and an unscoured chamberpot? She was a gentlewoman, I reminded myself. She would be horrified.

'What shall I do?' I asked Mother when, later, she brought me a cup of Oxo.

'I think you had better see her downstairs,' said Mother. 'The doctor said you can get dressed for a little while tomorrow, so you can probably get down the stairs all right.'

I agreed fervently. If Mother tidied up the living room it would look much better than the bedroom did.

'How long did they pay my wages for, Mummy? Did they send any?'

'Oh, yes. They're still paying them. A money order comes every week. I cash it at the post office.'

'That's awfully kind of them,' I said.

'Well, they're a charity. They should be charitable,' Mother said, with considerable venom in her voice. She picked up my medicine bottle and shook it.

The sudden elation in me died at her remark. I shivered. How cold charity could be.

As I sipped the scalding Oxo, I told myself that I was stupid, inept, untrained and deserved the impatience of the filing clerks and Mr Ellis, the irritability of the Cashier who had the unenviable task of making the charity's ends meet. Two of the social workers, the ladies of the green overalls, had, at my first Christmas with them, given me gifts, one of sweets, the other of a bottle of lavender, which I had promptly used as gifts for Mother and Fiona; so they knew I existed. There were days, however, when I wondered if I was really a person to the staff or whether I was just an inefficient piece of machinery. Mother had never regarded her servants as people; perhaps they thought of me like that.

I sighed, and dismissed the depressing subject. Anyone as unwashed, smelly, ugly and generally repulsive as me, I assured myself, was bound to suffer the opprobrium of those who could afford hot water and soap.

But the Presence realised I was a person. She had apparently ordered wages to be sent to me, and now she was going to call on me. She had sent me on a miraculous holiday which had given me the affection of Emrys Hughes, draper, during his last few weeks on earth.

At the thought of Emrys, tears of weakness began to flow. The battle to survive seemed too great to be borne and I wished I was with him.

'What are you crying for?' asked Mother. 'Come along, now. Take your medicine.'

Chapter thirty-one

Mother seemed anxious that we should make a good impression on the Presence; and on the day of her visit, she brought the tin basin from the kitchen and washed me all over with warm water. She had ironed my work skirt and she lent me one of her own blouses to wear. I was too weak to endure having my hair washed, so she combed it out and pinned it back from my face with a hair clip. All the time my heart went pit-a-pat at the thought of facing my formidable employer, and I was glad to rest before Mother supported me down the stairs.

To my surprise, she opened the front room door instead of the living-room door. Obediently, I tottered into the room and stared, unbelievingly, around me.

A small fire blazed in the hearth and gave a pleasant glow in a room made dark by an overcast afternoon. A pretty beige and green rug covered the floor; the windows were draped with pale green silky curtains. In front of the fire stood a new, beige settee, and at either side was a matching easy chair. In the window was a softly shining bureau. Over the mantelpiece hung a glittering, plate glass mirror. Reflected in it was a water colour painting hanging on the opposite wall. The picture was one painted for Mother when she was a young girl, and she had snatched it up when leaving our home; it was all she had of our earlier, more prosperous life, and she had never pawned it.

'Good Heavens!' I exclaimed. I was so startled that my weak legs gave way and I sat down suddenly on the settee.

'It looks nice, doesn't it?' said Mother, her face glowing. 'It's a little bare yet, but we'll soon add some more pieces. They delivered it on the Monday after you were taken ill.'

I replied truthfully that it looked extremely nice. I had more sense than to start a fight regarding the other ideas which shot into my mind. 'It's charming,' I added.

'I wasn't sure whether to choose beige curtains or green ones. But the green brocade seemed such good quality that I bought those.'

'They look lovely,' I assured her. 'Thanks for making a fire here.' My head was whirling with the effort I had made to get dressed and come downstairs, and my chest felt constricted and painful with the effort not to burst into helpless tears.

Mother smiled. 'I'll just go and tidy myself before your visitor arrives. It's fortunate that I did not have any work today.'

She closed the door quietly behind her, and I leaned back against the new upholstery. Mother was an intelligent, well-educated woman, but when I looked around me I doubted her sanity.

How many shillings each week was this new extravagance going to drain from us? I wondered. And if they felt compelled to buy something for the house, why not start with blankets and sheets or towels? Our beds still lacked the basic necessities to keep us warm and clean – and they had gone out and bought a drawing room full of furniture. I sobbed inside, not daring to cry aloud. And how much longer was I to go hungry – and to a lesser degree the other children, too – until the damned stuff was paid for? I knew that we had not yet finished paying for the furniture that had been repossessed. Would they never learn to be practical? I whimpered in feeble anger.

There was a quiet knock at the front door, and I hastily dashed errant tears away and sniffed. I had not got a handkerchief.

There was the sound of soft, refined voices in the hall, a familiar, slightly shuffling step. I eased myself round, with some difficulty, to face my employer as she entered. Somehow she did not look so awesome in these surroundings – just a frail, small, elderly lady with a genuine look of concern on her face, as she held out a little gloved hand to be shaken.

'How do you do?' I inquired politely.

Her eyes looked dreadfully tired, but she said, with a little smile, 'Very well, thank you. And how are you?'

'Better, thank you,' I managed to gulp.

Mother asked her to sit down on one of the easy chairs, and she did so. She loosened the fur collar of her dark winter coat, arranged her black handbag on her knee and crossed her ankles neatly.

Mother swished down into the other easy chair, and the Presence looked me up and down earnestly.

'You seem to have been very ill,' she said. 'You have lost a lot of weight.'

I nodded nervous agreement. I wanted to lie down, but did not dare to move.

'Has the doctor told you yet when you will be fit for work?'

Mother intervened. 'This is her first venture downstairs, so I imagine it will be a few weeks before she can do much walking.'

'I imagine so.' The Presence continued to gaze thoughtfully at me. I had the feeling she could have given a police description of me after such an intense scrutiny.

There was an embarrassed silence, finally broken by Mother, who inquired, 'Would you like a cup of tea? You must be cold after coming so far. Helen usually has a cup at this time.'

The Presence was drawing off her leather gloves. She glanced up at Mother, who had risen from her chair. 'I would enjoy one very much. Thank you.'

That got rid of Mother for a few minutes, which I had had an instinctive feeling the Presence wanted to do. She smoothed her wrinkled gloves between absent-minded fingers, as she looked round the room. I noticed that her thin face had fine, premature lines round the eyes and at each side of the firm mouth. She wore no powder or lipstick, and she had the quiet, deft movements of a nun.

'This is a pleasant place for you to sit, isn't it? I am happy that your family seems to be getting on to its feet again.'

I wanted to lean forward and put my head into her tweed-covered lap and bellow tearfully that, in my opinion, the whole room was an outrage to reason. Instead, I whispered, 'Yes, it is a nice room.'

'You have been with us for two years, now,' she said with sudden briskness. It was a statement, not a question.

I nodded, and she sighed as if the fact was cause for woe.

'We need an extra girl in the Registry Office, to look after the index cards and to help with the filing. Such a girl would have to relieve the telephone operator at lunch time. I understand that you can now manage the switchboard; and it has been decided to give the new position to you. Er – Mr Ellis is agreeable to this.' She looked at me expectantly, a suggestion of a twinkle in her eyes.

The sense of overwhelming relief I felt was so great that, at first, I could not speak. I opened my mouth and no words came. A promotion! No more making tea or having to go out in the snow, and less running up and down stairs.

'Oh, thank you,' I finally gasped, with such sincerity that she really smiled this time.

'Your salary would be twelve shillings and sixpence, payable monthly.'

I was in ecstasy. 'That would be splendid,' I whispered. I wanted to shout it from the rooftops, dance in the street. Life was beginning to move forward at last.

'You can tell your parents about it yourself,' she added, in a tone of voice which hinted something which I did not at first grasp. Then, as I heard the rattle of teacups in the back room, I realised that she was being very forebearing. In a period when children of the middle classes remained children until their majority, it would have been quite possible that she would discuss this promotion with Mother before telling me, particularly as she herself belonged to a still earlier generation. She had, however, left me the choice of telling my parents about the salary increase, or not. Did she, I wondered, understand something of the misery I was going through?

'You are very kind,' I said warmly.

Because our crockery was chipped and ugly and we lacked many essentials, like milk jugs, Mother brought the Presence a cup of tea with milk already in it, and proffered the cheap, glass sugar basin with its tin spoon.

The tea was graciously accepted and consumed, the bad weather discussed and good wishes expressed for my early recovery.

'We will see if we can arrange another holiday this summer,' the Presence promised, as Mother took her cup from her.

Mother made no comment. Her smile was thin and polite. With a jolt, I wondered if she would try to keep me at home again, on the excuse of chronic ill-health. Perhaps I would never return to the office. Perhaps she was just willing to accept the payment of my salary as long as the organisation was prepared to pay it.

I must have gone even whiter at the idea, because the Presence said suddenly, 'Helen is exhausted. I must go.'

Hands were shaken, and Mother showed my

kind visitor out. I thankfully lay down on the settee.

If Mother and Father could buy over a hundred pounds' worth of sitting room furniture, I meditated bitterly, then they did not need the extra half-a-crown a week I would be earning. I desperately needed to be able to buy soup for lunch each day, instead of once a week. I needed shoes and second-hand woollens to keep me warm. The money I was already giving to Mother was more than adequate for the small amount of food I received, for the coal and gas I shared, and for a small contribution to the rent. I determined that Mother should have the next rise in pay I received, but not this one.

'And if you think I am going to stay at home, you can think again,' I muttered to myself acidly.

Mother had been quite patient while nursing me, but, from sad experience, I doubted if that patience would extend past the day I managed to walk about.

Chapter thirty-two

The doctor feared that the infection of my ears would cause a loss of hearing, and he insisted that I should see a specialist. So, a few days before Christmas, Mother managed to bundle me on to a tram, and we went to the Ear, Nose and Throat Hospital.

Since I was very weak, we arrived early, in the hope of being seen without much delay by the specialist, who donated his services to the hospital.

When I looked up at the building, it seemed to touch the pale blue sky. Its tall, narrow windows, the stonework beautifully carved by long dead masons, seemed to be slender fingers pointing upwards. Mother propped me against the wall, as close as she could get to the pollution-blackened doorway, where a shabby crowd awaited the opening of the Outpatients' Department. A cold wind fluttered the stained raincoats of the men and the bundly overcoats of the women, some of whom hugged beshawled children to them. The wind pierced my own macintosh and Mother's woollen cardigan which I was wearing beneath it, and I shivered convulsively. Mother had on a second-hand leather coat, which she had bought to keep her warm while doing a short spell as a door-to-door vacuum saleswoman.

Every so often I would feel faint and would start to reel, and Mother would pin me against the building's wall so that I did not fall. After waiting about half an hour, just when I felt I could endure no more, the door was opened by a probationer and the motley crowd poured in, elbowing each other in an effort to be first.

We found ourselves in a large waiting room with lines of wooden benches, and we sat down, not sure what we were supposed to do next.

I fainted against Mother's shoulder and, when I came round, I heard an angry rumbling from the waiting crowd. Apparently, Mother had asked a passing nurse for a glass of water and the girl had said coldly that it was not necessary, that I would come round quickly enough.

This indifference had riled the out-patients and they spent some time talking to each other and to Mother, in furious whispers, about other hospitals where they felt they had been treated equally uncompassionately.

We sat for a long time and nothing happened, until a nurse came and sat at a desk in front of us. Mother left me in the care of an elderly lady sitting next to her, and went to inquire when we might be seen.

'The specialist usually arrives about eleven,' the nurse said. 'You will just have to wait.'

'Could my daughter lie down somewhere?'

'Ask the patients if they will move up, so that she can lie on the bench.'

But the room was packed, so I leaned against Mother in a lethargy which passed occasionally into complete oblivion. I was so bony that it was also very painful to sit on a wooden bench for such a long time.

Finally a young physician and a nurse arrived, and began to sift through the patients, to discover their reasons for attending the hospital. Our kind neighbour held me again, while Mother went to the desk to explain our presence. By this time I was so exhausted, I did not care whether I saw a doctor or not. All I wanted to do was lie down – on the floor, if there was no other place.

'You should not have to wait much longer,' the nurse told Mother. 'Doctor arrived a few minutes ago.'

At about twelve, having left home before eight o'clock, we finally were ushered into a lofty, poorly-lit office. A thin, grey-haired man in a white coat, a man with the gentlest voice and the kindest manner I ever remember, was seated on a little stool, scribbling on a note board held across his knee. Since I had come about my throat and ears, his elderly nurse took my coat from me and sat me down in a straight-backed chair.

The doctor, a famous surgeon, smiled at Mother, when she handed him a note from our physician, opened the envelope and read the description of my illness.

He put the note down on a nearby table, and, while he looked at my face, he asked Mother a few questions about the duration of the infection. I sat with eyes cast down, hoping I would not fall off the chair.

'Well,' he said, as he picked up a torch. 'Let me have a look.'

He peered very earnestly down my throat, and then with another instrument down my ears. I winced as the ears were stretched slightly by the insertion of the cold appliance. He then felt carefully round my neck.

Mother volunteered the information that I had been subject to ear infection ever since I had had the measles at the age of five. His expression as he turned to Mother was a bit puzzled; perhaps the exquisitely enunciated words from such a battered looking woman surprised him.

He turned back to me and said gently, 'Helen, I would like to examine your chest. Nurse will take your blouse from you and help you with your underwear.'

I nodded, and unbuttoned the heavy, cotton blouse, to expose the naked, bony chest beneath. I handed the blouse to the waiting nurse.

Both doctor and nurse gasped. The doctor glanced at Mother in a puzzled way, as if to include her in their shock. I was suddenly afraid that the doctor had spotted some deadly disease.

'Nurse, bring a gown,' ordered the doctor sharply. 'I think I had better take a look at Helen generally. Help her slip off the rest of her clothes.' He looked at me and smiled. I must have appeared to him to be scared beyond measure, as I gazed at him, pop-eyed, because he said soothingly, 'There is nothing to be afraid of, my dear.'

Mother had not expected that I would have to strip, and I saw her flush slightly, as I dropped my skirt off, leaving me garbed in a pair of worn, off-white knickers held up by a pin and a pair of rayon stockings supported by rubber bands.

Almost tenderly, the nurse slipped the stiff, white gown round my shoulders, and her carefulness frightened me more.

The nurse laid me on an examination table and the specialist checked me over, part by part. I must have looked ugly to him, with only a slight rise of young breasts above ribs that stuck out, a distended stomach with a fluff of pubic hair at its base, legs that seemed all bone. I could not see my own buttocks, but I knew that there was little fat on them. He pinched me in several places very gently. Then he wrapped the gown round me, and the nurse helped me to sit up.

The specialist turned to Mother, and in a voice which indicated a rage ill-controlled, he asked her, 'Mrs Forrester, what *has* happened to this child? An illness such as your physician describes could not have reduced her weight to this extent.'

Mother said uneasily, 'She does not have a very good appetite.'

'She is half starved.' He was furiously angry, and his voice rose. 'You will lose her unless you find some means of getting food into her. No child should have to suffer like this. What is the City thinking of? Is your husband on Public Assistance?'

'No,' muttered Mother. 'He works for the Liverpool Corporation.'

'And Helen?' He turned to me, 'Have you got work, child?'

I told him the name of the organisation which employed me. The nurse had put me into a chair, and I sat staring at him, aghast.

Hunger was painful at times, but most of the time

I felt lethargic and weak. I thought I was lazy, and I was always pushing myself to complete the work I had to do.

'I can't understand it, Mrs Forrester. You are, I imagine, an educated woman, and should understand something about nutrition. Your physician *has* expressed to me his anxiety for her general condition, though he sent her to me, of course, because of the ear and throat infections. But unless she can eat more and put on some weight, she will be subject to all kinds of illness. Her ears will heal – your doctor will explain that to you. Even in this city, however, it is some time since I saw such a shocking case of malnutrition. Did your doctor recommend a special diet?'

During this diatribe Mother had stared at him with an expression of blank disbelief. Now she flared up suddenly.

'Yes,' she snapped. 'And I have done my best to give it to her – but she doesn't eat it.'

In an instinctive defence of Mother, I interjected, 'I haven't been able to eat very much, doctor. My throat hurt and so did my ears when I swallowed.'

He looked at me almost contritely, as if ashamed of his outburst, and said to the nurse, 'Take Helen into the other room – there's an easy chair there. You can help her dress in there, while I talk to Mrs Forrester.'

The nurse picked up my clothes and wrapped the white gown round me. She put a hand under my elbow to help support me as we went towards the door. At the entrance, I paused, reluctant to leave someone who cared so much that I was thin and hungry.

'Thank you, doctor,' I said, forcing back tears of weakness.

I never saw him again.

As the nurse helped to dress me and told me what a wonderful doctor my new-found friend was, an outburst of words rumbled through the closed door. I could not hear what he was saying, but when Mother joined me she was weeping unrestrainedly, and this distressed me. I took her arm, to comfort her, while the nurse said briskly, 'Doctor will be writing to your G.P. You should go to see him in a few days' time.'

Without a word, the two of us went very slowly back through the hall and out into the street to catch a tram.

'Mummy, I'm so sorry. Please don't cry. What did he say?'

No matter what battles we had fought, Mother had suffered so much herself since we arrived in Liverpool, that I could not bear to see her reduced to tears by a stranger. The careworn woman, whose arm I leaned upon, was totally different from the pretty, fashionable lady I had known as a child. I wanted passionately to erase whatever bitter words the specialist had used when speaking to her in my absence.

Mother did not answer me at first, but heaved me up the steps of a tram which arrived as we emerged from the hospital. She handed the conductor two pennies and received our tickets, before she finally spoke.

'He is going to write to our doctor,' she said finally, with a trembling sigh. 'He will make some recommendations. You have nothing to fear. You have no disease.'

And that was all the information I could extract from her.

A few days later, I managed to walk the short distance to our own doctor's house, and spent a happy hour reading all the old magazines in his waiting room, and talking in laboured German to two German patients waiting to see him. They told me such horrifying tales of what was going on in Germany under Hitler that I felt my own suffering to be very small.

The doctor checked my ears, throat and chest again. The specialist's report, he said, had been optimistic about my hearing and he hoped I would not have much hearing loss. Afterwards, he sat down at his desk, and said very earnestly, 'Helen, you must eat as much plain food as you can obtain. Don't spend your pocket money on sweets – buy an orange or an apple. Clean up your plate at meal times.' He grinned cheerfully at me.

'Yes,' I agreed. How could I tell him that I had had no sweets during the four years I had been in Liverpool, except one or two which had been given to me? How could I tell him how empty my dinner plate had been for so long?

'And I want you to go to bed early and rest as much as you can during the next few weeks.'

Rest? With so many children pestering me with their constant needs? And I was now terribly behind in night school – my only hope for a better future; I would have to catch up somehow. Then I remembered the new job – that would be easier. So I nodded agreement again.

'And during the weekends you should walk in the park whenever it is sunny, to get fresh air. Perhaps go to New Brighton sometimes and walk there – that would be nice, wouldn't it?'

Poor, benighted man. Didn't he realise that the ferry boat to New Brighton cost twopence? Princes Park was there, however, and I often took Baby Edward and Avril for walks in it. So again I agreed.

As he scribbled on his prescription pad, he said, 'I wish your Mother had come with you. I would have liked to discuss your diet in detail with her. Tell her what I have said, and come to see me again next week.' He handed me a prescription. 'Have this tonic made up and take it regularly.'

I thanked him and went out and walked slowly down the steps into Parliament Street. After such long confinement, Liverpool seemed a beautiful place in which to walk. My eyes ran appreciatively along the fine symmetry of the big terrace houses which lined the street. Father said they had been built from money gained from the slave trade with America, but they were still beautiful to me. Even the stolidness of the brick Home for Incurables seemed lighter, more cheerful, than usual. The whole district was bathed in a mid-afternoon hush, that pause which occurs in suburbia before the homeward rush from the city. The only other person I saw was a woman on her knees scrubbing the marble steps of the Rialto Cinema and Dance Hall, and I paused on the other side of the road to watch her. Perhaps, I thought wistfully, now I have a rise in pay I could go to the cinema. People said that the floor of the dance hall was a particularly good one, and I imagined myself in a long dress twirling round it in the arms of the Prince of Wales, now a troubled exile, to the strains of a Strauss waltz. It doesn't cost anything to have dreams.

Chapter thirty-three

Many years later, Alan told me that one day, while I was out, some people came from the child welfare authority and threatened to take us all into care. He cannot remember the date of this, but I think it must have been during my convalescence, perhaps while I was at the doctor's surgery. It is hardly likely that our doctor or the outraged specialist would have left such a case of malnutrition unreported. It is also possible that my astute employer may have goaded officialdom into action. Brian's skinny condition had quite likely been noted during his stay in hospital. So several complaints were probably made.

Whenever it was, my parents must have talked their way out of it. In those days, few would believe that neglect or ill-treatment of children occurred in any but working-class homes; and once my parents' original social status had been established there would be a tendency to believe anything they said. From the day on which we saw the specialist, however, Mother saw that I received the same amount of food as the other children, and it was obvious that she gave priority to the buying of food over other needs. We still did not have enough to eat, but there was an improvement. I became concerned that in an effort to feed me, she would go without herself, and this caused a reciprocal concern for each other, which improved our relationship.

As soon as I was able to stay up for most of the day, Mother began to use me as a housekeeper again, and I was dreadfully afraid that, once again, I would become the family's unpaid general factotum. I never grudged helping in the house, but I did not want to be permanently at home.

Little Edward was now nearly four and could talk well. He was a pleasant, confiding small companion, always asking questions, like Tony did. I would sit with him on my lap, his untidy brown hair against my cheek, quivering inside at the thought of being shut into a kind of slavery without any rewards.

Long before I returned to work, I had taken out my text books and begun to study again. I pressed Fiona into reading aloud to me, so that I could practise shorthand and not lose speed. This bored Fiona terribly – she hated reading anything, but she was very good-natured and, on my behalf, she stumbled through business letters from the text book and the first few chapters of *Jane Eyre*. She would put down the book after two or three minutes, during which my pencil had scampered frantically across my notebook, and would ask bewilderedly, 'How can you stand it? Why bother?'

I would smile at her and say I liked it. Embryo maiden aunts must be able to earn, I felt, though I could not have explained it to her. I did not want to end up a nervous ghost in the house of one of my siblings, caring for their children, dependent on them for the smallest need.

Sometimes, when Edward or highly strung Brian had difficulty in going to sleep, I would sing irregular French verbs or German declensions to them. Brian chuckled at the strange words, but Edward only needed a comforting hum and did not miss Little Bo Peep or her friends.

Three of the children had not been up to the bedroom to see me at all while I was ill. Fiona, Avril and Edward tumbled straight into the big double bed on the other side of the room and usually fell asleep immediately, but I had not seen Alan or Tony, and Brian only immediately before he was sent to hospital. Now I was downstairs again, they looked as if they had all grown enormously during my absence.

Brian had recovered quickly, and he and Tony had found good friends amongst neighbouring shopkeepers' children; they played in their houses or in the street. They also went to choir practices and to the church services.

Alan had made friends with one or two other office boys and clerks, and his pocket money was sufficient to enable him to go to the cinema, to boxing matches and to play cricket.

Fiona did not make many friends. Like me, she had little money. She was also very slow moving, so that getting herself to and from school, keeping her scanty clothes clean and joining in an occasional game of tag or skipping with other girls in the street practically filled her day. Occasionally, on a Saturday afternoon, Alan kindly took her to the cinema, or she beguiled Mother into giving her twopence to go by herself. Continuous performances in the cinema had just begun to be common, and she sat all through the afternoon and two evening performances, seeing the same two films offered, over and over again. She would return about eleven o'clock at night, silent and bemused. As she approached her fourteenth birthday, she began to put her hair into rag curlers and to take a deep interest in her appearance. Boys in the streets around whistled after her, and she would run into the house blushing and bewildered.

Because I had such intense pain during my menstrual periods, a pain which could not be hidden from the rest of the family because I used to scream with it, she dreaded the onset of this natural cycle, but when it came it was painless and she was much relieved. When I saw this, I asked the doctor if my pain could be at least reduced, but he laughed and told me to take a couple of aspirins, assuring me that it would go away when I was married. Through the years I got the same reply from other general practitioners.

Avril, short for her age though sturdy looking, still raged helplessly when our parents quarrelled or whenever she was in any way frustrated. Like me, her birth had been bitterly resented, and in her first years she had been left almost entirely to the care of servants. Now, however, I noticed that Mother had begun to recognise a fellow spirit, for they were surprisingly alike, and the little girl clung to her mother in a very moving way. Yet another stray cat had attached itself to our household and Avril seemed to get some comfort from cuddling it and pretending that it was a baby. It submitted very patiently to being wrapped in a piece of blanket and held upside down.

As I waited for my lethargic body to gain strength, I watched the children come and go, each intent upon his or her own business. I began to realise that life does change; nothing lasts for ever. When I had first come to Liverpool and had been plunged into sudden, frightful poverty amongst coarse and scarifying people, it seemed as if we would always be small and helpless. But it was not so; the children were growing vigorously, despite poor food.

All growing things push against each other, each fighting for air, space and sustenance, and large overcrowded families are no exception. And I observed that, as each child grew in strength, it fought quite ruthlessly for a place for itself, giving very little thought to the plight of the others. I saw that the family unit was not as tightly locked together as my parents were fond of imagining. And I was plunged into melancholy when Mother preached to me the need to go without, give up my life to the care of the children. Why could they not help, too? I would ask angrily. And the retort was always the same, 'You are the eldest.'

But, in truth, they were better at avoiding it. Alan was the eldest boy and automatically more privileged; he was my father's hope. Fiona pretended to be much more stupid than she really was, and she was more frail. Brian and Tony kept out of the way, and Avril had such a colossal temper that even Mother was silenced by it. Amongst us toddled Baby Edward, serene and self-assured, too small to have to worry.

Too sick myself to do a great deal, I sat and watched them, corrected them if they seemed to be doing anything of danger to themselves, made the meals and the fires, and wondered once if they would go hungry for my sake.

The answer, I believed, was that of Shaw's Pygmalion, 'Not bloody likely.'

Chapter thirty-four

When I returned to work, the mood of the City seemed more cheerful. The previous winter it had been hung with crape for the passing of King George V; Edward VIII, my adored Prince Charming, had come and gone, and was an exile with his Mrs Simpson. Now we all looked forward to a coronation, that of George VI and his plump little Queen, Elizabeth. It seemed also that there was a trifle more work available, though the lines of unemployed were still very long.

I said a mental 'Hello' to Minerva, looking down from the dome of the Town Hall. Belief in ancient gods never quite dies – it remains, mixed with the myths and legends of one's people, in the background of one's mind; and I believed that Minerva would help her people, if she could, and even, perhaps, an ugly little stepchild like me. It was not an active belief to be expressed in prayers; but just a cosy feeling like that given by a St Christopher medallion or the ownership of a black cat.

I was still very weak, and was thankful that I now worked most of the time on one floor of the office, though I was constantly under the subduing eye of Mr Ellis. I was allotted a wooden chair and a corner of a table on which to do my work. I became very quick at the tasks given me; and, whenever I had the chance, I would retire behind the stacks of files on the excuse of helping to put some of them away, to read, spellbound, the files' contents. They were moving stories of human suffering, sometimes covering many years, set down in unemotional prose by succeeding social workers. In some cases, I was acquainted with the family concerned, and it was interesting to see a social worker's opinion of them. I chuckled sometimes, because the priorities of the family and those of the social worker were often at odds. Most of my neighbours had the aim of surviving with as little pain and as much immediate enjoyment as they could obtain.

I learned the name of the women I had observed on the way to night school. They allowed men to play with their bodies in the same way as cows allowed a bull. Now the files told me that this was wrong; it was sinful. And I began idly to wonder about the relationship of men and women and about love. Surely there was something more to it than the conversation of the mill girls I had met on holiday had led me to think. I came across the words fornication and adultery, Bible words that I had not previously thought about. The dictionary was not very helpful.

I remembered the knowing laughter of Cristina Gomez when she had referred to Alonzo's goodness as a husband; perhaps she meant more than the fact that he gave his wages to her each week. Perhaps the wild, unearthly dreams I sometimes had were prompted by my coming into the beginning of womanhood; I blushed when I remembered them.

In my isolation from anything that most other

girls had, friends, affection, parties, dances, I had missed the usual slow discovery of sex. Whispered stories told between girl friends, the hints of it in magazines, discreet warnings and indications from mothers, had not been part of my experience. No boy had ever approached me. I had never worked out why Emile Zola's *Nana* was so wicked; all she seemed to do was stay in bed. In our early days in Liverpool I could have been raped and I would not have understood what had happened to me. Perhaps it was fortunate that I had been so dirty, so grey in looks, that I merged with the grey-black city around me and had thus walked unscathed through streets that for centuries had been very unsafe. Now, I began to knit together the romance of the many novels I had read with the facts that the files and the mill girls had brought to my attention and to understand the happiness of Cristina and her husband. The thought of the Gomez couple brought home to me that whatever physical relation there was between husband and wife it could be an enriching experience. And I imagined that lonely single men bought that experience from prostitutes.

Now that I was in the office most of the time, I came into closer contact with other members of the junior staff.

We could find no common meeting ground.

I was still grubby and untidy, though our landlord had had our house fumigated and I no longer feared passing bugs to the other girls. Even the fleas in the house had been reduced. Occasionally I caught head lice from the other children, who picked them up at school; and once I had to go to work with my head smothered in a heavy ointment to eradicate them; this caused a lot of stares and some open laughter, because my hair was pasted down against my skull, like a boy's.

Like any youngster, I wanted to be included in the girls' conversation, much of which hinged on the films they had seen, the boys they had met and the radio programmes they had heard. Though I had not been to the cinema in Liverpool and we had no radio, I had read a great number of popular novels which had been made into films, so I could analyse the plots and discuss their themes. I sometimes broke into their gossip with an observation, which was usually received with stunned silence; and the conversation would be resumed, as if I had not spoken. This made me feel hopelessly stupid and I would be quiet for some time afterwards. When I made a mistake, however, they would address me brusquely.

The first purchases I made with my increase in salary were a bar of soap and a packet of soap flakes. These were used up within a day or two by the rest of the family, but now, with a little money, I tried very hard to collect a few more clothes and to keep them clean. I hunted through the oddments table at the pawnbroker's and I saved up for a pair of shoes from Marks & Spencers.

I soon discovered that to have spare clothes was very difficult. Frequently, I came home to find the garments pawned or on Mother's or Fiona's back. This made me furious and my wicked temper would rise and for days I would be in disgrace for the outburst. I rarely borrowed from Mother and always asked specially; she had several hats and sometimes I would beg the loan of a change of headgear. I was confused. How did other girls cope with such situations? I wondered. What should I do?

And the weakness from my illness persisted, despite the slight improvement in diet. The tremendous inborn strength which had carried me through years of hardship was gone. I was wracked with pains in my legs and sometimes in other joints, and the throat still tended to acquire threatening septic spots in it. I gargled with salt and water in the hope of clearing them, but it was only partially successful.

So the strain for the first few weeks after being ill was very great, and I did not take much notice of my successor, Sylvia Poole, except to help her a little until she knew the office girl's work. I was afraid to say much to her, because I expected to be snubbed. She had eyes as blue as speedwells, which stared, with considerable perspicacity, through thick, horn-rimmed glasses. Though much shorter than the rest of the staff, she seemed uncowed by them or even by the formidable Mr Ellis.

I lived all my life in fearful apprehension, but she seemed to view life with a calm confidence. She had a firm, though light tread, and all her movements were deft and certain. I could not imagine a voluntary worker daring to complain to her that the tea was cold or that there was too much milk in it. Such complaints used to send me racing up to the kitchen in nervous haste, to fetch a fresh cup.

In the privacy of the top floor kitchen, where at

first I helped her make the tea, she asked me, 'Have you been here long, Miss Foster?'

'Forrester,' I corrected.

'Er-Forrester. How long have you been here?'

'Two years.'

'As office girl?' The blue eyes glanced sharply up at me, as she rattled cups on to saucers. The pretty red lips curved in a grimace. 'I wouldn't like to do this job for long.'

I did not know how to answer. All the underlying terror of losing my job and not being allowed to take another seemed impossible to explain to someone of her temerity.

Her smile was sweet and friendly, however, and gradually I began to relax with her. She had a very pink and white complexion and the suggestion of a double chin, which indicated plenty of good food. She had a charm, a gaiety about her which I longed to emulate.

Finally, I answered her question.

'Yes, as office girl. The job seems to offer a future, Miss Poole.'

Again she made a disdainful moue with her mouth. She was a year younger than me, but her fearlessness and her self-assurance made me feel the younger of the two of us. To my astonishment, she did not seem to think my conversation stupid; and slowly I began to talk to her about all kinds of subjects.

I had theories of history, and she patiently submitted to their being unloaded on her. I had done considerable background reading on the current political situation in Europe and I read every newspaper I could, either at home or in the library, so that, however misguided my ideas may have been, I had many of them. I had recently acquired two pen friends in Germany, who told me something of what they were being taught. Their letters were loaded with references to 'our beloved Fuehrer', and we shared surprise at anyone so monstrous being beloved. The basement waiting room held an ever-increasing number of terrified refugees from all over Europe, sent to us for aid, so we were more aware than many people of what was happening to Jewry, to trade unionists, to honest priests, under the beloved leader.

When I described to her birds that I had seen or a flower peeping up between paving stones or how lovely the Greek church looked in the early morning sun, she did not snigger. And gradually the barriers went down.

Sometimes we would walk out of the office together to catch our respective trams – walking to and from work was impossible for me at that time because I was too weak – and conversation would pour out of me in torrents. All the pent-up knowledge, ideas, theories, came flowing out, to be tried against a cool and clear intelligence. In fact, for a long time I forgot the difference between a monologue and a dialogue. When I expounded on an idea that was particularly far out, she would respond, 'But don't you think, Miss Foster. . .' and I would automatically correct her, 'Miss Forrester'. She would politely repeat, 'Miss Forrester . . . don't you think that . . .'

And my idea would begin to take a more sensible outline.

Life suddenly began to be exciting, interesting. I could hardly wait to meet her again and share another reflection with her. Every joke, every amusing incident had to be recounted.

Her parents had managed to keep her in school until she was fifteen and encouraged her to go to night school; her desire for better education was nearly as great as mine. She wittily reduced the office staff to size for me, and I ceased to be afraid of them. Her respect for my ideas added a little self-esteem to that already implanted by Emrys Hughes.

One day, she became the target for the scorn of the other girls. She arrived with her straight brown hair transformed into a soft blond, waved and curled about her face. The improvement in her looks was remarkable and I said so. But to bleach one's hair, however good the result, was simply not approved of by lower middle-class society, and the staff retired behind the stacks of files to laugh and condemn.

As she helped me sort index cards, she said with a scowl on her pretty face, 'I don't see any reason to look dowdy all my life. I'm going to make the best of myself.' And undeterred by Mr Ellis's startled looks, she added, in the days that followed, a subdued make-up to her already good complexion.

I was fascinated by the transformation.

Instead of buying soup in Woolworth's restaurant, I spent one lunch time examining the contents of their cosmetic counter, and, greatly daring, bought a tin of Snowfire foundation cream and a box of face powder. Unfortunately, when I applied them, before the broken mirror stuck in our kitchen window, they did not transform me immediately into a beauty. The washed-out, sallow complexion was made somewhat whiter and the red acne boils were a little less apparent, but the black rings around my eyes looked even blacker, as did the thick black eyebrows. However, I hopefully applied these aids to glamour again when I went to work the next day. Nobody seemed to notice any difference.

When I discussed the matter with Miss Poole, like an old granny solemnly discussing a funeral, she looked carefully at my efforts, and said, 'What about buying a lipstick and some rouge?'

This shocked me. Mother had always used both rouge and lipstick and, when she was younger, heavy eye make-up. But I remembered the servants saying that she was fast. I did not want to appear fast.

'Wouldn't it be rather – um – fast?' I asked timidly.

'Of course not,' Miss Poole assured me firmly. 'I use them. Everybody does now.'

So I went without another lunch and spent sixpence on rouge and lipstick. They were the wrong colour for me, and I did not place the rouge correctly. With my hair combed back in a bun and two feverishly red spots painted on my cheeks, I looked like a Dutch doll.

This time, Mother noticed. And she laughed at me. Cross and crestfallen, I went to wash my face.

But Fiona, much less cut off from other girls than I was, had borrowed some women's magazines which showed how to apply make-up. In exchange for a chance to paint her own face, she brought these magazines out from under her mattress and let me read them. When Mother was out, we both tried to follow the instructions, vying for peeps into the bit of mirror, as we worked. There was a special diagram showing how to place rouge on a long, thin face. I was surprised at the improvement, though the magazine confirmed that the colour was wrong for a brown haired, green-eyed person with a yellow skin.

When I looked at Fiona's more successful efforts, I realised, with a shock, that she had grown up. She laughed at my expression of astonishment. Perfect teeth flashed between the gaily painted lips. She had carefully removed, with a wet finger, the surplus powder from her huge eyelashes and smooth, long brows, and her dancing, violet eyes were greatly enhanced by the powdered skin.

'Fi, you look gorgeous,' I exclaimed.

'Do you really think so?' she asked shyly.

'Oh, yes,' I assured her.

She looked down at her grubby, little girl's clothes, and sighed. 'Thank goodness, Mummy's going to buy me some decent clothes to start work in. She's going to get a cheque so that I can have a new coat and hat and everything.'

Such a pang of jealousy went through me. I remembered the exhausting battles I had fought and was still fighting to be able to work, to have a few clothes, even to get enough to eat. Here was Fiona taking it for granted that she would have no such difficulties.

'She hasn't asked you to look after Edward until he starts school in September?'

'She knows I'm no good at that sort of thing,' she replied placidly, as she took down the mirror and tried re-arranging her straight hair in a more sophisticated style.

It was true that Fiona had always appeared very helpless, when asked to help in the house. I looked at her sharply. She had picked up the family comb and was contentedly combing her hair. I had an uneasy feeling that she was much smarter than me.

'Good for you,' I said, trying unsuccessfully to keep acidity out of my voice.

Fiona put down the comb and turned to me.

'They can afford to pay someone,' she said calmly. 'There will be five of us at work, when I start.'

'Tell that to Mother,' I snapped bitterly.

Chapter thirty-five

As promised, the Presence arranged another holiday for me. This time, I had to pay my own fare and one pound towards the cost.

'Since you will receive a month's salary before you start the holiday, there should be no difficulty about that,' she said to me very pleasantly.

I was most grateful and thanked her effusively. I nearly danced out of her office. A holiday like the one I had had before would make me strong again, take away the pains in my legs. And I could, if I wished, sleep and sleep and sleep, until my head stopped aching and my eyes lost their bloodshot hue.

Filled with excitement, I dashed into the house when I arrived home and poured out the thrilling news to my parents, who were seated at the table, bickering as usual. It took a lot of effort on the part of both Father and me to persuade Mother that she could provide the necessary one pound.

'I'll save up my fare,' I promised, as I ate a slice of bologna and several pieces of bread and margarine, followed by gulps of sweet, weak tea.

In the weeks that followed, by halfpennies and pennies, I saved the fare, two shillings for pocket money and enough to buy some stockings, knickers and a petticoat, the first petticoat I had owned in Liverpool. The day before my departure I bought the ticket, put my few clothes together in a shopping bag, and talked gaily to a silent Mother about the beauty of the Lake District.

On the Friday night I handed her my month's pay, less the rise which the Presence had quietly given to me. This latter money I had to keep for fares, stockings and soup when I returned. Mother slipped the money into her handbag, without a word.

An hour before the train was due, I asked her for a pound to pay to the Holiday Home.

'I haven't got it,' she said.

I could not believe her. But it was true.

On the previous evening, while I had been fetching some milk from the dairy, the agent who collected for the Finance Company that provided the cheques with which she purchased clothes, had called. She was, as usual, behind in her weekly payments, and he had threatened court action; so she had given him my wages. She added coolly that, since I would not now need the ticket for the train, she would like to have it, so that she could get a refund on it from the Railway Company.

I spent my holiday sulkily watching Edward, while Mother commenced a full-time job as the representative of a sweet firm. Edward would go to school in September, and she felt she could undertake regular work. I began once more to fear that she would try to keep me at home.

Within two weeks her accounts were, as she put it, in a muddle, and she was dismissed. I breathed a sigh of relief as she returned to her demonstration work in shops, and the children cheerfully ate her samples.

In an effort to improve my wardrobe, I bought two black dress lengths from the pawnbroker and a sixpenny pattern from Woolworth's. I found that I could not cut the dresses out with the blunt, curved nail scissors which were all we had, so I begged a razor blade from Father and cut them out with that. It took me some weeks to hand-stitch them, but when they were finished, they fitted well; and even Mother said they looked very nice.

I had also bought from the pawnbroker a thick, brown coat. It was a nondescript garment which had suffered from being bundled up in his loft, but it was warm. And though it was summer time, I seemed to feel cold every time the wind blew, so I wore it daily.

Mother called at the office one day and asked for me. Since I was in the basement taking clients' names, Sylvia Poole asked if she could help. Mother said she wanted my coat and, in front of the other girls, a bewildered Sylvia gave it to her. I was even more bewildered, when Sylvia told me about it. And I was hurt by the gleams of amusement in the eyes of the other young staff members.

I was outraged when I returned home to find that the coat and my second, newly stitched dress were in pawn. But heated argument did not get it back, and I shivered into the autumn before I had saved enough money to redeem it.

I was again plunged into embarrassment at the office when Father sought an interview with the Presence. He wanted help to keep our many creditors off the doorstep. I am not sure what kind of a miracle he expected her to perform on his behalf, but he lost his temper and so did she. Their raised voices came clearly through the door panelling into the office in which I worked. She told him that, with five people working, his family was far better off than most.

'But there are seven children,' he spluttered defensively.

'One should not father children one cannot keep,' she retorted tartly.

The office was convulsed with laughter. Even Mr Ellis managed a subdued haw-haw, as he wrote in his big record book. I wished that the floor would open and close over me. I bent over the index cards and sorted them feverishly, while the private exit to the hall from the Presence's office was opened and slammed shut again.

Father raged, off and on, for days afterwards, and vented much of his frustration on me, as if I was responsible for my unbending employer.

I feared greatly that the Presence would lose patience with such a trying family. But she did not. On the contrary, she was particularly kind whenever she met me in the hall or on the staircase, and would stop to ask if I was well or how night school was proceeding.

A few weeks later, she was asked by the British Broadcasting Corporation if she could find someone who would give a talk on managing on a small budget. This was not an easy request to fill, because most of our clients were far from literate, and she asked me if I thought my mother could do it.

Mother was delighted. The offer meant a day trip

to Manchester, lunch provided, and a fee for the broadcast. We all encouraged her.

She spent hours writing out likely lists of expenditure, and then screwing them up and throwing them impatiently into the fire. Though she was very good at letter writing, the talk had to be written in a manner suitable for verbal delivery; and this she found extremely difficult.

I watched her struggle for several evenings, as I went about my household tasks. Then I asked her timidly if she would like me to try to write it for her. Much to my surprise, she thankfully agreed.

Since every day I read several files which gave detailed lists of family expenditures, I was able to compose a likely-sounding budget, based on Father's supposed salary plus my earnings. Then I wrote this into a chatty format and read it out, timing it by our solitary clock. It was a little short, so I added a recipe for fried herrings as a recommended standby for impecunious housewives – fishmongers nearly gave away herrings in those days.

While I stood nervously by her, Mother read it, and, with a sigh of relief, said it was excellent. I basked in her unexpected approbation.

She had a most enjoyable day in Manchester and delivered the talk without a hitch. It resulted in several complimentary letters from listeners and was reported in the *Liverpool Echo*. Because we had no radio, we could not hear her, but most of our neighbours did own radios and they were most impressed that anyone in our district could speak on it. They ceased to regard Mother as 'bloody stuck up', and

Mother found herself talking to respectful women wrapped in shawls or old overcoats, all of them anxious to discuss her wonderful budget, which actually balanced. Their questions confused her, since she had not made up the talk, and they must have been puzzled by some of her answers. The unexpected status that the talk gave her in our bedraggled community, however, helped her greatly. She was forced to communicate with our many kind neighbours and her isolation was broken. She had had to approach one or two of them before, when asking them to care for Edward, but this new relationship opened up their world and their suffering to her, and, though she often made sardonic jokes about them, she tolerated them much better.

Some of the mothers of the girls at work had heard the talk and reported it to their daughters. The daughters spent a considerable part of their lunch hours and tea breaks arguing with me that it was a pack of lies, and I found myself in the unenviable position of having to defend it as gospel truth, despite Father's request for help from the Presence. I said loftily that the debts Father had come to see the Presence about were old ones, and finally they retired to their respective gossip corners and left me once more alone. Sylvia Poole said nothing, for which I was profoundly grateful. Perhaps her mother did not hear it.

The unexpected success of my composition set a seed in the back of my mind which was to lie dormant for many years before it finally sprang to life, and flowered.

Chapter thirty-six

Pressed by youngsters who wanted to share the experiences of other children, Mother began to take us, on fine Bank Holidays, to New Brighton, a small holiday resort on the other side of the River Mersey.

Father refused to accompany us to its crowded beach, washed with the effluent of both Liverpool and Birkenhead, so Mother and I packed paper shopping bags with banana sandwiches and beer bottles filled with lemonade made from a concentrate. Down the sides we stuffed old pairs of underpants or shorts and our always dirty towels, so that the children could bathe.

We took the tram down to the Pier Head and caught the New Brighton ferry. The floating pier, pulsating gently beneath our feet, was always packed with people, anxious to spend a day away from Liverpool's heavily polluted air; and we held the children firmly by their hands lest they stray beyond the confining link fence and fall into the heaving tidal waters.

When the ferry boat's gangway slammed down, the crowd pressed forward while the passengers hurried off. Then, using prams and elbows to make a path, they charged on to the boat. Frantic voices floated out of the crowd screaming to our Aggie or our George to 'come 'ere afore you fall in.'

Pushing and jostling, we poured on to the upper

deck in search of a seat in the sun, so that we could nurse Edward and Avril. Edward invariably broke into howls of fright at the uproar and had to be comforted by having the pretty seagulls pointed out to him and the lovely shiny waves.

Then there was the excitement of watching the funnel belch smoke. One of the boys invariably got a smut in his eye, which had to be hooked out with the corner of a handkerchief or by carefully pulling down the red-edged lid.

Sweet air from the sea blew straight up the estuary, ruffling the surface of the great river. The Royal Liver Building and the Cunard Building, trademarks of the Port of Liverpool, receded, and the New Brighton tower, the lighthouse and the sturdy battery jutting into the river loomed up. The children went mad with excitement and rushed up and down the companionways and along the crowded decks, like small, wingless gulls.

At New Brighton pier, the mob poured off like black pepper out of a pot. It was a miracle that nobody fell off the gang planks into the water.

The beach always seemed to be full before we arrived, and yet, somehow, boat load after boat load of people were absorbed.

Heavy on the air were the odours of beer and fish and chips. Fathers and young men made straight for the public houses beyond the Parade, while mothers spread old blankets to mark their patch of sand. The children flew down to the water like startled seals.

Ice cream men dispensed dripping cornets, and Alan and I sometimes bought one each for the younger children, if we had money left over after paying our fares.

Occasionally, Mother sent me to a booth to buy a pot of tea – one shilling deposit on the teapot – and we drank hot tea, while the children guzzled the overly sweet lemonade straight from the bottles.

While a towel was held round the middle of each child in turn, they wriggled out of their clothes and put on the old pants we had brought with us, and then went dancing into the filthy water. It was remarkable that nobody caught any deadly disease from the sewage and chemical filled stream.

They came out shivering, splashing the water from their skinny bodies, their feet caked with a mixture of sand and mud, and stood round us while they devoured the sand-impregnated sandwiches. Then they would play tag in and out of the seated crowd. To go to the fun fair was beyond our resources, but the children were happy to be freed from constraints of traffic and narrow streets, and to be allowed to yell at the tops of their voices.

My grandmother had always forbidden me to go to the beach near her home on Bank Holidays, because it was filled with similar trippers. Nice people, I was taught, stayed at home on such days. I wondered privately what she would think of her grandchildren if she could see them.

To my mother, these trips must have seemed unbearably noisy and smelly, the people round her crude and boorish. Yet, in a way, the change did her good, too, and she always returned from them much more talkative and cheerful.

In the late afternoon, we made the long trip home, sun-reddened and weary, Edward and Avril tending to be fretful and quarrelsome, Brian and Tony still bouncing. Fiona, Alan and Avril, being very fair skinned, were usually as red as pillar boxes, and blistered by the unaccustomed strong sunlight. They groaned ruefully about it and, whenever possible, we bought a twopenny bottle of calamine lotion and sponged it over their backs and arms, while during the next few days they peeled painfully.

One August Bank Holiday, we spent the day at New Brighton in a crowd so thick that it was literally impossible by late afternoon to find a square foot of beach on which to sit. We were lucky, however, and the children stripped off and tumbled away into the water. The next day, on the front of a national newspaper, was a large close-up of the Forrester family, half undressed, with a caption describing the record-breaking crowd. Though we were not named, we were easily recognisable.

This made fuel for both Alan and I to be baited by our colleagues at work, and, as far as I was concerned, this seemed to confirm their poor opinion of me. The gulf between us widened. It made no difference, however, to my developing friendship with Sylvia Poole. Miriam, also, continued to be very kind to me, and she took me one Sunday for a hike into North Wales. I found that I did not have the strength to walk very far because my legs began to ache intolerably. We sat comfortably under a hedgerow, however, while she expounded to me the philosophy of Karl Marx and Engels. I discovered that we were both victims of The System; but her ideas seemed too radical for me to comprehend. I did learn, however, through this and many subsequent conversations, quite a lot about human beings caught in a radical belief, how the mind can be closed to argument, the path followed so narrow that even the biblical 'eye of a needle' seemed wide and liberal. I remained obstinately politically uncommitted.

Another unexpected pleasure came into my life when we discovered that the Central Hall on Renshaw Street held showings of old films. In an effort to give the poor of Liverpool an alternative to the public house, they offered a long programme for the price of twopence, and people flocked in from all over the city centre. I used to accompany Mother on any Saturday evening on which I was not giving a shorthand lesson, and it became a treat I looked forward to throughout the week, because it did not matter how shabby one looked; nobody was in a position to sneer.

Then Sylvia asked me to go for a walk with her one Sunday afternoon and to have tea with her family.

'I'll ask Mother,' I promised, rather desperately.

She seemed surprised that I had to ask permission to accept the invitation, but I could not tell her that I had been taught obedience like a peforming dog, and I rarely moved without permission.

I broached the subject to Mother, as I did the ironing on the living room table, while the rest of the family was out and Father was reading peacefully in the cold front room.

Mother was sitting by the fire with her feet up on

a poof made out of an old tin can, and she looked up quickly from the newspaper she was reading.

'What kind of a girl is she?'

Dread question. Miriam's degree had made her acceptable, but Sylvia had no such advantage.

'She's pretty – and she's clean – and she has nice clothes – her mother makes them,' I floundered, as I eased the iron round Father's second shirt; he had only two shirts, with four loose collars.

'Mm?'

'She speaks nicely.'

'Does she?'

'Yes.'

If she doesn't give me permission, I will go anyway, I silently swore to myself.

I set the iron on the fire to heat up, while Mother folded up the newspaper.

'Well, that sounds delightful,' Mother said warmly.

I stared at her, shirt cuff half folded back. Then I gasped, 'Oh, Mummy! I'm so glad you think so. I'm sure you will like her.'

Mother made a slight, disparaging gesture with one hand, as if to indicate she doubted that liking would enter into it. She had accepted the acne-pocked youths with their strong Liverpool accents who were Alan's friends, and the fact that Fiona occasionally played with rowdy local girls in the street. Tony, Brian and Avril sometimes sounded as if they had been born in the narrow street in which we lived, because remembrance of their former home had practically vanished. Perhaps Mother realised at last that we could no longer be exclusive, that she could not prevent her children adapting to their new circumstances, however unpleasant it was to her.

Now I had to approach the problem of getting a suitable dress out of pawn. Mother kept in her purse all the tickets for the many bundles of donated clothing and bedding that the pawnbroker had piled up in his loft for us.

'I could afford two or three shillings to redeem something, Mummy,' I said meekly.

'Yes,' Mother replied, a sudden razor sharpness in her voice. 'You have plenty of money.'

A year earlier such a remark would have stung me into a quarrel. Now, I was better able to keep control of myself, and I said as gently as I could, 'I'm trying very hard, Mummy, not to ask for anything, to pay for everything, so that you have one less person to worry about.'

Mother slapped down the newspaper and got up. 'You seem to be doing very well. You seem to have money for everything.' Her whole stance was unexpectedly filled with boiling resentment, as she shuffled over to the fire and poked the coals crossly.

I began to tremble at the sudden change in attitude. To gain time, I took the iron off the fire and wiped the soot off it with a piece of rag. I was clumsy and managed to sear my thumb against it. I winced, dropped the rag and popped my stinging thumb into my mouth.

I wanted to shriek at Mother that every penny spent for fares, every threepenny-bit for a bowl of soup at lunch time was painstakingly considered. I wanted to remind her bitterly that the last ninepenny pair of rayon stockings that I had bought had been taken from under my mattress and worn out by her. In consequence, I had had to appear at work with long black lines on my stockings where I had over-stitched ladder after ladder. I was still smarting from the giggles of the other girls and Mr Ellis's tart inquiry, 'Where d' yer buy stockings like them from?'

I bowed my head over the ironing again.

'Well, sometimes I do better – when I have a shorthand student.'

'Humph.'

She put down the poker and moved slowly round the room, picking up and putting into a pile odds and ends left around by the children. I looked at her back with pure hatred for a moment. Her legs were grievously lined with bulging, blue varicose veins and her shoulders were hunched like those of an old woman. Too much starch in her diet was beginning to make her fat around her waist. The anger in me gave way to pity.

Perhaps, better than all her children, I understood what had happened to Mother. I could remember her in the heyday of her beauty, when, at every function, she was surrounded by admirers. The sight of her now easily moved me to compassion. It was, however, like being compassionate towards an angry wasp.

As I began to get a grip on myself again, I wondered what she was thinking about, as she trailed around the grubby, ill-lit room.

The silence lengthened between us, till I felt the tension relax a little. Then I asked, 'Could I get my overcoat out? And the dress with the gold spots that I made?'

'I'll give you the ticket for the coat – it's in a bundle by itself. That dress is not suitable.'

'I don't know what else to wear.'

'There's a blue wool dress in one bundle. I intended to wear it for work – it came in a parcel from Mrs Walsingham some time back. You could borrow it. It fits me, so it will fit you.' She spoke in a weary, dull voice, and she did not look at me.

So the bargain was struck. I could borrow the dress once, for the price of its retrieval. I could have my coat back if I had the money to pay the pawnbroker.

I thanked her humbly.

Chapter thirty-seven

Sylvia had on a well-fitting, grey, pin-striped suit. Her golden curls peeped out from a tan-coloured sailor hat. Her immaculate shoes, gloves and handbag matched the wide-brimmed hat. The heels of her shoes gave her height, and she looked charming.

I was agonisedly aware of my old overcoat and lack of gloves. I wore the hat that Mother had had on when we arrived in Liverpool, a battered beige cloche. The coat was still badly creased from its sojourn with the pawnbroker, despite my frantic efforts with a hot iron. Underneath it, Mrs Walsingham's dress hung on my slight frame; I consoled myself with the thought that it was a very good dress, excellently cut from a soft blue wool. I had had more success in ironing it than I had had with the coat.

We walked soberly for an hour along silent Sunday streets. Occasionally, we met a young couple, dressed in Sunday clothes, strolling arm in arm, or pushing a pram with a befrilled baby in it.

Finally we arrived at a terrace house, similar to the one in which I lived. There was, however, a great difference in its aspect. The panelled front door had no dust on it; the window sills were likewise clear of dust. The front step had been swept and washed.

Sylvia took her key out of her handbag and let us both into the gloomy hall. The house smelled sweet,

I noticed, as I took off my crumpled coat and gave it to Sylvia to hang up on a peg in the hall.

She ushered me into a living room, smaller and darker than ours. It was stuffed with furniture, but its general air of cosiness reminded me of pictures on Christmas cards. All it lacked was a row of brightly coloured children's stockings hanging along the high mantel shelf, in expectation of Father Christmas's arrival. Instead, in front of the old-fashioned fireplace with its big cooking oven, stood a little, stout lady in a navy-blue dress with a tiny pattern on it. Her grey hair was combed softly back into a bun. Her complexion was rosy enough to suggest high blood pressure. Her hands were clasped in front of her, and her wedding ring was deeply imbedded in a finger swollen slightly, perhaps from years of washing with a scrubbing board. She seemed to me the epitome of all that was kind and motherly.

And mother me, she did. I was plied with tea and bread and butter and jam and home-made cake. I was warmed by the fire, and in a quiet, shy manner made to feel very welcome. I had talked without stopping to Sylvia during our walk; but now I felt shy, and Mrs Poole had to help me out with a question or two to keep the conversation going.

At one point, Mr Poole rushed in from another room. He was in shirt sleeves and waistcoat, his scant hair rumpled, his glasses slipping down his nose. How was he going to finish preparing his sermon when there was no more paper to write on? he demanded.

My presence was pointed out to him and he was

introduced hastily, but his mind was not on visitors and he shook my hand absently. As soon as more paper was produced from a drawer, he vanished immediately.

Mrs Poole told me that her husband was a lay preacher, in addition to his normal work as a city electrician. I did not know exactly what a lay preacher was, but was too shy to ask to have it explained to me. She added that there was one other member of the family, Sylvia's elder brother, who was out for the afternoon. She sighed and indicated that she was in some way worried about him. As she talked, I began to realise that I knew him.

Just before my fourteenth birthday, the Liverpool Education Committee had discovered my existence and had ordered me into school until I reached my birthday. Sylvia's brother had been a pupil in the same class as me. There were forty-five or more pupils in the class and discipline was, of a necessity, rigid. I remembered Chris Poole vividly, because he was a target for the sarcasm of every teacher who entered the room, and yet he did not seem to be particularly naughty. If there was talking on the boys' side of the room, it was invariably he who was reprimanded, though he might be one of several offenders. If a pencil was not returned to the teacher, he was the first to be checked for its disappearance. If the class fidgeted or something was noisily dropped on the floor, it was he who had to stand in front of the class as punishment. And the class was so conditioned that they took his guilt for granted, and laughed at his discomforture.

I recognised a fellow scapegoat and felt a sneaking sympathy for him.

I was never in trouble during that period of schooling. I was thankful for the orderly lessons and was happy to put in a phenomenal amount of work. But Chris, with all the exuberance of a thirteen-year old, obviously hated the inflexible confinement to a desk, hour after tedious hour.

If anything went wrong at home, it could be guaranteed that I would be the first person blamed; in the class room this happened to Chris. In Germany it was happening to the Jews. I had just begun to realise that majority groups will always find convenient scapegoats for their own shortcomings; the scapegoat is usually a small minority. In families it can be a minority of one.

So I understood Mrs Poole's general anxiety about her son better than she realised and could feel sympathetic about it. And by many small threads of congeniality a friendship grew up between Mrs Poole and me which was nearly as deep as that between her daughter and me.

I felt so enriched that I walked home from their house in a dream, feeling as if I was floating a foot off the ground.

Chapter thirty-eight

He was a short man, padded with layers of hard fat under his well-tailored grey suit, a man with a chin always blue, however well shaved. He stood silently staring at the ceiling of the lift while I took him up to the Committee Room, and I marvelled at the announcement that the Presence had that morning made regarding him. He had never spoken to me. How could such a rich man understand a very great need of the small person who politely opened and shut the lift gates for him? A need for entertainment. As he climbed the final staircase up to the Committee Room, I stared at his broad back with awed amazement.

'He's Greek,' said Dorothy disparagingly.

'He's in shipping,' Phyllis told me. 'He made a fortune.'

And I thought, very humbly, 'He's remembered how empty of fun life can be, if you have principles and no money.'

'Sylvia,' I whispered behind the files, 'He's giving us three shillings and sixpence each. The Cashier is going to give it to us.'

Sylvia's brow wrinkled up in doubtful surprise.

'It's true. It's a present to all the staff, so that we can go to the theatre. It's supposed to be the price of the very best seat anywhere. The senior staff are going to get more.'

Sylvia pushed a cardboard folder into the file, while she considered this information.

'You know, it's only sixpence to go to the Playhouse,' she said thoughtfully.

'Really?' I breathed.

'Yes. You queue up at the side of the theatre – you can't book.'

'I used to do that at home,' I said, without thinking. 'At the matinées.'

'Home?'

I giggled sheepishly, and did not answer. Liverpool was home, wasn't it?

The slip was revealing. Was I still waiting to go back home to the small southern town from which we had come? To a house now occupied by others? To a nannie who must have long since married and gone to live in the 16th-century farm house her fiancé owned?

Sylvia was waiting for an answer, another file held ready to push into the stack.

'Oh, I used to go by myself to the theatre – when I was about ten. Mother sometimes allowed me to go to the cinema if there was a suitable film – but I never went.' I laughed at the recollection, and added, 'There was a theatre in the town which had all kinds of shows – travelling ones – and I used to go there. I sat right up at the top of the topmost balcony.'

Sylvia laughed, and said she wished she had been there, too.

Mr Ellis heard the unseemly laughter, and reprimanded us. But later on I told her about Mother's lovely singing voice and how she had always belonged to amateur operatic or dramatic groups. When Brian was born and Edith had complained about the work load, Mother had formed the habit of taking me with her to rehearsals. I was a very quiet child, not much trouble to Edith. But it was a gesture on Mother's part and Edith had to be satisfied with it.

At first I sat and fidgeted in the frighteningly empty theatre and did not understand what was happening. I watched while adults walked about the stage with books in their hands and talked in loud, artificial voices. A gentleman seated in the front row sometimes shouted at them, and someone else occasionally rushed onto the stage and re-arranged the players and told them how to behave. But gradually I became fascinated as a story began to evolve in front of my eyes. There was nothing very experimental in the plays they performed and a child could understand them. Once I discovered the existence of dress rehearsals, I used to look forward to them very much. Sometimes, as I grew older, Father took me to the opening night. He always had a formal bouquet of flowers to be presented to Mother at the end of the performance, when the bows were taken; in fact, sometimes the stage looked like a garden because of the number of bouquets presented to the principals.

Father also arranged for me to go to the pantomime each year, whenever one was within reasonable journeying distance. And what pantomimes they were, filled with singing and dancing, magical illusions, uproarious Dames whose red and white striped pants always fell down below their skirts, and, of course, noble Principal Boys like Dick Whittington and lovely Princesses in silver gowns. A magic world, a paradise for children.

Since the kindly Greek had intended that his gift should be spent at the theatre, Sylvia and I decided that we would spread the money as far as it would go. By sitting 'up in the Gods', as the gallery was called, we could see seven plays at the Liverpool Playhouse.

Probably no one would have appreciated our solemn efforts more than the benevolent donor. We queued patiently, leaning against the side of the building. We always hoped to see the actors and actresses arriving at the stage door, but we never did. Instead, we were entertained by a tattered crew of mouth-organ players, concertina players, clumsy tumblers, and even an elderly tramp who would slowly put a brick down on the muddy street, lay his head on it and gradually raise his legs until he was standing on his head. He would remain poised uncertainly on the brick while a beguiling small boy ran up and down the queue with a cap held out hopefully. It was some years before Sylvia or I could afford to give him anything.

When the gallery door was opened, we would pay our sixpence and make the long, long climb up the stairs to the top of the building. Crouched on a bench, with our knees knocking the heads of the people in the next row, we waited for the curtain to rise. Coffee could be purchased at the back of the gallery, and I was torn with doubt as to whether our Greek shipowner would mind if I spent some of his money on a cup. I finally decided that it would not be honest to do so, and sometimes I used my soup money for coffee instead. One could become very cold and wet while waiting in the queue, and if I did not warm up quickly, my treacherous throat would begin to swell and the pain in my legs intensify.

But the excitement, the magic, was a tonic to a starveling like myself. Neither Sylvia nor I realised that we were watching the early efforts of some of Britain's greatest actors and actresses, who were being nursed along by a famous director, William Armstrong. Michael Redgrave and Rachel Kempston, Geoffrey Toone and Lloyd Pearson, peopled the shabby theatre with kings and queens and princes, and I fell hopelessly in love with each handsome face, as cloaks were swept over shoulders and swords were flourished.

I told my parents I had been given tickets for the theatre. I did not dare to say that I had been given money; it would have inevitably been squeezed out of me, by reminders that there was nothing in the house for breakfast or that Baby Edward had no socks; and I would have felt so guilty that I would have handed it over like a lamb. I kept the money from my occasional teaching earnings, and the extra half-a-crown that the Presence paid me, in a bag round my neck. But often the need was so great at home that I would have to give part of it for some necessity, and go without lunch or some other small luxury. Since my illness, it had been a grim necessity to hold on to sufficient money for tram fares; it was over a year before I was strong enough to walk to and from work again.

Minerva, sitting on top of the town hall dome,

smiled particularly on the Liverpool theatres of those days, as if to encourage specially her actors to create for two young girls a world of wonder which helped to make endurable the soot-blackened city outside the theatre walls. In those precious hours in the stuffy Playhouse gallery, tucked up comfortably beside Sylvia, I was happy as I had never before been happy in Liverpool.

Thank you, dear Minerva. Thank you for all that sweet content. I knew you'd help me.

BY THE WATERS OF LIVERPOOL

Helen Forrester was born in Hoylake, Cheshire, the eldest of seven children, and Liverpool was her home for many years until she married. She now lives in Canada. The first two volumes of her autobiography, *Twopence to Cross the Mersey* and *Liverpool Miss*, as well as her novels, *Liverpool Daisy*, *Three Women of Liverpool* and *Thursday's Child*, are also available in Fontana.

The author is most grateful to Naomi Lewis for suggesting the title of *By the Waters of Liverpool*.

HELEN FORRESTER

By the Waters of Liverpool

FONTANA/COLLINS

First published by The Bodley Head Ltd 1981
First issued in Fontana Paperbacks 1983
Twelfth impression April 1986

Made and printed in Great Britain by
William Collins Sons & Co. Ltd, Glasgow

To dear Robert
who helped so much

Chapter one

I was seventeen going on eighteen, and I had never been kissed by a man. It was not surprising. Who would want to court the favours of a gaunt, smelly beanpole? I was five feet four inches tall, and that was real height in underfed Liverpool.

As I strode primly along Lime Street, on my way to evening school, the men who hung about the entrances of the cinemas hardly spared me a glance. I was most unflatteringly safe. And this, in a world where women still took it for granted that they would get married, was very depressing. Girls did not look for careers – they worked until they got married. If a woman was not loved and cherished by a man, she must be hopelessly ugly or there must be something else wrong with her.

I tried not to care that no young man had so much as winked at me. I stuck my proud Forrester nose in the air and vowed to make a career for myself as a social worker in the charity which employed me. Dorothy Parker, the famous American writer, had once remarked that men seldom make passes at girls who wear glasses; and I had a pair of too-small horn-rimmed spectacles perched on my nose. There was nobody to suggest to a shy, short-sighted girl that she might occasionally take off the ugly impediment to show the sad, green eyes behind.

'Perhaps your yellow skin will improve, as you get older,' my childhood Nanny, Edith, had suggested; and she scrubbed my face harder still with Pear's Preparing To Be A Beautiful Lady soap. To no purpose. All time and our subsequent poverty had done was to add a revolting array of acne spots, spots that were made worse by the lack of soap, hot water and clean towels at home.

And here was the year 1937 rolling along. Soon I would be eighteen. And nobody, I felt, really cared what happened to me. To my mother I was a trying daughter who brought in a wage each week; to the rest of the family a pair of hands, very useful for cooking and darning socks.

It was seven years since Father had gone suddenly bankrupt, plunging us into a poverty so great that I was frequently surprised that the nine of us had survived it, seven skinny children of whom I was the eldest, and two equally thin parents.

I sighed as I trudged up the hill. Though Mother and Father now both had work, they were very poor managers, and we were still cold and hungry most of the time, surrounded by the unpleasant odour of neglect and poor nutrition.

I handed my small wages to Mother every pay day, except for three shillings and sixpence. This totally inadequate sum was supposed to clothe me, pay for lunches and tram fares, make-up and all the small things a girl at work was expected to have. Mother was bent on making me give up my employment and once again stay at home to keep house, something I dreaded; so she made it as difficult as possible for me to go to work.

I found pupils to coach in shorthand in the evenings, but I earned very little because my free time was extremely limited.

I was doing very well at evening school, I comforted myself. One day I might be promoted and earn enough to live on. My ugly, kind bookkeeping teacher had assured me recently that, if I took one more course, I would be able to become a bookkeeper. She had added that parents were always glad of a girl at home who brought in a wage; it contributed to their comfort in their old age.

She had put into words something I dreaded, something only a husband could save me from. I could be faced with spending the rest of my life maintaining and waiting on two irritable, shiftless, nagging parents, the usual fate of the daughter who did not marry. Because I was plain and shy and frightened of my mother, I knew I could be bullied into being a nobody, a nothing.

Some women with gentle parents found their care a labour of love. Not me. I knew I would be crushed as flat as a shadow. I had already had a spell as housekeeper, from the age of eleven until I was fifteen. It had been a nightmare, looking after six young children and two quarrelling parents. Mother had, before Father's bankruptcy, never had to care entirely for her children. We had had servants. In fact, I hardly knew her until we were plunged into a slum together. She escaped from her unruly brood by working as a demonstrator in department stores.

In a frantic effort to escape myself, I had at the age of fourteen raged and threatened, as only a fourteen-year-old can, until I got permission to attend evening school, to repair in some part my lack of education.

At fifteen, with the unexpected help of Miss Ferguson, a deaconess at the local church, I had fought another battle to take the job I at present held. Housekeeping was divided between a very angry mother and me.

I called Miss Ferguson my Fairy Godmother, and it was of this devout, cultivated lady that I was thinking, as I kicked a stone up Copperas Hill on the way to evening school. The street was quiet in the fading spring light, the misty air balmy – and I was shivering with pure fright.

Miss Ferguson had laid on my shoulders a fear worse than that of death, the fear of hell, Dante's hell.

How could she do such a thing? I wondered miserably, with a superstitious shudder. She was my Fairy Godmother.

She had first visited the family in order to recruit my two middle brothers, Brian and Tony, into the church choir. She knew them because all the children attended the church school. She had seen my situation as unpaid maid-of-all-work, and, perhaps to give me an hour or two of rest, she had pressured Mother into allowing me to go to church on Sunday evenings. At first I had no suitable clothes to go in, but once I could look at least neat, I thankfully attended.

We were Protestants, an important point in a city where the division between Protestants and Catholics was bitter and sometimes bloody. Children were aware from the time they could speak which side of the fence they stood on, and the implanted bigotry is to this day not entirely rooted out.

No amount of churchgoing could erase the vaguely erotic dreams which haunted me occasionally, or a terrible sense of empty loneliness. Ignorant, innocent, half-starved, practically friendless, my flowering body was trying to tell me of needs of which I had little notion. Almost all the myriad of novels I had read ended with the hero kissing the heroine for the first time. I had never considered what happened next. I felt a kiss would be the ultimate height of happiness.

But it was churchgoing which was causing my present unhappiness. As I turned into the big, gloomy evening school, which I loved so much, I was trembling with fear. Unable to concentrate on the shorthand teacher's rapid dictation, my mind was filled with scattered pictures of what had happened the previous Sunday.

Unaware of impending trouble, I had crept out of the back pew in which I normally hid my shabbiness, and battled my way up Princes Avenue through a brisk north-westerly carrying with it a spray of rain.

I was going home to a mother almost unhinged by her fall from considerable affluence, and to a fretful, delicate father, an under-paid, overworked city clerk. Liverpool was awash with the unemployed and the under-paid, and this governed all our lives. To a plain girl hurrying through the dusk, life seemed very hard. There was little physical strength in me. I was frail and always hungry, and I hugged my worn brown coat tightly round me for comfort.

Thankfully I pulled the string hanging from the letter-box of our row house. The latch lifted, and I was glad to step inside, away from the wind.

Miss Ferguson, Fairy Godmother and deaconess of the church, was seated in our old easy chair by the fire in our living room, undisturbed, it seemed, by the fetid atmosphere and the dirty chaos surrounding her. She must have been quicker than me in leaving the service and making her way over to our house, because she was already deep in conversation with Mother as I edged my way into the cluttered room. Her square pallid face with its cherry-red nose wrinkled up into a smile as I entered.

'Good evening, Helen.'

'Good evening, Miss Ferguson. Hullo, Mother.'

Mother was seated on a straight-backed chair opposite Miss Ferguson, and was smoking with long, deep puffs, the smoke like a fog round her head. Miss Ferguson seemed to be the only person able to penetrate beyond Mother's polite façade and fight her way through to the real, suffering woman beneath, and Mother was listening intently as Miss Ferguson continued their conversation.

Dressed in black, with wrinkled woollen stockings and flat-heeled shoes, her hair covered by a black coif, Miss Ferguson was very different from Mother's fashionable friends of so many years ago. But she was a cultivated woman, like my convent-bred mother, and it was a pleasure to listen to the hum of her soft voice.

I picked up an old fruit basket full of mending from beside the hearth and began my nightly task of darning the family's socks and stockings. Everybody's woollen socks or rayon stockings seemed to spring a hole or a ladder each day, and because we had so few pairs, they had to be darned ready for wear the next day.

At first, as my needle flew in and out, I did not take much notice of the conversation. Then Mother's voice penetrated. She sounded pettish. 'Helen's at evening school three times a week. And she is often out on Saturday evenings – either at the theatre with her friend, Sylvia, or teaching her shorthand pupil. Then church on Sunday evening – she's hardly home, to help me.'

I looked up quickly, just in time to catch a resentful glance from my tight-lipped mother.

Dear heaven! Now, what had I done? My needle slowed. Miss Ferguson knew how much washing, mending, ironing and cleaning, not to speak of child care, I managed to tuck into the time before and after work and during the weekends. She visited regularly and had seen me always busy. She now favoured me with a quick wry grin, and let Mother's complaints pass.

I looked at my flashing fingers as I darned. Broken nails and soot-ingrained cuticles, half-healed cuts and burns, all told of fires made, sooty saucepans scoured and food prepared. At work I hid my hands as much as possible.

'It is really time dear Helen was confirmed – I should have mentioned it before,' Miss Ferguson said persuasively. 'The confirmation lessons don't take very long – in fact, she may already know all that is required.'

So that was it. Well, I was quite happy to be confirmed if it pleased my Fairy Godmother, and thereby become a full member of the church.

'I suppose it is,' replied Mother. She flicked the ash of her cigarette into the tiny fire, which was almost lost in the huge, old-fashioned kitchen range. 'It is the time for the lessons – she really has to spend more time at home. I need her help.'

I let them continue to discuss the merits of Confirmation and the first Communion which would follow it, and went on darning and dreaming. Suddenly my heart jolted, when unexpectedly Miss Ferguson said, 'Of course, the dear child has never been to Confession. If she is to take the sacrament, she will need first to go to Confession. It would be a good idea, don't you think, if she got into the habit beforehand and went this week. Perhaps young Alan should think about it, too.'

I could feel myself going clammy all over. At that moment all the history books I had read, written almost entirely by Protestants, seemed to contribute to the sense of horror at anything which savoured of Catholicism – and Confession was surely a Catholic institution. In my nostrils there was suddenly the smoke and smell of the burning flesh of Protestant martyrs, made beloved by many a story; ordinary men and women, lords, priests, yokels, who had bravely faced being burned alive rather than acknowledge the Pope or the Mass – or confession to anyone but God.

I was weak on the theology of it, but I knew that Catholic Bloody Mary was the most hated Queen in British history, because she had tried to burn out of existence all signs of Protestantism. This unthinkable suggestion of Miss Ferguson's went against everything I had ever learned of my church. In a city riven down the middle by religion, it seemed incredible that a Protestant deaconess should ever mention Confession.

Needle poised, I burst into the conversation with a frightened squeak, a squeak of genuine horror. 'But we are Protestants. We say the General Confession during service. We make personal confessions only to God. I thought that was what being a Protestant was all about.'

Mother laughed, her delicate, superior, crushing laugh. 'Helen, we are High Anglicans. It is by accident that you have never been to Confession before. By chance, most of the places we have lived in have only low churches, so that when you were little you were taken to them.' She drew on her cigarette, and then added a little sharply, 'You seemed to have enjoyed going to a High Church recently.'

'In all the many months I stayed with Grandma I never went to Confession,' I protested. 'If she had gone, I am sure she would have taken me with her.'

Mother did not like being reminded of her mother-in-law, who had washed her hands of her shiftless son and would no longer have anything to do with us.

'Your grandmother was too old to walk further than the village church – and that church was low church.'

I pushed my fist into one of Brian's smelly socks and attacked another hole. My voice trembled, as I said flatly, 'Well, I'm not going.'

Miss Ferguson looked nonplussed, and her hands with their black cotton gloves fluttered helplessly.

Mother's heavily made-up face began to darken. 'Don't be ridiculous, Helen. It would do you good to go, to come face to face with your arrogance and bad temper. It might teach you to honour your parents, which would be a welcome change.'

Me? Confess? Tell some strange priest that there were times when I felt like murdering my mother? Times like this moment. Tell him that I had dreamed that I took all my clothes off in front of a man? I couldn't. I wouldn't. I could tell God himself these things in the course of the General Confession, because He had made me and probably understood His faulty work. But not a priest – not a man!

Much that I had let pass during my recent church-going suddenly fell into place. I had puzzled that the ministers of the church strode the streets in cassocks with black birettas on their heads, that servers assisted at the altar, that incense was used, the whole elaborate ritual. Now, the theatrical beauty of it, which had so impressed me, seemed suddenly to hide a basket of vipers.

Shivering but determined, I put down the darning into my lap and turned to Miss Ferguson. Her short-sighted eyes darted from Mother to me.

'Miss Ferguson, I couldn't do it. If I have to go to Confession, I might as well become a Catholic and do it properly. There wouldn't be any difference.'

Miss Ferguson found her voice and said rather hoarsely, 'There is a great difference, Helen. We do not accept the supremacy of the Pope. Our King is head of our church.'

Mother nodded agreement, her mouth pinched with her disapproval of me.

I felt as if I had been backed against a wall by a member of the Inquisition. I had never thought about the legitimacy of being allowed to worship as one pleases. I had no profound knowledge of my own faith. Most of my age group did not even attend church, though the majority, if asked, would say that they were either Protestant or Catholic – so great was the religious division in Liverpool.

To Liverpool Protestants, Catholics were people who lived in the worst slums because they did not know any better, and their greatest entertainment was attacking Protestant religious processions. They were not ordinary, kindly people at all.

I saw through Miss Ferguson's suggestion only the tortured faces of my own beloved martyrs. I ignored the fact that Protestants had, in their time, done their share of roasting hapless Catholics.

Miss Ferguson saw the need to reassure me, and she leaned forward and patted my knee. 'The first Confirmation classes will be held in a fortnight's time, my dear. Come along to the vestry. I am sure the good Father can explain to you much better than I can how good for the soul Confession is.'

'But – but . . . ,' I spluttered helplessly. 'Miss Ferguson, I can't – I just can't.'

The good Father! Not the Vicar. Childhood memories of gentle, vague scholars in clerical collars sipping tea in various drawing rooms made me want to rush back in time to them. I seemed to recollect that they only extolled the basic virtues. Where had they gone? I must have been asleep during the weeks I had been attending Miss Ferguson's church.

Mother was saying brightly that, since Miss Ferguson thought it wise, time would be found for my attendance at classes.

With her usual outward charm, she saw Miss Ferguson out of our grubby living room, into the narrow hall and finally out to the littered street. I knew very well that she would attend to me later in a very different fashion.

Though doubtless learned clerics were already discussing and challenging the concepts of hell and damnation and other long-held beliefs, eternal punishment for the heretic was a very real threat to a girl brought up by ignorant country servants and subsequently cut off from her contempories as I was. To defy one's parents for any reason was bad enough. To defy one's church was, in my opinion, likely to be much worse. As I contemplated Brian's tattered sock, I was shaking with fear of the spiritual forces which might be ranked against me. I wondered if I would be struck dead if I argued with the priests, actually raised my voice in a church building. And death was only the beginning of trouble for those cast out of the church. I might burn in hell for ever afterwards.

Nevertheless, quivering like a mouse before a cat, I determined on a last squeak.

Chapter two

I could remember Mother at the age of twenty-four, an elegant beauty with fashionable short black curls and large, pale blue eyes. Her fine legs were sheathed in the latest pure silk stockings, her skirts daringly short, so that a sudden flip of them would give a glimpse of ruffled silk garters trimmed with tiny roses or pearls, or French knickers heavy with lace. She attracted a great deal of attention from Father's war-battered friends, and Edith said she could get anything by merely fluttering her eyelashes. It did not work, however, when I tried fluttering my scant lashes, and I decided it must be something magical, known only to grown-ups.

The slightest argument or objection, the smallest frustration, would unleash her ungovernable temper, from which shell-shocked husband and servants would fly. I was terrified of her and would cling to Edith, seeking safety in her starched white lap. Edith always said comfortingly that she did not care a tinker's cuss about Mother's tempers; the job was handy for her. We lived conveniently close to the young farmer who was Edith's fiancé, and we frequently escaped to the warmth and laughter of his mother's farm-house kitchen. Alan, who was the child next to me in age, was also wheeled in his pram to the farm and got bounced merrily on many a rustic knee.

Now Mother was a middle-aged harridan, worn down by the illness she had suffered when my smallest brother, Edward, was born and by the privation we had all endured since Father's bankruptcy. Her figure was shapeless from eating too much white bread, her lovely legs horrible with varicose veins, hands ruined like mine, from washing, scrubbing, blackleading fireplaces, and lack of gloves. We rarely had hot water or soap, either for cleaning or washing ourselves, and face or hand creams were luxuries to look at through the chemist's window. All that remained of Mother's earlier self was a great charm of manner and a quick intelligence, when she felt like using either of them. Her scarifying temper had been further fed by her total unhappiness at her present state.

Like alcoholics, an improvement in my parents' lives could be brought about only by their facing their problems squarely and themselves determining on a new and careful path, in their case a financial path. But, like many alcoholics, they could not do it. So we all continued to suffer, despite the fact that five of us were at work.

Alan worked as an office boy in the city, and most of his small wages were handed back to him for tram fares, lunches and pocket money. Similarly, my pretty fifteen-year-old sister, Fiona, worked as a cashier in a butcher's shop. She earned the same amount as I did, but, unlike me, most of her wage was handed back to her for her expenses. Her clothes were bought for her, new, by paying for them by weekly instalments through a system of cheques. Companies issued cheques, commonly for five pounds, and with these one could buy clothing or household goods of one's choice at any store on the company's list. The clothing was often shoddy and expensive, but Fiona was at least as well dressed as any other girl travelling to work on the trams with her. I struggled to keep myself in clothes by buying them from the pawnbroker's bargain table.

Paying the cheque man was as much a worry to Liverpool housewives as finding the money to pay the rent, and it drained our income. We were permanently hungry, frequently cold and not very clean. Cleanliness is expensive. Our landlord had freed us from one plague of slum living. He had had our house stoved, so that we were no longer verminous, and our relief from bug and lice bites was wonderful to us.

Brian and Tony, who came next to Fiona, had inherited their parents' brains and they also had some of Mother's earlier vivacity and physical strength. Brian had won a scholarship from the church school to the Liverpool Institute, and I was very envious of him. Earlier, I had won a scholarship to the Liverpool City School of Art, but I had not been allowed to take it up. I had to stay at home to keep house.

Also at school was short, determined Avril, almost unnoticed unless she had a temper tantrum like Mother, and little Edward, beloved baby of the family, whom I had nursed along since infancy. Though Edward was not very strong, probably because of the lack of adequate food in early childhood, his mind was clear and he had the ability to apply himself with great concentration to whatever he was doing. He could already read well, and Father hoped that both he and Tony would also win scholarships. Neither Mother nor Father gave any heed to Avril's possible abilities as a scholar. She was only a girl.

The only other members of the family to attend church were Brian and Tony, who for nearly three years had sung in the choir and had enjoyed a remuneration of a shilling and eightpence per month, which they were allowed to keep. Now they sometimes acted as acolytes. Nobody, as far as I knew, had pressed them to go to Confession. They were, however, the cleverest of passive resisters and even if pressed would probably have placidly failed to turn up for it. Brian's hazel eyes and Tony's calm blue-grey ones could look as blank as a factory wall, with an innocence and incomprehension of stare usually seen only in the subnormal. They were a pair of cheery scallywags, most unlikely to be faced with the inner qualms and soul-searching which always afflicted me.

I was dreadfully troubled when Mother ordered me to stop being such a fool, and to attend Confirmation classes. I made no reply, because I had long since learned not to do battle when I knew for certain that I could not win. For several days I fretted fearfully about what I should do.

'Them as don't obey goes straight to hell,' Edith had assured me, whenever I was being particularly perverse.

And there was Grandma's soft voice whispering, 'Good children go to Heaven, dear. Only the wicked burn in hell.'

And the Bible from which I had learned to read,

under Grandma's tuition, was full of the horrors of what happened to those who did not obey the will of God.

As I sorted files in the office, I tried to comfort myself. 'It doesn't really happen nowadays. It is an allegory.' But the fear in me was almost a primeval one; it stuck in the back of my mind and refused to be shifted.

Mother was obviously used to the idea of Confession. It must have been reinforced when she was a child, because she had been brought up in a convent, the only Protestant amid a sea of Catholics. It was waste of time to appeal to her.

Walking home through the April rain, I prayed to God to tell me what He wanted me to do, and got no immediate reply. Confused, afraid, with a mind filled with myths, I turned to the only other person I could think of who might advise me. I would ask Father.

Chapter three

To get a little time alone with Father would, I knew, be difficult. A big family in a tiny house has almost no privacy.

I pulled the string hanging inside the flapless letter-box, in order to let myself in. I had worked late and then gone straight to evening school and had not eaten since morning, but I paused for a moment in the doorway to watch some men playing ollies in the gutter. The little white balls skittered over the rough roadway, almost invisible in the light of the street lamps. These men used to say disparagingly about our family that we talked 'with ollies in t' mouth'. Refined Oxford accents were extremely rare in slums.

The smell of the house hit me as I went into the little hall, a smell of warm, damp, much used air, with strong overtones of the odour of vomit.

All the family was crowded into the small, back living room. Old-fashioned wooden shutters had been closed across the curtainless windows and secured by an iron bar. A small fire blazed bravely in the big, iron kitchen range, and by it Father was seated bolt upright in the solitary easy chair.

His usual yellowy complexion was flushed red, and he was pounding his delicate, almost feminine fist on the arm of the chair, as if to emphasise forcibly something he had already said.

As I paused by the door, he almost shouted, 'I will not tolerate such an abomination. It is disgusting beyond words. She must leave at once.'

He was answered by an unintelligible babble from the family.

I thought for an anxious second that he was talking about me. I lived in constant, gnawing fear that my parents would withdraw me from my job and make me stay at home again to keep house; they were quite capable of taking such a decision without any prior discussion with me and of handing in my resignation directly to my employer. I was still under twenty-one.

With some trepidation I eased my way through the half-open door and into the room itself. The children's upturned faces looked sickly in the light of the single, unshaded electric bulb, and Edward turned his heart-shaped face, pinched with fatigue, towards me. He said simply, 'Bed.'

Though he was nearly seven, he was no great weight and I picked him up, and said, 'Yes, love.' He and Brian were the only children I ever knew who asked to go to bed. It was as if their strength ran out suddenly. I smiled at him, and added, 'I'll put the kettle on to heat and help you wash your knees and neck as soon as it is hot.' I looked cautiously round him at the family.

The centre of attention was Fiona. She was standing in the middle of the group, facing Father, and her wide eyes with their enormous fringe of long lashes showed signs of tears. She was almost cringing, her toes turned slightly inward, her arms across her breast as if to protect herself.

She said in a watery voice, 'It's not that bad, Daddy. I didn't go. I wouldn't dream of it.'

Nobody took any notice of me, except Alan, who grinned at me as I stumbled over his feet, on my way to the kitchen with Edward. 'I think it's funny,' he said to Father.

There was some hot water in the kettle sitting on the greasy little gas stove, so I poured it into the washing-up bowl and commenced to wash Edward. I could hear Father's choked voice. He said furiously, 'It is *not* funny. It is horrible. At the least, it shows a total disrespect for the dead – at the worst, it is perversion. They ought to be put out of business.'

Mother was laboriously cutting her nails with our single pair of blunt scissors, letting the ends drop into the hearth, and she murmured, 'It makes me shudder.'

I paused in my preparations to wash Edward's dirty knees, and left him sitting on the kitchen table drying his face, while I went to the intervening door and asked, 'What's happened, Daddy?'

'Pack of sickening necrophiles!' Father exploded again, turning to me.

Brian and Tony were sitting at the table, elbows on open exercise books. I saw Tony's eyes light up. A beautiful new word to be learned, to be used incessantly for at least a week, while he turned it over in his mind and tried it in every possible way.

Mother greeted me with a worried, 'Hello, Helen. We'll explain it later. Put Avril and Edward to bed – it's getting late.' She turned to the students at the table who were obviously most intrigued by the conversation. 'Hurry up, you two. Put your books away.'

'It's something about looking at dead people, Helen,' Edward whispered to me, as I returned to him, and rolled down his knee-high socks. His knees were very dirty and I scrubbed them with a piece of cotton cloth. There was no soap.

Avril had followed me out, and stood waiting for her turn to be washed. She said nothing, but her plain, round face beneath the straggling blonde hair was white, and I wondered if she were ill.

Edward struggled out of his woollen jersey and proffered a far from white neck to be washed. 'It's nasty,' he muttered.

Both children looked so bewildered and scared that I answered them with forced cheerfulness. 'It doesn't sound very respectful, I know. But I'm sure there's nothing to be afraid of. Dead people are just people who have shed an overcoat which has worn out. And the real people – their souls – have gone to Heaven. They are happy. It is only the people who get left behind who are unhappy – it's natural – they don't like being left.'

I tried to be soothing and matter-of-fact, while Avril perfunctorily washed her hands and face in the same pint of water.

Protesting crossly, Brian and Tony put their books together and heaved themselves between furniture and family towards the staircase and bed. Tony asked sulkily, 'How do you spell necrophile?' and was told angrily by Father not to be impudent.

I took the candle from the kitchen and eased Avril

and Edward along after the boys. Mother looked overwhelmed with fatigue, but she was not too tired to fire at Fiona, as I passed her, 'For goodness' sake, be quiet, girl.' Fiona sank down on an upturned paint can, which we used as a chair, and continued to whimper miserably.

Upstairs, I heard Avril and Edward say the small prayer which our nanny had taught me long ago, 'Gentle Jesus, meek and mild . . .' Then I tucked Avril into the bed she shared with Fiona and me, and put Edward into the one he shared with Brian and Tony, and left them shivering under the thin blankets to their individual nightmares.

Brian and Tony stumped grumpily round the room, pulling off their outer clothes and tossing them on to the bed rail. I put the candle down on an orange-box, which had been made into a dressing table by draping an old curtain over it, and told Brian to blow it out before he got into bed. 'Quietly, boys,' I pleaded. 'Let Edward go to sleep.' Then I ran downstairs again to the living room.

Alan had picked up a book and was flicking through it. Father and Mother were staring into the fire, Father rubbing his chin with quick, impatient motions. Fiona sat, her back against the wall, still crying. I was dreadfully hungry and quite apprehensive about what might have happened, but I went first to her and put my arm round her shoulders. She laid her head against my threadbare skirt. We never talked together – we had little in common except our sisterhood; yet we were often a comfort to each other.

'Daddy, what *has* happened?'

'She has to leave her job,' said Father, beating an impatient tattoo with his fingers on the arm of his chair. Mother nodded agreement. Alan put down his book and watched the scene with a look of morbid fascination, glancing expectantly from one to the other of us.

'Why?' I inquired, puzzled.

'She must,' Mother agreed, and then added crossly, 'It is not fit for a young girl – it is not fit for anyone to be there.'

Alan interjected with an unexpected chuckle, 'You could put it down to professional interest – after all, it's all meat.'

Mother was shocked. 'Alan! How could you say such a revolting thing?'

Alan grinned wickedly and folded his arms, as if enjoying the family's evident distress.

Father groped for words and finally said carefully, 'The butcher's shop in which Fiona is working is opposite an undertaker's. Sometimes the undertakers invite the butchers over to look at the corpses. I cannot believe that it is the undertaker himself who does this – I think it is some of his employees.'

Fiona lifted her face. 'It is, Daddy. They do it when he is out – and the butchers always wait until our boss has gone to market.'

'How awful!' I exclaimed. 'Imagine being stared at in your coffin by a pack of strangers. How morbid!' I looked down at Fiona's tousled head, and said to her, 'Perhaps you should look for another job.'

Fiona turned her face up towards me. She was so white that I thought she might faint. She said, 'They had a young girl there this morning – and she wasn't in her coffin – or even wrapped up. She was naked – and they were whispering and laughing afterwards about how they played with her. It sounded awful. So I was sick suddenly over the cash desk – and they laughed. After I had cleared up the mess, they sent me home early.'

Nausea began to overwhelm me. Vague tales I had heard, whispered amongst the beshawled women beside whom I had sat on front steps or in the park while watching the children play, began to surface in my mind and come together. I had always discounted their mutterings as rubbish. Now I realised that it was not rubbish. They had been disapproving about something which had really happened. I took big breaths to control my surging stomach. How could men be so vile?

'Heavens, I'm glad you told Daddy,' I muttered.

'I had to,' responded Fiona flatly. 'I was thinking about it again just before you came in – and I was sick over the floor.'

'Humph,' Mother almost grunted, 'I thought it was something else, but I was wrong, thank goodness.'

For a moment, I looked at her blankly and then remembered her bouts of morning sickness before every birth, and I said indignantly, 'Fi would never get herself into trouble. She's not that kind.' But a sudden, different fear for Fiona had been planted in my mind. Did she know anything about sex? I was still vague myself about the precise details of this mystery, but since I never expected to have a boy friend it did not matter in my case. It did matter for

Fiona. I knew that she was already meeting a local youth secretly and going to the cinema with him.

Father had been brooding during this exchange. Now he fumed, 'They should be reported.'

'Who to?' asked Mother.

'The police, of course.'

'Could the police do anything?'

'Oh, yes. It is a serious matter.'

'Oh, Daddy,' wailed Fiona, 'If you do tell the police there'll be such a rumpus in the shop. The men will say I'm a lying troublemaker, and the boss won't want to give me a reference.' She rubbed her wet eyes with the backs of her hands. 'The story will go all round the local shops, and then what will I do? With no reference, I won't stand a chance.'

She clung to me and I suddenly leaned limply against her. I was beginning to feel faint with hunger.

Chapter four

Fiona's situation was grave. When fifty youngsters were competing for even the most menial of jobs, lack of a good reference could be crippling.

'You can stay at home and keep house,' Mother said briskly. 'You spend all you earn – I never see much of it.'

'Oh, Mother, Fi only gets fifteen shillings a week, and she pays all her expenses – even buys some of her clothes,' I intervened vehemently.

Fiona's hands clutched convulsively against my hips. She, too, feared becoming the family's forgotten, unpaid maid-of-all-work.

Mother fumbled in her handbag for a cigarette and lit it from the fire with the aid of a newspaper spill. 'She would be more use at home,' she reiterated.

Father got up from his chair and moved restlessly up and down the narrow space between table and hearth which formed a passage between the front hall and back kitchen. He was very thin, and his grey tweed office suit with its shiny seat and elbows hung loosely on him. He looked haggard, as if this new problem was too much for him, and his face and prematurely bald skull shone pale yellow in the poor light. He took off his bent, gold-rimmed spectacles and rubbed eyes that were red-lidded and bloodshot.

'If I want to leave,' sobbed Fiona, 'I *have* to give a week's notice on pay day – that's Friday, and it's Friday night now. So it means I have to work almost another two weeks. And nobody is going to give a reference to a girl who leaves without notice – and how can I tell the boss the real reason I want to leave? It's too horrid!' She continued to dampen my skirt, as I held her.

Mother looked scornfully at her two daughters, her lips curled in disdain. 'Really, Fiona! All this fuss, when you could make yourself useful at home for once.' She turned to Father, and almost shouted, 'For goodness' sake, stop prowling.'

Father flung himself back into his chair, while Fiona cried, 'No.'

'She cannot mix with such dreadful people any more,' Father sounded off determinedly. 'What is the world coming to?'

'They leave me alone most of the time,' Fiona turned her puffy face towards Father. 'I sit in the cash desk and lock myself in. It has glass all round it. They tease me but they can't get in.' She moved uneasily against me. 'Only when I go to the loo sometimes . . .' Her voice trailed off.

Father started up. 'What?' he exclaimed. 'What happens then?'

'They chase after me and pinch my bottom,' she announced baldly.

'Oh, Lord!' Father was really shaken, as if he himself had never in his life pinched the bottoms of our maids.

Alan burst out laughing. 'That's better than being

whacked on your rear with a ruler, like I am.'

'Alan!' exclaimed Mother. 'What a lot of louts they must be.'

Father looked at his pretty daughter, speechless for a moment, and then said firmly, 'You will stay at home tomorrow, Fiona. Helen can phone from her office to say that you are not well. Then we will say later that you are not fit to go back. You can look for other work.'

'I'm not staying at home.' Fiona could be as woodenly obstinate as Avril and me, but she never seemed to draw her parents' wrath as fully as we did. 'I just have to get through the next two weeks as best I can. Then I'll leave. After all, I've put up with them for nearly a year now.'

Father looked at her aghast. 'You mean all this has been going on for a year?'

'Not all the time.'

'How frequently?'

'You mean going to see the – the . . . ?'

'Yes.'

'Oh, they run over every time the undertaker has a nice looking one.'

'And have they been pinching you all that time, too?'

'No, Daddy, only just recently.'

'You must have encouraged them, Fiona.' This from Mother.

'Oh, no, Mummy. I suppose they notice me when they've nothing much to do. Anyway, how can a *derrière* encourage anybody?' she asked innocently.

This made Father smile, even in the middle of his

disquietude. Fiona's flawless figure, now burgeoning, would in years to come cause many a heart to throb and provide a good deal of temptation.

Father's voice was very gentle, as he looked at his younger daughter. 'I am sure you don't encourage them, my dear.' He smiled knowingly at Mother, who did not smile back.

Alan began to whistle softly to himself and moved restlessly against the table.

'If I had a sheet of the butcher's notepaper,' said Mother suddenly, her face brightening, 'paper with his heading on it, I could write an excellent reference for Fiona.'

'Mother!' I exclaimed, scandalised. 'That would be forgery.'

'A new employer might phone the butcher to check it,' suggested Alan.

'I don't think so,' replied Mother, ignoring my outburst. 'As a demonstrator going from shop to shop, I carry written references – I've heaps of them, because all my jobs are short-term ones. I don't think anybody has ever telephoned to check them.'

Fiona looked up quickly, and then mopped her eyes agitatedly with my hanky which I had handed to her – it was the only one I owned. 'Mummy! Could you do it? Really?'

Mother looked as pleased as a Cheshire cat. 'I don't see why not.'

'If I go to work tomorrow, I can get the paper easily. I have some in the cash desk.' She straightened up, sniffed and rubbed her nose hard with the hanky. 'I could start looking for a new job on Monday.'

It took Mother and Fiona some time to convince Father that it was the most sensible way out. But he was genuinely worried about his favourite daughter, and he finally gave in.

Alan thought it was a huge joke, and asked Mother if she could do anything about forging pound notes. I thought she would strike him, but instead she laughed.

Though it seemed to me to be wrong, that it might be better if Father had a quiet talk with the butcher himself, I did not want to start a family row, so I held my tongue.

On Saturday, Fiona went to work as usual and returned triumphantly with the required sheet of notepaper. Mother concocted an excellent letter for her, written in a round, illiterate hand quite unlike her usual beautiful penmanship. She ended it with a phrase popular amongst tradesmen, 'And oblige your obedient servant', followed by a flourishing signature.

Father often bought a *Liverpool Echo* on his way home from work. The day's copy was lying on his chair, so Fiona and I spread it out on the table and conned the Situations Vacant columns very carefully, though it was nearly midnight.

We found two advertisements for office girls, and Fiona begged Mother's penny pad of notepaper from her, took the cork out of the ink bottle and sat down at the table, pen poised. She looked up at me expectantly. To my dictation, she wrote in a round schoolgirl's scrawl letters of application to both companies.

Mother looked disparagingly at her handwriting.

'Really, Fiona, I should have thought you could write better than that.'

But Fiona could not, and never did. The teaching of handwriting in the elementary schools was so poor that few people seemed to leave with anything better than an ugly, irregular hand. Good, flowing handwriting, like the right accent, marked one's place in the social scale, and Fiona's laboured, round letters indicated a girl with a poor background, in a world which was very snobbish. Only Alan, who had been taught in preparatory school, wrote the same exquisite Italian hand which my mother did.

Fiona had a natural refinement and an endearing gentleness, without a hint of snobbery. She floated amongst all kinds of people without difficulty. Her letters, however, did not produce any replies, despite the fast postal service which we enjoyed, and Fiona became very depressed. Mother thankfully set her more and more household tasks each morning, and then borrowed her fares and lunch money, which meant that even if she obtained an interview with a firm, she would probably have to walk to it.

I encouraged her to keep on writing applications and, as my office was close to the *Liverpool Echo*'s office in Victoria Street, I dropped her replies each day into the newspaper's letter-box.

I had hoped to have a talk with Father on that busy Saturday, because both he and I finished work at one o'clock on Saturdays. Every time I thought about the coming Confirmation lessons, my stomach clenched with apprehension and I longed to unburden myself to somebody. But he had spent the afternoon at the public library, and after he had eaten his tea, he went immediately up to bed. He had had a heart attack when I was a little girl, and occasionally pain in his chest sent him hastily to lie down.

Chapter five

'Why can't I sign on at the Labour Exchange?' asked Fiona fretfully. 'They might have a job for me.' She was helping me to clear the breakfast dishes, and without make-up she looked tired and not very well.

Mother was putting on her lipstick in front of a piece of broken mirror wedged into the frame of the back kitchen window, and at this remark, she paused and said to Father, 'She might be entitled to Unemployment Insurance.'

'If she was, she has forfeited it by voluntarily leaving her position.' Father was running backwards and forwards between kitchen and livingroom like a demented hen. 'Where can my hat be? Have you seen it? I'll be late.' He called to Brian who was about to go out of the back door to school, 'Brian, wheel the bike round to the front door, there's a boy, while I find my hat.'

'I'll be late if I do,' complained Brian, his dark, heart-shaped face sulky, as he clapped his school cap on to his head.

'Oh, rubbish,' replied Father. 'Go and get it. And don't wear your cap in the house – you are not a workman.'

Brian slammed down his satchel on to the floor, flung his cap on top of it, and went to do as he was bidden.

'Why can't I?' reiterated Fiona, plaintively.

'Do you want to stand in a queue with a mass of unwashed, vulgar girls?' asked Mother. She quickly licked her forefinger and ran it over her eyebrows to remove the surplus face powder clinging to them. 'There is no point anyway. They would try to put you into domestic service. Do you want that?'

'No,' muttered Fiona dejectedly. Neither she nor I had ever considered going into domestic service. Even in my most deprived days, when I began to fear I would die from hunger, I had never considered this way out of my misery. Both of us remembered the servants in our own house when we were small. With the exception of their weekly half day off and on alternate Sundays, they were never free from six o'clock in the morning until eleven at night.

No. No domestic service for Fiona. Being at home was a shade better than that; at least one could have a good cry in the privy at the bottom of the back yard.

Father found his hat under the living room table, where the boys must have been using it as dressing-up material. He grabbed the bicycle from a fuming Brian at the front door, and pedalled creakily away to work.

'Never mind, Fi,' I comforted. 'What about writing to some of the big shops in the city – they like to employ under sixteens. I'll deliver the letters – or Alan can.'

Fiona's face lifted a trifle. 'Who should I write to?'

'Um – er, try Lewis's or Blackler's.'

'I'd love to work for Owen Owen's or Boots.'

I was hastily getting into my coat and hat. Given

good advice on how to improve her appearance, Fiona would have fitted well into these higher-class shops, but she was untidy and grubby, despite the fact that Mother bought her new clothes as often as possible. I said with caution, 'You could try them.' I picked up the letters that she had written the evening before. 'I'll put these into the *Echo* office for you.'

'Come on, Helen,' shouted Alan from the front door-step.

Mother told Fiona what to give the children for lunch and fled through the back door to catch her tram. Suddenly poor Fiona was left standing alone in the dirty, cluttered living room.

Some time back, I had been very ill and for two years had not been strong enough to walk to work. Recently because I felt better and, anyway, could no longer afford the tram fares, I had begun to walk again. Alan had always been provided with tram fares, but he started to accompany me. This long march to and from the city was hard on shoes. We both had pieces of cardboard poked into our footwear to help to fill up the holes in the soles. I had painful ingrowing corns on the bottoms of my feet from the exposure of the tender flesh to hard pavement. At times it was like walking on knives.

We always went along the side of the Anglican Cathedral. It was the last of the big Gothic edifices to be built in Europe, and clearly on the morning air one could hear the tiny taps of the stonemasons' hammers, as if a band of elves were hard at work. In pouring rain the great building looked like a huge red sandstone peak, and I loved looking at it, though I had never yet plucked up enough courage to enter it – I feared I was too shabby. Alan did not share my cat-like interest in new territory, so when I suggested that we go into it together, he shrugged and asked, 'Whatever for?'

Along Rodney Street, with its charming Georgian frontages, its trim white front doors and gleaming brass plates, he made me stop several times. It was a street of medical specialists, whose cars parked in the street reflected their owners' status. Alan would pause to touch reverently a polished door handle or a new shiny mascot sitting proudly on a bonnet, and would point out to me the merits of the various makes.

Sometimes he would talk enthusiastically about the cricket matches which he played in the park. He was always the hero batting steadily against the opposing team's wicked bowlers.

Occasionally, he would ruefully rub his bruised bottom and mutter maledictions against the ruthless bookkeeper under whom he worked as an office boy. Older men were heavy-handed with their apprentices. They believed in knocking a young man into shape. They had never heard of bruised egos, and a bruised bottom was just one of the hazards of being young. Boys of fourteen found themselves a small minority amid older men and they learned their trade and how to behave, whether they liked it or not. Perhaps that is why in those days there was less vandalism and less theft. In big, soulless places like the docks, however, theft was a fine art.

I rarely talked to Alan about my own affairs. I was, after all, a stand-in mother to him. I listened. It was unusual for me to talk very much to anyone except my friend, Sylvia Poole. I never seemed to be able to stop talking to her. Ever charitable, Sylvia always said she learned a great deal from me. She certainly received a great number of lectures on British and French history.

Neither Alan nor I mentioned the necrophiles amongst whom poor Fiona had found herself working. To me it was another sickening facet of human behaviour to be shunned, condemned and put out of my mind. Alan had made a joke of it, and I wondered if he really thought it was funny. It must have been in his mind, because he said suddenly, as we hurried down fashionable Bold Street, 'You know, Fi is very dumb. She was lucky she didn't get raped in that place.'

'She's not so stupid, really,' I replied. 'She had enough sense to lock herself into the cash desk – like a doll in a glass case. She's so pretty. Too nice to be pushed around.'

I caught my breath as a stab of pain went down the side of my stomach. A familiar dull ache spread down my back.

My step faltered, and Alan paused to ask, 'Something the matter?'

'No. Nothing much. Just a little spasm. It will go.' I clutched one arm across my waist, to try to contain a second wave of pain.

'You look awfully white.'

'No. It will go,' I reassured him, and moved forward again, pressed by the crowd behind me hastening to work.

Alan must have been aware that each month I was seized by terrible, clawing pain lasting some eight to twelve hours. It was impossible to hide it, because I would faint from time to time. Yet I could not bring myself to tell him what the trouble was. Our National Health Insurance doctor assured me that it would disappear when I married, which was not much comfort to a born spinster. He never examined me. I took aspirin in large quantities. Mother bought me ground ginger to take in hot water and, if the pain struck while I was at home, I had the use of Edward's hot water bottle to hug. Nothing helped much. I wondered how I would ever crawl through the day's work. I had no sanitary towel with me to use, and no money to buy one. We used bits of old cotton cloth which we washed over and over again.

I did not consider returning home. People who missed too many days of work tended to be dismissed at the first excuse, and I had lost a lot of days through illness already. If I fainted in the office it would be all right. Women frequently fainted from overwork, lack of food and all kinds of untreated illnesses.

I felt a stab of another kind as we moved slowly onward. The pin holding up my panties had opened and scratched me, and in seconds they slid down my legs and lay round my ankles. Alan giggled, as did one or two passers-by.

Proud as hell, I felt so humiliated that I started to cry quietly, as I stepped out of them. It was not the loss of the panties that bothered me; it was their grey raggedness. They were tattered beyond repair, elasticless, patched on patches, in a world where a good pair could be bought for sixpence – and they were already stained. I did not know how to endure the look of disgust on the face of one nicely dressed woman who stepped round me. I wanted to scream at her that it was not my fault that I was not clean.

'Pick them up quick and put them in your bag,' said Alan, a grin on his face.

I did so, hastily cramming them down into the old-fashioned handbag, and we moved on quickly. Alan produced a hanky and I surreptitiously wiped my eyes. The pain was coming in low level, steady waves.

'Thanks,' I murmured, as I handed it back to him. The handkerchief was grey from poor washing. Sometimes it seemed as if we lived in a world which was made up entirely of shades of grey and black.

We came to the corner of Whitechapel and Church Street. Here our ways parted.

'All right?' Alan asked.

I hesitated for a second, wondering if he could lend me three-halfpence for a tram ride home. Fear of piling up more absences than my employer would tolerate made me say, 'Yes, thanks. 'Bye.'

I shuffled up to the office. What was I going to do? I would have to ask one of the girls for help. Would they again think me to be a disgusting object, lacking even basic commonsense to provide myself with ordinary sanitary requirements?

Filled with consternation, beside myself with pain, I climbed the six flights of stone steps to the cloak-room on the top floor.

Chapter six

There was no one in the cloakroom and it gave me the opportunity to attend to myself as best I could. I replaced the errant panties, pinning them firmly this time.

With eyes closed in pain, I washed my hands. The water belched forth from the tap, gloriously hot, and I thought how heavenly it would be to lie in a bath full of it, to ease the cramping pain. And the soap – how lovely it smelled.

There was a quick tap-tap of high heels on the linoleum on the landing. The door burst open and in flew the Head Cashier. She was a small woman, swathed in a green overall, a rigid disciplinarian. Today, her forbidding expression boded ill for anyone she met. I hastily busied myself drying my hands.

She ignored my good morning. 'Where are the girls?' she demanded. 'Everybody is late.'

I trembled. Without exception, all the younger employees dreaded this ferocious lady. Her Assistant was never known to open her mouth, and her Junior Clerk was so frequently reduced to tears that her eyes seemed permanently lachrymose and her nose was red from much mopping.

'Well?'

I started to say that I was going downstairs to work

immediately, when such a sharp, tearing pain hit me that I clutched the white roller towel and let out a moan more like the shriek of a woman in childbirth.

'Good gracious, girl! Whatever's the matter?' Her usual bitter expression vanished.

My senses were leaving me, and I whispered, 'It's my period.'

She was much shorter than me, and elderly, but she said firmly, 'Pull yourself together. Now, put your arm round my shoulder. I'll help you into the Committee Room. You can sit down there.'

Eyes clenched shut, mouth open as I continued to groan and gasp, I thankfully put my arm round her shoulder and she supported me into the adjoining room. She dumped me on to a wooden chair and then put three other chairs together, and assisted me to lie down on them. The wood of the curved seats was not comfortable, but it was better than having to stand.

A couple of books from the bookcase were put under my head. She arranged me on my side with knees tucked up in a foetal position. Then she stood back, hands on hips, and surveyed me.

I could not control the deep, primeval groans that burst from me, as the pain surged in ever greater waves. Tears would come later, when the agony was gone and I was left exhausted.

'Poor girl,' she exclaimed suddenly. 'It's worse than childbirth.'

Childbirth was something I hardly understood at that time, but much later in life I found that indeed she was correct.

'I'll get the office girl to make some strong tea,' she

promised, 'and I'll send up some aspirins.' The scarifying Department Head had vanished completely and a very understanding woman had emerged. She did not waste time telling me to be brave or to stop the noise I was making. 'You lie here and try to relax yourself – it might help.'

I whimpered, 'Thank you – but aspirins don't help much.'

'They should if you take enough. We'll try what four tablets will do.'

I curled myself up tighter, as another roll of pain went through me. 'Mr Ellis . . . ?' Mr Ellis was the head of my department, a man of few words, usually very tart ones.

'I'll deal with him,' she promised, and whisked out of the room.

It seemed a very long time before the door opened slowly and the office girl slid in with a tray of tea things. The girl was a replacement for my friend, Sylvia Poole, who had left to take training as a chiropodist. I wished frantically that Sylvia was with me. She was so sensible. I was very cold and was lying on my back, knees up, swaying them from side to side, unable to find easement, and threatening to fall off my perilous perch. As each peak of pain was reached, I would put my clenched fist against my mouth to muffle a shriek, and then moan, a noise which came from the depth of my being and had nothing to do with will.

The tea tray was put on another chair drawn close to me, and the frightened little girl, a mouse, aged fourteen, fumbled in the pocket of her blue overall.

'She said I was to give you these.' She handed me four aspirins from one pocket and then, very shyly, a sanitary towel from the other pocket. 'She said I was to help you while you put it on.'

That meant I had to get on to my feet and make a trip to the cloakroom. I lay with eyes closed, wondering if I could do it.

'She said to tell you to take big breaths,' announced the girl, watching me pop-eyed, as if I were something in a cage.

'Ask Miriam Enns to come and help me,' I winced. Miriam was a stenographer, one of three who worked in a small office next to the Committee Room. She was in her late twenties and had been very kind to me. A dedicated Communist, she tended to attempt to recruit quite ruthlessly, so I had begun to avoid her, since I was not politically minded. I was too engrossed in trying to stay alive, to sidestep Mother's terrible tempers, to educate myself, to be a good employee. To survive was all I asked of life.

Miriam came running. 'Whatever happened?' she asked. Her reddish hair drooped smoothly round a pixie face. She had a big mouth which could curve into a smile so sweet that one could hardly believe in the strong Party Worker lurking within. But she had the physical strength I needed very badly.

The moment she saw my contorted face, she understood. I had taken refuge before in her little office on several occasions when I had been struck like this while at work.

Miriam looked down at the tea tray and sent the

office girl away. 'O.K., love. Have the tea first. Have you got any aspirin?'

I opened my clenched hand, to show the four tablets.

She raised her eyebrows. 'That's a lot.'

I took a large breath, as instructed. 'The Cashier said – take four,' I gasped.

'Well, I suppose she'd know.' The Cashier was never referred to by name, only as She or The Cashier. I called her Madam when I had to speak to her.

'Oh, Miriam!' I nearly screamed.

'You'll be all right, dear.' She poured the tea and held it to my quivering lips, while I swallowed the aspirins. Then she sat by me and chafed my hands and talked about seeing a doctor.

'I did, Miriam, and he just laughed – said I'd be all right when I married.'

'The stupid fool,' she exploded. 'Consult someone privately.'

'Miriam, I don't have money for things like that.'

She was referring to doctors who practised outside the National Health system. I was registered with a National Health doctor and it was difficult to change one's physician under this system. I felt I was lucky to have one doctor on whom to call, never mind anyone else. In suggesting a private physician, Miriam was, for once, allowing her middle-class instincts to outweigh her socialistic convictions.

I choked down the aspirin, and then we staggered to the cloakroom like a pair of drunks. Miriam kept one foot against the door, so that no one could enter, while she helped me wash myself.

Back in the Committee Room, she rearranged the

chairs and I lay down again, while she ran downstairs to take dictation from one of the senior staff.

The pain did not go, and I longed for home. I suppose that the Charity could not afford a taxi to send me home – they were very short of funds – and I certainly could not go on the tram. The Society did own a car, but it was in use all day taking workers to visit clients in distress.

For a while, I continued to lie on the chairs, but then removed myself to the linoleum floor, where I could move more easily. The floor was very cold, but it was flat. Nowhere in the building, which housed some twenty-five women, if one included the employees of a tea company on the ground floor, was there a couch or easy chair for staff use. There was no place where one could eat a packed lunch, except for the minute kitchen adjacent to the Committee Room. Truly, the tailor's child is the worst clad, and we lacked facilities which were increasingly being provided by thoughtful employers.

Half way through the morning, the Cashier sent the office girl in with more tea and two more aspirins. Thirty grains of aspirin in little over an hour and a half did have some effect. The top edge of the waves of pain was less sharp. I lay with eyes crunched shut and wondered if the pain was a judgment on me for refusing to go to Confession.

I could not eat the slice of bread and margarine I had brought for lunch, but I drank eagerly a cup of coffee which Miriam poured for me from her own thermos flask. Miss Short, the Head Typist, kindly provided two more aspirins.

Forty grains of aspirin. I was not sure how much one could take without poisoning oneself. I knew that a hundred aspirins would cause death – it was a popular form of suicide amongst women. Mother took as many as twenty in a day. She had no physical pain to assuage, but she said they soothed her nerves; suffering from nerves was a socially acceptable ailment – Liverpool women often referred to 'Me poor nairves'. Mother also smoked twenty to thirty cigarettes a day, as did Father.

The pain finally lessened, and when the other clerks returned from their lunch break, I went downstairs and reported shyly to Mr Ellis.

'Oh, aye,' he said absently, when I said I was feeling better. 'Take t' index cards and sort them – there's a lot.'

I sat down at the corner of a table which was my place in the crowded room, and spent the rest of the afternoon sorting the little white cards into alphabetical order and then standing to file them in long wooden drawers. The aspirin and exhaustion combined to make me feel sleepy, and sometimes I felt as if I was floating on a sea of distant pain.

When the office girl brought in the afternoon tea, she also carried a message from the busy Cashier, who worked in the next room. How was I? Would I like some more aspirin? She spread out her grubby little hand to show two tablets. I swallowed them gratefully with the tea.

The secretary to the Presence – the Presence was my name for my austere employer – thundered away on her typewriter at the other end of the table, but on seeing me take the aspirin, she paused to inquire what the trouble was. Through tightly clenched teeth, I told her I had a monthly pain. She nodded sympathetically and renewed her thunder. The other clerks running about with piles of files in their arms had no time to stop to ask after my well-being.

It was the longest of afternoons. The noise and vibration of the typewriter in front of me, the sound of the buzzers and bells of the old-fashioned telephone switchboard behind me, the filing clerks pushing behind my chair as they ran to and fro, made the close-packed room almost unbearable. Clients crept in and out, to see the Presence in her office which led off the room I was in. Chairs were dragged across the floor for them to sit on and even that vibration went through me and made me hurt all the more.

It did come to an end, however, like everything else in life, and I had to admit to Mr Ellis that I had not completed my day's work.

'Humph, then we shall have to work faster tomorrow, shan't we?'

I agreed humbly, and put the remaining cards in the table drawer.

In the cloakroom, I met Miriam struggling quickly into her overcoat. She stopped to inquire how I was.

'Better,' I said. With my eyelids drooping with fatigue, I turned to hang up my overall.

'You usually walk home, don't you?'

'Yes.'

She buttoned up her coat and picked up her handbag. 'You'll take the tram tonight?'

'No.'

'For Heaven's sake, why not?'

I forced myself to look at her and said dully but honestly, 'I don't have any money.'

'Oh, child! Why didn't you say so before? I'll lend you twopence – you can pay me on payday.' She rustled round in her handbag and proffered the coins. I took them gratefully. I had been troubled all the afternoon wondering whether I would manage the long climb up the hill to home.

Liverpool trams swayed like a ship in a storm and I began to feel nauseated. I was glad when the vehicle came to a stop at the Rialto Cinema and I could descend, while its motor hummed like a hive full of angry bees as if to say it could not wait to let me off.

As I stood on the corner of Upper Parliament Street waiting for the traffic to clear so that I could cross the road, my eyes began to dim and I knew that I would probably faint. But where to take refuge on such a busy corner, with its lounging groups of unemployed men gossiping idly?

Facing me stood the Rialto Cinema and dance hall. It had a wide pillared entrance and a sweeping curve of steps. I could lean against one of the pillars, I thought, under the supervising eye of the girl in the cash desk. If I actually passed out, she would undoubtedly call for help for me. Two or three people obviously waiting for friends to join them were already standing on the steps. People would think I was waiting for a boy friend to take me to the cinema.

The Commissionaire glanced at me. He was a shrimp of a man in a gilt-trimmed uniform too big for him. I leaned against the wall of the entrance at the furthest point from him, and closed my eyes.

'You O.K., love?'

It was a man's voice. Wearily I opened my eyes. A man neatly dressed in a light raincoat, tightly belted, and a trilby hat rakishly tipped over one eye was standing in front of me smoking a cigarette.

I knew him by sight. He seemed to spend a lot of time hanging around that corner. Once, while I was buying groceries, he had come into the shop to purchase some cigarettes, and after he left the shopkeeper called him a damned pimp when speaking to another woman customer. 'Got three girls, he has,' she had said.

He had, however, the pleasant smile and easy manner of so many smart alecks making a living in the streets, and I answered, with a sob in my voice, that I was quite all right, thank you. I winced and turned my face away. He did not leave me. Instead, his voice quite compassionate, he asked, 'Like a cigarette?'

The steps of the cinema looked wavy when I again opened my eyes, and my legs threatened to give way. I glanced at the proffered case. It was finely worked silver.

'No, thanks, I don't smoke,' I responded.

'Try one of these,' he urged, poking at some small brown cigarettes in one side of the case. 'They're great for headaches – make you feel on top of the world.'

I sighed. 'It's all right, thanks very much. I'll be O.K. in a second or two. I live quite near.'

He helped himself to an ordinary white-papered

cigarette and threw the stub of the old one into the street. He tapped the new one on his thumb nail before putting it into his mouth, then closed the beautiful cigarette case and stowed it in an inner pocket. He produced a matching petrol lighter, lit the cigarette and exhaled leisurely through his nose. 'Yeah,' he said. 'I know you. Seen you often.'

At this I stared, pain forgotten. Then I realised that if I knew him by sight, it was very likely that he knew me as a local inhabitant. I smiled wearily and straightened myself up. His cigarette had not lit properly and he flicked his lighter on again. The tiny flame showed for a moment a coarse but not unpleasant face, with calculating black eyes. I felt I was being weighed up.

'What do you do, like – work?'

'I'm a clerk.'

He nodded, and I said goodnight, and slowly walked the short distance home.

It is strange to think that if, in the acuteness of my pain, I had accepted the Indian hemp which he had offered me and it had created sufficient euphoria to dull it, I would have wanted to obtain it again. Undoubtedly, he would have approached me again, anyway, in the hope of my becoming hooked. Then he would have promised me clothes, food and a flat if I would work for him, and I would have slowly sunk into the dregs of Liverpool.

But I knew from reading and from one or two cases I had seen at work what hashish could do to people, and almost instinctively I had refused

Chapter seven

The back living room seemed packed with people all talking at the tops of their voices. The family had long since finished its tea and, normally, I would have quickly eaten whatever had been kept hot for me in the oven which lay alongside the fire. Then I would have cleared the dishes and washed them up and put Avril and Edward to bed before going to night school. Tonight I had no strength left.

Mother, in a soiled house dress, was sitting in Father's easy chair, reading the *Echo*, her bare feet on a wooden chair – to rest her veins, as she always said.

'Hello, dear,' she greeted me amiably, glancing over the newspaper. Then she put the paper quickly down on her lap. 'Are you ill?'

Sometimes I was more afraid of Mother when she was being considerate than when she was quarrelsome. I answered carefully, using the polite expression for what had happened to me. 'I was unwell.'

'How are you now?'

'A bit better, thanks. I won't go to night school tonight – I'll hand my German essay in on Wednesday.'

I took out of my handbag the crumpled confectioner's paper bag which held the uneaten lunch of bread and margarine. 'I'll take this for tomorrow's lunch,' I added as I laid it on the table.

'Gosh,' exclaimed Fiona, 'You must be hungry.' She went quickly to the oven and lifted out a plate, using the hem of her skirt to protect her fingers from the heat.

I smiled at her gratefully, as she put the meal down in front of me, a tablespoonful of stewed minced beef, a potato and the inevitable pile of frizzled up cabbage.

'Mother bought some jam tarts and we kept one for you. Here it is.' She pushed towards me a second plate with a little tartlet in a paper case sitting on it.

Mother was watching me, as I sat down, and I asked if she could spare two aspirins.

'Of course,' she said, and got up to find them in her handbag. 'Would you like some hot ginger?'

Even in pain, this horrible thick concoction of ground ginger mixed with hot water was something to be avoided, so I refused it with suitable expressions of gratitude for her kind thought.

'Eat your tea and go to bed,' she advised, and returned to her perusal of the paper.

Edward put his tousled brown head out from under the table where he and Tony and Brian were playing cards. 'You can use my hottie if you've got a tummy-ache,' he offered. He loved lending his hot water bottle to other members of the family. Some kind soul, responding to the begging letters Mother wrote quite regularly, had sent it with a parcel of clothes. Since it was unpawnable, Edward had always had his bed warmed by it.

I laughed for the first time that day and thanked him, as he ducked back underneath the table. The healthy noise of play in the room was a godsend to me. So often my parents fought or the children squabbled and howled. Amity was something to be cherished.

Avril was playing by herself at her favourite game of dressing our latest alley cat in an old baby shawl and putting it to bed in a box. She was talking softly to the patient animal.

Mother had dropped the aspirins by my plate, and Fiona brought some weak tea, made by pouring fresh water over the old leaves in the pot. Mother leaned forward and poured a cup out for herself and for me. Absently, she popped two aspirins into her own mouth and swallowed them.

Father and Alan were seated on old paint cans, trying to rewind the thread neatly round the handle of a time-worn cricket bat that one of Alan's colleagues had given him. Both had nodded to me when I came in; now they started to argue as to the best way to secure the thread.

'Snap!' came a delighted shout from Tony under the table. 'I've won. I've won!'

'No, you haven't,' responded Brian indignantly. 'Something's wrong. All the Kings have been played before. There must be an extra one in the pack.' He had a most retentive memory, but neither Edward nor Tony would accept his contention. An altercation broke out, as they scrambled round in the tiny space, while they checked the incredibly battered pack of cards with which they always played.

I ate my tartlet, while Mother leaned down from her chair and shouted at them. The raised voices vibrated through my wracked body. The tartlet did nothing to assuage my hunger, and I considered eating the lunch which I had brought back home. But I was not sure that there was enough bread in the house to provide me with lunch the following day, so I left it wrapped up in its old margarine papers.

I went upstairs and took a piece of cloth from a pile at the back of a dusty, built-in shelf in the bedroom. These rags had been accumulated from bits of sheeting and garments bought from the second-hand shop and torn into squares. Mother, Fiona and I used the same collection for our periods, washing them again and again. We were always nervous of running out of them.

The pain was rapidly easing now, and I went downstairs again, through the living room where a fight between the boys seemed about to break out, through the little back kitchen with its clutter of unwashed dishes, into the tiny backyard, lined with brick, to the lavatory by the far wall.

We were lucky to have a flush lavatory to ourselves. There was still a number of courts in Liverpool, surrounded on all sides by houses containing a family in each room, where all the inhabitants shared two lavatories set in the middle of the court.

Ours was a dank, cold outhouse, and its pipes or its tank froze every winter, causing bursts which sometimes took our aristocratic landlord weeks to repair. Copies of the *Liverpool Echo* lay on the long wooden seat, for use instead of toilet paper.

When I returned, Fiona had filled the hot water bottle for me and I thankfully took it and went up to bed, leaving the family to cope as best they could with the work I usually did.

The bed I shared with Fiona and Avril now boasted a bottom sheet and three pillows with pillow cases. The linen was grey with poor washing with insufficient soap, and sometimes with no soap or hot water; but it indicated an improvement over earlier days when I had slept on a wad of newspaper covering a door set on bricks, with an old overcoat to keep me warm.

I crawled on to the lumpy, smelly mattress and drew the two thin blankets up to my chin. I placed the hot water bottle carefully on my aching stomach; it was so hot that it seemed as if it might skin me. The rest of me was very cold despite the comparative mildness of the weather, and my knee joints and ankles hurt quite sharply whenever I moved.

Then the tears pent-up during the day exploded and I cried bitterly until I could cry no more. I cried from weakness, from cold, from hunger, from despair that life would never get any better, a holocaust of loneliness, of frustration, which seemed to pick up brief pictures of the pain-filled day and whirl them maddeningly in my head. Despite my fear of burning in hell if I did not go to Confession, I began to pray passionately to be allowed to die.

But God evidently had other things in mind for me, because I continued to survive.

Chapter eight

I slept so deeply that I did not hear Avril or Fiona get into bed, but when Father's alarm clock clamoured its warning of six o'clock, I was automatically out of bed and on my feet in a flash, anxious to get into the kitchen before the others, in order to wash myself in private.

Father trailed down the stairs ahead of me dressed in the tattered remains of a camel-hair dressing gown his sister had given him for his sixteenth birthday – the only garment apart from what he had been wearing that he had brought from our old home. He went straight to the kitchen range to rake out the cinders and build a new fire, while I put a kettle of water on the gas stove for his shaving and for Mother's early morning cup of tea.

I filled the washing-up basin with cold water from the tap, stripped off and quickly washed myself from head to foot. Mostly I had to make do with water and a cotton rag – occasionally there was soap for my face. When the kettle boiled, I padded across the tiles, naked, filled a cup and handed it to Father through a crack in the door. He then shaved, without a mirror, in the living room, using an old-fashioned cut-throat razor and a stump of shaving soap. As soon as I had some clothes on, he would enter the kitchen and make Mother's tea, occasionally holding the razor dripping with soapsuds in his left hand, half his face still lathered, the other half shining clean. The early morning offering of tea was one of the few things Mother appreciated about Father. She always thanked him and drank the weak, scalding liquid slowly, while shouting instructions about clothes or breakfast to various members of the family.

Fiona was usually the main target of her criticism in the mornings. In all her younger days Fiona never managed to prepare her clothes or lunch for the following day. The fact that the boys took it for granted that their clothes, books and lunches would be prepared for them and that they could, therefore, be considered equally inefficient was lost upon Mother; girls were capable of looking after themselves; boys were not.

If the fire that Father had made did not catch, I tried again with it, while he washed in the kitchen. First, old copies of the *Echo* were crumbled up to make a base, then a small pyramid of wood chips, bought from the chandler in neat wire-bound bundles, was built, upon which small coals were laid. A match was set to the paper and, if the wind was in the right direction, the chimney would draw the flames upwards and the fire would catch. In addition to coal, we burned vegetable peelings wrapped in newspaper, worn out shoes, anything that would burn was burned. I had long since given up collecting rubbish from the streets to keep the fire going, because I felt we should be able to afford enough coal to give us a little fire, morning and evening. Nevertheless, despite five of us having work, the coal cellar was often empty, particularly in the autumn and spring, when Mother felt we should be able to manage without heating. At such times we kept the windows tightly closed and the damp, badly constructed house acquired an icy stuffiness, an unwholesome exhalation of nine half-washed bodies.

This morning, Fiona, wandering about in her grubby nightgown, kindly laid the breakfast table for me and fed Edward and Avril.

Alan had recently very proudly begun to shave with a safety razor. He was rather slow at it, because his face was a dreadful mass of acne spots, great pustules painful enough in themselves without an added nick from the razor. Sometimes the pimples came up on the back of his neck and the pressure of a stiff collar band aggravated them, until they became big open sores that took a long time to heal.

While Alan shaved, Brian and Tony washed themselves. They pushed and shoved against each other, as each tried to insert a finger into the tap, so that they were doused by the resultant spray. The stone tiles of the kitchen were often running with water by the time they had finished.

Avril and Edward, having been perfunctorily washed in warm water before they went to bed, got a quick wipe around their mouths with a damp cloth and a flick of the comb from either Mother or me.

Except for Mother and me, everybody ate a small dish of cornflakes with milk, followed by a slice of bread and margarine, sometimes with a little marmalade. Weak tea was the drink of the whole family.

In the interests of economy, Mother and I ate a piece of bread and margarine only.

Quite frequently, Mother did not work in the mornings, so often the children came home at lunchtime to a hot meal, usually of minced meat or of eggs, with potatoes and cabbage or carrots. When she did work before noon, a meal of bread and margarine and cold meats was prepared by Mother or me and left on the table for them, and we tried to provide something hot for them at teatime.

Father and Alan took a lunch with them of bread, margarine and cheese. Since I made up the lunches, I always made mine last, and there never seemed to be any way in which I could divide the small amount of Canadian red cheese so that I could have some without leaving them short. The severe illness I had suffered two years earlier had left me very apathetic about myself; it was enough for me if I could crawl through the day without incurring either Mother's or Mr Ellis's wrath and perhaps get a kind word from my dedicated night school teachers.

Mother was a demonstrator. She took short contracts with department stores who wanted to launch new kitchen gadgets, and she stood in the store and showed people how to use them. Occasionally, she did door-to-door selling for vacuum cleaner companies, family photographers, Christmas card publishers or sweet firms. When doing outside work, she wore an all enveloping leather coat which she had bought second hand. This protected her from Liverpool's damp, cold wind, and, despite its bulk, she still managed to look elegant in a faded way. She had a lovely carriage and an authoritative voice with a pure Oxford accent. She was a very good saleswoman.

Her supervisor in a vacuum cleaner company, who once called at the house, said admiringly, 'She could steal your front door key off you and sell it you back before you knew it had gone.'

Father received this doubtful praise in stiff silence, while his guest threw a cigarette stub into the hearth and smoothed his curled moustache.

I do not know what Mother thought of some of the men with whom she worked, but it is doubtful if their crassness bothered her much. She was so sure of herself, so certain of her social superiority despite our current circumstances, that she was to a degree armoured against them.

Father was different. He was abject in his failure and very easily hurt. His public school training, followed almost immediately by war service in Russia during the Revolution, had given him little preparation for a world which had changed completely by the time he came home. He might have survived better had the Depression – and a large family – not added to his difficulties. Like many soldiers returning from the First World War he was emotionally and physically drained by its unremitted horrors; there was little real strength left; and I could guess at the cold flame of hatred in his heart, when faced with a runt of a salesman, who was probably doing rather better than he was as a City clerk.

Mother came downstairs with the coarse white teacup in her hand, and paused when she saw me in the hall to ask if I felt better. I said I did. How could I complain of overwhelming fatigue to someone who looked like a haggard ghost herself?

As we stepped out of the house into a beautiful, rain-washed morning, glad to be away from a fetid, crowded home, Alan offered to pay my tram fare to work. He was shy about referring to my aches and pains of the previous day, but he was well accustomed to their occurrence.

'No, dear,' I said. 'I shall be all right. In fact, the exercise is good for me.' And I marched beside him down the street as if I had not a care in the world. I could not take his pocket money; but I loved him for the sheer kindness of the offer, and our conversation held more than its usual friendly warmth.

'The man from the furniture shop came last night – after you'd gone to bed,' he informed me, as we paused to look in the window of the bicycle shop at the corner of Bold Street; and he sighed over black enamelled frames and racing handlebars.

'Oh, dear!' I exclaimed. 'What now?'

'Threatening to take it away again.'

'Haven't they been paid lately?'

'Suppose not,' he replied gloomily.

'Oh, blow. It's such an appalling waste, Alan. Mummy and Daddy make the weekly payments for a while. Then the stuff is repossessed – but we still have to pay for it – it doesn't get us off the hook. It's so stupid. Really, they're absolutely crazy.'

'Humph.'

He was not very interested. He never used our front sitting room. His friends did not come to visit

– he always met them on the cricket or football field or in the park, where they would sometimes kick a tennis ball about in an impromptu game.

I was very interested, because payments for the furniture represented a heavy drain on our income. It was money that could have been spent on food and coal. Mother always hankered after some semblance of prosperity, and this was the third room full of sitting room furniture she had bought on the hire purchase system, while ignoring our frantic need for bedding and beds, coal, hot water and food. It was easy to obtain furniture for a very small down payment and weekly payments, laden with interest. Failure to pay resulted in prompt repossession of the furniture, without releasing the buyer from his financial commitment. So the loss could be a heavy one, particularly if one had nearly completed the payments. The three separate firms we had to pay or face being sold up entirely by the bailiff, swallowed enough money to have fed us well. Twice the sitting room had been emptied by phlegmatic furniture removers, well used to pushing their way into the houses of debtors. Now it seemed that it might happen again.

Chapter nine

The great port of Liverpool lies on a series of hills rising from the waterfront, and each day I climbed the long slopes from the city centre, on my way home. I passed concert halls, hospitals, surprisingly finely built Edwardian public houses, rows of little shops and tasteful Victorian houses, some of which were falling into decay. Every so often there was a newsagent's and tobacconist's shop, and I depended upon the hastily chalked newspaper headlines displayed on boards outside their shops to alert me to the big news of the day. They currently dealt with the crises of the Spanish war, about which Miriam frequently held forth passionately in the office. She foretold quite accurately that it was but a dress rehearsal for a much bigger conflict. They also announced the forthcoming coronation of George VI and his plump little Duchess, Elizabeth. Some of these shops were decorating their windows with souvenirs, coronation mugs, flags and brooches. A number of defiant people still wore pins and brooches with the insignia of Edward VIII, to show they thought that he should be the king, despite his intention of marrying an American divorcée.

I never saw a billboard that dealt with Liverpool's fearful slums, some of the worst in the country, nor the hunger in them. Occasionally an increase in the number of unemployed was mentioned, and a great march by workless men who walked all the way to London got some attention. The slums with their suffering inhabitants had always been part of the Liverpool scene; they were not interesting.

Trudging homeward through pouring, slashing rain, I had no particular desire to arrive. Too often more problems, more worries awaited me.

This evening, to my astonishment, there was good news. Fiona had received a letter asking her to go the following afternoon for an interview with a magazine-distributing agency. She was as agitated as an aspen in the wind, and while I ate my tea, she discussed with Mother what she should wear, as if she had a wardrobe full of clothes instead of a single blouse, a skirt and two dresses which were almost outgrown.

Mother was being most cooperative. She offered to lend her a hat which had recently been refurbished with the aid of a bright yellow feather and a new ribbon into what was known as a Robin Hood style. Mother knew that when a shorthand student had paid me a few days earlier I had bought a pair of rayon stockings, so she lent her those as well, despite my protests that the pair I had on could not be mended any more; they were laddered beyond redemption.

After returning from night school, I spent a couple of hours fuming as I oversewed ladders and darned heels, and then lengthened one of Fiona's dresses for her. It was after midnight before the hem was finally hand-stitched and pressed, but Fiona who had never learned to sew was touchingly grateful.

There were times when I wished that Grandma had not taught me how to use a needle. When I was a child I used to stay with her for long periods of the year in her house on the other side of the Mersey river, but she no longer had anything to do with us, because Father had quarrelled bitterly with his family.

Mother had learned from nuns who brought her up how to do fine embroidery for copes and altar cloths, but she was not adept at other sewing. She sometimes darned socks if I was too busy to do them or if I had, in a rage at the pressure put upon me, temporarily struck work. Nine people in near rags produced a lot of sewing, by necessity to be done by hand. My eyes were always tired from short hours of sleep, constant reading for night school and from my day-time work, all done with the aid of spectacles long since outgrown and in need of replacement. Quite often the work was done by candlelight, because we did not have pennies to put into the electric and gas meters.

Apart from Fiona's letter, there was a letter for me to give me pleasure. To improve my German I had a pen-friend. He was the son of a schoolmaster and lived, as far as I could judge from the map on the wall at night school, about forty miles from Munich. The idea was that I should write to him in German and he would write to me in English, so that we would both benefit. However, he soon fell into the habit of writing in German. This had for me one fortunate result. Because Mother did not know German, she gave up opening and reading my letters before allowing me to have them, something which I had always bitterly resented.

In early April, he had sent me some violets, carefully pressed, from his garden. His letters had taken a slightly sentimental turn, and he wanted a photograph of me. It was very thrilling, though Hitler's stern limitations on foreign travel and my poverty made it almost certain that we should never be able to visit each other. As a young boy, he had already visited England on an exchange plan, and that was how I originally met him.

When this pen-friendship first commenced, I had had the utmost difficulty in finding money for stamps out of the shilling a week allowance I had squeezed out of my parents. Miriam in the office had willingly contributed sheets of typing paper and some envelopes, and I usually wrote to him in my lunch hours, using the office kitchen counter as a desk because it was clean. I had a tiny pocket German dictionary which my German teacher had given to me, and as my grasp of the language improved I wrote with its aid ever lengthening letters.

Too shy and ashamed to tell him of the grim poverty into which we had fallen, of the filth, hunger and vermin which were my daily companions, I wrote as if we were still living in our old home and I was attending the local high school – a private school which took girls of all ages. I described the house, the servants and our social life. My grandmother and her home, shared with two aunts and a cousin, were also sources for description of English life. As time went on, I wrote of my hopes of becoming a qualified social worker in Liverpool, and he responded by saying that he would become a schoolmaster, like his father. We had lively discussions on books which we had both read and on religion, but he soon discovered that if we touched on politics or if I sent newspaper cuttings, the letters were not received, indicating censorship of both inward and outward mail, presumably in Germany.

I had also acquired a girl pen-friend in Stettin, through an offer, in the correspondence column of a Sunday newspaper, to put children in touch with each other. Judging from her photograph, she was exceedingly pretty, an ash blonde, and was the daughter of some small government official. She was impatient of my bad German, which was very good for me, but she gave me such long and involved explanations of German grammar and idioms that I sometimes did not understand all she said. She was one of a class of students who had been encouraged by their teacher to seek English pen-friends, and both sides seemed to get quite a lot of fun out of it. What neither side knew was that we had been drawn into a minor spy network, and this was to cause me no little distress when the war began.

Ursel, aged fifteen, and I were blissfully ignorant of all this and discussed the scary prospect of her father arranging a marriage for her, when she was passionately in love with a boy who travelled on the same bus as she did each day. When she was not correcting my grammar, she wrote pages on every detail of the young man. They had never got beyond smiling at each other – but for nearly a year her hopes ran high. At the age of sixteen, a marriage *was* arranged for her by her father, to the minister of her church, a man of forty, and the last letter I received from her a few days before the war broke out was from a young girl broken-hearted and pregnant. It would have moved even a bored censor. Poor Ursel – and the war with its repression of the clergy and its ruinous fighting was yet to come.

Chapter ten

Fiona went for her interview. Father provided her with threepence for the tram fares to and from the city, and she returned glowing with excitement.

'I think I've got it,' she said, as she took off the Robin Hood hat with its bright yellow feather and handed it back to Mother. 'They said they'd let me know – they want to see one or two other girls before deciding.'

She did not return my stockings, but she was so relieved and happy that I did not want to spoil things for her. I did not tell her that the phrase 'We'll let you know' was the stock dismissal of an unsuccessful candidate. She would learn the sad facts of job-hunting in Liverpool by experience. She had been fortunate in finding her first job, because few girls would want to work in a butcher's or a fishmonger's shop, and she was probably by far the smartest fourteen-year-old to apply.

I went on sweeping the living room's tiled floor and then worked my way over the small piece of coconut matting in the middle, briskly brushing the dust and debris towards the hearth.

'What kind of work is it?' Mother inquired. She was seated at the table, writing pad and bottle of ink before her, and she did not look up from her composing of a begging letter. She still occasionally wrote to perfect strangers asking for financial help, and quite frequently received compassionate replies enclosing a welcome pound or two.

Fiona sat down on the easy chair and clasped her hands in front of her. She replied eagerly, 'They would teach me to use a thing called an addressograph. It makes the labels to put on the magazines they send out. They've got hundreds and hundreds of magazines, lovely ladies' magazines and story ones – everything. They send them out to subscribers. They've got so many that they even have to have a van to take them to the post office.'

'Are there many on the staff?'

'No. Two gentlemen saw me – and an old lady who does the books. I don't think there was anyone else.'

'What's the pay?' asked Alan.

'Twelve shillings and sixpence a week at first, and then in two months' time – if I get quick at managing the machine – they'll give me fifteen shillings. Isn't it great?'

Alan looked amazed. 'Holy Cain! You lucky thing! I'm only getting seven and sixpence – and Helen's been working nearly three years – and she's only getting twelve and sixpence.'

I was actually receiving fifteen shillings, but I dared not say so. The precious half-a-crown difference was what had paid my fares during the time I had not been strong enough to walk to and from work, and now it sometimes bought me a bowl of soup in Woolworth's cafeteria when there was nothing left at home for me to take for lunch. My shorthand student, when I had one, paid me enough to cover my pair of rayon stockings every other week and the bits and pieces of clothing from the pawnbroker's bargain table.

Fiona laughed, looking suddenly like Mother when she was young and full of vivacity. 'I'm so excited.'

'It's lovely,' I agreed heartily. 'Lift up your feet, people.' They all automatically raised their feet off the floor, while I swept neatly in and out of the chair legs. Like an army, they put their feet down on the floor again in perfect unison when I reached the hearth and picked up the pile of dust between my hands. I threw it into the fire and there was an immediate outcry from the others at the horrid odour of burning hair, as it hit the hot coals.

Father had been sitting silently on a wooden chair at the opposite end of the table from Mother, while he drank a cup of tea left over from our meal. He rested his head on his hand and, except for the red acne rash across his nose and cheeks, his face was pale. Now he said, 'I'm very glad about the job, Fiona. What happened this morning about the furniture?'

All the joy was immediately wiped off Fiona's face. She said sadly, 'They came and took it – like they did before, Daddy. They just pushed past me and walked in when I opened the door.'

'Pack of bullies,' said Father angrily. 'And to think that we've already paid two-thirds of it. They might have waited.'

Personally, I thought the furniture company had shown the patience of Job waiting for their money at different times. But I knew enough to keep my mouth shut. I put the broom away and went upstairs to get my account books, so that I could do my book-keeping homework.

When I returned, Mother was saying, 'We could let that room. Nobody is going to let us have more furniture on the never-never plan for a while.' I smiled at her use of Liverpool's name for the hire purchase system, which never, never seemed to get paid off.

'Well, it might help to pay the furniture instalments,' said Father wearily. 'Some business girl who has her own furniture, perhaps?'

I sat down by him and opened my ledgers. 'She'd have to pass through this room and the kitchen every time she wanted to get water or go to the lavatory,' I pointed out.

'Oh, you always look on the black side of things,' Mother grumbled. 'I don't suppose such a girl would be home very much.' She folded up her letter and put it into the envelope. 'I'll advertise it in the news-agent's window. I wonder what rent I could get?'

'A small room rents for about seven shillings a week,' I told her, as I carefully made entries in my collection of books.

'How do you know?' Mother was cross. She licked the envelope and rubbed her hand impatiently across the back of it to seal it.

'Well, Mummy, I see details of dozens of people's incomes and expenses at the office. The first thing an interviewer does is to fill out a form about the client with all kinds of details.'

'I think that's about right,' Father agreed. 'I see

plenty of them, too. With no bathroom in the house, we can't charge much.'

'I'll try for ten shillings,' Mother said firmly. 'After all, this is a very respectable house.'

She wrote an advertisement on the back of an envelope and immediately went out to see the newsagent, who would, for twopence, exhibit it for a week in a glass case hung on his door.

Fiona had had an early tea before going for her interview and now announced that she was going to see a girl friend. Alan drifted off to play cricket with the other boys in the street. I should have gone to call Avril and Edward to come in because it was their bedtime, but for the moment I was alone with Father. He had picked up his library book and was looking for his place in it. I laid down my pen.

'Daddy, could I ask you something?'

'Yes, dear.' He closed his book again and peered at me through his spectacles. I noticed that the gold frame was bent, so that one eye was not looking through the middle of the lens, and it gave a curiously lopsided appearance to his face.

I reminded him of Miss Ferguson's desire to see me confirmed, and that she expected me to go to Confession before taking my first Communion.

'I've been so worried, Daddy. What is it all about? I never dreamed of having to go to Confession. I thought old King Henry VIII and Queen Elizabeth did away with such things in the Church of England? I'm so frightened, Daddy – is it wrong to refuse to go?'

He chuckled. 'Good Lord, no. There's nothing to be frightened about. The Church of England allows considerable latitude within its ranks – you must know that.' He sighed heavily. 'Both your Mother and I were brought up as High Anglicans – in fact, you probably know that your mother was actually brought up by Roman Catholic nuns, despite her being a Protestant.'

'Hm,' I agreed.

'But then there was the war. And, you know, it was difficult after that to believe in anything. We rarely went to church after that, except to get you children christened.'

'You go to the cenotaph every November 11th, no matter what,' I reminded him with a little smile.

'Yes, I do. But that's just so that my old friends – my dead friends, wherever they are – know that I remember them, that I have never forgotten them.' His voice was suddenly shaky. 'There were only three survivors, you know, from my old regiment – the three of us who volunteered for the Russian campaign.'

I could not bear the stricken look on his face, and I selfishly recalled him to my own predicament by asking, 'Must I go to a High Anglican church, Daddy? Couldn't I be confirmed somewhere else? Edith always took us to the village church – and they had very plain services, I remember – and neither you nor Mother said anything.'

Again he sighed, and then he looked up at me with a little smile. 'As far as I'm concerned, dear, you can go to any Protestant church you like, if it gives you comfort. I know you are trying to live a good life – and church will help to keep you out of mischief.'

Mischief was the last thing I was ever likely to get into, and I laughed, a laugh tinged with great relief.

'Really? Would it be all right? Could you talk to Mother about it?'

'Of course. Your Mother won't mind, and I expect Miss Ferguson will get over it; she will probably be offended at first, though, because you always seem to have been a protégée of hers.'

'She's been a fairy godmother – and I'm truly sorry if she becomes angry about it, but even for her I can't face Confession.' I picked up my pen and chewed the end of it, and then said passionately, 'I'd burn first.'

Father laughed. 'You're a real Protestant – but I'm glad for you that you seem to have a clear belief, God bless you.'

Such a weight rolled off my shoulders. The smell of sulphur and brimstone, the smell of hell, which had haunted me uneasily for days, rolled away.

I jumped up from my chair and leaned over to kiss his bald pate. 'Thank you, Daddy.'

He caught my hand and squeezed it, while he looked up at me earnestly. 'Religion is a private thing – remember that. If you can find a path to God which suits you, take it. I wish I could, but I am not able to feel anything any more – as I said, it was the war.'

I put my arm round his shoulders and sought in my mind for comforting words. 'Perhaps you will change as time goes on, and the memory of the war becomes less.'

He nodded. 'Perhaps.' But he never did.

I was the one who changed. Starting from Father's

unexpectedly wise counsel, I began to look at others' religions with a wider and more inquiring mind, as I moved about Liverpool and met people of all beliefs and all nationalities. Edith was fond of remarking that the gentry had too much book learning and not enough real learning, and it took a while for me to remedy this imbalance.

The ice between Father and me had been broken. Older now, I was more able to forgive and understand his weakness and in reaching out for his aid when I was so afraid, I think I had restored to him in some small part a sense of being wanted, being needed for more than the wages he brought in.

Whether his talk with me had alerted him to the possible code of behaviour of his sons, I do not know. He began, however, to check on where they went in their spare time and what they did. He made them all promise to tell Mother or me their destination whenever they went out. Nobody thought of Fiona and Avril. The boys all had lively, inventive minds and were fairly well mannered. They tended to draw friends to them, whose parents were glad to have them play in their houses, where they were under supervision. The boys also frequently played together, and this helped to keep them out of bad company.

Father's new interest in his children was wonderful to me. One of the most scaring things in childhood is the lack of an older person to turn to, to depend on for guidance and advice. Now, in a diffident, irregular way he was beginning to make his presence felt in the family, as if the trauma of the war and his financial ruin was beginning to be sloughed off. Though, in fearsome battles, Mother still shouted him down, he persisted quietly, using a strong sense of humour which I had not realised he possessed.

Chapter eleven

Two women came on separate occasions to view our empty front room. One of them was an elderly widow and the other a shop girl in crumpled black – black was the uniform of work in those days. The lack of a bathroom and an indoor lavatory made them both turn it down with supercilious sniffs.

A few days later, a young Irish labourer, cap in hand, came to see it.

'I'm sorry I am not prepared to let the room to a man,' Mother said, beginning to close the front door on him.

'It's not for meself only,' pleaded the youth. 'It's me wife and me baby.'

It is doubtful if anyone, except the poorest slum landlord, would have considered such a tenant. Labouring in Liverpool meant casual work at rock bottom wages – and a consequent difficulty in paying the rent. A baby meant noise and a lot of washing to be hung out. And Irish people did not have much of a name for cleanliness.

I saw Mother hesitate. The careworn white face with its red-rimmed, pleading eyes must have touched some chord in her – perhaps she remembered when she had canvassed from door to door, trying to find a landlord who would accept seven children. 'Is your wife with you now?'

'She's waitin' at t' corner.'

'Ask her to come. She'd better see it, too.'

Joyfully, he turned and bawled up the street, 'Mary, coom 'ere.'

A plump, cheery woman wearing a black shawl, with a young baby wrapped in the front of it, came panting up to the doorstep. Her rosy face, and thick light brown curls bobbing round her shoulders, reminded me of Edith, our nanny. They both had the same country-fresh look. Her expression was one of sudden glowing hope.

Fiona and I were longing to see the baby, which seemed very small, and when we had all trooped into the bleak front room, from which even the curtains had been removed by the hire purchase company, Mother asked if we might see it. Its tiny puckered face under a clean, frilled bonnet was tenderly admired by all of us, as it placidly slept.

' 'E's only six weeks,' his mother announced proudly as she wrapped the shawl back over him.

Mother stood in the middle of the unvarnished square of wooden floor, where the carpet had lain, and explained the disadvantages of the room. The young couple were irrepressible.

'Och, I can keep a couple o' buckets o' water in t' room. And Pat will be gone to work before most of yez is up.'

'We're all away during the day,' Mother informed her, 'except for a little while when the children come home to lunch.'

'To be sure,' responded Mary, with a wide, sweet smile, 'I can do me washing and cooking while you're all away.'

'You can hang the washing out to dry in the back yard,' said Mother. 'Come and see.'

We all went out to view the tiny, sooty yard with its lavatory near the alley door.

'We could keep our coal in the corner here,' suggested Pat. 'I could roof it over with a bit of a tin roof, like.'

'Where are you living now?' asked Mother, as we returned to the house and entered our living room.

'We're living with me Mam,' replied Pat. 'It's too hard on Mary, though. Me Mam isn't an easy woman, I know. When we was in Dublin we was living with her Mam, and that was all right, wasn't it, Mary?'

Mary nodded agreement, and sighed. We all understood. In Liverpool–Irish families, daughters frequently brought their husbands to live in their family. Husbands escaped from their mothers-in-law by going to work and then in the evening going down to the local pub for a drink. The young wife, however, had recourse to no such escape route if faced with her husband's mother – and the result was battles so bitter that they sometimes spilled out into the street and caused a street fight, a welcome entertainment to the onlookers, but unpleasant for the combatants.

As we showed the young couple round, I had become more and more resentful of Mother. I believed that she was raising the couple's hopes, without having any intention of giving them the room. Now, to my astonishment, a bargain was struck; a rent of ten shillings a week, plus one shilling for electricity, payable in advance.

'If you want to use the gas stove in the back kitchen, you will have to put your own pennies into the gas meter,' Mother instructed them. It seemed fair, but in practice we were more likely to benefit from gas left over by them than they were from us, because we always seemed to run out of gas and money before we had finished cooking. We had to try to complete the job on whatever bit of fire we might have at the time.

'We'll bring our gear over on Saturday afternoon,' Pat said. They both thanked Mother gaily, and through the undraped window we watched them laughing and talking together, as they hurried up the street.

Mother was the strangest person, I thought. There were layers of her character of which one caught only a momentary glimpse. Our tiny house would now have twelve people living in it, all using the same outside lavatory and the same cold water tap. The inconvenience of people trailing through our crowded living room and kitchen at all times of the day and night would be indescribable. Our frequent bitter family rows would be heard clearly by these strangers, the details in due course to be gossiped to the neighbours. The clash of uneducated Roman Catholic Irish with upper class Protestants was something I dreaded. Yet, watching Mother's drawn face, I was sure she had taken the family in out of compassion. Admittedly the rent was more than half the rent of the entire house, but nothing could compensate for the overcrowding and loss of any small privacy we had.

Mother and I went back to the living room and

were met by a barrage of questions from the children, who had watched in silence the small procession to and from the back yard.

'Yes, they are coming to live with us,' Mother told them. 'You will have to be quiet so as not to wake the baby – and be polite to them.'

Alan raised his eyebrows and made a rueful expression at me, while Fiona just shrugged her shoulders. Father was out having a drink with a young colleague with whom he had recently become friendly. Fortified by several glasses of beer, he received the news optimistically when he came home. Perhaps he felt, like me, that a week of such an arrangement would see the end of it.

Chapter twelve

To my surprise, Mother accepted my diffident announcement that I would prefer to be confirmed by another church, with only a fretful, 'What am I going to say to Miss Ferguson? Really! Don't you have any consideration?'

I was much too shy to go to see Miss Ferguson myself, and I do not know what explanation Mother gave her. I never saw her again, though I did hear her once when Mother sent me to borrow a shilling from her, with the plea that we had nothing for breakfast – which was true. Mother had already coerced out of me the few pennies I had, so feeling very sick at heart I had trudged to her flat, through dark streets, where the gas lamps gleamed dully through a sea mist.

The lady with whom she lived answered the door. She did not know me, and when I inquired for Miss Ferguson I was told that she was having a bath. Fearing Mother's scathing tongue if I returned without the shilling, I nervously whispered the reason for my visit. She left me standing in front of the open door while she went to consult the bather. There was a mumble of voices in the little apartment; then clearly I heard Miss Ferguson say, 'Better give it to her. Get it out of my bag – it's on the dressing table. I'm tired of that woman – she never pays back.'

I wanted to turn and run. Miss Ferguson probably lived on a pittance, unless she had private means. The stranger was, however, hastening down the hall towards me, at the same time feeling inside a small black handbag. When she reached the door, she unsmilingly handed me a silver coin and shut the door on my muttered 'thank you very much'.

I stood looking at the offending woodwork and wanted to throw the coin at it. Mother had lost a good friend for the sake of a shilling – which she could have easily saved had she not smoked.

Mother received the money with triumphant relief, and sent Avril out to buy bread and margarine, milk and cornflakes.

So kind Miss Ferguson vanished, as far as I was concerned, into a dish of cornflakes. Fairy godmothers do tend to depart when their work is done.

When Pat and Mary and the baby arrived, it was clear that they regarded Mother as a fairy godmother. They brought their bits of furniture on a handcart; it took two journeys. An iron bed frame was put together in the room, with much bumping and rattling of metal slats which had to be woven across the base. A wool-packed mattress tied with string was banged down on it, making the slats again vibrate in tuneful protest. A wash-stand with a marble top, innumerable galvanised metal buckets, a pile of enamelled wash basins with a few dishes laid inside the top one, two chairs and a small table, some iron saucepans, a tea chest of assorted garments and blankets with a chamber pot perched on top, a fine old handmade cradle on rockers, all were piled into the room. There was only one small cupboard, which had once held a gas meter, and I wondered how everything would fit in.

Mary pinned up over the small bay window a pair of dusty looking lace curtains. They did not give much privacy when the light was on, but they looked fairly tidy from the outside. It was only from occasional glimpses through the curtains when I passed in the evening that I was aware of the muddle of their lives. Nobody to my knowledge entered the room.

The young couple evidently decided that to make the situation bearable for both sides, they should be as invisible as possible. We were barely aware of Pat, except as a shadow going out to work through the front door as Father and I came downstairs each morning. He spent half of Sunday in bed with his wife, judging by the giggles we heard and the pinging bed slats. Mary once said primly, 'Men must have their rest on Sundays.'

To use the lavatory in the yard, they went out the front way, walked past three houses and then down a side alley which led into our back alley, and came back in through the yard door to the privy. They rarely pulled the chain, but at least they did not come through our living quarters. Nobody commented on this long tour they had to make so often, and I doubt if the family appreciated their consideration.

While we were out, Mary cooked huge quantities of stew in an enamelled wash bowl on the gas stove. I sometimes saw her hurry through our living room with this vast amount of steaming meat and vegetables, smelling so savoury that I was envious. I think she cooked enough at one time to last two or three days and that she heated portions of it on the fire in their room. I once caught a glimpse of the room's interior when I opened the door for her when she was thus laden. Three big pails of coal and three of water were ranged against a wall. A pile of washing was flung into a corner. The baby's cradle stood close to the fire. The wash-stand was littered with utensils for cooking, the mantelpiece laden with anonymous bottles and jars. The table and chairs were, I knew, set in the bay window – I had seen them as I passed – and the rumpled bed was against the hall wall, behind the door. The wooden floor was bare and grimy, but it had been swept. A thick effluvia of human living rolled out, a mix of stew, onions, baby's faeces, sweat, urine, and steam from the washing drying on a string hung from the mantelpiece. It added itself to the neglected grubbiness of our part of the house. I hastily shut the door after Mary's, 'Thanks, luv.'

After a few days, we discovered that Mary had found an old built-in wash boiler in a corner of the coal cellar. Rather than use a similar one in the corner of our kitchen, she had carried water downstairs and had boiled her washing in it by making a fire in the tiny grate underneath. She did all her washing down there amid the clammy smell of coal dust and cats. Then she hung the clothes to drip in the back yard, before bringing them to finish drying in her room. She was very resourceful.

I probably saw more of her than the others did, because I was almost invariably the last person to go to bed; I often did my night school studying after everyone else had gone up to bed. She would slip apologetically through the room several times, carrying buckets of coal and water or a pile of washing from the back yard. She also emptied buckets of dirty water down the kitchen sink.

Occasionally, while I was studying by candlelight because we could not afford a penny for electricity – candles cost a halfpenny – she would hasten in with a penny because they also were plunged into darkness. I always continued with my candle, because I felt it would be unfair to switch on the light and help use up their pennyworth.

On Saturday night, Pat, with a shy grin on his face, would knock on our living room door and hand to whoever opened it, eleven shillings. They had no rent book and never asked for a receipt. Their trust was moving.

Because of the poor quality of the building, any raised voices could be heard in the next room, and they must have suffered from the continual squabbling of the children and the bitter, screaming rows between my parents.

Sometimes they themselves quarrelled. In their case, it was not always a verbal spate. There were the sounds of screams, scuffles and thumps, while the baby howled untended. Fortunately, perhaps, our children found it funny rather than frightening. Most of the time, the baby was quiet, cosied against his mother's ample breasts or rocked in his warm cradle by her foot on the rocker, while she knitted.

Occasionally, Mary would stop in her late night promenade to ask me what I was doing. She smelled strongly of milk and perspiration, but she had a glowing life about her, an eager effervescence that I wished was mine. She was endlessly curious about us and boundless in her praise of Mother. I began to see Mother in a slightly better light. 'To be sure, she's a great lady,' Mary would remark at times, and I wished I could feel the same about her.

One night, I had been wrestling with a difficult task which my English master had set me. I was to read a book of essays by William Hazlitt and comment on it. I was very tired and could not concentrate and was asking myself why I bothered, since it would make no difference to my marks, when Mary, carrying a pile of dirty washing, entered without knocking.

She paused, smiled and asked, as an opening gambit, 'How are yer, luv?'

Relieved to be temporarily delivered from Hazlitt, I put down my pen and pushed the cork into the ink bottle.

'Not bad, Mary. How are you?'

She looked at me hard. 'You bin cryin'?' she inquired solicitously.

I had cried, after everyone had gone to bed, letting the tears drop on to my books. Mother had paused on her way to bed, and had asked me with a hint of contemptuous curiosity what I was going to wear for my forthcoming Confirmation. Her attitude was cold, as if she were poking idly at a half-dead beetle on the floor.

I had never seen a Confirmation, and it was with a sense of shock that I received the information that I would be expected to appear in a white dress and veil – a fact which was confirmed by the head of the church's Sunday school, the following week, when after the evening service she announced to the congregation that veils would be loaned by the church.

In a world which still judged people by what they wore – a moment's consideration of a person's dress would establish his position socially – I was in a difficult dilemma. To buy odd garments to cover me was hard enough; to buy a dress for a single occasion was impossible. I would, presumably, need white stockings and shoes as well, which would never be worn again.

Mother had not offered any answer to her query, so there was not much hope of help from her. I said, tight-lipped, that I did not know what to do, but I would think about it, and opened my books and got on with my homework as best I could with a mind in a nervous flutter. Life never seemed to get any better and this additional problem made me cry with dumb despair.

'We all have a little cry sometime or other, Mary.' I tried to smile.

'Oh, aye,' she agreed. 'I like a good cry meself sometimes. Relieves you, like.'

I nodded and piled up my books. I would have another try at Hazlitt tomorrow during my lunch hour.

Mary shifted the washing round in her arms. It reeked.

'What's to do?' she persisted.

I sighed. 'Well, Mary.' She was always Mary,

never Mrs O'Neill, to all of us. It marked the difference in class. 'Well, Mary, I'm going to be confirmed.' And I went on to explain the problem of the dress.

Mary was thrilled. Confirmation was a great event, she burbled, though in her opinion it should have taken place when I was seven. 'Och, you'd look like an angel, in white,' she assured me, looking my beanpole figure up and down. 'Surely your Mam will get you a frock?'

'She can't afford it,' I defended Mother. 'And I don't have a penny,' I added frankly.

Mary clicked her tongue. '*My* Mam got me one – and for sure we didn't have much money. It's a very special occasion.' She glanced down at the washing in her arms. 'Look, luv, just let me take me washing down. We got to think how to do this.'

She tripped down the stone steps to dump the washing in the copper. When she came up she had a coal smudge on her apron and was dusting it off impatiently. She stopped in front of me, and announced almost defiantly, 'If you can't get a dress any other way, I'll lend you me wedding dress.'

'Oh, Mary!' The offer was so kind, but Mary's figure was rotund and anything of hers would have hung on me. Yet her dress must have been almost a sacred relic to her amid her present hard circumstances. I hesitated.

She must have read my mind. 'It's proper nice – and it'll fit near enough,' she said. 'I was real thin when I was married.' She looked down at her enormous bosom and giggled. 'Marriage agrees with me. I'll have a word with your Mam.'

When I came home the next evening, Mother greeted me with such enthusiasm that I was frightened. But, according to Avril, Mary – dear Mary – had indeed been talking to her, pointing out that other than my marriage or my funeral, Confirmation was the greatest day of my life, even if it was to be performed by a Protestant bishop.

Before I even got my coat off, Mother was saying, 'Just come and look.'

Laid on a chair, with a sheet of newspaper under it so that it was kept clean, was an open dressmaker's box with a large pile of white tissue paper in it. Mother carefully parted the tissue, took out a dried sprig of orange blossom and laid it on the table, while she gushed, 'Isn't that sweet? It's from her wedding bouquet.' Then she carefully lifted out a pile of lace and shook it. It was a charming, long sleeved white dress.

I gaped as I looked at its shimmering whiteness, its absolute purity of line. 'Mother! It's lovely. It's perfect. They must have spent a fortune on it.'

Mother laughed. 'Well, you should know by now that a working class wedding is a great event. And they spend money on them.'

Mother carefully folded the dress back into its tissue. As she lifted the package and handed it to me, a few grains of lavender fell from it. I bent over the box's contents and sniffed. It smelled like Grandma's sheets and dresses, with a lovely perfume of fresh lavender.

'Mummy's going to buy you some white shoes and stockings – and a petticoat,' interjected Fiona. 'Aren't you, Mummy.' She said it firmly, as if to reinforce the decision.

'Of course,' said Mother, without blinking an eyelid. Fiona winked at me. Mary, she told me afterwards, had swept Mother along on such a flood of excitement that Mother had said she would apply to the finance company for a cheque for a pound, to cover the purchase of these accessories.

To persuade Mother to buy me anything was little short of a miracle and, with the box still in my arms, I knocked on Mary's door, and went in to thank her. She blushed as I kissed her. Then heaved her baby round on her lap to offer it her breast, and muttered, 'It's nothing, luv. Nothin' at all.'

So, for the first time I entered the echoing hollowness of Liverpool Cathedral. It was overwhelming. Soaring pillars of tawny pink sandstone, huge stained-glass windows, their myriad colours reflected on the smooth grey stone floor, a welter of beauty for a sensitive seventeen-year-old, a fitting place for God to dwell. Surely, I thought, God Himself is present here.

Mother and Fiona had entered by another door, and I stood alone for a moment almost afraid to advance into such a place. Then a lady from the church fussed forward, led me into a corner, pinned a veil over my newly washed hair and straightened my dress. 'You haven't got any gloves!' she exclaimed, throwing up her hands. I looked down at my work-reddened hands and then at the hands of the other boys and girls, standing soberly near me. Everyone had on white gloves, except me. I blushed to the roots of my hair. All the sense of oneness with the beauty around me vanished. Would God ever forgive the lack of white gloves?

It was my fault. I had never thought of gloves. I blamed myself, never thinking that Mother, experienced in all things appertaining to etiquette, might have reminded me.

'I suppose you'll have to go without,' said the lady testily. 'Pull your sleeves down as far as you can.'

Hanging my head, I stood alone in a corner, waiting to be marshalled into a procession according to height, and tried to turn my thoughts again to the spiritual aspect of the ceremony, but I could not recapture it. All the pleasure and hope of my beautiful dress was lost, all the tender belief that I was approaching God like a bride ready to offer what little virtue I had to His service was gone, shot down by an impatient woman and the lack of a sixpenny pair of gloves. Ironically, I could have bought them myself, one of my shorthand students having paid me the night before. I began to shiver.

Two by two we advanced towards the old bishop sitting in front of the altar. We knelt before him and he placed his hands firmly on our heads, so that we should not rise prematurely. He said in a loud sonorous voice, 'Defend, O Lord, this Thy child with Thy heavenly grace, that she may continue Thine forever; and daily increase in Thy Holy Spirit, more and more, until she comes to Thy everlasting kingdom. Amen.'

I was so innocent that I expected to feel different after the magical words had been spoken. But I did not. I was still shivering, disconcerted by the importance of outward and visible signs – like gloves – as against the inward and spiritual grace which I had hoped to acquire that day.

Mary had said firmly to Mother that I must have a photograph of myself, to celebrate the event and as a keepsake, so the sixpence which could have been spent on the missing gloves was expended at the local photographer's, who took the first picture of me since I was a little child. Until I looked into his mirror when tidying myself ready for the photograph, I had, of course, no idea what I looked like, because at home we had only a small piece of broken mirror. The photograph was better than I had hoped.

The photograph shows a slender girl with small curves in all the right places. She is dressed in a plain lace gown with the uneven hem which had been fashionable a few years earlier. She has long slender fingers, delicate ankles, and small feet encased in white satin shoes. Her face, clothed in horn-rimmed spectacles too small for her, is as plain as the back of a Liverpool tram.

Chapter thirteen

I was now eighteen, going on nineteen, a plain, silent girl still struggling to stay alive, no longer quite so devoted to the church, deeply distrustful of the motives of those whose lives touched mine, a young woman without hope.

I had been promoted to the Stenographers' Room, working side by side with Miriam, thankful to be at last delivered from the sniggering girls downstairs. My shorthand was almost perfect, thanks to good evening school teaching; my typing was still very faulty because I had taught myself. I had consequently not received a rise in salary, just an improvement in status.

Miriam had for a long time worked very hard to raise money for the volunteers among her Communist associates who went to fight against Franco in the Spanish Civil War. Now, as her fingers flew over the typewriter keys, she raged that the war was lost to the Fascists and soon Europe would be plunged into a much bigger war. She threw herself impetuously into aiding the many Spanish children who had been sent to safety in England and into consoling the wounded, disillusioned returning volunteers.

There was a number of active Communists on our staff, earnest women toiling as social workers in the depths of Liverpool's appalling slums. Despite their desire to recruit to their party, I kept well back from their political endeavours, partly from the fact that my personal life was so full of work that I could not cope with anything as abstract as political beliefs, and partly because of the scarifying stories Father had told me of Communist excesses he had seen during his military service in Russia.

Several stenographers had come and gone during my employment with the Charity, but the Head Typist was still the devout Roman Catholic who tried regularly to save Miriam from her misbegotten ideas and me from the clutches of a heretic church. She was a dear and almost everybody was fond of her, no matter how cross she got about hanging participles and bad spelling. Between her and Miriam I learned to disagree with other people's beliefs and yet have respect for them.

At one point the Charity was so short of funds that she instituted a fine of one penny for every sheet of paper that Miriam and I wasted as a result of typing errors. Miriam promptly said, 'Not bloody likely!' and since I had little money to spare to pay fines, we smuggled screwed up balls of paper containing our typing sins out of the room, by quietly stuffing them into our overall pockets or down our necks. Occasionally, we had the most remarkably lumpy figures.

My life had settled into a dull, fatiguing rut. Ever fearful of unemployment, I clung to my job. Each January or February, I went down with influenza or bronchitis and, in my emaciated state, usually took a month to recover. The Presence always sent my wages to me, no matter how many weeks I was away, a rare generosity in those days.

A few more jobs were becoming available in the beleaguered city. Shadow factories were being built, with an eye to war; and an army of bricklayers and other building workers, though thankful for a small pay packet, cursed with pain as their blistered hands and aching backs got used to working again.

I began to have a faint glimmering of hope that, despite my lack of education, I might be able to find a better job or, by continuing my evening school studies, become well enough informed to join the more privileged green-overalled social workers.

Students came to our office from the Social Science Department of the university, to do some practical work. Our workers gave them lectures, taught them how to interview and took them to see our clients in their homes. Some of the students were horrified at what they saw and were afraid of visiting alone.

In the Committee Room a large bookcase began to be filled with volumes on the theories of social science. Whenever the lecturer forgot to lock the bookcase, I borrowed books for a night or two and read them, slipping them back into the bookcase when the room was empty. Sometimes the theories and the interpretations of statistics made me laugh, and I thought of the shrewd exploiters of social assistance amongst whom I lived. Some of our neighbours knew every trick and used extremely agile brains to obtain what they needed from the many agencies in the city; it was almost like a business to them. They were all poor, but it was often not the most needy who received the most help. Now, three generations later, this swindling has become an art, and some people live very comfortably with it. They would probably do equally well if they turned their astuteness towards earning a living. Crying poverty, however, can be a good excuse for shrugging off the weight of responsibility for one's life.

The books opened up to me the world of theory, and I began to understand that there were people who spent their lives trying to find the underlying principles upon which society and nature itself were built. Pondering upon theological questions was something to which my history reading had introduced me; now I became interested in what might be going on in the university. It was further intensified by a casual conversation with one of our older students, who told me that he had been a weaver for twelve years and had, during that time, managed to study enough to matriculate. He had also saved enough to put himself through university. For a moment my ambitions soared. Then he said, 'I couldna ha' done it without me Mam and Dad. They just asked a bit for me food – and they gave me a room to work in – you need a room of your own to do aught. Me Dad was really good. He went without to buy me books and me Mam took in washing. Soon I'll be able to help them.'

The ambition flopped like a balloon with a leak. My parents took from their girls; they did not give. They might occasionally encourage verbally, but they would not help. Any money they had, any ambition they felt, was channelled to the boys. Fiona, Avril and I were always just useful wage earners.

Alan, nearly six feet tall, though very thin, joined the Auxiliary Air Force and clumped about in strong black Air Force boots. He shone them to a jetty perfection every Sunday morning. He had an Air Force uniform, with brass buttons which were also polished with the aid of endless tins of Brasso. He learned to press his uniform himself, a radical decision brought about because once when pressing his trousers I had burned a hole in them.

Every Saturday and Sunday, he went to an airfield to be trained, first in ordinary drills and physical fitness programmes, then to work, as he said, on *real* aircraft with *real* tools. The planes were Hawker Hind biplanes, which went all of one hundred and seventy miles an hour. He was thrilled, and concentrated on the work with passionate intensity. His thin wrists strengthened as he learned to use tools, and the regular exercise broadened his shoulders. He began to walk with more self-assurance. He was paid for his service and was allowed to keep the money in addition to his pocket money.

He was generous by nature, and he would often treat the younger children to the Saturday matinée at the Rialto Cinema. They ate ice cream sandwiches during the intermission and had a wonderful time shrieking encouragement to film heroes like Tom Mix as, on his white horse, he galloped after the 'baddies', who always rode black horses.

Fiona, after spending two miserable weeks in suspense, had been engaged by the magazine dealer and was very happy, working the addressograph and, when business was slack, reading all the magazines, from *True Confessions* to *Good Housekeeping*, not to speak of a number of American magazines for men, which, she told me, were utterly shocking. Her employers treated her like one of the family. She was soon earning fifteen shillings a week, the same as me. She paid half of it to Mother for her food and kept the rest for travelling expenses and pocket money. Mother still bought her clothes, which put her away ahead of me financially.

Every night she went to bed with her hair in curling rags, until she could afford a permanent wave. I wanted such a wave, too, but had not the faintest hope of being able to afford it. I had no time to put my hair in rags, so I still had long hair pulled back into a bun.

Her boy friends multiplied, so her entertainment was paid for by a series of devoted swains. Sometimes, she would beg me to tell a more ambitious one at the front door that she was out, while she slipped through the back door to meet someone else. Her social life became one of the first family jokes at which we all laughed.

It was apparent to me that Father was now earning more than he used to. He, too, began to have a modest social life, when he met his colleagues at various public houses in the city. Several times he went to concerts at the Philharmonic Hall, newly rebuilt after a disastrous fire, which Brian and Tony had enjoyed watching. He managed to buy a suit and an overcoat and occasionally shoes and shirts.

Cinemas bored him, so he did not go to them. He did not give any more money to the home, which caused constant flareups between Mother and him. His main argument was that to retain his job he had to have a minimum of clothing, which he would certainly never get if he did not buy it himself. To that end he had to save some money. Mother would come flying back at him, that he smoked and drank too much, to which he would promptly retort that she spent most of her evenings at the cinema – she went at least twice a week – and that she also smoked like a proverbial chimney. Then they would rake up every possible transgression since the day of their marriage, and accuse and counter-accuse until the family fled or was reduced to tears and impassioned pleas to them to stop.

Though Mother was now very strong physically, she was feeling the effect of the change of life, something I had never heard of until Miriam mentioned it in connection with her mother. Mother's temper was so unpredictable that if she was more unbalanced than usual we did not notice it. She complained, however, of being overly hot and she sometimes looked as if she had fever. Miriam called these attacks hot flushes and advised me to be patient with her and encourage her to rest. I made a great effort to hold my tongue when she was being particularly vicious in her remarks, and tried to help more in the house when she obviously did not feel well.

At nearly nineteen I was an adult and better able than I had been to assess soberly what was happening to any of us. Once Mother realised that I understood what was happening to her, she seemed glad to be able to speak frankly to me about it. I encouraged her to see the doctor from time to time, and though there was no real aid then for this intense physical upheaval, he was able to comfort her by assuring her that it would pass.

Rest was possible, because she did not work full time, and when all the children were at school she could go to bed in the afternoon and get up late in the morning. Whatever cleaning and washing there was to be done was usually achieved at the weekend when I was at home. She began again to read regularly, and drew real enjoyment from the great storytellers of the time – Edgar Wallace, Jeffrey Farnol, P. G. Wodehouse, Rafael Sabatini and many others. She had been a librarian before her marriage and she liked to discuss what she had read. In me she found a willing listener.

Through her guardian, who owned a string of private libraries, she had met many of the early twentieth century writers and in those days had read much more deeply than she did in her later years. It dawned on me that her knowledge of literature had in part guided me, because every time I was ill – which was at least twice a year – she would bring me her own choice of books from the public library to read in bed. It was she, I recollected, who had brought me the first books I read on Japanese and Chinese history and travel books on South America, a continent I had never thought about before then and a fascinating area for further study.

This shared love of books formed a slender bridge

between us, and I began to find it easier to talk to her, though on a shallow level, about other concerns in which I was interested, like the war we were all afraid would break out and about the refugees pouring in from Europe.

Mother feared for her sons. She dreaded them being butchered as her own generation had been, though I once heard her remark that she had 'done her duty to the nation by producing four sons.' The idea that to produce soldiers was the duty of a mother shocked me beyond measure, but to women of her age, of the officer class, it must have seemed natural.

As a result of the battle-axes being laid down between us, though never buried, at the time of the office Christmas dance I felt brave enough to say that for once I would like to attend.

'Do you think you could help me buy a second-hand dress?' I begged humbly. 'I have never been to the office parties before, and Miriam thinks I should – I might meet some of the Committee members – and that might help me with promotion later on.' Miriam was nothing if not practical, despite her ideals.

Mother pondered over this, and said, 'I'll see.'

A few days later, she came home with a long white rayon taffeta dress, which she had bought from a girl she knew in one of the stores. My share of the cost – five shillings – was paid in two instalments, as my shorthand student paid me. The material of the dress was delicately patterned in fine red and green stripes and at the back it had long ruffles running from waist to hem. The sleeves were short and puffed and the low V-neck had a diamante clasp tucked into it. Though it was not particularly fashionable, it fitted me and Fiona said it looked quite pretty.

The white stockings bought for my Confirmation had, because of their colour, survived Fiona's marauding, so they were ready to hand, and Mother gave me the pawn ticket so that I could retrieve the white satin slippers and the petticoat from Uncle's.

The pawnbroker was Jewish, portly. What hair he had was curled tightly round a bald patch. The light of the bare electric bulb above his high counter shone on his olive face and made his heavy watch chain glitter. He was an old friend.

While the apprentice went up into the loft to retrieve the cloth-wrapped bundle, I told him shyly about the dance, and then confided that I had not been to a dancing class since I was eleven and feared I might not be able to dance.

'T' boys'll soon learn yez,' he assured me with a grin. 'Eee, now, I wish I could coom meself. But me wife'll never let me off the hook, yer know. Proper hard case she is.'

I laughed. 'I think the girls are allowed to bring a boy friend – but, of course, I haven't got one.'

'Aye, give yerself time, luv. You'll soon find one.'

I smiled, feeling suddenly a little flattered by his pleasantries, though I did not think that boy friends were likely to enter my life.

*

I sat quietly on a chair at the edge of the dance floor

for the entire evening, watching the colourful dancers.

'What else can you expect?' I asked myself. The other girls had each brought a partner. Miriam did not come, having Party affairs to attend to. Except for an elderly gentleman, who, after bowing and making a polite inquiry, brought me a dish of ice cream and a glass of lemonade, I was left alone. After a few moments of laboured remarks about the inclemency of the weather, the gentleman was drawn away by a more thoughtless and equally bored Committee member. I ate my ice cream and sipped the lemonade with what I hoped was a look of jaded sophistication, and at about half-past ten I went to the ladies' cloakroom and retrieved my old brown coat and outdoor shoes. After putting on these shabby garments, I put a carefully reserved silver threepenny piece in the attendant's saucer. She looked up from her knitting and said, 'Thank you, Miss,' a slight surprise in her thick, Liverpool voice.

It was drizzling as I dawdled back up the hill from the city restaurant in which the dance had been held. I held up the long dress from the wet pavement and the satin shoes hung from the fingertips of my other hand. Occasionally, I heaved a great sigh. The whole great expense had been for nothing.

Only Mother was up when I entered the living room. She was sitting with her feet braced high against one side of the big kitchen fireplace, her dress slipped back above her knees, to ease her veins. She laid her book down on her lap, and asked, 'Well, how was it?'

'A flop,' I replied, laying the precious slippers carefully down on a chair. 'I didn't get a dance.'

'You didn't stay till the end? It's only eleven now.'

'I could not sit there – through the night – until one in the morning – it would be too humiliating. Not one of the girls even spoke to me.'

Mother bit her lips. 'I'm sorry, dear,' she said, and she sounded as if she really was. Then after a moment, as I peeled off my coat, she added some sound advice. 'You'll have to stop looking like a frozen rabbit. Men don't like plain girls – and girls who look both plain and dull never get anywhere. You must smile – look gay.'

I sighed, and tried to smile. 'I expect you're right,' I agreed.

The next day the pretty dress, the petticoat and the beloved white satin shoes were bundled up in a white cloth and returned to Uncle.

Chapter fourteen

Nineteen-thirty-eight was the year that Mr Neville Chamberlain, our Prime Minister, sold Czechoslovakia down the river, in order to gain time for us. The word 'appeasement' entered our vocabulary, appeasement of a raving lunatic called Adolf Hitler, who with his Panzer divisions was mopping up the map of Europe. It seemed that after every visit Alan made to the cinema, he would remark that the Paramount news reels had shown the takeover of another country.

At first we all felt a sense of relief when an ailing Mr Chamberlain, supported by his black umbrella, came home from Europe and announced, 'Peace in our time'. It was peace bought at the expense of Czechoslovakia; and it seemed that gradually in the city a great sense of shame welled up. 'Letting a pack of bloody gorillas loose on them,' I heard a station porter say angrily.

The sacrifice *did* gain us time, we all knew that, time to mobilise the fleet, time to extend the barracks just off Princes Road, to fill factories at Speke with the machinery of war, expand the fire brigade, plan the evacuation of the city, time to write innumerable pamphlets which fluttered through our letter box on what to do in an air raid, gas attack, food shortage, petrol rationing, evacuation of school children – it went on and on.

A pile of gas masks in neat cardboard boxes arrived on our living room table, to make the children giggle and shiver nervously as we tried them on, and were suddenly converted into anonymous, long-snouted aliens.

It was taken for granted that if we had to go to war our cities would within a few days be flattened by air raids. Liverpool was our paramount western port, a legitimate target. I found that I was not much afraid at the prospect of death, only of being half dead beneath a mountain of rubble. I wondered if in such a situation I could commit suicide by swallowing my tongue as it was said the poor suffering Ethiopians did. Death – to be dead – did not seem to be much worse than being alive.

Mother fervently thanked God that only Alan was old enough to be called up. Alan was wildly excited, and spent every moment he could at the airfield. Father, who had fought the war to end all wars, looked particularly pinched and sad as he read the headlines in the *Echo*. He went out and bought himself a small atlas from the local tobacconist, and with more perception of the future than our army generals, spent evenings plotting the advance of the Japanese in China, a fray which had been pushed to the back pages of the papers.

I had my usual dose of flu during February, and it left me with a cough which was a nuisance to the whole family. I determined to try to save up for a holiday. I discovered from a book at work that there was a Girls' Holiday Home on the seafront at Hoylake in the Wirral, across the river. They charged about a pound for a week's stay, not a very large sum, though it would take me a long time to save it, and the shilling or so train fare.

I instituted an iron discipline. No trams at all, no twopenny cinema shows of old films at the Central Hall, only a penny bun for lunch instead of a threepenny soup, and, most difficult of all, making my easily laddered rayon stockings last longer – the main difficulty was keeping them out of the clutches of Fiona and Mother. They cost ninepence a pair and were my biggest single expense. I relooped ladders with the aid of a darning needle, an eye-straining, time-consuming job. I darned and redarned the heels, which badly fitting secondhand shoes tended to wear through very quickly. The money saved was carried in a little cloth bag on a string round my neck, and no matter how much Mother whined I never admitted its existence.

After a bitter battle, Mother managed to squeeze out of me a further two shillings and sixpence from my small wages. This left me with exactly one shilling to cover all my needs, and in a desperate position. Any money for my own existence had to be earned by teaching shorthand to pupils in their homes.

Six or seven shillings would feed a woman quite well. What I ate at home would cost about three shillings, so Mother was doing quite well out of me. My one joy during this period was going to the theatre with my friend, Sylvia, the money for which was provided to all the staff by a kindly Greek interested in the work of the Charity who employed me. I used to live for those evenings spent tucked up on the topmost bench of the Liverpool Repertory Theatre, one of the finest repertory theatres in the country.

The village in which the Girls' Holiday Home was situated was the village in which Grandma lived. I had spent many months of childhood with her. I used to cuddle up by her side while she taught me to read from the Bible; and, from dog-eared sheets of music, how to read the notes.

Grandma was short, plump, and always dressed in black silk or satin, skirts almost touching the floor, a boned, white lace modesty vest filling the neckline in a long vee-shape from her tiny pink ear tips to her waist. She had a hearty, merry laugh and could be very witty. As she shook her head the front curls of her snowy wig bounced gently on her forehead. When she went out to shop in the village a huge hat was skewered with long hat pins on to the top of the wig. The hat was always heavily trimmed with black, grey or white satin, sometimes held by a large diamante brooch or by a bunch of dark red cherries – very dashing – or black feathers. Because going to Liverpool to buy a new hat was an exhausting operation, my two aunts who lived with her would periodically retrim her hats for her. I accepted as natural that her clothes were always black, as were those of her very dignified circle of lady friends. Widows wore black, and a few of the older ones wore tiny black bonnets like Queen Victoria's, with a black veil which could shroud the face or be flung back, according to the official depths of one's mourning. Victoria had set the fashion for widows, a fashion nearly as repressive as that for widows in India. Grandma had been a widow for forty years. In its almost unbearable boredom, it must have seemed to such a lively woman like a life prison sentence.

Dare I go to see Grandma while I was in Hoylake, I wondered. I had dreamed for years of doing so, had wanted to run away to her when first I faced the appalling poverty of Liverpool. Father had not attempted to get into touch with her, as far as I knew, since their final quarrel when he went bankrupt, and of latter years I had refrained from visiting her because of his bitter remarks that I would not be welcome. But Father was her baby, who had arrived long after his nearest sister, and they must sometimes have wanted very much to see each other. He had also managed to quarrel furiously with his two sisters who lived with her. They did not approve of the gay life he had led nor did they approve of Mother, who, they felt, was not quite a lady, having worked for her living.

During our early years in Liverpool, a small parcel postmarked Hoylake, would arrive from time to time. It always contained a pair of very soft, finely knitted children's combinations; there was never any note. Avril or Edward would rejoice for weeks in the warm comfort of the garments. Mother always wrote a polite thank-you note to Grandma -- nothing more. I wondered sometimes what Grandma thought about during the long afternoons when she must have sat, as was her custom, in her sunny lace-curtained sitting room, cat on knee, and knitted. Did she grieve? Or was she sustained by righteous indignation? Had she any inkling at all about what was happening to us, that we looked like children who had suffered in an Indian famine?

After a noisy row with Mother about my duplicity in saving for a holiday and about my grim determination to go on it, regardless of the fact that Edward needed new shoes, it was with mixed feelings that I carried a shopping bag containing a change of clothes down the long slope of King's Gap to the sea. It was said that King William's troops set sail for Ireland from here, to fight the Battle of the Boyne, a battle celebrated annually by Liverpool Protestants with a great procession, in defiance of Roman Catholic wrath.

The wind from Liverpool Bay blew my hat off as I turned to walk along the Promenade. Along here, in a bright red brick house which was a nursing home, I had been born in a bed relinquished to my labouring mother by a wounded soldier, who lay on the floor in the passage while I yelled my first unhappy breath. Because the nursing home staff were swamped by wounded men, this man tended my mother and washed my nappies for her, while Father fought in Russia and did not know for a long time that I was born.

I ran my hand along the iron rail of the Promenade. Here, as a six-year-old, I had squeaked delightedly when a young fisherman picked me up and ran agilely along the top of the iron railings while the incoming tide lashed at the wall below us. From here, I had once or twice sailed out in his fishing boat with his brothers. The boat was a bouncing cockle of a craft which stank of fish. No wonder I am never seasick; my introduction to the sea was so happy. Grandma must have wondered once or twice why my discarded clothes smelled so badly. I never told her because officially I was spending the day with a lonely small boy who lived on the sea front. I did not like him, so when sent trustingly down the road to his house, I just went on to the beach and messed about amongst the fishing fleet, if it was in.

As far as I could see, there was no fishing fleet any more, not a sign of a sail or a net; only small pleasure craft heeled half over in the sand, waiting for the tide to come ripping in past the Hoyle Bank and round Hilbre Island and set them dancing.

The Holiday Home was spartan, but I rejoiced in clean sheets and shining floors. I was allotted a small windowless cubicle in which to sleep. It was stuffy with much use, and the whole building smelled of a mixture of floor polish, cabbage and cats.

I left the door of the cubicle open and sat down on the narrow bed and read innumerable notices on the wall telling me not to sit on the bed, to turn off the light, to be in at ten p.m., not to smoke, to come to meals promptly, etc. I wondered what to do. Girls cursing under their breath stumbled past to other cubicles, pushing heavy suitcases ahead of them.

The near darkness of the cubicle was becoming depressing, when suddenly the suitcases of two girls jammed in the narrow passageway. They swore ripely and richly in strongly accented German. Then they stood and laughed at each other. I jumped up eagerly to lend a hand, and between the three of us we managed to move the cases, though we left a long scratch on the varnished wall of the passage.

The girls were the daughters of Swiss hoteliers. They had been working in England for nearly a year as servants, in order to perfect their English. Their employers had sent them to the Holiday Home while they themselves took a vacation. They, too, had very little money. We were reciprocally pleased with each other. I could understand their German and they could follow my accentless English. It was a joy to me to show them the Wirral.

At low tide, carrying our shoes and some sandwiches, we paddled out to Hilbre Island, stopping to watch the shrimps tickling our toes, and the local people bent double as they dug for cockles and mussels. We watched the sea roar in again round the tiny island, while we hunted for seashells along its shore. In the evening, when the water had silently retreated, we strolled slowly back across the wet sand, while the hills of North Wales went purple and the lights of West Kirby began to wink out ahead. As we walked, I pointed out to them the stumps of a great primeval forest sticking out of the sand, and we imagined tiny brown men in coracles drifting round the mouths of the Dee and the Mersey.

Puffing in the boisterous wind, we walked the length of the great seawall which held back the tide from the villages of Moreton and Leasowe. Behind the wall rich market gardens showed neat squares of different shades of green. Dutch dike specialists came from time to time to inspect this great sea wall and it was much admired. Father used to say that the best cure for a cold was to walk its length and let the wild clean air from the Bay blow the germs out, which probably was not quite what the builders had in mind.

We scrambled down into an abandoned quarry, in the hope of finding some of the nests of the innumerable birds who made it their home. We did not find a nest and we had a panicky few minutes before we managed to haul ourselves out, dusty, breathless and laughing. There were no birds except sparrows in our street in Liverpool, and the riotous singing in that quarry was like a Polish choir going full belt.

Inland, we discovered small villages in winding lanes, and we would walk along them singing softly together, enjoying the great swishing trees and eating penny ice creams bought from minute village shops.

I was happy with my gay companions. Good though very plain food helped my famished body, and the cough lessened. But all the time I thought of Grandma.

One day we passed along the road in which she lived, three giggly, gawky girls, two in light sleeveless summer dresses, one in a winter skirt and crumpled blouse, and I glanced quickly, almost frightenedly, at the house which meant so much to me.

It looked exactly the same as I remembered it. Lace curtains draped round the windows, wrought-iron gate, straight red-tiled path to the front door, carefully swept and washed, and a patch of neatly cut lawn with a few recalcitrant daisies scattered on it like stars.

I do not know why it is that some front doors look more closed than other shut doors, but to me Grandma's door looked that day particularly blank and forbidding. I did not sleep much during the night as I wondered whether if I knocked and it were opened, there would be any welcome inside.

Towards the end of the week, the two Swiss girls became acquainted with two young men who had been caulking a rowing boat on the shore. I had walked up to the village to buy a small gift for Mother, a peace offering.

On the Friday, the girls received an invitation from the boat caulkers to go out for a row, so I had my last afternoon in Hoylake to myself. At first I sat in the gloom – on my bed – and read the notice which said that one should not use the bedroom in the daytime. I felt very lonely in the deserted Home, and chewed my thumb unhappily.

Then, as if propelled by instinct alone, I got up and quickly washed my hands and face in the communal bathroom, changed my blouse, galloped down the stairs and ran along the Promenade, not pausing for breath until I was faced with the slope of King's Gap. My battered handbag was clutched in one hand, while with the other I tried to stop the hairpins falling out of my hair in the playful breeze.

Breathless, I opened the gate and ran up the familiar path, as if afraid that if I were observed from the windows someone would stop my entering.

I knocked.

There was no response. Perhaps everyone was out.

Shyly, I knocked again, and there was the sound of the well-remembered step of one of my aunts.

She opened the door, looked at me blankly, and then smiled. 'Why, Helen!' she exclaimed.

Still panting, I asked, 'Is Grandma at home?'

My aunt hesitated, and then said, 'Yes, she is. Do come in.'

I entered and paused in the doorway, while the feeling of the house rushed over me. The grandfather clock was still ticking its friendly tick, the house still smelled sweetly of flowers, polish and women's perfumes. No odour of tobacco or cooking. The antique china pieces still decorated a small shelf above the sitting room door, through which my aunt had vanished, her pink-striped Macclesfield silk dress flicking behind her, as she shut the door after her.

As breath returned to me, panic also invaded. What was I going to talk about?

My aunt was back in the hall, and saying, 'Go in, Helen.' She gestured with one thin, delicate hand. She closed the door behind me as I went in, and I could hear her going upstairs. I felt the same fear that I always did when the Presence sent for me to scold me for typing errors.

The room was shadowed in comparison with the bright sunshine outside, and for a second I could hardly see the figure seated near the fireplace in one of the chintz-covered easy chairs.

I caught my breath sharply, as if someone had stabbed me with a pin.

A tiny, shrunken person, swathed in black seemed engulfed in the chair. Beneath a white wig which appeared too large, two dim blue eyes smiled at me in a face hung with paperwhite folds of skin. The familiar brooch on the lace under her chin looked big and clumsy. Hands which seemed only bone and blue veins rested on a shallow china bowl of green peas, and on a small table by the chair was a basket full of pea shells and a brown paper bag, which presumably held more of the vegetable.

I stood awkwardly in front of her. 'Granny,' I said, while inside my heart cried. I had forgotten what great age did to the human frame. To me she was eternal. I was suddenly and brokenly aware of all the years that I had missed being with her. She was in her nineties, and though I did not care very much about death for myself, I wanted her to live for ever.

'How very nice,' she said, in a weak but clear voice. 'Come here, dear.'

I went to her and carefully kissed the papery cheek. She smelled sweetly of Yardley's lavender, as usual, and her lace modesty vest was fresh and white. 'Sit down, dear, and tell me about yourself. Bring that chair close to me.'

So I brought a straight chair and sat knee to knee with her. While we shelled peas together, I told her about the Holiday Home and about my job and how I hoped one day to be a social worker. Somehow, I could not bring myself to tell her about the frightful privation we had endured, nor about the steady hunger and cold, the lack of blankets, woollens and coal from which we still suffered. She had obviously been ill and I was not too certain that she comprehended all that I was saying to her.

When the peas had all been shelled, she leaned her head against the back of the chair and closed her eyes. I stopped talking, and she reached out her hand. I held the fragile fingers, while she rested, and thought about a small girl whose hand she had held through many a walk to the village. Now, it was I who was holding her hand.

After a while, my aunt came briskly into the room, and said, 'It's time for your walk, Mother.' She picked up the bowl of peas, the brown paper bag and the basket of shells. 'Perhaps Helen would like to go with you.'

'Certainly,' I agreed.

Grandma opened her eyes and looked at me. There was a slight twinkle in them. 'Yes. We'll go together. It will give Aunt Emily a rest.'

A long black coat was brought in by Aunt Emily and the old lady was eased into it. Carpet slippers were exchanged for tiny button shoes, which Aunt Emily did up. A hat as monumental as I ever remembered, trimmed with a touch of white – Grandma's only acknowledgment of summer – was carefully pinned on by Grandma herself. Then she sat down on a straight chair for a moment to recover from the exertion.

'How long for, Auntie?' I asked.

'About half an hour. Keep off the Promenade. The wind is too much for her.'

I nodded, and she opened the door for us. Grandma carefully crept across the rugs, and I eased her down the single step. She shuffled forward along the red-tiled path.

It seemed a terribly long way to the gate, and miles to the end of the road. However, Grandma silently concentrated on walking, and we turned into King's Gap, away from the sea. After about five minutes on the gentle slope, Grandma gasped, 'I think I have to sit down, dear.'

'Oh, goodness!' I looked wildly round for a bench or a low wall. The nearest place was a wooden seat about a hundred yards away. I pointed it out.

Grandma was panting, her mouth a little open. 'It seems a long way.'

'It is closer than returning home, Granny. I could carry you.'

She smiled up at me with the bright flash that I had known as a child, as if her mind had reverted to its old clarity. 'No, no. Don't be afraid, my dear. We will do it a step at a time.'

It was the longest hundred yards I have ever walked, but we finally got there and sank thankfully on to the weathered seat. I put my arm around Grandma's shoulder and she leaned against me and closed her eyes. It was like holding a small sheaf of wheat, the same sense of easy crushability.

I looked down at the top of the satin-trimmed hat, now pushed askew because she had laid her head on my shoulder. My old enemy, despair, washed over me. Memories shot through my mind, a belief in her inherent goodness, gratitude for the skills she had passed to me. She had taught me more subtle things than reading and sewing, to put on a cheerful face so that one does not depress others, to face with fortitude what cannot be changed, daily courtesies, which always surfaced when I was with people of my own class. My aunts, too, had been very patient with a silent, obstinate little girl.

Now I knew in my heart that Grandma had come

close to the end of her allotted span, and I did not know how to face the idea. I wanted to wrap her up in cotton wool, like something infinitely precious that must be preserved at all costs.

But nothing I could do would stop the remorseless march of the years – and it was obvious that the aunts were caring for her very well.

The return was accomplished by slow shuffles and pauses, a trifle more easily since the mild slope was downwards. Grandma did not say much, except for an occasional deprecating chuckle at her own inadequacies as she stopped to pant.

The front door opened as we approached up the path, and I pushed Grandma ahead of me up the step. She stopped for a second when safely landed, and then toddled into the hall. My aunt said, 'Thank you very much indeed for taking her out. She has to rest now.' She began to close the door, and added, with a bright smile, 'It must be your tea time by now.' Then she quietly shut the door.

I looked dumbly at the blank piece of wood in front of my nose, hardly able to believe that it was truly shut. A slow burning flush flooded my face and I turned angrily away and marched down the hill to the sea. The wind rushed up to meet me and helped to cool the fury within. I dropped over the railings of the Promenade on to the deserted powdery sands, and turned towards my favourite place, the Red Rocks.

Until the water began to lap close, I did not think of the tide cutting me off. I hastily took off shoes and stockings and paddled quickly the last few yards.

Such was the respect for property instilled into me that it never occurred to me to climb the sloping walls which protected the private gardens running down to the beach, and walk through to the road, and so save myself from the icy water.

I sat down on the rocks at a safe elevation and wrung out the hem of my heavy skirt. Then, cross-legged, chin in hand, I watched for a long time the tide race in and the sailing boats set out from Hoylake and West Kirby. I forgot about tea at the Holiday Home and was aware only of the pain inside me.

The sun sank slowly down in the centre of the sea, leaving an emerald green and bright pink sky. Grandma had a little oil painting which she said Turner had painted of that sunset. The painting was dark from years of being too close to the smoke of the fireplace, but as a child I had loved to run my fingers round its elaborately carved gilt frame.

With twilight, it became cold, so, shivering, I put on my shoes and stockings and clambered over the rocks to the road, and with head bent with grief and no little sense of humiliation I plodded along the almost deserted road back to the Home.

Chapter fifteen

At home, Mother had recovered from her vexation at my daring to go for a holiday. She was further mollified by the gift which I had brought her, a pretty box covered with sea shells. Both she and Father were intensely interested when I told them that I had been to see Grandma.

'Did she ask about us?' inquired Mother.

I looked at them both sadly, and had to admit that she had not asked a single question about the family, not even about Father.

'She's very weak,' I defended. 'I'm not sure that she is quite aware of what is going on around her. And, of course, I got cut off rather abruptly from her, when the door was shut on me. I had imagined that we would talk more over a cup of tea – or something.'

Father's voice was acidulous. 'I'm surprised they let you in.'

In June of 1939, a strange man presented himself at our door. He was small, dressed in a belted raincoat and a trilby hat. Father had answered the door and thought he was a salesman. He was just about to say, 'Not today, thank you,' when the man said, 'You must be Mr Forrester?'

Father agreed that he was.

'I am sorry to tell you that your mother has died,'

the stranger baldly announced. He then went on to say when the funeral would be held.

I had been standing on the staircase watching the scene, and the cold words bit into me. I wondered how much more they must have hurt Father. He looked very white, as he ushered the visitor into our living room. Our tenants in the front room had recently found a house and left us, so our home smelled a lot better – but the sitting room was still bare of furniture. I followed them into the living room.

Mother was introduced as the visitor edged his way into the crowded room, and when they were all seated Father asked how Grandma had died. My eyes misted, as I leaned against the door jamb. I remembered the little wraith with whom I had walked. It would not have taken much to blow her out of this life.

'She died in her sleep – from a stroke,' the visitor said. He went on to explain that she had had a stroke a year earlier and then, more recently, a series of smaller ones.

Father and Mother sat quiet for a minute. Then Father realised he had not inquired who the man was, and now he did this. The man gave his name and said he was a friend of the family. He had business in Liverpool, so had been asked to convey the news of the death to us.

Father closed his eyes. Despite the gravity of Mother's expression, there was a bright gleam in her eyes, which I did not understand.

Father said he would attend the funeral and looked inquiringly at Mother. Mother nodded negatively. 'Mrs Forrester will not attend.' He looked unhappily at me. 'If my eldest daughter wishes, she will accompany me.' I lowered my eyelids and made no response. I had not thought about the funeral.

Politenesses were exchanged and the man was ushered out. 'Unfeeling bastard,' exclaimed Father, as he came back in. He sat down slowly on his battered easy chair and put a shaky hand over his eyes.

'I'm sorry, Daddy,' I said gently. 'After all, he was a stranger – he didn't *have* to come.'

After some dithering, I decided not to go to the funeral, though as a child I had been very fond of my aunts. I was afraid they would think ill of me, because I had no mourning clothes and no money to buy any. I said to Mother, 'I would have to ask for a half day off – and every office boy who wants to go to a football match says he needs time off to go to his grandmother's funeral – and I've had so much sick leave that they might feel I was imposing on them by asking for more.'

Mother sighed, and agreed. 'Remember your grandmother as she was, dear, when you were little.'

She had understood, and she had called me 'dear'. I was grateful to her.

The day of Grandma's funeral was overcast and rainy in Liverpool. Mother stitched a black band of ribbon, culled from an old felt hat, round the left arm of Father's overcoat, a sign of mourning for those who could not afford black clothes. He shaved slowly and carefully that morning and gave his shoes a tremendous polish in a kind of dumb honour to his mother. I checked that his socks did not have holes in their heels, and wept all the way to work.

When he arrived home in the evening, he was emotionally exhausted. For once, Mother fussed round him. She made him tea, and put more coal on the fire to dry the legs of his trousers, which were soaked, as were his muddy shoes and socks which were put inside the fender to steam on the hearth. He had walked all the way to and from James Street station, because he did not have enough money for a tram, after paying the train fare to Hoylake.

'Did they give you anything to eat?' I asked, as he sipped the scalding brew from his cup.

He nodded negatively.

While Mother sat with him, I went into the kitchen, made toast, and in some bacon fat fried the solitary egg sitting on the shelf. Fortunately, all the children had gone out to friends' houses to play, so the house was quiet.

Father was not accustomed to so much attention, and after he was warmed and fed and had returned to sit in his easy chair, he cheered up a little.

'They all stood on one side of the grave – and I stood on the other. I felt like a pariah. Nobody spoke to me, except the solicitor, who said I had better come back to the house with them for the reading of the will.'

Again I saw the sudden gleam in Mother's eye – and this time I understood it. Grandma had quite an estate to leave. The unlit cigarette between her lips quivered.

Father sighed heavily. 'You will remember that years ago, my brothers and I signed an agreement that the contents of Mother's home should not be broken up but would be left to my sisters, so that they were assured of a home.' He paused and took off his spectacles to rub his eyes. Then he laughed, a small deprecating laugh. 'That was before your uncles died – and in the days when we had a home worth speaking of.'

Mother nodded. She tore a piece of newspaper from the *Echo* on her lap and started absently to fashion it into a spill.

'Well, of course, that still holds,' continued Father. 'Then in her will she left all her own property – that's the dowry she brought with her when she married father, to the aunts, so as to give them a better income to live on, I suppose – I don't think they have a great deal themselves.'

Mother leaned towards the fire to light the spill and then with the flame she lit her cigarette, puffed and blew the smoke towards the blackened ceiling.

'What about your reversionary interest?' she asked.

'What on earth is a reversionary interest?' I interjected.

Father turned to me. 'Well, dear, you know your grandfather died when I was a little boy. He left all his property to your grandmother for her lifetime. This meant that she enjoyed the interest – rents – whatever else he had – but she could not touch the capital. The capital was to be divided between his children or their heirs, after your grandmother died.'

I knew my grandfather had been far from poor, and I gasped. 'Does that mean we actually get some money?'

'Well, I had hoped so, though I think that the estate has not prospered because of poor management by his executors. Anyway, the thing is that when you were young, I borrowed from one of your aunts against my interest. Not against all of it by any means.'

He stopped and stared into the fire. Then he took out a cigarette, leaned over and lit it from Mother's.

'Well, what happened?'

'I signed a legal agreement in which I promised to pay interest on the loan – I had expected to pay the loan back quite quickly. I could not repay – and I forgot about the interest until today. She claimed the interest for ten years – and that wiped out my share.'

'Good God!' exclaimed Mother, cigarette half way to her mouth. 'Did she really?'

'Yes.' Father sighed again. 'She was legally entitled to it. Only it never struck me that a sister would actually charge interest.'

I made a face. Father was so unbelievably innocent at times that I wondered how he had survived at all so far.

'Well,' I said slowly, 'I suppose if she had had the money invested all these years, she would have got interest on it – and if she had not spent it, her capital would have increased substantially.'

'True,' said Father sadly. 'She was entitled to it.'

Mother clicked her tongue in exasperation, and unthinkingly stabbed her half-finished cigarette out on the bars of the fireplace. She flung the stub angrily into the unusually cheerful blaze.

And I sat quietly thinking of my usual obsession – cold. I thought of a frigid bed, where I lay with aching limbs beside a restless Avril, whose feet seemed always to be icy, and a patient Fiona who folded her arms tight across her chest and never complained. I dreamed of white sheets and a pile of fluffy blankets piled on top of us – and, yes, a hot water bottle each. And of the boys, inadequately clad, despite their school uniforms paid for by the city, often with wet feet and no gloves. Alan at least had his Air Force boots and a really thick Air Force uniform, so that he was warm during the weekends, but he must have been cold in bed, too. Our house was jerry built and the heat of our single fire was soon dissipated.

I thought wistfully that a small capital sum, if my parents used it sensibly, would save us so much misery – though I had to admit that our present circumstances were a little better than they had been.

'Never mind, Daddy,' I tried to reassure him. 'One of these days, we will have all the basics of life again and be quite comfortable.'

He smiled at me, looking suddenly very like his mother.

Mother looked as if she were about to cry.

A few days later, a small parcel came by mail for me. It contained a watch, and it had come from Hoylake. I presumed it was Grandma's and was delighted that she had remembered me. It was a neat gold one, with a black moire ribbon wrist band, and I put it on with tender pleasure. I never left it off my wrist, so it was never pawned.

Early in the war, when I had enough money to afford it, I took the watch to a reputable jeweller to be cleaned and adjusted. He asked my name, opened the watch and took it into a back room. A moment later, he returned very fast, his face most forbidding. 'We sold this watch to . . . ' and he named my cousin. 'Please explain how you come to have it.' He waited, lips pursed, eyes accusing.

My mouth fell open with shock at the abrasive tone. I licked my lips and swallowed, not knowing what to say. I knew I still looked like a skivvy, a kind of person who would never normally have been in his shop.

'It was left to me by my grandmother,' I faltered. 'The lady you mention is my cousin who lived with her.'

'When?'

I gave the date of my grandmother's death. I was very frightened. I feared he might call the police and accuse me of theft.

'What is your cousin's address?'

I gave my grandmother's address, where I presumed she still lived, and said, trembling, 'She probably bought it as a gift for Grandma.'

The address obviously tallied with the one he had, so he said slowly, 'I see.'

He pulled out a receipt, made it out in my name and, without apology or explanation, handed it to me. 'Ready in a week,' he said.

Badly shaken, I went out of the shop and stood on the pavement and watched unseeingly the rush of lunch hour pedestrians. Because I was obviously so poor, I had been treated as a possible thief. I was outraged.

I never forgot the arrogant jeweller, and I felt a most unchristian satisfaction when his shop was blown up later in the war.

Chapter sixteen

I was nineteen going on twenty and I had never been kissed by a man, other than an occasional peck from Father. I had never gone to an adult party and only once been to a dance. I had never since I was eleven played any games, did not know the meaning of the word *fun*. It seemed as if there was nothing but work in the world. The only real pleasure was my regular visits to the Repertory Theatre with Sylvia and an occasional walk with her.

The dogs of war who were to eat my generation were howling through the streets of Europe. The basement waiting room of the Charity for which I worked was packed with woebegone, nerve-racked Jewish and Trade Union refugees from every country in Europe. Upstairs, in the Interviewing Department, lay a Dictionary of the Languages of Europe and this was handed to non-English-speaking clients, so that they could at least establish for us which country they came from and which language they spoke. We could then obtain an appropriate interpreter. My French and German, though far from perfect, became suddenly useful.

In the parks, trenches were dug as air raid shelters. I remembered stories my father's friends had told, when I was little, of flooded trenches rotten with corpses and preying rats, and I felt sick.

For my twentieth birthday on 6th June, 1939, Friedrich, my ever faithful German pen-friend, now a young officer in the Luftwaffe, sent me a small ivory edelweiss on a gold chain; in his part of Germany the edelweiss was, in the olden days, given by a boy to his prospective bride. It was a lovely gift, the first piece of jewellery that I had ever owned, except for Grandma's watch, and I sighed regretfully over it – an English woman would certainly not be approved of as a wife of a Luftwaffe officer – and I wished that he had followed his original intention of becoming a schoolmaster. With the gift came a charmingly sentimental letter. In answer to a rather depressing letter from me, he assured me that his beloved Fuehrer would never plunge Europe into war. All Herr Hitler wished was to see all German-speaking people united under one flag. One day German travel restrictions would be lifted and we would meet each other and how wonderful that would be.

It could, of course, be that Friedrich was right and all our newspapers were wrong. As an Air Force officer, he might know more than I did of what was happening. Sometimes the *Express* gave the same view as Friedrich, and it was a big newspaper – it should know.

With the edelweiss in my hand, I dreamed wistfully. He had no inkling of the many other problems which I faced. The previous Christmas I had wanted to send him a present, a real challenge for me. I solved it by buying a torn sheet from the second hand shop, for a few pennies. The sides of the sheet were still good, and from that material I had cut six handkerchiefs, and hem-stitched them. The drawn-thread work was trying to the eyes, but the result was attractive. Then I embroidered Father's initials on three of them and Friedrich's on the other three. I had ringed Friedrich's monogram with a ring of tiny roses, all done with white cotton. Both recipients had been delighted.

'What on earth would Friedrich think,' I wondered, with a wry grin, 'if he knew where his gift had come from? What would he think if he saw my home?'

Our sitting room had once more been furnished on the hire purchase system, and we had finally managed to pay off the debts for which we were still responsible on the earlier sets of furniture which had been repossessed by the furniture stores. Father had also bought, on the same plan, a radio which was a great joy to all of us.

The radio ran on batteries and we had periodical crises when new batteries were required. The wet battery had to be recharged about once a week; and I soon learned, after carrying it down to the shop to have this done, to walk down the street with bare legs. The acid from the battery tended to slop down one's legs and burn them. Legs heal eventually – stockings do not. I still carry faint marks on my legs from those acid burns.

Despite the fact that five wages were now coming into the house, none of us earned very much. My parents still had little idea of how to manage a small income, with the result that we were still very poorly fed, often cold, and lacked proper changes of clothing. Shoes still got lined with cardboard to fill the holes in the soles, and I still sat at work with my feet firmly on the floor so that the other girls would not notice the holes.

Mr Ellis, with his formidable tongue, had been replaced by a gentle elderly lady, who was invariably polite and kind to me. Without saying anything, she seemed to understand a little of what was happening to me and the consistent effort I was making to educate myself. She sometimes asked me what plays I had seen – she also received theatre money, as it was called by the staff – and what books I had read recently.

Perhaps it was because of her recommendation that one morning the Presence sent for me.

'Oh, my goodness,' I groaned to Miriam. 'What have I done now?'

The Presence smiled, actually smiled, when after knocking timidly I entered her office.

'Sit down, Miss Forrester,' she ordered briskly.

Nervously I perched on the edge of her visitor's chair. If I had to sit down to hear it, she must have something quite devastating to say.

'Miss Forrester, we are expanding our Bootle office. The District Head at present runs it with the aid of voluntary workers. She does, however, need someone on whom she can rely to assist her. We have decided to appoint an Assistant District Head, and I would like to send you out there.'

I gaped. Presumably I would be a kind of Girl Friday – but the designation of the post put me close to the rank of the long envied green-overalled social workers. The post could lead to further promotion. Perhaps a living wage.

'The salary would be seventeen shillings and sixpence a week,' Miss Danson added, and swivelled herself round to look at me for the first time.

A rise in pay of half-a-crown would just cover the additional long tram journeys out to the north end of the city. It would not stretch to anything more. But it was a break at last.

I smiled. 'I would like that very much,' I assured the Presence enthusiastically, putting to the back of my mind how much the tram journeys would add to my already incredibly long working day.

Full of excitement I broke the news to Mother. She refused to believe that the rise in pay had been so little. 'It amounts to nothing, really,' she fretted. 'They must have given you at least five shillings?'

'They didn't, Mummy, I assure you. But I will get training in actual casework – and that is worth something.'

So, for half-a-crown more than I would have received had I been unemployed, I took on considerable responsibility and continued to live largely on hope.

Bootle had more unemployment, more overcrowding, more pollution, more ignorance, more huge Roman Catholic families floundering in poverty than I had ever seen before. It was even worse than the badly hit south side of the city. No wonder the patient, delicate-looking District Head needed help. With only the Society's small funds available to us, it was like being asked to shovel out a rubbish dump with a teaspoon.

I plunged in to help, but found the greatest difficulty was within myself. I had been so crushed by the staff of the Head Office that I tended never to do anything which I had not been asked to do. I had little natural initiative; only a kind of slave-like mentality. And this had, with much trial and error, to be slowly overcome. If I was to join the green overalls, all of whom had degrees, I realised sadly that I had a long way to go.

One night, as I sat huddled on the tram from Bootle, I pondered over my inabilities, not at that time very clear about what ailed me, knowing only that change I must from the frail, drained woman for whom nobody cared very much, into a more dynamic person. Otherwise, I feared, I did not have much to look forward to in the future.

Left alone with Father one Saturday afternoon, I asked him tentatively if he could think of any other kind of work to which I might aspire. Without a second's thought, he came up with a very good suggestion. 'You might be able to pass the entry exams for the Civil Service by now – they give you quite a wide choice of subjects, you know.'

Half believing, I made inquiries and found he was correct. Father became interested, and I found a schoolmaster willing to coach me in Geography, the weakest subject amongst the rag bag of subjects which I could offer. For five shillings a lesson, half of it contributed by Father, he came to the house in the evenings, and began to teach me about winds, tides and currents and how they affected the layout of the world. And I was hooked. Nobody in my childhood had taught me anything beyond the names of rivers, cities, countries, seas and where they were. Night school was finished for the season, and, fascinated, I studied earnestly from the books he lent me. He came four times. Then I received a brief note from his wife that he had been called up. Reluctantly I returned the books.

A few weeks later, the Civil Service cancelled its examinations for the duration of the war. Nobody seemed to know at that time how they would recruit any staff they would require.

Frustrated, I threw myself once more into an effort to improve my social work.

Chapter seventeen

As war began to breathe down the back of our necks, our socially isolated family received unexpected visitors.

A fussy, elderly man who lived in the next street arrvied to show us how to put on our gas masks. He was apologetic to the ladies because their hair styles were likely to be disturbed by the straps, since it was essential that the masks fit tightly. He recommended our keeping our hair short. He also warned us that mascara was liable to melt and run down our faces while we had our masks on.

Fiona was the only member of the family who used mascara, and she continued placidly to brush it on in front of the piece of mirror wedged into the kitchen window frame. It made her already huge eyelashes even more seductive. She brushed her hair up into the newly fashionable high sweeps round her face, and at the back bouncing curls fell to her shoulders.

My bun got so tangled up with the straps of the mask that it was as well that there never was a gas attack.

The air raid warden knocked peremptorily on our door. He lived a few doors away from us and had been unemployed for years. He had a reputation for being utterly lazy, but he took his present duties very seriously, and demanded to see our blackout curtains.

We had none. We had no curtains at all upstairs, except for a short net curtain across the front bedroom window. We did have, however, the original big wooden shutters of the house in the downstairs rooms, and had always used these instead of curtains in the living room. The warden agreed that these would make excellent blackout and a good defence against flying glass. He tutted like a maiden aunt over the bare bedroom windows, and ordered us to buy black cloth and make curtains.

'Or yer can paste double layers of brown paper over t' panes. Another thing you can do, is make wooden frames covered with thick paper and fit 'em into t' windows each night, like.'

Mother said frostily that we would just have to manage without candlelight in the bedrooms. She was not going to blot out the daylight with brown paper, and she could not afford curtains or frames.

The warden stuck his blue chin in the air and replied that the windows must be covered – by law – in case the flare of a match or other casual light flashed out of them and brought German bombs down upon us.

Mother was not going to take orders from any local oaf, and retorted, 'What rubbish!'

The warden stood firm. 'I tell yez, you'll be fined if you don't cover 'em,' he warned, his dark Irish face grim as he held his temper in.

Muttering maledictions, Mother went out to buy blackout material for the front bedroom. Then, in the copper in the basement, we dyed two of our few sheets and pinned one over the back kitchen window, which lacked shutters, and one over the window of the boys' bedroom. The girls' bedroom window remained bare and, since we could not show a light, we had to fumble round in the dark when going to bed.

The warden was not satisfied. The windows should have sticky tape crisscrossed over them, to stop shattering glass from flying into the rooms. Mother said she would see to it, but she never did, and the patient warden finally acknowledged defeat. Resignedly, he recommended that we sit on the basement steps during raids, that being the safest place in the house.

A school teacher came to explain the need to evacuate Brian, Tony, Avril and Edward to the country, in the charge of their teachers. She was a faded, middle-aged woman in a worn tweed suit, and the children stood around the room and stared at her, as she spoke.

She inquired if we had any relations to whom they could be sent. 'You might prefer that to their going with the school.' Her artificial teeth clicked as she pushed them into place with her tongue.

'No,' replied Mother. Father cleared his throat.

'There are the aunts at Hoylake,' I suggested tentatively. 'Could Avril go to them?'

'I doubt if they would take her,' Father interjected, and it was finally agreed that the children would leave with the school.

Dismayed at the thought of filthy, lousy evacuees from Liverpool or Birkenhead being billetted on them, the aunts had the same idea as I did, and the next day a letter arrived suggesting that they should take in two of the children. Father roared with laughter at the thought of how suddenly important their long-neglected nephews and nieces had become. He turned the letter over and over in his hand, and remarked, 'I can't remember when one of them wrote to me last.'

Mother looked as if she had been caught between the devil and the deep blue sea, and I tried to reassure her.

'They were always very kind to me when I was a child,' I said quickly. 'None of the children will come to harm with them.'

So, as German tanks ploughed across the Polish border, Tony and Edward, with a pitifully small amount of luggage, went off with a school teacher, to meet the aunts they had never seen. I will never forget their tight, white little faces. A stony-faced Avril, determined to be brave, went with them, to live nearby with a friend of the aunts; and for the first time in her memory knew what it was to have good, new clothes bought for her, sleep in a properly equipped bed and be decently fed. Brian, like a young soldier, went with the school to Wales and lived with a postman who was also exceedingly good to him. Despite much kindness, none of the children came through that traumatic time without scars.

The government provided an allowance for the evacuees' board. But later on, they demanded that parents contribute to this cost. On the day they announced this, Mother decided that she could not bear to be parted from her darlings any longer, and they were brought home. If she had to maintain her children, they might as well be at home, air raids notwithstanding. When the raids became very heavy, under pressure from the school, they were re-evacuated, this time to strangers, and they were very unhappy. However, when the Government again demanded money, Mother brought them home. They were thankful to return, despite the danger.

In June, 1939, Alan went gaily off, for the second year, for his annual training camp with the Auxiliary Air Force. It was to be two weeks long and was to be his holiday. We knew that, like the first one he had attended, he would be out in the countryside at a Royal Air Force base being well fed and would be enjoying himself working with tools. He would also be paid, and would return home looking well and with pocket money to spend. Before he went, he bought himself a new sports jacket and trousers, so that off duty he would look smart, and we teased him before he went, about all the feminine hearts he would break during his free evenings. He was happy.

He did not return. There was no letter to say what had happened, and Mother was in a panic. Father said that a number of young men from his office had also not returned from various military training camps where they had gone as Territorials for their summer training. It was part of the national call-up.

About a month later, the postman delivered a small sack containing Alan's unworn sports jacket and trousers. Mother wept. 'He must be dead,' she mourned, and pawned them next time she was short of money.

Father reminded her that the Forces were very good at telegraphing the news of deaths. No news was good news.

Three or four months later, he arrived home on forty-eight hours' leave. He looked even thinner than when he had left us, but it seemed as if he had grown a foot. He had finished an arduous square-bashing, through which all regular recruits had to go, and was now again thankfully working on planes. He was tired and slept most of his leave, but he was still enthusiastic and went back to his base quite cheerfully.

He had obviously had a tough training period, so we refrained from reminding him that we would have been glad of a letter to say where he was. Now we had an address, both Mother and I wrote to him regularly.

Mother forbade me to write to the evacuated children or to go to see them. I was very angry about this, but gave in sulkily when she said, 'Seeing someone from home will upset them.' Despite her argument, she went out to Hoylake to see them and she would never say how she got on with her in-laws. I could not really understand her objection to my going, but she may have been jealous for a long time of my particular position as surrogate mother, and wished to reassert herself with them.

Anyway, I obeyed. I was finding it increasingly hard to face up to Mother. My new job amid appalling squalor, in addition to the long journey out to Bootle, was draining a character already crushed and e[illegible]

It seemed as if the whole population of the country was on the move, as men were called up and women shut down their homes and went back to live with mother, as the children vanished into the countryside, and drafted workers got sent to distant war factories. Lonely youths far from home spent much time cultivating girls who would invite them to their homes, to compensate a little for spartan Victorian barracks or bare, comfortless workers' dormitories. Fiona's dates multiplied exceedingly, and into our emptied house began to drift a curious assortment of men of all nations and all social classes, to eat our rations and warm their wet feet at our single fire, to have their socks darned and their buttons stitched on. Mother was in her element as a hostess, and we all hoped, as the war progressed and the other boys were called up, that somewhere in the world Alan, Brian and Tony were being taken care of, too. I think this was the best contribution that Mother ever made to society, as she tried to feed and comfort the strangers at our door.

Chapter eighteen

To say that in the summer of 1939 we were scared would have been an understatement. Almost everybody in Liverpool was obsessed by a dread of the unknown. The tenseness of men's voices and their slightly hysterical laughter, the grim shut-in look of women whose sons and husbands were being called up, the problems of beleaguered city officials suddenly faced with putting into effect elaborate programmes, which had been concocted by equally harassed civil servants sitting at desks in far away London, all contributed to an almost unbearable tension as we waited.

Much preliminary work had already been done during the year of time bought for us by Mr Chamberlain during the infamous meeting in Munich in 1938. Now, there was a great urgency, and everybody's life was thrown into confusion.

Father was transferred by the City to work amongst the increasing number of refugees from Europe, who were arriving in Liverpool. He was shortly to be nearly overwhelmed by the arrival, in waves, of battered contingents of the Polish Army and Air Force. Later, he was transferred to the staff dealing with the inadequate Rest Centres provided for the bombed-out. They had originally been meagrely provisioned to discourage people from settling down to live in them rather than seeking new accommodation. The frantic needs of bewildered households, often without menfolk, could not be met. The more houses that were damaged, the more people crowded the Rest Centres and the less likelihood they had of finding alternative accommodation. Father worked like a demon.

In the meantime, we waited, fearing the future and yet unable to visualise what it would bring. Mother had been working as the representative of a greetings card firm. In August, she found herself politely dismissed, in the expectation that the paper for such a business would be severely rationed. She decided that she could, now the children were away, take a full-time post, and she was thankfully snapped up by a big bakery firm, whose bookkeeper, a Naval Reservist, had vanished into the navy. Mother could keep books because, at one point, during the First World War, just before my birth, she had taken the place of a man in a bank, and she said that she was the first lady cashier in Liverpool. The salary offered seemed enormous in comparison with what the rest of us were earning, and she was able to buy herself some new clothes and send some extra clothing to our frightened little evacuees at the aunts' house. We now had five less mouths to feed, and this made a great difference. I had cornflakes for breakfast as well as a piece of bread and margarine, and occasionally marmalade, which I had not tasted for many years. There was no shortage of food in the shops and we were not rationed until several months later.

This better salary which Mother was able to command made me even more ambitious to join the ranks of the green-overalled social workers. But the longer I worked in the Bootle office the more I realised that lack of education was going to hold me back. Anyone new coming on to staff had a degree. It was not that I could not do the work. I understood only too well most of the problems that bedevilled our ever increasing flood of clients, and as the war came closer I could sympathise with the middle-class women who began to consult us.

Men in good positions were called to the army, where they earned fourteen shillings a week, seven shillings of which they had to allot to their wives, so that they were eligible to draw a dependant's allowance. These allowances were so pitifully small that they hardly paid the rent for many people. Women threatened suicide as they were increasingly bullied by hire purchase firms, mortgage companies or rent collectors because they could no longer pay. A few employers sent their employees' wives sufficient money to bring the allowance up to their husband's wages, but many, faced with profound changes in their businesses due to the war, were unable to do this. My colleague and I read up the laws on contracts till our eyes glazed and learned to find technicalities upon which we could break hire purchase agreements and so release our desperate clients. Finally, organisations such as ours were able to pressure the government into declaring a moratorium upon serving men's debts, and so keep the wolves from the door until the end of the war.

So experience poured in upon me – but at the back of my mind there was always the nagging thought that if I was ever to make progress in the world of social work, I would need that precious piece of paper, a degree. And I had not had the opportunity to matriculate.

On 1st September, all the lights of the city were turned off. It created a darkness which townsfolk had not faced before, and we blundered about like people suddenly blinded, and were touchingly grateful for a lighted match or the spark from the trolley of the electric trams to give us a bearing. At first we endured the blackout with shivery, laughing fortitude, but after a while it became a frustrating curse, a maddening tedium. It was dangerous, too, as traffic tried to move about in such dense darkness and pedestrians stumbled over unexpected steps and hazards, like the fire hydrants, wandering dogs and cats, and parked bicycles. I once walked into a letter box and went home with a streaming, bloody nose. We learned how beautiful the stars were and, until the bombing began, rejoiced in moonlit nights.

All schools were closed, because in principle all children were evacuated with their teachers. This meant that for the first time for years, I not only had no children to care for; I had no studying to do. All places of entertainment were also closed, with the exception of public houses which were small and had only a limited number of people gathered in them. I was accustomed to cramming my life with study, with house cleaning, with care of many of the children's needs and with tutoring in shorthand. My current shorthand student, a cripple, had been evacuated to Southport and I had not yet found a replacement, so although I worked long hours I sometimes found myself, late in the evening, sitting with Mother over a cup of tea, not knowing what to talk about. If I introduced a subject, I could never be sure that she would not take offence and begin one of her irrational rages, so I tended to sit in dismal silence, and leave her to talk if she wanted to. Her favourite subject was Father's backslidings or some incident in the office when she had bested an adversary. I felt sorry for the office.

Mother was herself undoubtedly at a loss. She was not in the least interested in me and, I think, endured my presence as best she could. Her usual retreat, the cinema, with its long programmes and two new films a week, was closed to her. She had no friends – I do not recollect her ever having a bosom friend, though in our palmier days she had many close acquaintances and admirers. Father sometimes asked if she would like to go with him to his favourite pub, 'Ye Hole in Ye Wall' in Hackins Hey, and have a drink. She would always respond tartly that, 'Ladies do not go into public houses.'

Looking back, I find it odd that neither of us at that point volunteered our help as wardens, telephonists, first aid personnel or anything else. Half the town was enrolled in some service or other, while we sat stiffly over our tea. For my part, I think it was both mental and physical exhaustion. Having to walk most of the distance to and from work and spend the day coping with other people's woes, many of them quandaries unheard of before, was a heavy strain. I rarely reached home before eight o'clock, a home where I still never had enough to eat. There was a limit to the number of the world's woes which I could take upon my skimpy shoulders.

In Mother's case it seemed as if there was a whole section of her which did not function at all. She never managed to bring any real order into her life, never mind into ours. The bright and intelligent mind, of which I sometimes caught a glimpse when she cared to talk about books, seemed to have been buried amid the wild, superficial gaiety of the post-war years and the disasters which had subsequently befallen us. Perhaps she was hopelessly drained, too.

So there she sat, drinking tea and popping aspirins into her mouth, while Poland was decimated and we waited for our turn.

Father bought two second-hand suitcases. The few spare clothes we had were packed into these, together with family papers, like birth certificates, marriage lines and army discharge papers. One case was kept by my parents' bed and one by mine, so that if the house caught fire from incendiary bombs, we could run outside with them. When the air raid siren went, we shot out of bed, grabbed our clothes and the cases and fled to the doubtful safety of the cellar steps. There were several false alarms at first, when the sirens howled, the anti-aircraft guns in the park rumbled, searchlights swung across the sky and part-time wardens ran along the streets, pushing everyone indoors. Still the bombers did not come.

We began to feel safer.

Mother bought some cheap dress material, striped in green and tan, and I stitched pretty covers, complete with shoulder straps, for our gas mask boxes. I also made each of us a matching turban and scarf. Mother, Fiona and I sailed out in these feeling very smart and up-to-date. After a while, like everyone else, we discovered what a convenient receptacle the gas mask box was. We left the gas masks at home and used the box to carry make-up, lunches and the inevitable cotton pocket handkerchief. When rationing commenced, Mother found that the ration books fitted very conveniently into hers.

With no student to tutor, I had very little money of my own. I not only walked to town, which was the first stage of my journey to work, I walked half way to Bootle as well, trudging a couple of miles along Scotland Road, a dreadfully poor area, and Stanley Road, to reduce the amount of the tram fare. I cut out lunch, except when there was enough bread in the house for me to take a slice of bread and margarine.

Rumours went about that one could earn huge sums in the new factories out at Speke, which were going into war production. I thought about this and then decided that after the war I could be out of work and walking the streets with hundreds of other unskilled workers. To become a qualified social worker as quickly as possible still seemed a good idea, if I could achieve it.

No one could complain to us that our work was not essential. Daily we filled an ever-widening gap between official mandates and the protesting, unhappy victims of them.

I missed very much my fellow typist, Miriam Enns. She lived too far away from me for us to meet socially, and anyway I had no money to pay for coffees in city tea shops, which would have been one way of seeing her. Gradually, I lost touch with her.

Sylvia Poole was working for a firm supplying medical aids, like bandages and cotton wool, and her company became very busy. We did, however, manage to go for prim little Sunday walks together, and, because of the slackened pressure in our house, Mother agreed that she should occasionally come to tea. Tea was a simple meal of bread and margarine and jam, followed by a cake bought from a shop which sold leftovers from a big bakery. Much to my delight, Sylvia and Mother got along famously, and Mother began to look forward to her coming, and would suggest that I ask her.

It was ironical that the commencement of a world war which threw the lives of millions into turmoil should at first give me a little more leisure. During the long walks home, I began to think of myself as a person in my own right and tiny independent wistful longings floated in the back of my mind. I had always had it drummed into me that I was a possession of my parents, to be moved around, fed or not fed, bullied or ignored, as they saw fit. I had fought against it instinctively for years, but I had always lost, excepting in regard to going to night school and obtaining my current job. Now, in little flashes, I began to wonder if one could not, after all, exist without somebody else's permission. But I was an exhausted bag of bones, worn out with years of intolerable strain, and the slave mentality which I had acquired was not going to be easily shed.

On Sunday, 3rd September, 1939, Father kept the radio on from early morning. He did not go for his usual walk. Mother and I went about our normal Sunday tasks of cleaning, cooking, washing and ironing, feeling particularly subdued. Even Fiona, who took little notice of anything which did not directly concern herself, got up earlier than usual, and wandered restlessly about the house, while we waited to see if Hitler would continue the war in Poland, despite the Allies' ultimatum. A tremendous, ominous silence lay over our old, black city as people stayed close to home. No children played in the street and no traffic passed along it. The old men who played ollies in the gutter did not come out for their customary game.

I read again a comforting letter which I had received from Friedrich the previous day. Our dear Fuehrer was apparently still uniting the German race and I was not to be afraid, just to keep on writing to his home address. Earlier in the week, I had received a hysterical letter from Ursel. Her husband, a minister, had been arrested for a sermon he had given defending the Jews, and she was terrified. How the letter got past the German censor is beyond me, unless they had become a little less efficient as a result of Germany's having to supervise so many newly acquired countries.

At eleven o'clock, we gathered in the living room to listen to the BBC. The tired voice of our Prime Minister, Mr Chamberlain, announced that we were at war. As we all stood up while the National Anthem boomed over the radio, we looked at each other. Mother and Father, veterans of that war to end all wars, Fiona, beautiful in spite of her hair curlers, a face as blank as the page of a new exercise book, and me with Friedrich's letter still in my pinafore pocket, all of us assured by our newspapers that we would be buried under the ruins of Liverpool within hours of the declaration of war. Would Friedrich be one of the bomber pilots, I wondered, fingering the gentle letter? Or was he at this moment too busy killing innocent Poles?

It seemed incredible, impossible. The weight on my chest was unbearable. I said in a grating voice, 'I think I'll make a cup of tea.'

Chapter nineteen

A few evenings later, mildly surprised, like everyone else, that I was still alive, I languidly hung up my coat in the hall, the same old brown coat so often pawned, now near the end of its days.

The door into the living room opened suddenly and I blinked in the light from the room's bare electric bulb. Fiona, with a piece of toast in one hand, stood in the doorway, and said with something like awe in her voice, 'Helen, you've got to go down to see the police.'

'What?'

She was obviously intrigued at this unexpected call for her eldest sister, and with a cheek swelled with toast, she repeated, 'You have! To see the police.'

Thoroughly alarmed, I forgot my hunger and hastened into the room. Father and Mother were seated at the table. They had just finished their evening meal, and thick white plates rimmed with bacon fat were scattered round the soiled cloth.

'Mother! What's wrong? I haven't done anything.'

Father answered me. 'Only Fiona had arrived home when they came. They left a message to say that you should go down to a place in Lime Street – and take with you any correspondence you had received from Germany.'

'Oh, my God!' I muttered. 'What would they want that for?'

Mother put her knife and fork neatly together on her plate. 'We don't know, Helen. We hope it isn't serious.'

'Am I supposed to go tonight?'

'It is nearly eight o'clock,' Father replied. 'They can wait. I'll take you down tomorrow evening. Try to get home early.'

Throughout the night I tossed sleeplessly, wracked by nervous fears. Had I broken the law in writing to Germany? Would they shut me up in an internment camp? Should I burn all the carefully kept letters and say I had none to show them? Friedrich had been courting me by mail. What would they say about that?

In the morning, as I washed myself in cold water in the kitchen, using a bit of Father's shaving soap since there was no other soap, and Father built the living room fire, I shouted to him to ask his advice. I made a clean, blushing admission of Friedrich's sentimental advances. As soon as I had my underclothes on, he came into the kitchen to wash his hands and get his razor. While I made Mother's early morning tea, he slowly lathered his face and thought about what I had said.

'We'll take the letters with us,' he finally decided. 'They will look so innocent – I am sure the police will understand. If you destroy them, they may become unduly suspicious – people do usually have some of the letters they receive, lying in drawers or desks.'

'O.K.,' I agreed reluctantly.

Because Father was a little behind in his shaving, I took Mother's tea up to her, and she broached the same subject as she huddled in the meagre bedding.

'Your Father and I were talking about your going to see the police. He says you must look nice. What are you doing about your clothes?'

Only twice before had Mother discussed clothes with me, at the time of my Confirmation and when she had helped me to buy the dress for the office dance. Now she sounded quite anxious.

I saw the point. A nicely dressed middle-class girl would be treated with greater respect.

'I hadn't thought about them. My coat is a mess, and I haven't needed a hat since the warmer weather started. No gloves. Social workers don't have to look smart, thank goodness. The turban and scarf I made for the spring don't look bad, though – I could wear those.'

Mother sipped her tea. 'Your Father is very worried. Could you buy a coat in your lunch hour? I have a pound that you can borrow.'

I was flabbergasted. I never looked for help from Mother – and now she was suddenly offering it. She *must* be worried. She earned very much more than I did, but I had not expected such a sudden change of mood.

'I could try, Mummy. C & A Modes might have something in their sale.'

'I don't think there is anything in the pawnbroker's which will fit.' Mother sipped the scalding hot, greyish brew thoughtfully.

Suddenly, I wanted a new coat passionately. I forgot about the police. I remembered only that I had never had a *new* overcoat since I was a child. 'I'll try, Mummy,' I said eagerly. 'I can pay you back bit by bit as soon as I get a new shorthand pupil – you'll remember that Miss Bennett was evacuated to Southport last week – but I have advertised for someone else.' I whistled under my breath. 'I'll have to go into town from Bootle, in my lunch hour. If I'm late back, the office will just have to put up with it for once.' I felt reckless in my longing for a coat.

At lunch time I had about ten minutes to find a garment at half-price in which to impress a suspicious police force, an impossible task.

Breathlessly, I looked through the racks of new stock – heavy winter coats just put on display – until a white-haired lady asked if she could help me. 'I've a pound to buy a coat,' I confessed frankly to her, and she was unexpectedly sympathetic. She suggested a lined mackintosh, and my face must have fallen, because she said, 'Come over to the back here. There are one or two items which were missed when we were putting away the summer stock after the sale yesterday.'

And there it was, a soft woollen coat, beige, with a narrow braid trim in orange and green round the collar. The top front button was missing, a loose thread marking where it should be.

'Try it on.'

I did. It fitted neatly on the shoulders and round a twenty inch waist. I twirled slightly, and the flared skirt swished round legs that I was astonished to see were slender and shapely. The turban, a hemmed length of tan cloth touched with green flecks, which I had made from a design in a magazine which Fiona had brought home, blended very well with the coat. The assistant tightened the belt slightly and stepped back.

I glowed, and inquired carefully, 'How much is it?'

'Nineteen shillings and eleven pence – marked down from thirty shillings.' She rubbed her chin thoughtfully, as she surveyed me. 'I think I can find you a similar button. The collar would nearly hide it, if it doesn't quite match.' She went to a table, opened a drawer and ran her fingers through an assortment of buttons and belts. She turned triumphantly with a beige button between her bright pink fingernails.

I apologised to my superior at the office for being five minutes late, and plunged into work. Later when a moment of calm arrived and I had made a cup of tea for both of us, I told her that I had to go with my father that evening on some special family business and asked if I could leave promptly.

She sighed and the weary lines under her eyes deepened. 'Of course,' she said. She was only about seven or eight years older than myself, and I wondered suddenly if our clients were worth the sacrifices she made for them. Since leaving university, she had given all her young days to them, given them her life, working far into the evenings and at weekends to try to find help for them. And I wanted to do the same thing. Or did I?

Father had to pay my tram fares into the city, because I had spent my last travel money for that week on the additional trip going to and from the dress shop. In a brown paper bag lay practically all Friedrich's letters and most of Ursel's passionate epistles, including the last terrified cry. The pride in the new coat had gone and had been replaced by feelings akin to panic.

Father was grave and, at first, silent. On the tram, he murmured to me to answer any questions put to me, and then he qualified the remark by adding, 'And don't say anything more than that. I will introduce us.'

We were passed from a uniformed constable, to a sergeant and then to a plain-clothes policeman, as we worked our way into the bowels of a building in Lime Street. This was not the police station – it bore all the marks of makeshift offices hastily set up. Father had assumed like an overcoat the quiet air of authority and the cultivated language of the public school man that he was, and this outweighed his cheap clothes, and had its effect. The higher one was in the social heirarchy the more carefully the police handled one.

Finally, we were seated at a small table sheltered by a cloth screen, which looked as if it might have started life in a hospital fifty years before. The room was a large one, containing a number of tables similarly set up, and men and women sat round them whispering and shuffling papers, like relations going through desks after a funeral. I stared up at a high ceiling, finely moulded as if for a ballroom, but covered with dust and drooping spiders' webs. Pale green walls were discoloured from ancient water leakages and the passage of many people.

Two new plain-clothes men joined us. One sat opposite me at the table, the other one perched on a stool slightly at a distance half behind me. Nervous as a new climber faced with a precipice, I clenched my hands on my lap and braced myself for whatever might come.

It was an ordeal. The fear of internment, perhaps imprisonment, haunted me, though at no point was either mentioned by my interrogators. At times I thought I would surely faint before it was over.

Once our relationship and our names were established, Father sat quietly. I produced the letters and laid them in two neat piles before the man at the table. He was middle-aged, with deep lines criss-crossing a craggy face. Small, hard blue eyes glittered between reddish-gold eyelashes. Thin, tightly curled hair had been plastered down each side of his head with a heavy application of strongly scented pomade, an odour combined with the heavy smell of stale cigarette smoke. He and the man behind me smoked incessantly, and the pile of cigarette butts rose in a dirty white saucer on the table. I was offered a cigarette, but whispered that I did not smoke. A battered packet of Player's was offered to Father, and he took one and smoked it slowly, while he listened.

A young man in a shabby blue suit had pulled another chair forward and sat down. He had brought with him a small pile of writing paper, some folders and a couple of well-sharpened yellow pencils. He had arranged a shorthand notebook on his knee and was taking notes of everything that was said. This threw me into further alarm. I shifted myself fractionally, so that I could see what the young man wrote. My own shorthand was first class and I had often transcribed from the other typists' work. I had no difficulty in reading what he wrote, even at an odd angle. If he doesn't get it down correctly, I will correct him, I promised myself, like a terrier prepared to defend its territory from a Great Dane, all bombast and no clout.

Age? Place of birth? All the addresses I had ever lived at – Father had to aid my memory about this one. Jobs? Schools? My short time at school was explained by Father as being because of Mother's bad health – but these were not school officials, they were detectives. Religious affiliation? Friends?

Friends? Had I really only two? Miriam and Sylvia? Boy friends? Only Friedrich? Was I sure? No casual men friends that I met only occasionally?

'No,' I snapped indignantly. 'I'm too busy.' Why could not they see that that was a stupid question to a girl who looked like me?

'Why did you study German?'

I looked at him dumbly. Why did one study anything? Because one wanted to know.

'I wanted to make up my lack of ordinary education,' I told my grim interrogator cautiously.

'Most people learn French.'

'I am learning French as well.'

'Humph.'

We sat silent for a moment, looking at each other. The blue eyes were cold and hard, mine a little moist because I felt physically weak and helpless. Why were they bothering me like this? I wanted to ask. But

Father had warned me only to answer questions, not to ask them.

I half closed my eyes, so that the detective should not see the tears threatening. Under my lids I took a quick look at the shorthand writer's notebook. On his current page, the record was correct, right down to the exact wording of Father's interjection about my schooling.

The detective was reading Friedrich's letters. Apparently he read German easily and was flicking from one page to another quickly.

'How did you come into contact with Friedrich Reinhardt?'

I half smiled. I was immediately whisked into a train lumbering northwards towards Crewe. I was travelling alone, as usual, on my annual visit to Grandma's. On the window seat next to me sat a boy about two years older than me. He was dressed in a grown up suit of unusual cut, rather shabby. He was slim, hair dark and slightly wavy, with a heart-shaped face and a flawless white skin.

The train was a local one which stopped at almost every station, and at each stop the boy would peer anxiously out of the window. Two adults in the compartment, a middle-aged husband and wife, had, after staring at both of us, opened newspapers and retired behind them.

Very shyly, the boy had turned to me and asked, 'Pardon me. Where are you travelling?' His accent was foreign.

Equally shyly, I had peeped up from under the brim of my panama school hat, and whispered,

'Liverpool,' as if it were important that the other travellers did not hear me.

'I must the train at Crewe leave. A man comes for me there.'

'I change at Crewe. I will tell you when we arrive.'

'Much thanks.' He relaxed his vigil of station watching, and I sat the doll I had been nursing down on the seat beside me and arranged its skirts modestly. He smiled at it, rather patronisingly, and I smiled at him. Boys never understood what a friend a doll could be.

It was the beginning of a long friendship, all of two hours. I left with a note of his address and the promise to write. It was a simple address, the name of a village near Munich. Neither of us did write, of course, and the slip of paper was lost before I returned from Grandma's. But the address was not lost. It stayed in my mind with the picture of a beautiful youth and a lovely train journey through the green Midlands of England. When I began to learn German and the class was encouraged by the teacher to find a German pen-friend, I had remembered it like a nursery rhyme and all the other odds and ends which children keep in a mental rag bag.

'How did you get the name and address of Reinhardt in order to write to him?'

I jumped at the sharp repetition of the question. The granite face before me was formidable. I told him.

'You have a remarkable memory.' The tone was heavily sarcastic.

'Children remember all kinds of things,' I responded woodenly.

'What was he doing in England?'

'He was going to stay with English friends of his father's – friends from long ago before the war – to improve his English. It was already quite good. He could talk about almost anything – but not correctly.'

'Where was he going?'

'To Manchester.'

'And where had he come from?'

I was getting fed up and snapped back, 'I didn't ask him.' Father cleared his throat reprovingly.

I thought I was being grilled thoroughly but when, after what seemed hours, we finally got down to Ursel's letters, questions about Friedrich seemed nothing.

I had been put into touch with Ursel when I had replied to a letter in the Sunday *Observer*, which Father had once bought. The letter offered to put children in touch with pen-friends in Germany. I had asked for a girl friend. The detective told me that my letter of so many years earlier had been found by the police in the file of the man who wrote the letter to the *Observer*, a known Fascist.

I stared at the detective unbelievingly. 'Who on earth would bother to retain such a letter? And why are you interested in such a silly thing as two girls writing to each other?'

The detective did not answer. He was reading one of Ursel's letters. Perhaps he did not like his work being considered silly.

Then he launched his attack. Question after question. Small things that Ursel had asked about, matters

I had long since forgotten. How had I replied? What did this paragraph or that one refer to? Questions until I was dizzy and bewildered. Finally, Father intervened to remind the detective reproachfully that I was only a young girl.

'Twenty is not a young girl,' retorted the detective tartly. 'Please be quiet. I have my work to do.'

Father was obviously getting very upset. But he did keep quiet.

Nine o'clock. Ten o'clock by the timepiece on the wall. I began to think we would never be allowed to go home. And I still did not understand what all the fuss was about. I was floundering in bewilderment.

At about eleven, it came suddenly to an end. The man who had been sitting quietly nearly behind me, said, 'I think that will do, Tom.' He swung his heavy body round to look at me. 'We will have a summary typed up. You can sign it and then you can go. If you change your address you must let us know immediately.'

The curly-headed detective stood up and stretched himself. Unexpectedly, he asked quite pleasantly, 'Would you like a cup of tea?' He picked up Friedrich's and Ursel's letters, shuffled them into a neat pile and put them into a folder handed him by the stenographer.

I nodded silently. Father said, 'Thank you.'

The three men went away, and I turned to Father, 'What . . . ?' I began in a quavery voice.

Father said very softly, 'Don't say anything.' He made the smallest possible gesture towards the screen half-surrounding us, and mouthed, 'Listening.'

I swallowed, and said in a normal voice. 'I hope they bring the tea.' If they were listening, they might as well be reminded of their promise. Then I sat with hands crossed on my lap, like a tabby kitten tired of play, and watched people coming and going through the door.

After a little while, a bald-headed elderly constable in uniform brought two cups of tea, with Marie biscuits tucked into the saucers. 'There you are, Miss, Sir,' he said politely, as he put the cups down on the table.

We ate the biscuits and drank the tea in perfect silence, while we listened to the rise and fall of innumerable muffled conversations in the huge room. Men in uniform, men in civilian clothes, occasionally women of various ages and classes, were ushered through. How late did the police work? I wondered.

At five to twelve, the curly-headed detective returned, bearing several sheets of closely-typed paper. 'Sorry you had to wait so long,' he said quite cheerfully, and plunked himself down on his chair once more. He started to read the closely-typed sheets very carefully, running his forefinger along each line. I noticed that he had lost his little finger and I sat watching the slight movement of the stub as the non-existent finger tried to adjust to the movement of the others.

The stenographer and the second detective joined us at the table, their faces looking nearly as rumpled as their navy blue suits.

The summary of the conversation was handed to me, with the request to read it and sign it.

Father uncrossed his legs and leaned towards me. For the first time he looked tense.

'Read it very carefully, Helen. If for any reason you feel it deviates from what was said, I am sure the officer will have it altered.'

The officer sighed and looked at his watch. He blew through his lips, making a soft pooh-poohing sound, and then agreed, 'Yes, it can be altered.'

I was no lawyer but I was used to reading contracts, new laws and government directives and interpreting them to our clients. The stenographer had composed a very fair summary of what had transpired. A lawyer, no doubt, would have queried every sentence, but I did not have such an adviser. In fact, it never occurred to Father or me that we could have demanded the presence of a lawyer, though I cannot imagine how we would have managed to pay him anyway.

I borrowed Father's fountain pen, and signed.

Chapter twenty

The signature had a galvanising effect. The stenographer, hovering in the background, was dismissed. The detective who had been the observer at the interview seized a weather-beaten trilby from an old-fashioned hat stand nearby, clapped it on his head, said 'Good night,' to us, and 'See you in the morning, Tom,' to my diligent questioner, and fled after the stenographer.

The big room seemed suddenly nearly deserted. Tom leaned back in his chair and stretched himself. He rubbed his eyes and grinned like a schoolboy at Father and me. The rocklike hardness of his expression vanished completely and we were faced with an average Liverpudlian, who might have been a small businessman of some kind.

'How are you going to get home?' he asked Father.

Father did not have a watch, so I looked at Grandma's watch and said to Father, 'It's half past twelve. We shall have to walk.'

Father rose and nodded to the detective.

'Like to wait a few minutes? I'll drop you in my car.'

Father was looking completely worn out and both of us had to be up by six the next morning, so I smiled impulsively at the detective, and said, 'That would be lovely.'

The detective gazed slyly at me through red eyelashes. 'Forgiven?' he asked.

My smile died. 'You have to do your work,' I replied. 'But I wish you'd tell us what it is all about.'

He stood up, moved around the table and then perched himself on the edge of it, facing Father. 'Well, I can tell you this. Your daughter is not what we are looking for. We are quite satisfied about that.' He stopped, and again blew his soft pooh-poohing sound. 'We're checking everyone known to have any association with Germany. We could have a Fifth Column here, ready to betray us – you must realise that. Your daughter's letter about a pen-friend was found in the files of a known Nazi, when we picked him up. He had a neat little espionage system going, you know. Linked up children in one district in England with a single class in a German school.'

I gasped, and he grinned at me.

'The English letters addressed to one school in Germany were read by German intelligence before delivery.' He paused, and shrugged. 'You can appreciate how it would work. Kids write about where they live and what their father does for a living – whether he has been called up or sent to work in a new factory. Undoubtedly, questions were suggested to the German children for them to ask their pen-friends; I've checked enough piles of correspondence like Helen's to realise this. If they had enough letters they would get a very good picture of what was going on in a given town in England – and Liverpool, being a big port, would be of particular interest.'

'Good Lord!' exclaimed Father. 'You mean that Helen had actually become part of this?'

'Yes.' He turned and grinned down at me. 'But her pen-friend had left school early to be married. I gathered from her letters that she was married at sixteen?'

'She was,' I agreed sadly. 'She was terribly unhappy. Her husband was a Minister in her church – and he was nearly forty.'

'So, you see, she could not be prompted in her questions – without telling her how she was being used. And from her last letter I gather that her husband was in deep trouble with the Nazis.'

I sighed, and nodded agreement.

'But why put me through all this . . . ?' I gestured helplessly.

'Had to be certain, my dear. And you work in a place where many of the staff are highly politically minded.'

Dumbfounded, I stared at him. I thought of Miriam and her high ideals – and then I remembered that,only the month before,Russia had signed a non-aggression pact with Germany. I whistled under my breath, an unladylike habit learned as a child from a shepherd.

'From Communists, Conchies, Catholics and Cranks, good Lord deliver us,' the detective was saying to Father. He glanced again at me, sitting frightened in my chair. 'What's a pretty little thing like you doing, working in a place like that? You should be out enjoying yourself – dancing.'

I was deeply offended and said loyally through

gritted teeth, 'The ladies I work with do a wonderful job. I sometimes think they prevent this city from bursting into riots from sheer misery. At least people can talk to us about their troubles.'

His red eyebrows shot up and he made a face. 'Well . . .' He swung off the table, and abruptly changed the subject. 'I'll get the car. You know your way to the front door?'

We agreed that we did, and we stole down quiet corridors where lights still burned behind closed doors, to wait in front of the building.

At first, after the light inside the building, we faced a wall of complete darkness, but gradually our eyes became accustomed to it. Familiar Lime Street began to emerge. The outline of St George's Hall loomed against the sky in front of us. Intermittent flashes from the shaded lights of cars lit up for a moment the squat block of the War Memorial or the finely-cast fish whose tails held up the lamp-standards. Other than the occasional sound of a car engine the busy city was absolutely quiet, and I jumped violently when above my head a sleepy pigeon cooed once.

'I'm glad we don't have to walk home in such darkness,' I remarked to Father. I was deeply angry at the detective's derisory remarks, but the safety of his car would be welcome.

'I should buy a torch,' replied Father, 'and you should get one, too.'

I shrugged. When would I be able to afford a torch? I wondered suddenly if Father knew that Mother received practically all my salary, and that to all intents and purposes I worked for nothing.

'Could you lend me fourpence for my fares tomorrow?' I inquired hopefully. 'Now I'm out at Bootle, it is too far for me to walk. I'll pay you back as soon as I get a student.'

'I can,' Father replied. 'I won't have to pay our fares back tonight, thanks to friend Tom.'

A small car swooshed around the corner and drew up at the kerb. We felt our way carefully down the steps. The door was opened from within and the front seat tipped forward, so that I could clamber into the back seat. Father sat by Tom, and as we swept through the empty streets, they talked fitfully about the invasion of Poland by the Germans and the sinking of the *Athenia* by German submarines.

When we stopped in our deserted street, I leaned forward and asked, 'May I have my letters back sometime, if I come for them?'

Tom laughed. 'Not till the end of the war, luv – round Christmas, probably. They have to stay in our files until it's over.'

'That's not quite fair, is it? You said I wasn't what you were looking for.'

'Can't be helped, luv.' He turned round to look at me over his shoulder. 'You should forget about your German boy friend. Find yourself a nice English lad.'

I drew in my breath crossly. I resented Friedrich being termed a boy friend. It seemed to belittle him. But one does not argue with the police. Father had got out of the car and was holding the front seat forward for me. I slid out as gracefully as I could, and paused for a second to shake my skirts straight again.

The detective leaned across the front seat towards

us. I saw the flash of his teeth as he grinned. 'Remember what I said, young lady. Cranks, Conchies, Communists and Catholics – get out of it. Enjoy yourself while you're young.'

I seethed with anger. Father bent and shut the door, after saying good night and thanking the man for the lift.

'The abominable bigot!' I exclaimed furiously to Father, as he felt around in his pocket for the house key. 'I had no idea police could be so narrow minded. I could cheerfully have shot him.'

Father sighed. 'They are like the rest of us.'

Father had been so good about coming with me to the interview, that I did not want to argue with him, so I swallowed my flaring temper and did not answer him.

The letters never were returned to me. They probably still lie in some dusty crate of war-time files of the CID, a gentle record of innocent young people touching each others' lives across a mighty gulf.

Chapter twenty-one

'Mummy, I haven't got enough clothes,' wailed Fiona, oblivious of small matters like a full-scale war. 'I can't wear this dress *again*, going out with Reg.'

So Mother retrieved some bundles from pawn. Since they contained all kinds of garments, I benefited by the addition of a summer dress and a blouse to my small wardrobe. Both Mother and Fiona were considerably plumper than I was and these garments were too tight for them. This did not stop them 'borrowing' them – and anything else of mine left clean and folded on the shelf in our bedroom. The resultant burst under-arm seams were left for me to repair, which I did with savagely bad temper. I had also to wash and iron the garments.

When I turned on her in anger, Fiona would say mildly, 'But your things are always ready. I don't have time to see to my clothes.' And it was with difficulty that I refrained from hitting her.

Mother always helped herself, with the remark that I was welcome to borrow anything of hers. But she, like Fiona, rarely washed or pressed her clothes until she had nothing fresh left to wear. Anyway, both Fiona's and her clothes hung on my wasted frame.

The absence of the children and Alan considerably eased the financial strain. Mother's excellent salary meant that there was a little more food in the house, though frequently it was not the most nutritious kind. I still lacked lunch quite often, but a proper, though modest, breakfast helped me through the day, and there was a little more on my plate at night. There was far less work to do at home, no studying and no student to teach, so the awful strain on me began to slacken, despite long hours of work and travel. Yet I was totally miserable.

One weekend, Mother brought home some cheap wallpaper with a garish pattern of bright red cherries and green leaves printed all over it, and we covered the dingy grey walls of the living room with it. Emboldened by the improvement, Mother bought some cotton curtaining in similar colours, but emblazoned with roses, and we stitched curtains and, also, padded seat covers for the upended paint cans which formed some of our seating. The effect was very cheerful.

We still lacked sufficient bedding and sheets, and as the autumn crept on the increasing cold began to make my legs ache abominably. The bedding from the boys' beds had been pawned the day they were evacuated.

A general boredom set in as the fear of being bombed to death receded. I spent some weekend evenings with Mrs Poole and Sylvia. Mrs Poole, a professional dressmaker, showed me the proper way to cut out and fit a dress. But I could not afford to buy any material.

It seemed that nobody was interested in learning shorthand in such uncertain times. A small advertisement in the *Liverpool Echo*, paid for with the last fee of my evacuated student, brought no result.

Despite my anger at the derogatory remarks of the detective, he had sparked in me the idea of looking elsewhere for a better paying job, and I began to scan the Situations Vacant columns of the *Echo*. I wanted a position in which I could use my burgeoning experience in social work. I did not particularly want to be a secretary, for which type of position I was quite well qualified, unless it could be to a private person. There were still a few people in those days who had live-in secretaries, and in a big private house I felt that to a degree I could return to the kind of life which I had known in childhood. I wrote in reply to several such advertisements and received one response from Chester. An interview was arranged in the Adelphi Hotel. I did not get the job. My poor clothes, despite the new overcoat, and my generally neglected and unhealthy looks, together with a gauche, painfully shy manner, made it certain that I would never obtain a post in a private house. A more cultivated and presentable young woman would be essential.

With time to think, my inadequacies became even more painfully apparent to me. Yet I seemed shut into a situation of such acute penury that it was impossible to alter myself very much, and I cried myself to sleep a number of nights.

I had never discussed the situation at home with Sylvia. I shrank from trying to explain to anyone the hardships we had been enduring and the weird, bewildered lostness of my parents. Much of the time they seemed to float in a mist through which they were incapable of finding their way, though, as I pondered, I realised that Father had been trying recently to reach out to his children. Looking back, it is clear that Sylvia and I rarely discussed our personal feelings or our emotional life. We fed each other with talks about political events, books, theatres, history – a lively intellectual stimulation, almost bereft of the giggles and gossip of ordinary youngsters. Perhaps Sylvia had other friends who fulfilled this youthful need, but I did not.

There was no one to whom I could confide my shy desire to look chic, to learn to behave appropriately, become a normal middle-class girl again, groomed and cared for. Even the working-class girls who lived round me knew how to take care of their hair and their skin.

Wistfully I thought that if I had a little money to spend on pins and setting lotions, Fiona would show me how to do my hair. Mother spent a lot of time showing Fiona how to use hair tints and face creams and make-up. She bought her a fair amount of clothing and all this, added to a natural beauty, made her stunning to look at. All she had to do was smile in a lift or in the café where she had her lunch and it did not take long for well-heeled young men working in the city to find a polite way of approaching her and making a date. She was introduced by them into a circle of young people where she was accepted and was invited to parties, balls and dances. She soon learned from the more refined girls that she met how to deport herself, and this, added to her normal gentleness, made her quite popular amongst them. She sometimes amused me in bed by telling me of small incidents that indicated that she had succeeded where I had failed; she was on an upwardly mobile path. I wondered if I would ever learn to put a teacup down on a table without upsetting it, enter a room without tripping over the rug, the small social etiquette of when to take off gloves and hat, when to shake hands and when to greet a girl with a kiss; such small things, yet so important in a world still ruled by etiquette.

At twenty I was still wearing the glasses bought for me ten years before. The frames were hopelessly small and had not been improved by several poor repairs. A few years later much of my clumsiness disappeared when I was able to buy a new pair and see properly again.

But I had no money for hairpins, never mind expensive things like spectacles, and now no money for make-up or lunches or even stockings. Few people in those days had the courage to ask an employer for an increase in pay, and I lacked the courage of a mouse. My fear of unemployment had been enhanced by the lack of response to my tentative efforts to obtain another post. And I still owed Mother the pound she had lent me for the coat, about which she had reminded me caustically only a week before.

The visiting of clients in their homes, which I had been doing since my transfer to the Bootle office, had taught me that, though many of them were in dire straits, a great number of them lived far more comfortably than we did. They were simply better managers. Strangely, the war had not made much difference to the number of unemployed, but increasingly they seemed to be finding ways of earning small sums to augment their parish relief. They talked quite frankly to me about these little jobs, trusting me not to make a record of the information. If I had reported them, any money they earned would have immediately been deducted from their meagre allowance from the Relieving Officer. The women cleaned the homes of the more prosperous, the men did gardening, worked as handymen and sometimes as casual labour on building sites. No matter what time I called, there usually seemed to be a fire in the grate. What they most suffered from was overcrowding in dilapidated, verminous houses, lack of bathrooms, hot water and indoor lavatories, things that they could not themselves do a great deal about. Their rents were controlled at such a low level that it was in many cases impossible for landlords to find the money for repairs, renovations or fumigation.

At home, we never learned to manage so successfully.

One Saturday, after a visit to a client, I had to spend twopence in a public telephone box to check something for the woman concerned, with my superior in the office. Afterwards I was in great distress when I realised that, though I would have the twopence returned to me eventually, I now had no money to pay my fare back to the centre of the city. I would have to walk there, and then the rest of the way from the city centre up the hill to our house. I was already sorely troubled that I had no fares left for the following week also.

I thought I would never reach home as I trudged along Stanley Road. I was dreadfully tired and still badly undernourished. At St Luke's Church, I sat down on the steps because I felt I could go no further. People passing glanced at me curiously, so I shut my eyes until the world had stopped swimming around me.

It was a mild day, sunny enough for the rays to fight their way through the cloud of pollutants that veiled Liverpool on the few days when it was not windy. I should be able to manage four or five miles, I told myself, now that the situation at home had eased.

Jumbled, chaotic thoughts wandered through a dulled mind, as I sat trying to get my breath. The detective had suggested that I should enjoy myself, go dancing. He must have been crazy. Things like that cost money. Even to volunteer, say, as a part-time air raid warden, which would have given me new friends, would need a few more pennies for fares, for the odd cup of coffee, possibly for uniform. Eyes still closed I put my head down on my handbag on my knee, and laughed.

'Are ye all right, luv?'

An elderly newspaper seller had shuffled across the road and was bending over me solicitously. I looked up, startled. Small kind eyes stared at me through cheap metal-framed glasses balanced on a bulbous red nose.

'Yes, thank you. Yes. I had to rest a moment, that's all.'

'Thought you was goin' to faint.'

I smiled up at him. 'No. I'm fine now, thank you very much.'

He grinned and toddled back to his little table of newspapers.

With gritted teeth I made myself climb the hill.

At the Rialto, leaning one trench-coated shoulder against a stucco pillar, lounged the pimp who had once offered me a cigarette. I wondered if his girls felt much worse than I did. He said good night as he always did, tipping his rakish trilby hat as he did so. He must have found me rather a joke, because I looked so prim, yet despite his despicable occupation, I always smiled and replied politely, 'Good night.'

This night I was almost shaky enough to ask him for a cigarette, to quell my hunger and soothe the great tide of unhappiness which was threatening to engulf me. It beat in my head, choked my throat. Years and years of suppressed misery welled up; thoughts of all my lost girlhood, all the possibly happy, irresponsible years lost in grinding poverty and an incredible weight of work, marched past me and jeered at me, as if to say, 'You think you were *entitled* to live and laugh and be happy? Don't kid yourself. You've got years and years of semi-slavery before you – and nothing much else.'

The house was incredibly quiet as I entered. I shivered. Without the children, I felt bereft of a reason for living.

Father and Mother sat on either side of the fireplace reading the paper. For once, they were not quarrelling. The puppy recently brought home by Brian slumbered unheeding on the coconut matting, his back braced against the warm fender, the current stray cat curled comfortably on top of him. It was a great friendship. Fiona must long since have gone out with a date.

Both parents looked up and said, 'Hello.'

I responded with a small, tight 'hello' back, and went straight to the kitchen to fill the kettle at the sink. When I twisted a knob on the gas stove, gas hissed out of one of the rings and I thankfully lit a match and put it to the ring. I could make tea quickly.

There was a slice of commercially cooked ham on a plate in the kitchen, and I called, 'Is the ham for me?' My voice sounded as if I were being strangled.

'Yes,' Mother called back, and I heard the rustle of the newspaper as she turned the page, and it grated on my raw nerves. I took two pieces of bread from a packaged sliced loaf, dabbed some margarine on them and put the ham between them. When the kettle boiled, I asked Mother and Father if they would like tea; if so, I would make a full pot. They both decided to have some.

With agitated hands, cups were somehow rinsed under the cold water from the tap and assembled on the table with the ham sandwich. I sat down in front of them and looked at them. My throat felt tight to choking point. Within there was a rising feeling of panic. In a minute, I thought frantically, I am going to scream – and scream – about nothing.

That was it. Scream about nothing. Scream about the void which was me. About a non-existent person, with no meaning to anyone else but me – or perhaps Sylvia. My God, how I wished she was there.

Moving like a zombie, I poured and distributed the tea. I bit at the sandwich and rolled the cottonwool bread with its stringy piece of ham round my mouth.

I chewed, but could not swallow it, trying all the time to control the irrational hysteria rising in me.

I took a big breath, then sipped some tea to help the sandwich down. I choked.

Hand to mouth, I fled to the kitchen sink and succeeded in spitting out the offending piece of sandwich. I began to cry.

It was as if a well-locked lid had suddenly burst from a gas tank, because of uncontrollable pressure from within. I could hear myself groaning and screaming, as I clung to the edge of the sandstone sink, frightful primitive cries of a creature beyond help, writhing as if in pain.

Pain it was. All the pain, all the suppressed grief of nine dreadful years, coming to the surface, now that some of the intense load had been lifted, the revolt of a human creature nearly pressed out of existence. Screams of awful mental anguish.

Chapter twenty-two

In a flurry of dropped newspapers, Mother and Father were beside me in a second.

'Good God, Helen! Whatever's the matter?' Father's face was shocked.

But I could not answer. I was far away, outside the tortured being standing at the sink, totally unable to take command again of my normal territory. I shrieked like an air raid siren out of control.

Mother took my arm and shook me. 'Stop it, Helen! Do you hurt somewhere?'

Hurt? I hurt all over. The shrieks became wild laughter.

Father seized me by the shoulders, turned me towards him and administered a great slap across my face.

It was partially effective. Mind and body snapped together again. With a hand to my stinging face, I continued to cry helplessly, bellowing like Avril in a tantrum. But I no longer laughed or shrieked. And this was no trantrum. It was like the cries of someone just bereaved. Mother put her arm round me and led me into the living room. 'Sit down,' she ordered, and parked me on a straight chair by the table. I laid my head on the table and continued to cry helplessly. 'Tell us what is the matter.' Her voice was unexpectedly concerned, and somehow the unusual tone caused greater paroxysms of tears.

Father, standing anxiously beside me, produced his dismally grey pocket handkerchief, and proffered it. I took it and wept into it.

Mother pulled up another straight chair and sat down. 'Are you ill?'

I nodded negatively. I could not put into words what ailed me. How can you say to the person most responsible that you are broken-hearted?

'Perhaps you'd feel better if you lay down for a little while,' suggested Father. In the Victorian and Edwardian world from which he came, women were entitled to have the vapours, a tearful manifestation of low spirits. They were usually persuaded to lie down and have smelling salts and brandy administered to them, until they could rise and face their terribly narrow world again. The connection struck me immediately and caused fresh storms of sobs.

'Nervous breakdown?' Mother whispered to Father, and I wanted to scream again.

'I hope to God not,' replied Father, as if I was not there. And that was the root of the trouble. To both of them most of the time I was not there – I did not exist. I rubbed my face on the dirty cloth and howled.

Mother patted the back of my head. 'I think bed is best. Come along upstairs, and when you are rested you can tell us what the trouble is.'

I was too far gone to care what happened, so I was led upstairs, kicked off my shoes and lay down on my bed. Mother brought a blanket to cover me, as I continued to cry. It was as if I would never be able to stop.

Father sat on the edge of the bed, while Mother went to fill Edward's hot water bottle.

'What's the matter, old lady?' Father asked, while Mother was downstairs

'It's all too much,' I nearly shrieked. 'I'm so tired. So tired and so lonely. I work hard – I never stop – and I never get anywhere.' I wept on, while Father sat, quiet, on the bed.

'I feel so weak – and I'm always hungry. And I've no money to buy anything at all – and I wonder if I ever will have. And nobody seems to notice or care. Nobody cares a tinker's cuss.'

I turned on my face and roared into my knobbly pillow.

Father caught one flaying hand in his own tiny hands, which went white at the slightest cold because his heart was so bad.

'Don't say, that, dear,' he responded, as if hurt to the quick. 'You're my Helen Rose. I care.' He started to unclench my fist and to rub my hand as if it were cold. 'Things are much better than they were, dear.'

'They are for everybody else,' I wailed, 'Not for me.' He continued to rub my hand. 'I wish I was dead,' I raved.

Mother came in with the hot water bottle. I took it from her and put it instinctively to my stomach, where the pain usually was, and curled up round it in a foetal position. I began to hold Father's hand as if it were a lifeline.

The room was nearly dark, so Mother lit a candle and put it on the mantelpiece. Then she, too, sat on the edge of the bed. There was silence, except for the sound of my weeping. The concern of both parents was undoubted, but in a corner of my mind which was beginning to function it appeared to me that it was the fear of the scandal of mental illness, rather than concern for me as a person, which bothered them. Probably this was unfair, but such was the distrust built into me since infancy.

I do not know for how long I cried. The storm began gradually to retreat, until I was sobbing occasionally, eyes sealed tight. The warmth of the blanket and the hot water bottle began to relax me, and I lay exhausted.

I lay quite still, too drained and fatigued to speak. Father still patiently held my hand, waiting for me to recover. Mother began to fidget round the room. 'Feeling better?' she inquired.

I looked dully at her silhouette against the candle. 'Yes, thank you,' I muttered, and then added hesitantly, 'I'm sorry.'

'That's all right, dear. You rest now. I'm going to attend to the blackout, and then I'll make some fresh tea and bring it up.' She turned briskly to Father, and said, 'You had better stay with her.'

'Of course,' Father assured her, and gave my hand a little squeeze. He must have been getting cramp from my holding on to his hand for so long, but I felt that if I let go, and lost the human contact, I would slip back again into hysteria.

I heard the big shutters in the living room being slammed and the iron bar being threaded across them, and then the ting of the rings on the blackout curtains which we had so painstakingly hand stitched; there were small thuds as Mother put some books along their hems to hold them flat against the window, so that light did not seep through. I began to cry again. The thought of the war made me feel even more helpless.

Father carefully put my hand down. 'I'll blow the candle out – the Warden may spot it.' He went over and blew out the small flame, and the odour of the smoking wick permeated the room. I watched him, still sobbing. He turned and looked out of the window through which the faint last afterglow of the sunset filtered. Over the chimneys of the houses huddled close to the back of our home, the thin, pencil line of a searchlight swept slowly across the sky.

Between huge, shuddering sobs, I said, 'I'm sorry to make such a fuss, Daddy.'

He turned and came slowly back to me. Seated on the bed, he faced me and asked, 'What happened?'

I tried to compose myself, and in unhappy gasps, I answered, 'It's nothing really, Daddy. I'm stupid. I spent my return fare from the office on a telephone call for a client. So I had to walk home from Bootle – and it seemed the last straw. I'm so tired – I feel I want to die with it.'

'You've had a lot of illness, I know. But I thought you were quite well.'

'I suppose I am.' Still weeping, I pulled myself up to a sitting position.

He sat looking anxiously at me, while I tried, not very successfully, to control myself.

'It wasn't exactly being without the twopence to

come back to the city – it was the whole thing. Everybody in the family – all their needs – seem to be considered – but never me. I haven't a penny. I can't find another student to teach. No lunch, no make-up, no clothes. I'm desperate for new stockings.' My voice rose with a hint of hysteria again. 'If it wasn't for the Greek gentleman who gave us theatre money again this winter, I would never have been able to do anything. Even to visit Sylvia costs tram fares.'

'Have you told your mother?'

'Oh, Daddy! Ever since I went to work, she has done her best to make it impossible for me to stay there. She wants me home as a cheap housekeeper. She wouldn't give me a penny.' I put my head in my hands and cried some more.

'She paid for a coat for you recently.'

'She *lent* me the money – and she wants it back.' I nearly screamed in fury, 'And I only got that in the hope of not having the police on our backs – that would have been a real scandal, wouldn't it? Nice families don't get called in by the police, do they?' I put my head on my knees and lamented like a wind on the moors.

Father put his arms around me, the first time I ever remember him doing so, and did his best to comfort me.

A very subdued Mother brought me tea, which I drank. Then as my sobs subsided, she suggested that I try to sleep. Still shuddering, I thanked them both and obediently lay down like an exhausted rabbit in a thorn bush.

Chapter twenty-three

Through my troubled sleep, I was aware of a first-class uproar in the living room below. The battle between Mother and Father was joined again while I lay in bed on Sunday morning – the first Sunday I ever remember staying in bed, except when I had been ill.

Shattered and demoralised, I lay by Fiona, crying softly and listening to the enraged voices going back and forth. I wondered if I was indeed losing my reason.

A little more food had come my way. We had a fire more often, and usually there were enough pennies to provide a minimum of gas and electricity. These were solid gains, for which I should be grateful. I did not realise that it is not the actually starving who revolt – they are too weak – rather, it is the underfed, the underprivileged, who feel that the system could provide more for them. My system – my family – had taken my money, my work, my affection – and had given very little. I felt betrayed and forgotten by those who should have had my interest at heart, and I wept on.

Fiona stirred, stretched and shivered in the bedroom's clammy stuffiness. She heard my snuffling into the pillow, whipped around and lifted the blanket cautiously off my shoulders.

'What's the matter, Helen? Have you got a tummy-ache?'

Slowly, I turned my face towards her. She looked quaint with her hair neatly rolled up on hairpins secured under a net – Europe might be in flames, but Fiona set her hair every night without fail. The deep, violet blue eyes looked down at me with alarm.

'I don't really know exactly what is the matter, Fi. My tummy's all right. I just can't stop crying.'

She rolled close to me and put an arm round me. 'It must be something.'

I curled up close to her and cried into her shoulder, while she made soothing noises and stroked my long straggling locks.

Between sobs, I began to tell her about not having a student to teach and my resultant penury. She was a good listener and by no means as stupid as she sometimes led our parents to imagine. 'This last few days I've realised, Fi, that without an education – with no degree – I'll never be able to be a real social worker. I might do the same work, but I would not be as well paid. And night school doesn't provide degrees.'

Fiona smiled. 'You're clever – and you can write shorthand and type. You could get a really good secretarial job.'

'Not the way I look,' I lamented. 'My clothes are all right nowadays for social work – one shouldn't look too smart. But a secretary must look really nice.'

'You should ask Mummy. She'd buy you some clothes – she's got plenty of money – she buys all mine.'

I felt the hysteria returning. I burst into further muffled wails. 'Mother expects me to manage.' I did not want to remind her that both she and Mother preyed on me for the bits of clothing I managed to obtain for myself.

Fiona pushed my hair back from my face and said earnestly, 'I didn't think you were interested in clothes and things like that. You're always too busy.'

'Nobody thinks.' I shot at her bitterly. 'I just don't really exist where most people are concerned.'

She stared at me uncomprehendingly, as the tears came down on her nightgown in rivulets.

She hugged me tightly. 'Please, please, don't cry, Helen. If clothes are the trouble, it's easy enough for Mother to get them.'

'It's not only that,' I wept. 'I want to have fun and go dancing, like the detective said.'

This made Fiona lean back and look at me in astonishment. 'Really?'

'Well, of course I do,' I nearly bawled.

'I thought you liked studying – and books – and helping people.'

I gave up, and cried on, and a bewildered Fiona held me tightly, until her nightgown was thoroughly wet.

Downstairs Father's footsteps echoed in the hall and a moment later the front door slammed. The key hanging from the letter box by its piece of string made a protesting rattle against the wooden panels. Father, I guessed, was going for his usual Sunday morning walk and drink at Peter's, a famous public house near Catherine Street.

Mother's slippers flip-flapped up the stairs and I clung closer to Fiona. Over me crawled my infantile fear of Mother, primitive, childlike, ridiculous, but nevertheless overwhelming.

'How are you feeling?' she inquired to the back of my head buried in Fiona's shoulder. 'Crying again? Come on, that won't do. There's no need to weep so much.' The voice was kind, a little weary.

Fiona, bigger and stronger than me, pushed me away from her and eased me round to face Mother.

I made an effort to check the waterfall, and sniffed and said, 'I'm sorry, Mummy.'

Fiona burst in. 'Mummy, she's feeling miserable. But all she really needs is to look nice to get another job – and have some boy friends – and things.' She spoke cheerily and patted me. 'Isn't it, Helen? That's all.'

In part she was right, so I nodded. How could I explain my frantic need to feel that someone cared, that another adult loved me enough to really care what happened to me.

Mother had not yet washed, and she looked as badly as ever I did, with her dyed black hair in a ruffled mop and the lines on her pasty-white face looking as if they had been etched in. But she laughed, an unusually natural laugh, and sat down with a bounce on the bed. She spoke with determined cheerfulness.

'Your Father and I have been discussing the matter,' she announced.

I tried to stop crying and to listen. I did not know that I had frightened them both very much by my sudden collapse, which they feared was the beginning of a complete breakdown, with all its future slurs on the mental stability of the family. In those days one was, to most of the population, either sane or insane – and insanity marked the whole family, not just the victim.

'We think that you and Fiona must be treated alike.' I felt Fiona stiffen beside me – and suddenly I wanted to laugh, in spite of her sympathy. Did she fear being reduced to my circumstances? Mother continued, 'Daddy and I can manage if you pay into the house the same amount as Fiona does – and we'll get you some clothes out of pawn.'

I gazed at her dully. I wanted her to take me in her arms. I didn't care about the physical help. I was mentally begging her to love me, to tell me that she would do what she could to help me, sympathise, comfort.

She was waiting for my reaction, and shrugged her cardigan up closer round her neck. She became uncomfortable under my gaze and said suddenly and defensively, 'You were always so keen on managing alone.'

I was astonished, and I stopped crying. How could she rationalise the situation like that? But there was no strength in me. After all, hadn't I wanted to be treated like Fiona? And, as far as physical needs were concerned, that was what she was offering.

I had no stamina left. One cannot argue a person into loving one, so I ignored her last remark and said, 'Thank you. It would help a lot if I paid like Fiona – and I would be grateful for some clothes.' I leaned against Fiona and tried by closing my eyes tight to stop a further flood.

There was silence for a moment, while Fiona hugged me close, and then Mother said, 'Your hair is a mess. Lady Fayre is having a sale of perms. They're down to three and sixpence. I'll stand you one, if you like.'

Fiona burst in enthusiastically. 'You should, Helen. You should. Betty is a wizard on hair.'

I crushed down the pain within, and said, 'That's very kind of you, Mummy. I would love to have my hair done professionally.'

Mother really was trying to be supportive; I realised it, and I added, 'Thanks, Mum,' while I clung to the comforting warmth of Fiona, and I lay quietly while the two of them swiftly planned my physical rebuilding.

Chapter twenty-four

I sat bolt upright in the hairdresser's shabby, white, wooden chair, while Betty, a plump and gloriously brassy blonde, first removed the too small, black-rimmed glasses and then pulled out the hairpins which held my bun in place. She ran her fingers through the tumbling locks and spread them on my shoulders.

'Goodness, you've got lovely hair, Miss. So thick. I'll put a brightener in the rinse.'

I had given Betty *carte blanche* as to how she did my hair, so I smiled and said, 'Thank you.'

She took her scissors out of her pink overall pocket and snipped and shaped. Rolls of nut-brown hair joined the piles from earlier customers, drifting about the floor. She leaned me over a grey sink, which smelled of old soap and hair, and scrubbed my head with light experienced fingers, and then towelled it half-dry. Strand after strand was rolled on metal curlers, which hung round my head like so many small, clock pendulums. Cotton wool was then poked between them to protect the skull. I gasped as the curlers were doused with a chemical that smelled like ammonia, and I snatched the towel from the sink edge, to protect my smarting eyes.

Betty laughed, and threaded the curlers into plugs dangling from electric wires attached to a kind of chandelier hanging from the ceiling. She turned on a wall switch and after a second or two a strong smell of burning hair was added to that of the ammonia-like lotion. I peeped over the towel. Wisps of smoke were rising from the curlers. 'Good heavens!' I exclaimed in alarm, and instinctively tried to jerk my head away, but I was firmly suspended from the ceiling.

'Be careful,' warned Betty, 'or you'll bring the whole thing down on your head.'

Quite undisturbed by the smoke, Betty had seized a broom and was shoving the mass of cut hair into a corner, while she sang under her breath. I froze in my seat and was relieved to find that the curlers ceased to smoke.

I began to relax, and Betty went to gossip with her apprentice, who was setting another customer's hair. The apprentice looked most fashionable to my untutored eyes. She wore her hair parted down the left side, smoothed back from her face and caught in a hair slide. A loose wave nearly covered her right eye. At the shoulder the hair was turned under in what was called a page-boy. Her eyebrows had been plucked to a pencil-thin line, the expressionless face powdered to a smooth whiteness and the lips painted with a purplish lipstick to a full pout. I sighed.

My mind was dull and lethargic, sodden with weeping, which from time to time tended to burst forth without warning. I felt I never wanted to face another whining client, no matter how pitiable her state, never open another book to study, never do an iota more of housekeeping or child-caring, never ever have to face another fight.

But life does not stand still. It has to be faced, somehow dealt with. I was shamefacedly silent before the family.

On the Monday evening after my collapse, Mother had announced that she was going to the pawnbroker, and had enrolled a protesting Fiona to act as parcel carrier. 'Somebody I know might see me,' she wailed ineffectually. Now a pile of crumpled garments awaited washing and ironing or sponging and pressing, to get the smell of the pawnbroker's loft out of them. I was grateful but still leadenly depressed.

That same evening, Father had gently suggested that we might go for a walk together, and I had thankfully accepted. Numbly, I had walked beside him down the hill towards the town. We strolled along Bold Street, looking in the shop windows. It was still light enough to see their contents. Because of the blackout, no illumination had been turned on, and, since rationing had not yet begun, the windows were still filled with goods. It did not seem to have occurred to shopowners that, if we were bombed, the glass would be blown out and their careful displays ruined or looted. Wholesale looting by fellow townsmen was as yet an unbelievable idea.

Father began to play his favourite game of If I Had a Million I Would . . . With this million, he would build and furnish a huge house. I slowly began to join in. We chose furniture and curtains and rugs out of Waring and Gillows'. We filled the larder with peaches in brandy and caviare from Cooper's in

Church Street, and the butler's pantry with silver knives and forks and serving dishes from Russell's. Russell's clock struck as we walked, its little figures coming out and performing as the strokes went on, and I felt a poignant need for Baby Edward, who loved this clock, and was now trying to be a model small boy for his aunts.

We went up Lord Street and filled our imaginary wardrobes with clothes from Frisby Dykes and the many gentlemen's shops; passed the statue of Queen Victoria standing firmly above Liverpool's most popular public lavatory, and down James Street. Here we were amongst the offices of the great shipping and food companies which had their business in Liverpool. Each door had a pile of sandbags round the entrance.

The city was very quiet, as we continued on. Its peace and the pleasant conversation, my Father walking by me as he had done when I was a child, had its effect. I began to feel more cheerful.

'Let's go right down to the Pier Head,' I suggested, quite unaware that this small decision was to make a big change in my life.

The sharp wind, clean and bracing, blew up from the river, sending little eddies of abandoned wrapping papers scurrying across the sets of Mann Island.

Father held his trilby firmly on his head and I took my hat off, as the playful breeze struck us while we walked along Georges landing stage and watched the busy river glinting in the sunshine. A transatlantic liner was moored by the Princes landing stage, and, by common consent, we went to peep at it through the open gates. A good-humoured guard warned us that we must not go through the gateway, unless we had business with the ship. I looked with awe at the great Cunarder, a queen of the Atlantic.

'Nice old girl, isn't she?' remarked the guard, nodding his grey head towards the ship. He laughed ruefully, 'Not that I'd recommend a trip on her at present. It's much too lively out there for comfort.'

My hairpins were falling out in the wind, and I held on to my loosened bun while I smiled at the guard and nodded, though the thought of the German submarines lurking in Liverpool Bay was no laughing matter. Some men standing near looked as if they might be crew from the ship; they were laughing and talking as if they did not have a care in the world.

Suddenly, as Father chatted with the guard, my hair rolled down my back and was lifted up by a particularly strong gust of wind. I snatched at it and knocked off my glasses. The same gust blew up my skirts, and to the amusement of the men talking, I tried to grab at the falling glasses, the flying hair and the revealing skirts.

One man, standing with feet giving to the rise and fall of the floating dock as if used to it, laughed at me and came forward and rescued my glasses, fortunately unbroken. He was a burly young man, heavy shouldered, and with a big fair moustache, unusual for those days. As he handed me the spectacles, he looked so jolly that, unhesitatingly, I laughed back when the errant wind flicked the ash off his cigarette on to his suit. Struggling with my flying locks, I thanked him, and with Father turned towards the protection of a shed on Georges Stage. I screwed up my bun again, and we took the tram home.

It was a happy walk and I suddenly felt much better. I forgot the young man. But he did not forget me.

Betty undid a roller and tush-tushed over it, rolled it up and slipped it back into its electric outlet. 'Won't be long now,' she remarked, as she leaned against the sink and lit a cigarette. Through the cigarette smoke, she looked me over in a casual, friendly way. 'Yer sister says you never go anywhere. But, yer know, yer could do quite well for yourself – if yer wanted.' She turned to her assistant who was standing turning the pages of a magazine, while she waited for her customer's hair to dry under a noisy machine. 'Couldn't she, Dawn?'

Dawn flicked her cigarette ash into the sink and strolled over to look me over, as if I was a pony up for sale. She nodded, and smiled at me. 'You got lovely legs.'

'Wait till I've finished her hair. You won't know her,' promised Betty. 'If you like, luv, I'll make your face up, too. Just so you can see what a difference it can make.'

'O.K.'

Underneath still surged a fearful depression hard to control, despite Mother and Father being so helpful, an emptiness of spirit, a lack of hope.

I was unable to talk truthfully and naturally to my parents, was certain in my mind that as soon as I seemed better, their interest would wane again. I missed the children and the letters from Friedrich and Ursel, all of whom had at least diverted my mind from our grim surroundings. I had not seen Sylvia for some days and determined that some of my new pocket money would be spent in order to see more of her. But even with her, there was a holding back, a reserve, a sense that I would never make her understand what the years had done to me. That trust was to come later on, but its time had not yet arrived.

I was thrust under a spray and Betty's scarlet tipped fingers scrubbed away the ghastly smelling solution. In apprehension I watched her brush out the tiny tight curls until I looked like a South Sea Islander. 'Goodness, Betty. What are you doing?'

Betty laughed, and sloshed highly scented setting lotion over my head. Cold trickles ran down my neck. 'Haven't you ever had a perm before, luv?'

'No,' I admitted shyly. 'I've not been to a hairdresser before.'

'Well, I never. You wait. Proper pretty it will be.'

And proper pretty it was. Soft curls finally haloed my thin face, a deep wave disguising the high forehead.

Betty stepped back and looked at me, head on one side. 'Now, when it grows, I'll set it for you with a bush of curls at the back – you could put a big slide in to hold them. T' perm'll last a few months, if you vary the style a bit.' She leaned over me, and picked up a pair of tweezers from the shelf in front of us. 'Now hold still.' She put a heavy hand on my forehead, and gave a quick series of painful tweaks with her tweezers. 'See, I took a few hairs out between your brows – makes a difference, doesn't it?' It did.

She took her own make-up from out of her handbag and swiftly rubbed vanishing cream into my face, touched the cheeks very lightly with rouge, carefully crayoned the lips with a slightly mauve lipstick, added a little length to the heavy black eyebrows with a dark pencil, and stood back. 'Come and see, Dawn. What she needs is very soft make-up, looking so young, like.'

Dawn, her customer combed out and sent on her way, strolled languidly over. 'Very nice,' she opined. 'Boy friends won't know you.'

I blushed under the rouge. 'I don't go in for boy friends.' Then at their startled looks, I added, 'Never had time.'

'For crying out loud!' Betty exclaimed. 'You've missed your vocation – you could do real well for yourself. You look as nice as the next girl – and you walk a lot nicer. Why Nick was only saying the other day, you got style – only needs bringing out.'

Astonished, I asked, 'Who's Nick?'

'Oh, you know him. Everybody does. He knows you. He was in this morning, fiddling with everything as usual. Saw your name in the Appointments Book. He knows every girl in the place – it's his business.' She giggled.

'But I don't know him,' I insisted, preparing to get up from the chair.

'Oh, yeah, yer must do. He's often around the Rialto – wears a light coloured mac most of the time – proper smart.'

Enlightment dawned. 'Oh, yes. He says good night

sometimes.' I paused, and looked at her distrustfully. 'But he's a pimp.'

The girls grinned knowingly at each other. 'Sure. He's set up a lot of girls in his time. Buys 'em clothes. Finds them flats. He's fair. Trades under a lamp-post, he does. Yer should get to know him better – you'd do fine with him. He moves his best girls into real good districts.'

I was shocked. 'Oh, Betty. I'm not that kind.'

Betty's face lost its smile, and hardened. 'We're all that kind, luv, when times are like they are. Better'n slaving in service or standing on your feet in a factory all day – or being so clemmed like you are.'

I looked at her steadily. There were lines under the heavy make-up. I got slowly up from the chair. Did she find it better than being a hairdresser who had to cut prices to the bone? 'Thank you, Betty,' I said very gently, and I took out from my otherwise empty handbag the three and sixpence which Mother had given me, and handed it to her, while Dawn drifted back to her magazines.

Betty smiled very sweetly at me, as she put the money into the drawer of a chipped, white counter. She replied a little sadly. 'There, luv. Don't be offended. You take care of yourself – and keep that innocent face of yours. Some nice lad'll know a good thing when he sees it – and take proper care of you.'

'You're too flattering, Betty,' I teased her. 'I'm not cross.' She meant to be kind and I did not want to leave her with the feeling that I condemned her way of life. I knew from my work that, too often, it carried with it its own tragic punishments.

Chapter twenty-five

I went back to work on the Tuesday after my collapse, and did my best to cope with the mob besieging our waiting room. It was a week later, however, when I walked into the office with hair permed, face made up, dressed in a good blue tweed suit and a plain white blouse, and caused a modest sensation.

'My goodness,' exclaimed my patient colleague, her pale face turned upwards from a mass of untidy files lying on her desk. 'I can see you won't be with us long, if you go on looking like that,' she added archly. 'You look very pretty.'

The inference that I might be whisked off to the altar at any moment made me smile weakly, as I teetered on my second-hand high-heeled shoes towards the door, and hung one of Mother's old hats on the back of it. The hat was navy blue and Fiona had donated a bunch of artificial sweet peas to retrim it. Both Mother and Fiona had been unexpectedly kind in helping to renovate a crushed young woman. But the inner woman remained squashed.

It would be nice to be able to say that we lived in amity ever after. Far from it. Mother continued to nag at Father and rage at me, between short bouts of better humour. Father still drank more than he could afford, still lost his temper over small details. Mother and Fiona, rushing to get ready for work, still purloined any clean clothes I had. But the total of garments between us was greater.

The amount of expense money and pocket money seemed wonderful. It bought a meagre lunch, stockings, and make-up from Woolworth's. I bought some much needed panties and a petticoat, all as yet unrationed. I was close to having the comforts of the working-class girls who sat facing me on the long benches of the trams, as I went to work. I was servilely grateful to my parents.

I was so afraid of offending people, particularly Father and Mother, that I was finding it increasingly difficult to show any originality, to use my own judgment. For years, I had continued a deadly routine of night school, of being an exact and obedient employee, an inoffensive helper at home – except when human nature had its say and I burst into a temper.

Now at aged twenty I wanted to strike out, find a new life for myself. To learn to act, not just react. I had been brain-washed too long into the idea that I lived by courtesy of other people. Touched as yet lightly by the first ripples of tremendous social change which was to affect all women, I determined to change myself not only in appearance but in character, to assert myself, to be a whole woman in my own right.

'I am me,' I cried inside. 'And I want to be me.'

Mother agreed to Sylvia's coming to tea. I wanted to learn from this most faithful friend's outlook on life. She was so balanced, so sensible.

Sylvia came. Her hair was, as usual, carefully blonded, swept upwards from the back to form a crown of curls on top of her head. The fairness complimented speedwell blue eyes and a dimpled, merry face. She talked with Mother and made her laugh. They got on splendidly.

Sylvia had always taken a course or two at night school, and because all schools were closed she was wondering, like me, what to do with her spare time. Now, as she sat like a neutral zone between Mother and me, I made a great effort to advance an idea made possible by the advent of some pocket money.

'You know, Sylvia, how clumsy I am – I'm always dropping things or falling over something. And I was wondering if I learned to dance – that would help me. After all, you learn to be precise in your movements when you dance.' I paused doubtfully. I did not dare to say in front of Mother that the detective had left with me this idea of dancing, having fun. I feared her scornful laughter, in spite of her recent efforts on my behalf. 'I wondered if we could go together?'

Sylvia drew in a deep breath. She was a nonconformist by religious persuasion, and with a sinking heart I remembered suddenly that nonconformists do not dance. Perhaps I've shocked her, I thought miserably.

Fiona interjected, 'I never had to *learn* to dance – I just picked it up.'

I ignored Fiona. I hoped that dancing was all her devoted retinue had tried to teach her, but in my jealous heart I always knew that, though Fiona seemed so pliable, her escorts would not be allowed to step out of line. She had a firm fastidiousness bordering on the prudish – she enjoyed the turmoil she created, but she would laugh and slip away from any man who presumed too far.

I concentrated on Sylvia. She was happily ladling jam on to a thin wafer of bread and butter. A quarter of a pound of butter had been bought specially for her, and the bread had been cut as it used to be cut in our long ago world of cooks and housemaids.

'Everything is shut,' she said ruefully.

'There are two or three dance studios tucked into old houses round here,' I reminded her. 'One of them says on its noticeboard that it charges only a shilling for a group lesson.' What was Sylvia thinking? Was she feeling wicked at the idea of dancing?

'I used to go to ballet school when I was little,' I went on, 'until a wardrobe fell on top of me and injured my foot – and it was great fun. After that I dragged the foot a bit, but I should be all right for ballroom dancing.' I could not mention that such a corrupt person as Nick said that I walked well – and had style.

She made a little moue with her mouth. 'That must have hurt. Of course, I'll come if you would like to go.' She giggled as if she thought it might be fun.

'You can dance already,' Mother protested. 'Why waste money? We sent you to learn ballroom dancing, when you made such a fuss about not going to ballet school any more.' She looked at me accusingly, as if I should now emerge, twelve years later, a perfect dancer – like a moth crawling out of a chrysalis and taking flight.

I did not say anything. I sensed the beginning of a fight which I had not the strength to undertake.

'Oh, she'll have forgotten,' Sylvia assured Mother briskly, as if she understood my need to be rescued before I fled back down my mental burrow. She turned to me, and added firmly, 'See what day they take beginners, and give me a phone call at the office. I'll come.'

Chapter twenty-six

The black taffeta dress with tiny gold spots on it was redeemed from pawn and carefully pressed. I had made it several years before from a length of material bought from the pawnbroker. It had been cut out with a razor blade and hand stitched. The taffeta smelled old, but the dress had not split anywhere. New black lace frilling was sewn into its neckline. Also redeemed were the white satin slippers I had worn at my Confirmation. I dyed them black. They had satin bows on each toe, and I was entranced by them; they looked so delightfully frivolous. Cinderella was about to go to the ball.

Cinderella, however, was not actively expecting to meet a prince. At the back of her mind lay the memory of the pleasure of moving rhythmically to music, a faint picture of a small girl in a short black velvet tunic standing in front of a mirror and slowly rising on her first pair of points, a child dreaming of being a cygnet in *Swan Lake*.

The cygnet was still rather like a duck, as she climbed the stone front steps to the porticoed entrance of the dancing school. The paint was peeling off the front door, and the steps looked as if they had not been swept for a generation.

Emboldened by a tiny crack of light from under the

door and the distant sound of a gramophone, Sylvia rang the bell.

The door was opened by a thin man in a light grey business suit. Hair was plastered back from a middle parting, above a rather sickly face. Grey eyes, as sharp as the Warden's when looking for illicit cracks of light, surveyed the two of us.

We both smiled politely, while the unfriendly stare continued. Then suddenly the man grinned. 'Come in, come in,' he invited, and led us into a big, dimly lit hall from which a wide staircase led upwards into total darkness. He closed the door quickly behind us, and inquired, 'Are you beginners?'

We assured him that we both had to start from scratch. 'Well,' he exclaimed jovially, rubbing his hands, 'Tonight's the night. We'll soon have you on your feet.' He pointed to a cupboard under the staircase. 'Put your coats in there. Bring your handbags with you – we mustn't lose things, must we? Then you can give Doris here your shilling.'

As we took off our coats, I observed a smiling middle-aged woman in a frilly dress covered with a pattern of large orange flowers. She held a record in her hand, and put it down on a small hall table, while we paid her.

'Ever been dancin' before?' she inquired in a friendly voice.

'No,' we murmured bashfully.

'Oh, you'll enjoy yourselves here. You'll like the people. We're fussy who we have in. No trouble – ever.'

Trouble in connection with a dancing school had not occurred to me, and I wondered timorously what she meant, but the man came bustling in from the hall saying, 'I'm Norm,' and led us further into the ballroom.

The ballroom had been contrived by the removal of the walls between the dining room, sitting room and breakfast room in the original house, so that the dance floor ran from front to back of the building. Three sets of windows were heavily shrouded with blackout curtains. The walls were a faded, frowsy grey, and battered bentwood chairs lined two sides. A large glass-fronted cabinet stood in an alcove at one end. On a small table, by the door through which we had entered, stood a big wind-up gramophone, flanked by an untidy stack of records. Two girls in summery dresses sat, legs crossed, on the far side of the room. Cigarettes dangled from their fingers, and they glanced casually over at us, and then continued their animated conversation. A couple of young men in neat suits with wide flowing trouser legs and big, gaudily striped ties were sprinkling chalk on the hardwood floor which, alone, showed evidence of care. The surface had been lovingly refinished and the wood glowed.

Norm seated us near the other girls, and said, 'I'll be back,' as the doorbell rang. Doris put on a record, and the young men rubbed the chalk lightly with their feet along the line of dance.

Men and women in their twenties and three or four much older couples began to fill up the room. Most of them seemed to know each other, and, while they waited, they gossiped in thick nasal Liverpool accents. Doris changed the record to a quick-step, winding up the gramophone like a mangle. She and Norm then swept out on to the floor and danced, while everybody watched. Since this was only the second time I had seen adults dancing, I was no judge, but the couple made a production of a basically simple dance. An infinite number of graceful variations was introduced, and, oblivious of their audience, they smiled at each other as if sharing some rapturous experience. It was a wonderful exhibition of perfectly coordinated, flowing movement; the shabby room was for a few minutes a theatre. I did not know then that I was looking at two of the best ballroom dancers in the north.

With hands clenched tightly on my lap, knees and ankles primly together, I sat on the edge of my chair, mesmerised by the charm of the dance. Now Doris and Norm gave a little bow, the audience clapped, and they retreated towards the gramophone. After a moment of consultation with his partner, Norm strode into the middle of the room, rubbed his hands together, and said, 'Now, most of yez learned the basic steps of the waltz last week. Now I want you to try out what you learned, and then we'll learn how to do a turn. Take your partners, please.'

The two girls smoking near us screwed their cigarette ends into a saucer of nub ends on the floor by their chairs, and rose to partner each other. I flashed a tiny, scared smile at Sylvia, who was sitting leaning back in her chair with a bright smile on her face. A young man, immaculately neat, acne scars all over his face, crossed the floor to her, and, with work-roughened hands clasped before him, bowed and asked her, 'Would you like to dance?'

She blushed, pushed her handbag surreptitiously further under her chair with her toe, and with a cheery grin at me, announced, 'Well – er, I can't dance.'

The young man went pink, and replied that he could not either. Undaunted, they went out on to the floor, and the young man put his arm round her waist, clasping her as if she might run away at any moment.

I was alone, feeling a little rejected. Would nobody ask me?

Norm was checking his flock, and when he found everybody paired off except me, he bowed and said, 'Let's dance, love.'

I remembered how to stand, and put my hand correctly on to his shoulder. He smelled nicely of carbolic soap and brilliantine. 'Now, everybody,' he called, 'remember, one and two, one and two, one and two.'

A very firm hand at my waist and an equally firm grasp of my right hand led me off correctly, without a word being said, except for the chanting count of 'one and two'. We circled the floor. After the first few steps the beat of the big band music relaxed me and I allowed myself to flow with my partner. 'Good,' he murmured approvingly, and twirled me into a simple variation. 'Very good.'

'You can dance already,' he said puzzled, 'and you're very light.'

I blushed to the roots of my hair, as if I had done something wrong. 'Well, I learned as a very little girl, but I thought I'd forgotten,' I confessed. Then I got up enough courage to say shyly, 'I think that it is your good guidance. I've never seen anybody dance like you and Doris. I wish I could be that good.'

He seemed as pleased with the compliment as if I had presented him with yet another gold cup, to add to the collection in the cabinet. Then he said, 'Oh, aye. You might be if you stuck at it.' He added earnestly, 'You'd have to find yourself a good partner, though. We've got a few silver medallists as come here – working for their golds, they are – and we've got one gold medallist – other than ourselves, that is.'

As the record came to an end, he led me over to Doris. 'We'll try the turn now,' he said to her. Then he added, 'Been telling this young lady, what's your name, luv, that she could win a silver if she worked.'

Doris nodded. 'I was watching you.'

I said shyly, 'My name is Helen Forrester. I didn't know one could get medals for dancing.'

'Of course you can,' replied Doris. 'A silver means you're good – and a gold you can teach.'

I looked at her open-mouthed. She had just bounced right at my feet a most interesting, brand new idea of how I might earn a living. Long ago, a country doctor had broken it to me very gently that I could never be a ballet dancer, because I was going to walk always with one foot turned slightly in. My dancing teacher confirmed it. I was sent to learn ballroom dancing, because every middle-class girl was expected to be able to dance. I had been very unhappy amid hordes of other little girls, and small boys dressed in sailor suits with whistles hung round their necks or in Eton suits with stiff white collars. Nobody had seemed to notice the turned foot – and neither, apparently, had Norm or Doris.

Doris was saying proudly, 'You should look at our cups in the cabinet there – proper collection of 'em we've got. Going to try for the world championship soon.'

None of us seemed to think it strange to talk about entering dance competitions, when we expected to be bombed out of existence before too long.

'How exciting!' I exclaimed, with genuine enthusiasm.

'Needs a lot of work,' Norm said, as he sifted through the worn records. He picked out a record and handed it to Doris to put on to the gramophone. While she was doing this, he leaned against the table to rest his feet, and said to me, 'If you're serious, you should come for lessons at least twice a week, and then come to the dance on Saturday night for practice with different partners. See how you get on, like.' He smiled at me, and I agreed, and then said shyly, 'I think I'd better go back to Sylvia.'

Sylvia was making rueful remarks about broken toes to the girl next to her. I sat down primly on the edge of the chair beside her. I was determined to continue the classes, and I hoped she would come with me, so I said soothingly, 'Never mind. A few lessons and we'll all improve.'

My dance with Norm had not gone unnoticed, and the moment we were told to take our partners to learn the turn, a gawky young man with a nervously bobbing Adam's apple was at my elbow, bowing with old-fashioned politeness to ask me if I cared to dance.

I jumped up eagerly, like an unpopular child suddenly asked to join in a game.

Norm, I discovered, was a stickler for good ballroom manners, and he stormed down the room towards one youth who asked a girl in a pink blouse, 'Worm, come and wiggle.'

'If that's how you're going to address a nice young lady, you needn't bother to come again,' he snapped.

The nice young lady immediately sat up straight, folded her hands in her lap and lowered her eyes.

The boy made a wry face, swept her a low bow, and inquired, 'Madam, would you care to dance?'

She nodded assent and rose gravely, leaving her cigarette balanced on an ash tray. Satisfied, Norm turned to his class.

Sylvia's pretty face and cheery manner assured her of partners, and I sat out only one dance. From this predicament I was rescued by Doris, who took the man's part and guided me very well through the basic steps of the slow foxtrot, which I had not danced before.

As we groped our way carefully through the unlit streets, towards the stop where Sylvia could catch a tram home, I was animated, flushed with excitement and exercise, yet scared that for some reason I might not be able to afford to go to the class again.

Sylvia's face was scarcely visible, but from the tone of her remarks she seemed to view the evening with an easy good humour and would tolerate another evening like it. My spirits sank a little, and I wondered if she could possibly understand what a lifeline it seemed to me.

Chapter twenty-seven

After a couple of weeks, Sylvia gave up attending the dancing classes, because of the long distance she had to travel in the blackout.

I went on my own. All the girls there were very nice to me, though they never gossiped with me or shared their jokes. Norm and Doris were conscientious teachers; and I began to gain a little self-confidence.

The dancing of the silver medallists at the Saturday evening dance showed a finish which owed much to almost daily practice. I was astonished at how much time working-class people were willing to spend on it, unlike the upper classes, who had many other sources of entertainment. Amongst Norm's pupils were older married couples who had met at a dance club, and had danced together all their adult lives.

To dance had been my first ambition in life and the first to be crushed. Its relaxing rhythm now began to heal the wounds that earlier years in Liverpool had so painfully inflicted upon me.

If I wanted to continue to dance, I had also to learn to be courteous and sociable. Such skills are normally learned within the family and their circle, while playing games, attending parties or church or clubs. By extreme poverty and the need to be a surrogate mother, I had been cut off from all the contacts that a young girl could normally expect to enjoy. Now, at twenty, I was an ignorant novice, trying to pick her way amid people who would have roared with laughter at most of the ideas with which my brain was cluttered. It was not easy.

The young men must have had many quiet laughs at my clumsy efforts to be agreeable. I was painfully shy with them, and soon became aware that they treated me a little differently from the other girls present. It was subtle, but it was there. I was an oddity.

I never lacked partners, because I swam on to the dance floor with the ease of a baby duckling learning to swim. All of them wanted a good partner with whom to practise, regardless of whom they eventually escorted home after the dance.

One brave youngster, curly haired and with the physique of a boxer, did one Saturday evening ask if he could take me home. I looked at him with short-sighted bewilderment and assured him that I was quite capable of seeing myself home. He looked stunned for a moment – perhaps he had never been refused before – and then he grinned in a friendly way which seemed to indicate approval, and said, 'That's O.K., luv,' and went to ask somebody else. Word of this rebuff must have gone round the class, because nobody else ventured to ask.

I went to the classes as frequently as I could afford. At first I was too shy to go to the Saturday night social dances, feeling that my dress was too shabby for a formal dance. The other girls seemed to have innumerable dresses.

I was so accustomed to working as a social worker amid a sea of unemployed, that I had never realised that even if unemployment was 33%, that still left over 66% of people in employment.

Now I was entering a new world of highly skilled artisans, where the division of the sexes was amply demonstrated by the fact that the women, whether married or not, congregated on one side of the room, while the men stood on the other side. Occasionally, bored by the lack of conversation, I would talk with Norm and Doris and learned much about their dancing careers and their hopes of expanding their business when the war was over – maybe after next Christmas.

I discovered that I was supposed to talk to my partners while dancing, and I spent anxious moments trying to think of something to amuse men whose main interests were football, football pools, girls and learning to dance so that one could meet more girls.

Finally, I hit on the question, 'Do you work round here?' This usually got an immediate answer, and then I would ask what their job was. This usually called forth a monologue which lasted until the dance ended. As I was escorted back to my chair, I would assure them that it had been a really interesting conversation and I had no idea before how hard men worked. It was true. Many of them worked very hard in hot, dirty, dangerous places, and I soon admired their tenacity, and the fact that they never seemed to realise how brave they were. One of them had spent most of his working life setting the stones of the Anglican Cathedral, and was very angry at having been brought down to street level by a government call-up, to build air raid shelters.

I met mechanics and carpenters, electricians and apprentice plumbers, machinists, pattern makers, draughtsmen, shipyard workers, slaughtermen, engineers of every description, bakers and others who worked in Liverpool's huge food industry, occasionally a man in an ill-fitting uniform home on his first leave; very rarely, a seaman or two. They were all scrubbed from head to heel, hair clipped close to their heads like Roman soldiers, dressed in well-pressed Sunday suits.

The top earners were girls who worked for Vernon's and Littlewood's, the companies who ran the football pools. Other girls were shop assistants, waitresses, factory hands in the biscuit factories or stocking works or the Dunlop Rubber Company. They dressed most elaborately, and I gathered from overheard conversations that they spent hours shopping for exactly matching hats, gloves and shoes, and in setting each other's hair. Like the girls I had worked with in the head office of my employers, they talked only of men, films and clothes.

On Sundays, I often went for a walk with Father. He gave me not only time but long and stimulating discussions of subjects which interested him. There was little that he had not studied of the life and times of Louis XIV of France, le Roi Soleil. We would discuss the King's policies, his strengths and failings, the details of his palace of Versailles, which Father had visited a number of times in his youth, and the lives of his advisers.

At night, we turned on our rickety radio, and Mother, Father and I listened to the nine o'clock news, as if it were holy writ. Then we would sweep the seeking needle slowly across the dial, while we tried to pick up news from France and Germany; and more than once I heard Hitler making a speech which sounded all the more terrifying because I could not always understand all of it.

Both Father and Mother benefited from a quieter home. Father never said whether he missed the younger members of his family and he never went to see them, probably because he flinched at the thought of having to meet his sisters if he did.

So, while Poland fought for its very existence, I danced my way back to a modicum of mental health, and we all waited for the holocaust to begin. The thought of it sat at the back of everybody's mind, a weight only hinted at by some stray remark – but there, all the same. At that time in the war, it was as if a conductor had raised his baton ready to begin a symphony, and the tiny pause before the orchestra played the first chord went on and on and on, the players frozen in their seats.

Chapter twenty-eight

People who did not drink were thankful to find some entertainment still open to them, and Norm was having to turn people away. 'T' floor might collapse and land us all in t' cellar, if I get too many dancing at the same time,' he explained, his thin face earnest. His skin looked yellow from too many late nights, on top of a job in a grocery during the day.

To me, the vibrations of the floor suddenly became something in which to take a personal interest.

Normally the Saturday night dance brought out the best dancers, Norm's treasured silvers and gold, and they now became fretful at the overcrowding. He consoled them by quietly opening up on Sunday night for them. Fortunately for him, the police had plenty of other work on their hands.

I still occasionally went to church on Sunday evenings, though the religious ardour of my early teens had gone. There was still enough natural light for the services to take place. The days of services in semi-darkness, as the winter approached, were yet to come. I would sit in the back pew, as usual, and wonder how I should make a life for myself, and sometimes ask divine help. Ever since I had arrived in Lime Street station at the age of eleven, torn from all that was familiar to me, I had seen clearly the need to obtain an education, despite my parents' objections, and then find an occupation to make me financially independent. What else could a plain girl look forward to? Now the war had made life even more complicated. Though I had not been able to find other employment, there was a steady flow of women, bereft of their menfolk, leaving their homes to take men's places in the work force. There was a call for volunteers for the women's services, in the Army, Navy and Air Force; but because I had no formal educational qualifications, I shrank from being thrown into the lowest rank to do unskilled, menial tasks. Less and less, I wanted to spend my whole life in the sea of sorrow in which I was at present working. I was recovered enough to feel compassion for the flood of widows caused by the sinking of the *Athenia* and the *Courageous* and a myriad of small ships which had been caught far from home at the outbreak of hostilities, and were now trying to creep back to Britain through seas menaced by U-boats. But sometimes I longed for laughter and cheerfulness. And so, while the collection clinked into the church plate, I fretted absently.

August and September saw Fiona's young escorts increasingly likely to be in uniform. It was clear that *my* dancing partners were going to be the war's privileged class; their skills were needed in the factories, much too precious to be wasted on the battlefield. It seemed that the war was going to be actually fought by the upper classes and by life's eternal losers, the unskilled.

It was Saturday, the day on which Hitler and Stalin formally abolished the country of Poland; and the clear moonlight made a fairyland of black Liverpool, beating its slate roofs into silver sheets, softening the ugly row houses, making the grubby window-panes glitter and the eyes of the many slinking cats in the alleys into blazing emeralds, as if there could not be a war in progress. It was a night of calm in which to look at the newly rediscovered stars.

Swinging my dancing shoes on two fingers, I strolled leisurely along the avenue to the dance club. Except for the bottom step, the imposing front steps and porch were in deep shadow, but I ran up them absently with feet that had become familiar with them, and stumbled clumsily into a small group of people waiting to be let in.

'Ow!' exclaimed a male voice, as, confused and apologetic, I stepped back on to a foot.

A shaded torch flashed for a second on my face, and then was turned downward to aid the shuffling and giggling group to see.

The owner of the torch assured me, 'It's all right. I think I'll live.' I was aware of a solid rock of male figure leaning against the portico.

''lo, Helen,' one of the waiting girls who had seen my illuminated face greeted me.

'Hello, Gloria,' I replied, smiling into the darkness. 'How are you?'

She did not have time to answer, because the door was opened by a grinning Norm, apologising for being so long. 'Had to go upstairs and turn a light off,' he explained.

Seven of us, four men and three women, hurried into the dimly lit hall. Though the electric light was swathed in red tissue paper to dull its rays, Norm shut the door quickly, before the ever vigilant warden could complain.

The gramophone was playing a scratched record of *Three Little Fishes and a Mother Fishie, too*, as we took off our coats and changed our shoes – woe betide anyone who stepped on Norm's precious floor in anything but dancing shoes. I always put on my little satin slippers with a feeling of pure joy.

I did not know the other people who had entered with Gloria and me, so I wandered into the ballroom with her. The dance was already in full swing and the floor was crowded. Doris looked up from her gramophone records and remarked, 'You're lucky. There isn't room for any more.' She surveyed the crowded room, and then added, 'This won't last, now the big dance halls are opening up again.'

'Why not?' I queried. 'It's a friendly place.'

She sighed. 'Well, we depend on regulars, and if they keep on transferring men around the country, like they are doing, there won't be anybody left for you to dance with, luv. Our John's got to report to some dump in Hull tomorrer. And he hasn't even got a place to stay.'

Our John was her brother, a pattern maker, so I commiserated with her, while the old house shook gently with the boom of the music and the movement of the dancers.

Gloria and I were soon claimed by men who knew us and were swept away into the mêlée of dancers. Above the music, I could hear Norm greeting some of the people who had come in with me, as if they were prodigal sons. 'Where you been all this time? What you doin' now?'

My partner deposited me, breathless, on a chair on the far side of the room from the door, where the re-union was continuing with much back slapping and laughter. My perspiring partner, the bricklayer who was really a stone mason, bowed and left me, to join the male cohorts near the door. I smiled briefly at the girl sitting next to me, but did not talk. She was with her mate, her close girl friend, and absorbed in a deep conversation about what *he* did and what *he* said last night.

I was still panting, when I thought I heard my name mentioned in the group of which Norm was the centre. I looked up quickly, just in time to see Norm hastily lower a finger pointing at me. Apparently slightly embarrassed, he turned his back to me and continued the conversation, in which Doris was also included.

The cigarette smoke made the room blue, hazing faces, dimming lights and adding a further deposit to the walls and ceiling. After a slightly longer break than usual Norm shouted, 'Take your partners for an old-fashioned waltz,' and after a doubtful start the strains of The Blue Danube filled the room.

Two young men were standing before me, both wishing to dance. One was a stranger.

'Like to dance?' asked the old acquaintance, with a surly look at the newcomer.

I was about to rise, when the stranger said shamelessly, 'Little Miss Helen promised this one to me when we came in.'

I opened my mouth to rebut this indignantly, but he had already leaned down and put his hand firmly under my elbow to help me up. Before I even had time to look at him properly, I was out on the floor, making apologetic faces to the other man over my partner's shoulder.

What the man lacked in finesse, he made up in energy. An old-fashioned waltz takes more vigour than its later counterpart and was always a test of endurance for me. Nevertheless, I was laughing breathlessly by the time the Blue Danube managed to reach the sea and come to an end. We had not spoken a word, and I had hardly glanced at my partner's face, except to note that he must be in his thirties. Lines, which would soon look like seams, etched a ruddy skin lightly, and there was little of the softness of youth. The face was vaguely familiar. The arms guiding me were extremely strong.

With a final spin, he whirled me to the narrow end of the room with its case of golden trophies. We flopped on to two rarely used chairs, and he pulled a handkerchief from his top pocket and mopped a perspiring brow. Blue eyes beneath fair, bushy brows laughed at me over the damp cotton. I was panting like a Pekinese and could not speak. The eyes were so merry, though, that I had to smile back. It was as if we suddenly shared some naughty secret.

'Well, little Miss Helen, how was that?'

'Fun,' I gasped. 'But, really you told an awful lie.'

'I spend nights dreaming of meeting her again – and she calls me a liar when I do.' He slowly tucked the crumpled hanky back into his pocket, then leaned back in his uncomfortable chair, hands lying loosely on his thighs. He looked at me, with a slight smile curving under a heavy, though neat moustache somewhat yellowed by tobacco smoke. Strong stubby fingers showed faint signs also of cigarette smoke, as did most people's.

Though subjected to a fairly intense examination, I did not feel shy – only bewildered that he claimed to have met me before. He was so relaxed, however, that he conveyed it to me, and when I had regained my breath, I said perplexedly, 'I'm sorry, but I don't remember meeting you before – yet you knew my name?'

'A girl on the steps called you by it – and, anyway, Norm sent me over to dance with you – thought you'd like me. Do you?'

I burst out laughing, embarrassed by the question. I did not know what to reply. 'Well . . . well . . .' I looked again at him, and then added bravely, 'Of course.'

He grinned, more at my confusion, I think, than at the reply.

'Did I . . . ? Were you . . . ? Did I tread on you on the step?'

'Yes,' he responded, with a twinkle, 'You trampled on me. I'm very hard done by tonight.'

I was sober. 'Did it hurt very much? I'm so sorry.'

'I thought I was crippled for life.'

'At least you didn't swear.'

'I save that for recalcitrant machinery – and occasionally for other things. Are you accustomed to men swearing at you?'

'No. But they do swear sometimes – under their breath. And at work I've been sworn at by angry men once or twice.'

'Have you? Where do you work?'

'Well, I'm a social worker – and sometimes men don't like the advice you give them – or the advice you give their wives – and they get very miffed.'

The smile had gone from his face, and he said, 'Well, I'm blowed. You don't look like one.'

'Like what?'

'A social worker.'

'What's wrong with them?' I asked sharply. But a quickstep burst from the ever-faithful gramophone and, without answering, he got up and held out his hand to me to dance.

He held me quite closely and guided me into one or two variations which I think he had invented himself. His suit was navy blue and I was careful not to brush my powdered face against his shoulder. After we had circled the floor in silence, he asked me in a genuinely puzzled tone, 'What's a nice girl like you doing in a place like this?'

I turned my face up to his. 'It's most respectable,' I parried.

'Aye, it is. Norm takes care of that. But you're different. You don't belong here.'

His accent was that of a north country man, but he did not have the thick nasal Liverpool accent of the other men present. I grinned wickedly, and inquired with deceptive quietness, 'And what is a nice man like you doing in a place like this?'

That made him jump. 'What? Me?' I felt the quiver of laughter in him. '*Touché*,' he replied.

We danced half way round the room before he answered. Then he said, 'I came with one of my friends and his wife. I sometimes do in winter. They're great dancers – they learned here.' He twiddled me into one of his fancy variations, and I felt the smallest sigh go through him. 'I rent a room in their house – to keep my gear in – and to sleep in when I'm in Liverpool.'

I glanced up at his face again. The mouth under the moustache was set and he looked suddenly weary. He became aware of my gaze and looked down at me, and smiled.

I was feeling tired myself, so I asked, 'Would you like to sit out the rest of the dance?'

Pure mischief glinted in the blue eyes. 'That's an idea.' He guided me round until we reached the door, and under the benign eye of Norm leaning against the gramophone table, he danced me into the empty, chilly hall, and sat me down on the carpeted stairs. They smelled of dust. He squeezed in beside me. There was just room for the two of us, and he put his arm round me, ostensibly to make more space. It was exceedingly comforting, quite the snuggest feeling I had ever experienced. And I felt quite safe. Norm was only a few feet away. It struck me that Norm had allowed this man to do something he would never tolerate in anyone else. Nobody was allowed to linger in the dark hall. Everybody was kept firmly under his paternal eye in the ballroom.

'Do you know Norm and Doris well?'

'Pretty well. Been coming here occasionally for years. Makes some company when I'm ashore, if all my friends seem to be out.'

He wriggled himself more comfortably in beside me. 'Mind if I smoke?' I assured him that I did not mind, so more wriggling ensued while he retrieved cigarettes and matches from his jacket pocket. Before flicking out the match, he held it and it lit up his face. It was not a particularly handsome visage; it was somewhat battered, though full of laughter lines. The nose looked as if it had been broken long ago. The eyes were lively and intelligent. The match, of course, lit my face as well, and I wished suddenly that I was as lovely as Fiona. I had never sat alone with a man other than my father, and never close to one except Emrys Hughes during a holiday when I was about fifteen, a charity holiday obtained for me by the Presence. And Emrys Hughes had been old enough to be my father. This man was young and I wanted to continue sitting by him; it felt very nice. He had already slipped the packet of cigarettes into his top pocket, when he said contritely, 'I forgot to ask if you'd like one. Would you?'

'No, thank you. I don't smoke.'

There was a small silence between us while he drew on his cigarette, which I broke by asking, 'Do you go to sea?'

'Yes, Miss. Engineer. Got my Master's, though. And how did you know?'

'You walk like a seaman. And what is a Master's?'

'Master's Certificate. One day – maybe – I might get a ship of my own.'

'Master of your fate?' I teased.

'And Captain of my soul.' The voice had an odd, defensive note in it. The hall was cold and I began to shiver.

His arm tightened round me, and he exclaimed, 'You're getting chilled. Come on, little lady, let's dance.'

So we danced, and I heard a great deal about the problems of being an engineer. Then he was silent as he led me round the room. I forgot that there were other men with whom I normally danced. I was content to let myself float in the arms of this most peculiar man, a man who looked as tough as an old boot, yet with a speech that was almost as civilised as my own.

I remembered suddenly that he had not told me where he had met me before, and I wondered if perhaps it was a long time ago, when I had stayed with my grandmother. He might have lived in the same village.

Chapter twenty-nine

Norm put on the record with which he always closed off the evening, a waltz called *Who's Taking You Home Tonight?*

My partner was very quiet as we slowly circled the floor. He looked down at me and asked, quite humbly, 'Can I see you home?'

I was suddenly flooded with shyness. 'It's all right,' I murmured, turning my face away. 'You don't have to bother. I'm quite safe by myself.'

My face felt flushed. I looked up at him and was subjected to a sober, searching look. He sighed, and agreed, 'You're quite right, my dear. When are you coming here again?'

'Tuesday, all being well.'

'Well, I'll see you here. It'll be a day or two yet before we sail.'

The information that he would shortly leave Liverpool, perhaps sail out of my life as swiftly as he had sailed in, was not pleasant. I was suddenly painfully aware of the U-boats sitting outside the Bay, reminded of the mourning women in the waiting room. I licked my lips and smiled up at him. 'I'll be here – but I may be late.'

'That's my girl,' he said more cheerfully and did a flamboyant, wild spin which would have made Norm wring his hands in horror had he spotted it.

'I don't know your name,' I ventured.

He laughed. 'God bless my soul! You don't, do you? Well, it's Harry O'Dwyer. And Doris said yours is Helen Forrester, right?'

'Yes,' I whispered. What was I doing? I must be crazy.

He whirled me into the corner reigned over by the collection of gold cups, and stopped. The last few bars of the music slowly trailed to an end, and Norm turned off the lights, except for the one over the gramophone table. He always said it was romantic to do so.

For a moment he held me close to him. It seemed to me that life had stopped, and he and I were suspended in a warm, cosy space of our own. Then, slowly he let go of me, and said, 'It's been a good evening, hasn't it?'

I came out of my trance, and agreed. 'It was fun.' With my hand still on his shoulder, I laughed softly, and asked, 'Before you go, tell me – where have we met before?'

'Don't you remember?'

'No.'

'Dear me. And I always thought I was such an unforgettable character!' He chuckled. 'Remember walking on Georges Landing Stage with an old man – your Dad, I imagine?'

Enlightment dawned. 'You were the man who kindly picked up my spectacles? And you wanted to meet me again – you said something about it earlier this evening? You really did?'

'Of course I did, dear, innocent, little Miss Helen,'

he mocked gently. He took my hand and led me over to the door, through the crowd making its way into the hall. He gave a small old-fashioned bow, and said, 'See you Tuesday.' He went away to join his friends and the crowd closed round him.

In a daze, I went to retrieve my shoes from the untidy pile in the big hall cupboard.

'My, my!' exclaimed Gloria, while she poked in the pile of shoes. 'You *have* made a conquest.'

I was offended, stood up straight suddenly and hit my head on the chin of a girl jostling me from behind. I apologised, and then said to Gloria, with a quiver in my voice, 'What nonsense! Me? I may have made a friend, Gloria.'

We crawled out between the pressing bodies, each with shoes in hand, and she said, as she wobbled on one foot while she put a shoe on the other one, 'Why not? Don't be upset. You're a proper nice girl – always said so. Keep yourself to yourself. And he's a fine looking fella.' She jabbed an elbow in my side, and added, 'Wish you luck, I do.'

Disarmed, I laughed self-consciously. 'Oh, Gloria.'

She giggled at me as, with shoes on, we straightened up. 'Lovely hair he's got.'

'Who's got lovely hair? Have I?' Her husband came from behind and put his arms round her waist, while I tried to remember what kind of hair Harry had.

'Not you, you old so-and-so,' she replied affectionately. 'You're going bald on top. That man Helen was dancing with.'

My face was scarlet. I heaved myself into my coat. I wanted to escape from their frank appraisal.

Her husband took his face away from its resting place on his wife's back, and gave her a push. 'Get away. You've got the girl all upset. She's as red as a beetroot.' He turned to me, his plain pasty face friendly. 'Don't take any notice of her. She's always looking for romances.'

I did my best to smile, but my lips were tight. I was nearly dead with embarrassment as I said, 'Good night,' and followed the crowd down the dark steps.

The blush slowly dissipated in the sharp September air, and I marched steadily home in the moonlight, trying to face the fact that the evening had been different from any evening I had ever spent – and that I could hardly wait until Tuesday. Common sense was saying, 'Don't be a fool. He's a sailor. Girls in every port. Experienced. And you're not much of a catch, despite Mother's efforts with clothes and things. Perhaps he won't even be there on Tuesday.'

Mother was still up when I arrived home, but I could not bring myself to tell her about the strange engineer. I feared her sarcastic tongue and the amused discussion that would probably go on behind my back. And suppose he did not come on Tuesday – I could not bear public humiliation. Mother, however, was anxious to discuss Fiona's latest escort. 'She's gone out to dinner at the George and then to dance,' she announced. 'He's a fully fledged General from the barracks. Said he saw her every morning waiting for the tram and had wanted to ask her for ages. So suitable, don't you think?'

'How exciting,' I responded absently, as I poured a cup of tea from the pot on the hob. I wondered if

Mother realised that Generals, usually men of good family, did not pick up girls from tram stops with any particularly honourable intention. I was anxious. Mother babbled on, however, and finally with no further comment I went to bed.

Probably Mother did not see Fiona's General in the same light that I did. She would think of him as an equal making himself known to an equal, a situation where he would tend to be much more careful of Fiona. I hoped wildly that Fiona was as big a prude as I thought her to be.

As I shivered in bed, I ticked myself off for being so stupid as to spend money on dancing, when what I really needed was a pair of thick blankets on my bed. I was as stupid as my mother, I upbraided myself. I determined to try to save up for this very expensive item, and the ache in my legs the next day reinforced the resolution. And then I remembered that if I bought a blanket, Mother would pawn it the first time she was short of money.

That week I cried for a city. Warsaw, brave, defiant old city, faced its final martyrdom, as German troops entered it. No point any more in trying to find its valiant voice on the radio. Another tragedy to add to that of the submarine, *Thetis*, which at that moment lay in Liverpool Bay while frantic efforts were made to raise her, though her crew were long since dead. In the office, my senior colleague faced not only supplicating hordes, but an ever growing pile of government instructions which had somehow to be read and understood and explained to our volunteer helpers. Her eyes were nearly as blackly ringed as mine. She scarcely stopped to eat and took a load of work home every night.

I often worked late at the office, but I never took work home. I could not face it. I walked a razor's edge. Though slowly recovering from years of privation, I was still by any normal standards in very poor health, still not well fed or properly warmed. Dancing had proved a real mental therapy but I tired easily. The war added its daily strain of perturbation. I worried about Alan and fretted about the children, though they were probably better looked after than if they were at home.

On Tuesday, as anticipated, I worked late. The trams taking me home seemed to crawl through the darkness. I ached with impatience. The house was in darkness, and I was greeted by an ecstatic dog and a note from Mother, who had thankfully gone to the cinema now it was open again. 'Gone to Rialto. Boil an egg.'

I duly boiled an egg, shared a slice of bread and margarine with the importuning dog, washed up a collection of dishes and made up the fire. It seemed as if invisible hands pulled at my skirt and made me slow. I washed carefully and then, holding the candle in my left hand, I made up my face. In its flickering light, I combed my curls softly round my face, peering anxiously into the piece of broken mirror wedged into the kitchen window. Would he be there?

Norm had left the front door unlatched, as he usually did on lesson nights, so I let myself in. I stood quietly in the big hall, shoes still dangling on my fingers, and stared through the open ballroom door.

He was there. Draped over a chair by the gramophone, if such a solid block of manhood could be said to be draped. He was talking to Norm. Neither man noticed my entrance, so I took a good look at him, and such a wild delight filled me that I wondered for a moment what was happening to me. Gloria was right. He did have nice hair of a nondescript fairness. He wore it a little longer than was the fashion. Without brilliantine, it curved comfortably round his forehead, a forehead which already had fine lines in it. Even relaxed, he radiated a considerable self-confidence. It was quiet, but it was there. It offered no direct threat, yet it suggested a powerful personality. Despite his easy manner and his light banter with me, he appeared a man not to be trifled with, either by a drunken seaman – or a flighty young woman.

I bit my lip, feeling hopelessly inadequate, and wondered if I should tiptoe out again. Where did he come from? Who were his people? His speech put him a cut above Norm's other customers, yet he was not what Father would have called a gentleman.

The sound of his hearty laugh rolled through the door, and plucking up courage, I changed my shoes and sidled in diffidently. I could already feel a blush rising up my neck. What was one supposed to say? How should I behave?

He had seen me. He immediately got up and came over and ushered me in. 'Hullo, little puss,' he said, and grinned all over his face, emphasising the lines on it.

He was so totally friendly that, as I opened my

handbag to pay Norm, I smiled back feeling more relaxed, and said, 'Hello.' He might call me little puss, but he himself was not unlike a dignified, amiable St Bernard dog. If he had had a tail I am sure it would have wagged in big, slow sweeps.

He put his hand over my bag and clipped it shut. 'It's fixed,' he assured me.

'Oh, but I can't . . . you can't,' I flustered. I looked appealingly at Norm, who assured me, 'Gentleman's privilege, luv.'

I swallowed, and said doubtfully, 'Well, thank you,' and allowed myself to be led to one of the chairs at the side of the ballroom, out of the way of the stumbling tango beginners. He sat down beside me, one arm curved along the back of my chair. 'I was afraid you weren't coming.'

I apologised for being late and said I hoped he had danced with someone else.

His response was scornful. 'With that bunch?'

'They're nice girls.'

He pursed up his mouth. 'Not my cup of tea.'

'Why do you come, then?'

'I came to please my landlord's wife last time. This time I came to see you.'

'Really and truly?' I smiled at him, flattered.

'Well, of course.' The gramophone struck up a quickstep. 'Would you like to dance?' he asked, unenthusiastically.

We danced. He was very quiet, and at the end he asked, 'Couldn't we go somewhere and get a cup of tea – and talk a while? There aren't any really nice places round here, but I know one which is very respectable.' He looked round the shabby, smoke-filled room. 'We'll never be able to talk much here – and I'm sailing Thursday night.'

I looked up sharply. I was suddenly afraid for him. Fear must have shown on my face, because he said, 'Don't be scared. I'll take good care of you. Ask Norm – he's known me off and on for a long time.'

'Mother will be expecting me home soon after eleven,' I dithered, while my pulses beat madly.

'I'll get you home in time. Promise.'

He looked so wistful and inside me was stirring a crazy pleasure at being singled out by him. 'Please, little Miss Helen.'

'I'll get my coat and shoes,' I said, trembling inwardly.

Chapter thirty

We sat down opposite each other in a steamy little café. We were the only customers. A fat, white-aproned woman stood behind a small counter laden with two hissing gas rings with bubbling kettles on them. An assortment of plates covered with glass domes held sandwiches and buns. The woman came over to our plain deal table, and said, '’lo, Harry, me luv, what is it tonight?'

Harry looked inquiringly at me, and I said primly, 'A cup of tea would be very nice.'

Harry ordered two teas.

'Would your young lady like something to eat? I've got some fresh bath buns – or you could have something hot?'

I was, as usual, hungry, but I had no idea of his financial situation, so I said with a smile at the friendly soul waiting in front of us, that a bun would be lovely. His young lady, indeed!

Harry was grinning at me like a small boy. He nodded towards the retreating female. 'Come here for years for most of my meals, when I'm ashore. It's quiet. Jack's wife gives me breakfast – I eat my other meals out, so as not to intrude on them. He's First Mate, and it's like a permanent honeymoon there when he's home. Ma here keeps me well fed, don't you, Ma?' He looked across at the counter, where a large pot of tea was in the making. Ma looked up and smiled and said she did her best.

'Why do you have to work so late?' he asked, stirring two spoonfuls of sugar into the cup of tea I had poured for him. I bit into the huge bun brought me on a thick white plate. 'It's the sinking of the *Athenia* and the *Courageous*. Every boat that goes to sea seems to have Bootle men on it – and we're looking after their widows.' Then I remembered, as his face sobered, that he went to sea, too, so I added hastily, 'I'm sorry, I should not have mentioned it.'

He sighed heavily, and put his elbows on the table and clasped his hands, big well-shaped hands with scarred knuckles and very short nails, broken in places.

'That's all right,' he said and was quiet, biting absently on his knuckles. 'I'm a Bootle man myself. My Mum and Dad still live there. Dad's retired. He went to sea – ship's purser.'

'You don't stay with them?' I inquired, guardedly.

'No.' He appeared to be cogitating over the question and continued to chew his knuckles. 'I'm too old to be bothering them now. I got used to living away from them – for a while Mam wouldn't have such a limb of Satan over the doorstep.'

'What?' Despite a mouthful of glutinous bun, I had to laugh.

'It's true,' he said ruefully. 'She's still a bit edgy with me.'

Still laughing, I asked, 'Whatever did you do to offend her so?'

'Decided I'd never make a priest – so I went over the wall.'

It was a totally unexpected answer, and I stared at him in astonishment. 'Really? A priest?'

'Yes. Why not?'

I nodded. Why not? So many Catholic families hoped to have one child enter the church, either as a priest or nun. The child would be brain-washed almost from infancy, so that it would never consider doing anything else. But this was the first rebel I had ever met – or even heard of.

'Did you study for it?'

'Yes. At first I thought I'd make it. Then it was as if part of me was dying inside. Don't know how to explain it. Like being slowly strangled, if you understand.' He was spreading out a watery ring on the table, and the blue eyes glanced up at me, as if to judge how I was taking his admission. 'I guess I didn't have the necessary discipline.'

'What did your teachers do?'

'Oh, them. They were very good. They made me mull it over good and plenty – because it costs money to educate a priest – and I think some of them really cared. But they don't want discontented men, and finally I left – with their blessing. They did it without making me feel guilty. But my Mum – that was a different matter.'

'What about your father?'

'Oh, he's a real old philosopher. Nothing gets him. But he does what Mum says while he's home. He's got to live with her! Neither of them takes kindly to him being home all the time. She's used to running the place – because of him being at sea all the time.'

I had seen enough seamen's wives to understand

the matriarchal set-up. 'So what did you do?' I asked.

'Never even unpacked after I came home from the seminary. Got shown the door. God, she was furious. I went to stay with my married brother for a day or two. Then I got a job sweeping out a warehouse. I didn't know what to do – jobs are as scarce as hens' teeth. Then I met a pal – a lad I'd known at school – and he got me a job with him aboard a miserable little tub – Goddam awful boat – excuse the language – and I was as sick as a dog the first week. It was rough – my God, it was. But having a pal aboard a bit older than me made all the difference – saved me from the worst, till I got to know the ropes.'

'Are you always sick?' I asked. I wondered with dim horror what the worst was. All the seamen I had ever interviewed spoke of vermin, poor food and low wages.

'No. Never been sick since, oddly enough.' He smiled at my empty plate, and signalled Ma to bring another bun.

'Don't you go to see your mother?'

He sighed. 'Yeah. But she's never forgiven me and never lets me forget it. So I don't go every time I'm ashore. I give her a little allotment, so that if ever I stop one she'd get a bit of a pension. See my dad more often and my brother.'

I looked at the old, young face in front of me, the openness and geniality of it, and wondered how any woman could be bitter enough to show a son like that to the door.

'Your mother doesn't realise what she is missing,' I said impulsively.

'Och, you're a sweetheart,' he said with sudden cheerfulness, and drank up his tea.

'Being used to study must have helped you pass your exams to be an engineer – though it is so very different.'

'Well, I had to start from scratch. But grammar school is a good place for learning to learn – and the Fathers at the seminary certainly reinforced it. They wouldn't have any backsliding. You can learn anything if you're really set on it.'

The room was hot, and he opened his navy blue jacket, to show a creased waistcoat with a watch chain across it. He also wore a wrist watch with an expanding gilt band. Inwardly I smiled at the creases on the waistcoat. I could not remember seeing a merchant seaman whose clothes were properly pressed. I suppose, if they took them to sea, they kept them rolled up. And this man had no one to look after him ashore. He picked up the conversation again, and continued, 'I don't drink, except the odd glass of wine – tried as a youngster, of course, and threw up a good many times before I gave up. So I've time to read – makes you a bit cut off from your mates at times – and I saved – so it was easy for me to take time out for Courses.'

'It's unusual for a seaman not to drink. I thought they all *lived* on rum, more or less.'

He laughed. 'Get away. There's always a few that don't. My father never did.'

'Well, what do you do when you're in a strange place?'

'Sometimes there's a Sailors' Home or some place,

where you can get a game of billiards – or you can go to a show or a match or into the bazaars. There's another chap, a Methodist, and he doesn't drink either, so we sometimes go together.' He looked at me slyly, and added, 'Pick up a girl occasionally.'

'Do you consider that you picked up me?' I asked tartly.

He grinned, hesitated, and then said, 'No. I hope I've made a permanent acquisition.'

I was so happy that I simply glowed. It must have been obvious to him, because he caught my hand across the table and gave it a hearty squeeze. For a moment we were united, and then bashfully I withdrew my hand, and asked shyly, 'What else do you do?'

'Well, not a great deal. Often enough, you're too busy to have much time ashore. I read a lot – take a pile of books with me. Get fed up at times – particularly not having a home to go to.' He lit a cigarette and blew a neat smoke ring into the air. 'Enough of this old man. How about you?'

This was a question I had been dreading. What should I tell him? How could I explain my odd parents? If I explained my origins, would he think I was swanking and despise me?

My unease must have shown on my face, because he said gently, 'It doesn't matter, luv. I can see you've had a bad time – it's written all over you.' Then he leaned forward and took my hand again. 'I don't care what you are – or anything. I know a good thing when I see it. I did when I picked your specs up off Georges Landing.'

He astonished me. Did I really show what had happened to me? Or what did he think I was – something dreadful? I sat looking down at my hands clasped over my handbag on my knee. I had to acknowledge an overwhelming desire to keep his interest, and was mortally afraid of not being able to do it. I wanted so much that he should think well of me.

He was sitting, elbows on table, a long ash on his cigarette, as quietly as if he were waiting for a badger to emerge from its burrow in the evening light.

The silence between us continued, until he began to smile at me, and as if to help me, began to talk again.

'You know, a man in my position doesn't often get the chance of meeting a decent woman like you – unless you strike lucky. When you don't have a home base, you can be cut off, like. And when you start out to be a priest, you try not to think about women – in that kind of way, if you know what I mean,' he muddled on, going a bit pink himself.

I smiled back at him. 'Yes, I understand. You wouldn't be taking out the girls who lived near you – the ones you'd normally meet – when you were in your teens, for example.'

He chuckled. 'Right.'

Suddenly I felt more at ease. 'Well,' I said, 'I've been cut off in a way, too.'

He looked at his wrist watch. 'Do you feel like walking home?'

I nodded agreement, and he signalled to Ma. She eased herself round the counter and he paid her. With his money in her red hand, she smiled down at me in a most approving way, and winked at Harry. I blushed yet again, and, as I rose, I thanked her.

Harry ushered me through the narrow door of the café and somehow his arm stayed round my waist as we slowly walked up the hill. He had a sailor's eyesight and steered me safely in the dark, overcast night. The whole city seemed still.

'Tell me how you came to be cut off, too,' he demanded.

It was easier talking in the dark, to a comfortable, warm presence strolling by me. A man I felt to be honest deserved honesty, so slowly, sometimes with pain, I told him what had happened to our family and its consequences to me.

He heard me through, with only an occasional exclamation. As we neared our street, I fell silent. What is he going to think of such a crazy family? I wondered. So unbalanced, not established, unpredictable except in their stupidity.

'You poor kid,' he said compassionately, and tightened his arm round my waist.

At the top of our road, he stopped and turned me to him. He paused, as if considering something for a moment, and then very carefully kissed me on the cheek. 'What's your office phone number?' he asked. 'I'll be busy now. Won't be able to see you until we dock again. I'll phone you as soon as I'm back – and we'll make a proper date. Officially, I'm not supposed to know where we're going – allow five weeks. O.K.?'

I was trembling in his confining arms, with a scarifying, overwhelmingly strange feeling within me.

'Yes,' I whispered.

'Which is your house?' he asked.

'It's the seventh – no, the eighth – down on this side.'

'Right. Just in case I can't get you on the phone, I'll know where to find you.'

'Do you have an address?' I asked nervously, trying to sound normal when I felt far from normal.

He immediately gave me the address of his lodgings. I wanted instinctively to put my arms around him and beg him not to go, but I was too shy.

A number of short voyages and happy reunions later, he told me that to gain my full confidence was harder than making friends with the disillusioned ship's cat, who regarded the cook as his sole friend, and then persuading the beast to come on to his lap.

Chapter thirty-one

Five weeks seemed an interminable time. When the thirty-five days were over and there was no telephone call I was nearly distracted. Harry had told me the name of his ship, and certainly no one had come into the office to claim a pension because the ship was lost – in those days of official silence about the total number of our losses, this was the most likely way I would have known if it had gone to the bottom.

On the forty-first day I could bear it no longer, and with elaborate casualness I asked Norm if he had heard anything.

Norm dusted one of his records, and said that almost certainly if Harry's pal from the same ship was missing, he would have heard about it – so the ship was still afloat. If it had docked, Jack's wife nagged him so much to be taken dancing that they would have been in the room that minute. He grinned knowingly at me. 'He's a proper nice lad, isn't he? I knew you'd like him.'

I nodded and smiled – and sighed.

'Don't you worry, luv. He'll be back like a homing pigeon. He needs a girl like you.'

But I did worry. Something wonderful, something precious, had plunged light-heartedly into my miserable existence, and I could not bear to lose it. I knew of so many little ships limping home damaged, or lost at sea. I realised to the full what many of the stony-faced women who came to our office for advice were going through.

Fiona, secretive and sour-faced, announced to Mother's disappointment that she did not like her General and had dropped him. Fiona had more sense than she was ever given credit for.

She stayed at home one night and set my hair for me. I was tempted to tell her about Harry. Yet, as she chatted on about films she had seen and dances she had been to, I thought better of it. Surrogate Mums listen; they are not expected to have anything to confide. Secretly, I dreaded ever having to introduce a man friend to Fiona. Her charm, her sex appeal, were overwhelming, like Mother's in her younger days. I would not stand a dog's chance against such competition.

Mother was fretting over a Government demand that parents contribute towards the billeting allowance made to the hosts of evacuees. The sum suggested was six shillings for each child, a little over half the allowance. Both parents grumbled that they could not afford it, though they could now afford to smoke, to drink, to attend the cinema or concerts. They had grown used to having money in their pockets, as I had with my little allowance.

I dreaded being returned to my earlier impossible penury, and I again advertised for a shorthand student, still without result. I had continued to apply for jobs advertised in the *Liverpool Echo*.

Unemployment was still very high, and employers could obtain stenographers who had matriculated.

Few of the men who interviewed me bothered to examine the sheaf of certificates which I had received for my night school endeavours. I was also still very poorly dressed in comparison with other girls who worked in offices, though I had now taught myself to make and alter underwear and dresses quite successfully. Not that I had the use of what I made for very long. All too frequently painstakingly hand-stitched petticoats and renovated dresses were borrowed by plumper Mother and Fiona, to be left dirty and with seams burst. I raged impotently and tried hiding my single change of underwear under the mattress. To no avail. I was a rotten, greedy bad-tempered daughter and sister who did not trust her relations. My despair about Harry did not improve my patience.

Another worry was that Mother began to justify avoiding paying the billeting charges for the children, by saying her darlings must be homesick and want to return. It certainly would have been cheaper to have them at home, because the price of food was still low – and we did not eat well anyway.

I brought a storm of recrimination down on my head by reminding Mother that, though Liverpool had not yet been bombed, there was no guarantee that it would not be soon. I wondered bitterly how much real affection she had for her children; she did not seem to really miss them very much. This idea strengthened my mistrust of Mother, despite her keeping her word to me regarding her share of my salary. I found myself even less able to talk to her, except for common courtesies.

After forty-two days I gave up. Either Harry's ship

was lost, or he had abandoned the clumsy hobbledehoy he had picked up. Probably the latter, I told myself acidly. Moodily I slammed files on to shelves, typed letters and was sent out to visit invalids or the elderly, who were always remarkably sweet to me.

'Miss Forrester,' called my colleague, holding up our solitary telephone. 'A call for you. Make it quick, because I have a lot of phoning to do.'

I blenched with the surprise of it, and almost snatched the instrument from her, 'Hello,' I murmured.

'Little Miss Forrester?'

'Yes.'

'Harry here. Look, sweetheart. We've just berthed. It's going to be a quick turnaround this time. Could you meet me at Mrs Ambleton's place – you know, the little café we went to – tonight, seven-thirty, eh?'

'Yes,' I breathed. 'Oh, yes, of course.'

'Wait for me if I'm late?'

'Yes.'

'I'll be there. 'Bye.' The phone clicked as he rang off.

In a dream I handed the receiver back to my intrigued colleague, who was smiling questioningly at me. 'Thank you,' I said, and then added, 'I'll check how the waiting room is doing.' And I fled, down to the unused basement of the house which was our office, pushed open a creaking door into an old kitchen wreathed with cobwebs, shut myself in, and burst into tears with relief.

Chapter thirty-two

While my colleague was out visiting a difficult case, I made a fast call to Fiona and asked her to tell Mother I would not be in for tea. 'We'll be sending out for some sandwiches to eat in the office while we work,' I lied merrily. Fiona had obviously been expecting a call from someone else, because her lively 'Hello' turned to 'What, you?' when she heard my voice. She promised, however, to relay the message.

'Where's Harry?' asked Ma through a cloud of steam from her kettles.

'He's coming,' I puffed, as I took off my darned woollen gloves and loosened my coat.

'Like a coop o' tea while you're waiting, luv?'

'Yes, please.' My eyes were on the narrow door. I was dreadfully hungry, but I was so happy, so wonderfully, wonderfully happy.

Eight o'clock came and went, and slowly my hopes shrivelled. Three men went out, and a man and a girl came in and sat down to a meal. The smell of sausages was tantalising.

He came in slowly and, for a moment, until his crumpled face broke into a lively grin, I hardly recognised him. He was dressed in beige twill cotton trousers, a blue shirt open at the neck, worn under an open black leather jacket. His face was almost without colour, except for red rings round eyes so weary I wondered how they stayed open. In one hand he carried a flat white paper bag. He came towards me eagerly, whipping off a navy blue peaked sailor's cap, as he approached.

'Eh, I'm that glad to see you,' he said, putting his arm round my shoulder for a second, before turning to swing into the chair opposite me. 'Thought I'd never get loose. How are you, luv?'

I was all curled up inside with pure joy. I wanted to hug him, and I am sure my face glowed, as I said, 'Oh, I'm all right. What about you?'

He looked exhausted, as if he should have been in bed, instead of meeting a stray girl in a café; and my happiness flowed out in compassion for him.

He grinned, and said, 'Well, I'm starving. Have you had your tea?'

I nodded negatively while my eyes dwelt on him, and he called to the beaming, fat lady, 'What have you got, Nell?'

She offered steak and kidney pie or sausage and mash, with steamed treacle pudding to follow.

Over a huge helping of pie, I repeated my question, 'What about you? You look worn out.'

'Been chasing all over the bloody Atlantic, if you'll pardon the language.' He began to eat quickly, as if he were indeed starving. 'Convoy got scattered – it was slow as a company of snails, anyway. We made it home on our own – we're fast compared to most freighters.'

A shiver of dread went through me. I refrained, however, from asking any more questions. Time enough to talk when he had eaten his dinner and unwound a little.

Between mouthfuls, I kept glancing up at him, amazed that he had thought of me first when he came ashore, that he really was sitting opposite me.

He caught my questing eye. 'Never stopped thinkin' about you,' he said, with a piece of kidney balanced neatly on his fork.

The tell-tale flush flooded my face. I wanted to say, 'I never stopped thinking of you.' But I was too proud to commit myself. This kind, comfortable man might soon get fed up with my long silences and my gauche ways.

'I'm so glad you got back safe,' I finally managed, a bit primly.

He leaned back and laughed. 'Wasn't too bad, luv. I was thankful to see Blackpool Tower, though, I can tell you.'

I thought about the sea mines being laid by both combatants, of surface raiders, of the dreaded U-boats, as yet only flexing their muscles. Suddenly I felt the icy Atlantic waters with its surface mist drifting over struggling men. I felt the choking water in my own lungs, and I asked impulsively in a strangled voice, 'Do you have to do another voyage? Can't you stay ashore – do something else?'

His eyes were intent on me, speculative. 'No, little Helen. We all have to go back. Even if I decided to swallow the anchor – and I might – I can't do it until this little ruckus is over. What about some pudding?'

I tried to console myself with a piece of steamed pudding big enough for a hungry lorry driver.

Steamed pudding did not help much. I was in love. I knew it. In love with someone I was seeing for only the third time. It was ridiculous, absurd, stupid, certainly unwise. Then I told myself piteously that there was no harm in loving, as long as one did not expect anything in return. As always with the children, perhaps I could give him love without consideration of what I would get out of it. Physical love I would have to be careful about, but that was only part of it – it was the commitment which mattered.

I need not have worried about being left with an infant to care for. I was dealing with a most unusual man, who, however he felt, was very much in command of himself. It was almost disappointing not to have to fight for one's honour.

We spent the rest of the evening riding backwards and forwards on the ferry boat, crossing and recrossing the Mersey river. Tucked in the curve of Harry's arm, it was a good place to talk and get to know each other.

On the first trip, he put the white paper bag on my lap. 'I brought you a present,' he announced.

Surprised, I picked up the bag hesitantly. 'May I look?'

He nodded expectantly, and I opened the bag, touched material and carefully drew it out.

It was a dress, and I did not need to totally unfold it to know that it was a very good dress. The colour in the poor light was either tan or dark red. It had tiny pin tucks running the length of the bodice on which was pinned a discreet leather flower touched with gold. It had long sleeves, and could, I guessed, be worn for any occasion.

'Harry!' I exclaimed, blushing. 'It is too – too

much – you should not have done it – but, oh, it's beautiful. Thank you very much.'

His arm tightened round me. 'Didn't know your vital statistics, but I found a girl the same size, I think. Like it?'

I shook it out and admired its fine leather belt, its plain skirt, and turned starry eyes up to him. 'It's perfect,' I said. 'I've never had anything so beautiful before.'

Our faces were very close together and I thought he would kiss me, but he didn't. Just hugged me tighter.

'Thought you'd like it. Went down to the garment district in Manhattan and looked around. My pal often buys things there for his wife. They've got everything there – stuff that goes to the good shops.'

I was overwhelmed. 'You shouldn't spend so much on me,' I protested.

'Humph. And who else would I be spending it on? That's the trouble with me. Never had anybody I wanted to buy presents for, for years.'

I laughed, and carefully folded up the dress and put it back into the bag. How I was going to explain it to Mother and Fiona or stop them from borrowing it, I had no idea. I could not explain my happy acceptance of it even to myself – and from a Roman Catholic, to boot.

We sat talking together, warm and happy, two odd, extremely lonely people, neither of whom had had very much out of life except work, and yet matched like a pair of gloves. I wondered what had happened to my passionate belief in my church, feelings strong enough to make me refuse confirmation from a church which demanded that its members go to Confession.

This remembrance made me turn to him and snuggling close, say, 'Harry, I have to tell you – you know, I'm a Protestant.'

He chuckled unexpectedly. 'I thought so. Do you feel very strongly about it?'

'I'm not sure. I used to feel that no other religion was a true one. But the more I see the more I realise that nobody can really say that.'

'Well, not to worry, my dear. Times they are a-changing. We'll talk about it some more another day.'

Nevertheless, we continued to talk about beliefs, though not very deeply, and then about ships' engines – very deeply and far out of my depth. Finally, we came round to the war, which was always at the back of everybody's mind, and in this regard Harry said, 'Y' know, I've never been out of work since I went to sea – and I've saved. Since the war began I've been getting danger money – and it is going to add up. So I was thinkin' of buying a house – I know it sounds daft – but I'm fed up with not having a place of my own. I want a decent place and I've been bickering with a chap out at Allerton who's got a few new houses for sale. Would you like to come sometime and look at one with me?'

I was a bit staggered, and my mind leaped ahead with all kinds of wild hopes. Remember, I told myself, don't expect anything. 'I'd love to,' I assured him. 'It must be miserable not having a home.'

'It is,' he said, looking at me positively wickedly.

To be able to buy a house – to have the money to do it – seemed to me an almost impossible ambition. Presumably, however, he knew what he was doing.

'When do you sail again?'

'Couple of days,' he replied soberly. 'Real quick turn around. Never know what they'll do next. They're even shifting crews around to other companies, as if they were ruddy pawns.'

'It's happening ashore, too,' I said.

He eased himself around, in order to look at me directly, 'Like to come dancing tomorrow night? I can get loose for a few hours – they owe me plenty. We can go to the Rialto, if you like.'

'Let's go to Norm's,' I suggested. The Rialto seemed suddenly a cold and alien place.

'Okay, and I'll try to think of a nice place for coffee afterwards.'

He said he would get the overhead railway back to the dock, and saw me on to the tram with only a gentle peck on my cheek. It was very disappointing. He told me later that he was so afraid of scaring me off and yet his time ashore was so little.

I did not have to account for the new dress, because everyone was in bed when I arrived home, and the next morning they all rushed off to work without remembering that they had not seen me the previous evening. While Fiona was washing herself in the kitchen, I hid the pretty garment on a hanger under my old brown winter coat, which was by this time too decrepit even to be pawned and was sometimes used as a bed cover.

I tore home that evening and shared tea with Mother and Fiona, because Father was working late. It was unusual for me to lie, but that night I lied like the proverbial trooper. I said I had bought a new dress from a well-known second hand shop which dealt in high class clothing, and was going to press it to wear to the dance club that evening.

When Fiona saw it, her eyes widened. 'You lucky thing!' she exclaimed. 'Do you think they'd have anything to fit me?'

'Probably they would,' I responded non-committally, as I carefully ran the flat iron over it on the kitchen table. To press such a garment without an ironing board was a skill learned from patient experiment.

It was a tan shade which suited my sallow complexion, and it fitted very well, too well, I hoped, for either Fiona or Mother to get into it. 'It *is* a nice dress, more like an American fashion than an English one,' Mother said quite innocently, leaving me tight-lipped and silent. 'You should go and have a look, Fiona, and see what they have.'

I could imagine what Mother would say if she knew a man had given it to me, and particularly if later that man dropped me. I could not face such humiliation. The less said the less humiliation there would be.

He was there, waiting for me, joking with Norm and Doris, all dressed up in creased navy blue. He whistled when he saw me. I had not been able to see myself in the dress, because we lacked a long mirror.

Doris said, 'Golly, you look nice, Helen!'

I looked across at myself in the long ballroom mirror and knew that I looked good. And I felt good, more sure of myself. The girl in the mirror was much as I had imagined myself growing up to be, if disaster had not struck the family first. I had agonised over having to wear black shoes and carry a black handbag with a tan dress, but they were an elegant contrast.

We danced and we danced until the end of the evening, oblivious of anyone else. He looked less weary and I was so happy.

Afterwards, five or six of us stood in the misty moonlight outside the front door, chatting casually. I was carrying my walking shoes, meaning to go home in my dancing shoes. Harry offered to put the shoes in his raincoat pocket – there was no doubt that I was going to be escorted home this time.

One of the girls laughed, looking at my satin-clad feet. 'Goin' to dance home?' she asked.

'I could dance all night,' I replied lightly, glancing up at Harry. 'I could dance the length of the avenue.'

'Get away, now.'

I laughed. 'Bet I could.'

'Bet *we* could,' said Harry, joining in the laughter, and he put his arm round me and, whistling a slow waltz, he turned me away from the cheerful little group, and we danced away down the pavement.

I was shyly quiet in the warmth of his arms. The other young people called, 'Tara, well. Enjoy yourselves,' and their voices faded as they walked in the other direction.

'I'd like you to meet some of my friends,' Harry remarked, as we danced to our own peculiar music down the empty avenue. 'I've a few old friends, mostly married, round Bootle.'

'I'd like that very much,' I said.

'We'll do it next time I'm home. They're more like your kind of people than that bunch are.'

I was no longer sure what my kind of people were, so I did not answer. But I felt that any friend of his was likely to be pleasant to know.

Only the sound of our shifting feet broke the silence. I was afloat in happiness. There was no beginning to life and no end, only the perfect now in the arms of a semi-stranger who meant everything to me, a stranger who was already planning to introduce me to his friends, take me into his life.

Half-way down the avenue he stopped, and holding me tightly, lifted my face and kissed me, a kind of kiss I had never imagined and I never wanted to stop. But he did stop it with a quick sigh, and a resumption of our slow progress, while all kinds of wild and wonderful feelings raced through my slender body.

'Love, I know this is too quick. But I want to marry you, if you'll have me – soon as I can get a house ready to put you in safe and sound.' He ignored my gasp, and went on, 'I'm askin' you now, because I'm away so much that I could lose you to somebody else.'

I was struck dumb, and he urged, as he stopped dancing again, 'Be my girl – I'll never let you down, I promise. I've always wanted a wife like you – someone I could really talk to – and so pretty.'

'Are you sure, Harry?'

He laughed. 'I know a good thing when I see it.'

'Then, of course, I will. I can't think of anything

I would like better. And I'll try to be a good wife – I know how to keep house – and, oh, Harry, I want to make you happy.'

Instinctively, I lifted my hand from his shoulder and touched the tired face, and whispered, 'I love you.'

'My girl – my little Miss Helen!' He swung me off my feet in a happy whirl, and then we went on dancing, dancing down the avenue into the Liverpool mist.

March 1950

March 1950

'Goodness me!' exclaimed Mother. 'What have you got there?' She looked askance at me, as I staggered through the kitchen door into the marshy back garden, with a huge drawer from the dresser in my bedroom. The drawer was stacked with papers, some of them in neatly tied bundles.

'It's all the letters I received during the war – all my love letters, too. I can't very well take them to India, so I thought I would burn them in the old bomb crater in the garden.'

I must have looked a little stricken, because Mother said very kindly, 'Yes, dear. Burn the lot. India is going to be an entirely new start for you.' Age had mellowed her a little and I was grateful for her quick sympathy, though she was still very difficult to live with.

Father looked up from his paper sadly. He did not want me to go so far away. He hoped my fiancé would find a post in England and that we would return soon. He was a much plumper and better dressed father now, and in good health. We had become friends and we would miss each other.

I thankfully dropped the drawer on the dew-spangled grass in the bomb crater, and stood panting with the effort of lifting it. Across the flat market gardens at the bottom of our land, I could see the sea wall which protected the district from becoming fenland again. It was dull mist-covered country, but I felt it was my country, because it was so close to where my grandmother had lived. Behind me stood the small, though pleasantly comfortable, bungalow which had sheltered us since 1941, when a bomb had made our Liverpool row house unsafe. The grass-covered crater at my feet had been caused by a small bomb which had fallen on our first night in our new home. Now in March, 1950, I proposed to incinerate in it the record of all my past life. Before me stretched a brand new path, totally unrelated to all that had gone before. I was going out to India to marry a gentle Hindu professor of Theoretical Physics, whom I had met in Liverpool when he was taking a doctoral degree at the university.

How strange life was. I was to give up a very promising career, take on a new country, a new religion, a new language, for this quiet person who had come into my life so unobtrusively that it was some time before I really noticed that he was there. And yet I was content, happy about it.

I crumpled up some newspaper which I had brought into the bomb crater, and set a match to it. Then one by one I opened out and dropped into the flames letters from all over the world from my three brothers, Alan, Brian and Tony, all of whom had served in the war and come home safely. They were now launched on new careers, determined to make up for the time lost. No letters from Baby Edward. He was now ensconced in Liverpool University on a scholarship. He had been kept out of the Forces by an untreated dislocated shoulder caused by a fall in childhood. Letters followed from umpteen men who had danced with me, taken me out, in some cases proposed to me, while like a lost soul I had searched frantically to find someone like Harry. But no one can take the place of somebody else. They have to be loved in their own right. I knew that now, but it had taken me a long time to learn it.

Here it was, a little clipping from the *Liverpool Echo*, with his picture: 'O'Dwyer – Henry, aged 33, lost at sea, beloved son of Maureen and John O'Dwyer, and loving brother of Thomas and sister-in-law Dorothy. RIP.'

It was as if the flames were burning part of me.

Woodenly, I continued to throw letters on the fire. Very few letters from women. My girl friends had been fortunate, like me, in spending the war at home. None from Fiona, just married and living close by, or from Avril, who was still living at home. Avril was taking the first uncertain steps which would eventually lead her to a full and satisfying teaching career, to marriage and four bonny children.

A form letter from the Petroleum Board offering me a post at £2 14s 6d a week – three times my salary in the charitable organisation. How I had leaped at it. A living wage at last.

I started on a packet of letters tied with blue baby ribbon and, half choked with smoke and misery, threw them one by one on to the fire. Dear, highly articulate Edward, six feet tall and built to it, had taken nearly two hours to propose to me, while marching along the road to Birkenhead Park station, when he had missed the local train home and I had decided to walk part of the way with him. It had taken me only ten seconds to accept.

Half-way through I could not continue. I snatched some of the letters back and have them still, a tiny bundle with another obituary culled from the *Liverpool Echo*. 'Parry – July – killed in action, aged 32 years, Edward, very dearly loved younger son of Mrs Parry, Orrell Park, his loving and sorrowing mother.'

That was 1944 – the invasion of France. I thought I was a Jonah, so after the war I concentrated on finding a career and discovered it in a packaging company, where women had a chance to rise in the business. I joined all kinds of social clubs and societies and made a number of good friends.

Now I live in western Canada with my dear Professor and our son. As I write, it is the beginning of 1981, and I have trunks full of letters, a much, much happier collection. Pictures of Fiona's and Avril's beautiful weddings, and those of the boys – what funny hats we wore; snaps of a dozen or more nephews and nieces; letters from my publishers accepting the manuscripts of *Twopence to Cross the Mersey* and *Minerva's Stepchild,** in which I described the sufferings of our family when we first came to Liverpool; lovely letters from my kind Indian in-laws. And my husband's long letters written to me from India before I went there and others from time to time when he has been away from me for a few days. How much I owe him for making my life anew. We came out to this wealthy, snowy country so that he could better continue his research, and here was born our son.

My cup runneth over.

*Published in Fontana as *Liverpool Miss*.

Helen Forrester

LIVERPOOL MISS

The continuing story of Helen Forrester's poverty-stricken childhood in Liverpool during the Depression. The Forrester family are slowly winning their fight for survival. But fourteen-year-old Helen's personal battle is to persuade her parents to allow her to earn her own living, to lead her own life after the years of neglect and inadequate schooling while she cared for her six younger brothers and sisters. Her untiring struggles against illness, caused by severe malnutrition, dirt (she has her first bath in four years), and above all the selfish demands of her parents, make this true story of courage and perseverance heart-breaking yet heart-warming.

'Records of hardship during the Thirties or earlier are not rare; but this has features that make it stand apart' – *Observer*

'An impressive record of what it is like to be very poor . . . written with a simplicity which is moving and memorable' – *Homes and Gardens*

'The story of a young girl's courage and perseverance against adversity . . . warm-hearted and excellent' – *Manchester Evening News*

Harry Cole

POLICEMAN'S PROGRESS

Being one of four policemen coping with the drunken, sex-mad, middle-aged, pear-shaped Clara, or sitting out a night with the neighbourhood ghost, or calming wayward Rosie, the local prostitute, who'd had her 'Bristols' bitten, must have been a lot more fun than digging out the late and seventy-year-old Elsie Morton, rotting in bed after not being seen for some weeks, dealing with violence, or bearing the news of fatal accidents to bereaved families.

PC Harry Cole, now nearly thirty years on the Southwark force, has done it all and there's consequently many a tale to tell. He produces his account of life on the beat with a combination of good humour and honesty that makes *Policeman's Progress* a rich mixture of riotous and serious reading. Harry Cole's loyalty to the force, but also his obvious sympathy for all reasonable human eccentricities, make one feel that he would be a good man to have around when there's trouble.

Harry Cole

POLICEMAN'S LOT

It's a policeman's lot to be involved with eccentric human behaviour and bizarre happenings, with personal dramas and social occasions, accidental disasters and deliberate wrong-doings. PC Cole, after nearly thirty years on the beat, has seen it all; and whether he's investigating the case of the exploding sewer cover or refereeing at a drunken Irish party, withstanding the abuse of the Gay Liberation Front or sorting out the imaginary fears of a lonely old man, it's his sense of humour that often seems the saving grace.

Katharina Dalton

ONCE A MONTH

Once a month, with demoralising regularity, over fifty per cent of women feel tired, confused, irritable and incapacitated due to the effects of premenstrual tension. Many others are indirectly affected – husbands, children, colleagues, workmates and friends.

Premenstrual syndrome is responsible for the timing of half of all criminal offences in women, for half of all suicides, accidents in the home and on the roads, hospital admissions, incidents of baby battering and alcoholic bouts. These are the calculable effects – how much greater are the less obvious changes in a woman's daily life, in her behaviour, appearance and health?

The problems might seem insurmountable – but are they? This book is a popular and easily understood account of menstrual difficulties by a doctor with many years of professional and research experience in their causes and treatment. Katharina Dalton shows that in most cases women can treat themselves, and that in severer cases progesterone treatment can be highly effective. It is a book which many readers – male as well as female – will find informative, sympathetic, helpful and above all practical in relieving the suffering caused by premenstrual syndrome.

Helen Forrester

TWOPENCE TO CROSS THE MERSEY

Helen Forrester tells the sad but never sentimental story of her childhood years, during which her family fell from genteel poverty to total destitution. In the depth of the Depression, mistakenly believing that work would be easier to find, they moved from the South of England to the slums of Liverpool. Here Helen Forrester, the eldest of seven children, experienced the worst degradations that being poor can bring. She writes about them without self-pity but rather with a rich sense of humour which makes her account of these grim days before the Welfare State funny as well as painful.

'The clarity with which utter privation is here recorded is of a rare kind' – Gillian Reynolds, *Guardian*

'. . . records, with remarkable steadiness and freedom from self-pity, the story of a childhood that – even if it was all forty years ago – most people would have set down in rage and despair' – Edward Blishen, *Books and Bookmen*

'. . . her restraint and humour in describing this stark history make it all the more moving' – *Daily Telegraph*

TWOPENCE TO CROSS THE MERSEY

Helen Forrester was born in Hoylake, Cheshire, the eldest of seven children, and Liverpool was her home for many years until she married. For the past twenty-seven years her home has been in Canada, in Edmonton, Alberta.

The other two volumes of her autobiography, *Liverpool Miss* and *By the Waters of Liverpool*, and her novels, *Liverpool Daisy*, *Three Women of Liverpool* and *Thursday's Child*, are also available in Fontana.

HELEN FORRESTER

Twopence to Cross the Mersey

FONTANA/COLLINS

First published by Jonathan Cape Ltd, 1974
Reissued by The Bodley Head, 1979
First issued in Fontana Paperbacks, 1981
Seventeenth impression February 1986

Made and printed in Great Britain by
William Collins Sons & Co. Ltd, Glasgow

To the Liverpool City Police

Chapter one

Liverpool is a city through which visitors pass on their way to other places. It is to them a dull world of shipping and commerce which sprawls untidily along the north bank of the River Mersey. Many of them will not know that it has a sister port, Birkenhead, on the opposite bank, which is linked to it by ferry-boats, a railway tunnel and a road tunnel. Beyond Birkenhead lie the small seaside towns of the Wirral peninsula and behind them is pleasant countryside. My widowed grandmother lived in the Wirral, and here, while visiting her, I spent the happiest days of my childhood, on sandy beaches or in wind-swept gardens. I remember with love the rain-soaked hills looking out on to stormy seas and the turbulent estuary of the Mersey.

It used to cost twopence to cross the river on the ferry-boat from Liverpool to Birkenhead. Twopence is not a very large sum, but if one has no money, the river is a real barrier, and, during the Depression years, was an impassable one to many of the poverty-stricken people of Liverpool.

Not so many years ago, I took my little Canadian-born son to see Liverpool and the places of my childhood.

'Did you live here when you were small, Ma?' he asked incredulously, his strong North American accent sounding strange amid the thick, nasal speech around him.

'Yes, I was in Liverpool for part of my life.'

'My, it's dirty! Do you mind it being dirty?'

I smiled, seeing it all through his stranger's eyes, eyes accustomed to new buildings, miles of neon signs, miles of prairie golden with wheat or diamond-white with snow.

I laughed down at him a little ruefully.

'Yes, at first I did mind. Not now, though. I soon learned that people and cities which do the hard, unpleasant work of the world can't help getting dirty. Liverpool's a wonderful place when you get to know it.'

He looked at me derisively and said, with all the cold logic of a five-year-old, 'They should use more soap and—wash the streets.'

My smile faded, as cold shadows of winters past crept over me. That was how I had felt, when first I had really looked at the city and not passed through it as a traveller. God, how I had minded the dirt! How terrified I had been! How menacingly grotesque the people had looked; children of the industrial revolution, nurtured for generations on poor food in smoke-laden air, grim and twisted, foul-mouthed and coarse, shaped in this strange gloomy world to serve the trade to the Americas. And I, a middle-class girl of the gentler south-west of England who had been shielded from the rougher side of life by a private school system and obedient servants, had nearly gone mad with panic when, with little warning, I had been thrown amongst them. Gone was the protection of money and privilege; I had to make what I could of this grimy city and its bitterly humorous inhabitants and share with them their suffering during the Depression years.

I clutched my son's confiding little hand in mine, as, for a second, I felt again the fear which had enveloped me that January day in 1931, when, at the age of twelve and a half, I arrived in Liverpool, not to pass through it as I had done before, but to live in it.

It seemed to me that it was not my son's hand which I held so tightly but the hand of my youngest sister, Avril, and that I could hear her snivelling, as we looked out from the entrance of Lime Street Station and saw, through icy, driving rain, a city which seemed to be slowly dying, unloved and unsung, in the Depression of the nineteen-thirties.

Chapter two

'Shut up, Avril,' I said sternly, between chattering teeth. 'Everything is going to be all right.'

'I'm cold and I'm hungry.' The wail threatened to become one of three-year-old Avril's howling tantrums, as she started to kick off her patent-leather shoes and tear at her blue satin bonnet-strings.

I loosened the wet elastic of my black school hat from under my chin. The hat, as usual, had been crammed down on top of a large ribbon bow, which held my front hair ruthlessly scraped back from a too high forehead. My spectacles were sprayed with rain and I could not see very well as I peered short-sightedly down Lime Street.

I lifted Avril up and hugged her to my damp school uniform.

'Behave yourself,' I ordered sharply. 'We are all hungry. You must be brave until Daddy comes back to collect us.'

Fortunately, I did not know that my father, at that moment walking the streets of Liverpool in search of shelter for his sick wife and seven children, had no real idea of what to do to mitigate the catastrophe which had struck him. I presumed that adults always knew what they were doing and the likely outcome of their actions. I did not know that my mother, lying on a stretcher in the ladies' waiting-room, her six-week-old son beside her, was sweating with pain after a major abdominal operation and was bordering on a nervous breakdown. I could not understand why we could not go to stay with my grandmother, who lived only a few miles away in the Wirral peninsula. No one had told me she had quarrelled violently with her son and his wife, whom she condemned jointly as worthless spendthrifts, and would have no more to do with us.

Busy with childish affairs of school and girl-friends, I had noticed only that during the last few weeks my parents' friends were not dropping in for a drink as frequently as usual; in fact the house had been almost free of visitors for a couple of months.

Alan, who was a year younger than I, had pointed out to me a few months earlier that Mother's wonderful collection of Georgian silver had vanished from the antique sideboard on which it was normally displayed, and I had asked my mother where it had gone.

'Girls should not poke their noses into the business of grown-ups,' I had been told tartly, and I had retreated to Alan for consolation.

'Perhaps it has been sold,' he had whispered uneasily, as he ran his fingers through his corn-coloured hair.

'Why?' I asked, my eyes goggled in surprise.

He stared at me reflectively, his wide, blue eyes troubled. 'I don't know. There is something wrong. Mary Ann packed her suitcase and left on Saturday.'

Mary Ann was our housemaid, a jolly, outspoken girl.

'I thought she had gone home to visit her mother for a few days—that's what she told me.'

'I don't think so. She seems to have taken everything with her. She even asked Cook for her curling-tongs back—Cook was always borrowing them.'

Our uneasiness grew while Mother was in hospital, until an idle word from a school-friend gave us a clue.

Father had done a mysterious thing called 'going bankrupt', a not uncommon occurrence in the world of 1930, but strange to me. I had heard vaguely that going bankrupt was an American disease which had struck Wall Street in New York, and that Americans committed suicide when this happened to them; mentally, I saw dozens of them hurling themselves off the tops of skyscrapers, and I wondered where Father would find a skyscraper.

Father was a public school man who had been sent to boarding school by his widowed mother when he was only six years old; he had left it at nineteen to join the army in 1914. My mother, an orphan, had been brought up by nuns. Neither had had any training in the management of a family or a domestic budget, and they had enjoyed a high standard of living by being permanently in debt. Further, they had had seven children. Bankruptcy was inevitable, once the Depression set in and dividends dried up.

The remainder of our servants left in a body, while Mother was still in hospital, and I was left to manage the home as best I could, until we moved to Liverpool. One of our unpaid domestics took the opportunity, while my parents were absent, to take away my mother's entire wardrobe, leaving her only the outfit she had been wearing when she was whisked into hospital.

Father had no knowledge of the legal rights of a bankrupt to clothing and bedding, so he sent the key of our house to his main creditor, a moneylender, with instructions to sell the house and its contents, and to reimburse himself from the proceeds. From a misguided sense of honour, he left everything we possessed, except the clothing in which he and his family were dressed, taking only a pair of blankets in which to wrap my mother and the new baby, Edward. Then, with his last ten pounds in cash, he bought tickets on the train to Liverpool, which was his birthplace.

He remembered Liverpool as a bustling, wealthy city and hoped to find employment there, perhaps as an accountant, in a shipping company. Having lived for years in prosperous, southern market-towns, he could not visualize what the Depression was doing to the north of England. He could not imagine that a man who desired work would not be able to find it.

Liverpool looked a dreadfully dismal place to my untutored eyes. Water swirled along the gutters, carrying a horrid collection of garbage. Across the road, the fine Corinthian pillars of St George's Hall looked like a row of rotting teeth, and to my right, down William Brown Street, marched a series of equally large, black buildings. When I peeked farther out of the station I could see the entrance of a big theatre, the Empire, and farther along at the corner was a public house, the Legs o' Man, near which a number of seamen stood laughing and joking, oblivious of the rain. Much later on, a sailor told me that sooner or later everybody in the world passed the Legs o' Man and if you waited long enough you could meet there anybody you cared to look for; certainly, it was a great meeting-place.

Along the pavement men in shabby cloth caps shuffled from litter-bin to litter-bin to sift through the garbage for food and cigarette-ends. In the gutter stood four unemployed Welsh miners, caps held hopefully out while they sang over and over again in sad tenor voices 'Land of our Fathers' and 'All through the Night'.

'Are you lost?'

I jumped and Avril stopped wailing. A policeman, water running down his cape and helmet, was bending over us, his red face concerned.

'No, thank you,' I said primly, and, since he continued to look down at us doubtfully, I added, 'Mummy is in the waiting-room.'

He smiled in a friendly fashion.

'Better go back to her, luv,' he said, 'Lime Street is no place for a nice young lady—and ye'll get wet.'

Reluctantly, I retraced my steps to the waiting-room.

Father had been away four hours or more. Baby Edward had not been fed and was crying lustily. Brian and Tony, aged six and five respectively, were playing tag round and round the high, varnished benches. Despite his determined effort at playing, I could see that Brian was afraid. Taut and dark as an Indian, so highly strung that he suffered constantly from nightmares, his little hands were clenched tight and his heart-shaped face was grim. Tony was playing the game with his usual cool care, watching his elder brother closely so as to anticipate every move he made. His mind seemed to work with such intelligence that it was as if he had been born with a brain already mature and furnished with knowledge. Sometimes when I stroked his silky, flaxen head I was almost unnerved by the idea of the latent power beneath my hand.

Fiona, aged nine, was still sitting silently by my mother, nursing her favourite doll, her huge, pale-blue eyes wide with dumb fear. We all loved Fiona with unquestioning devotion. She never had tantrums as Avril and I did; she never seemed to get dirty or forget her table manners. I always had a book in my hand, hated to miss school and loved an argument; Fiona adored her large doll family, accepted school but learned little. She was our placid refuge when we had been spanked, which was not infrequently, but now *she* needed asylum.

Mother lay on the stretcher, her eyes closed, her face ethereally white. An empty teacup on the bench beside her spoke of the kindness of the lavatory attendant, who stood leaning against her cupboard door, smoking a cigarette and regarding us curiously. There was no one else in the waiting-room.

None of us had eaten since breakfast, a meal of toast hastily consumed, and now it was after four o'clock. I knew that my mother had no money in her handbag, so it was no good offering to go and buy something to eat from the station restaurant.

I went up to my mother. A tear lay on her cheek.

'Are you all right, Mummy?'

'Yes, dear. I got up and walked for a few moments a little while ago.'

'You'll soon be better, Mummy?'

'Yes—yes, I have to be.'

I picked Edward up from beside her and, holding him against my shoulder, tried to stop his healthy bellows for food by walking up and down with him and patting his tiny back.

Alan had been kneeling on a bench by the window, watching the horses and drays in the station yard. Now he came and walked with me. We did not talk; both our hearts were too heavy.

I knew that Mother had been ill after Edward was born and had been in hospital until Christmas Eve, a scant eight days ago. I realized, with a sense of shock, that Christmas and New Year had passed uncelebrated, lost in a foggy nightmare of quarrels, recrimination and general disorder in the house. Mother had discharged herself from hospital, before the doctors thought she should, so that we could come to Liverpool.

As I clucked sympathetically at Edward, it seemed madness to me to embark on such a journey. I could not understand why the moneylender could not wait a few days more before taking legal action, so that Mother could get a little stronger before she moved. I had no conception of the panic gripping my parents, a panic which had made them lose completely any sense of proportion. They had been brought up in a little world of moneyed people, insulated by their private means from any real difficulties or hardships. When there was no money, they had no idea what to do, beyond trying to obtain a 'suitable' position. A moneylender was, to them, a ruthless Scrooge, and I do not think that it occurred to them that if he had been apprised of Mother's illness he might have had a little compassion. And so they compounded their troubles to an unnecessary degree.

My relief was overwhelming when my father, soaking wet, came into the waiting-room, with a muttered apology to the attendant. He went straight to my mother. She opened her eyes and surveyed him sullenly.

'I have obtained two rooms. Not very good. Just for a week.' He sounded breathless and on edge. 'Had to pay in advance. Walked back. I'm going to get a cab.'

My mother closed her eyes, and my heart sank. They were trying not to talk to one another again.

Father vanished again into the vast cavern of the station, and Mother told me to help the boys get their overcoats on.

A few minutes later, Mother was carried on the stretcher with the aid of a porter to a taxi-cab, the children trailing behind and the baby and Avril still crying. The procession caused some interest in the station, and I remember my face burning with embarrassment under the shadow of my velour school hat. Well-bred people, I had had it drummed into me, did not draw attention to themselves.

Mother crawled into the cab, and the porter folded up the stretcher, which belonged to the railway company. Somehow we all squeezed into the taxi, a hungry, forlorn group too tired to talk.

Chapter three

A stout, untidy blonde opened the door to us. A suffocating odour of unwashed bodies, old cooking and cats rolled over us. The woman beamed at us, however, and welcomed Father like an old friend. She helped him assist Mother into a room so shabby and so dirty that I could honestly say that I had never seen anything like it before. Next to it was a bedroom with two double beds crammed into it. There were no sheets or pillow-cases, just greasy pillows and grey blankets.

Mother sank on to a broken settee, while our landlady looked us over.

'You can keep coal out back and use t' kitchen and bathroom. There's eight other tenants upstairs and me and me sons on the top floor, so keep as quiet as yer can.' Her battered face showed pity. 'Ah'll give yer enough coal to start a fire. Coalman'll be along the street this afternoon and you can get some then.'

The room was very cold and Mother looked round it disdainfully, but she said 'Thank you' in response to this offer of fuel.

'Come on, luv,' the landlady addressed me. 'There's a booket in that cupboard. We'll fill it and you can bring it back.'

After a trip through linoleumed passages and a littered, stinking kitchen to a coal-house by the back door, I staggered back with a bucket of coal, some wood chips and a newspaper. After much anxious effort, Father got a fire going. It was the first time he had ever made a fire.

Tony and Brian, usually the best of friends, had been bickering irritably for some time, and they now turned on Alan, who was himself fretful with hunger. Furiously, he cuffed the younger boys and made them cry.

Father snapped at him to stop.

Alan, usually so cheerful, stopped, and said heavily, 'When shall we be able to have something to eat?'

'How much money have you?' asked Mother. She had sat silently staring into space, while we had divested ourselves of our coats and Father had lit the fire.

Father went through his pockets, and laid the results of his search on the settee, so that we could see the small pile of coins in the light of the bare electric bulb hanging from the ceiling.

'Two and ninepence,' he announced helplessly.

Thirty-three precious pennies would buy quite a lot in those days, though they would not last long in a family the size of ours.

In a dull monotone, Mother upbraided him bitterly about the mess he had got us all into, and Father snarled back that she had never been any help to him. Finally, Edward's wailing drew his attention to more immediate concerns, and he said, 'There is a little corner shop down the road. We could at least get some milk for Edward.'

'And for me,' said Avril, thrusting her small chin aggressively forward.

'Be quiet, Avril,' I hissed, afraid that my parents would start to quarrel again.

'Won't,' replied Avril defiantly, but she did keep quiet thereafter.

Finally, it was decided that since Father was already wet through he might as well get a bit more wet by going out to the shop and buying all the food he could for the money he had.

When he had departed, the children crouched around the miserable fire, and Mother managed to change Edward's nappy. We had only three nappies with us, and the baby had not been changed since we had set out that morning. He was, therefore, in a disgusting condition. Mother gave me the nappy she had removed, told me to find the bathroom, wash the dirty garment and bring it back to dry by the fire. I wandered off, sick and dejected, and did the best I could with cold water and no soap in a Victorian bathroom which stank of half a century of neglect.

Afterwards, Alan and I went to the kitchen, where a few dust-covered dishes were strewn along open shelves. We collected them and washed them under the only tap and, with frozen fingers, carried them back to our room. With nervous and uncertain gestures, we laid them on the table, which was covered with torn, stained oilcloth. We also had hopefully brought with us a saucepan and a frying-pan, since there was no stove in the kitchen on which to cook.

Our spirits rose when Father returned with milk, two loaves of bread, margarine, tea, sugar and a small packet of sausages. He had also brought a twopenny packet of Woodbines. With cigarettes in their mouths, our parents became a little more civil to each other.

Under Mother's instructions, I made a feed for Edward and then fed him: he was ravenous and took the whole small bottle full. Father cooked sausages on the smoking fire, found a knife in the kitchen and cut the bread and spread it with margarine. We sat around on whatever we could find and ate a sausage apiece in our fingers. He managed to boil a pan of water and make tea in it. Mother drank much and ate little, refusing a sausage which was happily snatched up by Avril. Father finally ate, and only afterwards I realized that he had not had a sausage, and I felt a crushing sense of guilt about it.

Our landlady called down the stairs to say that she could hear the coalman coming, and my father looked aghast. The coal donated by our landlady was already nearly consumed and we had exactly a penny left. We could do nothing, and sat hopelessly silent, as the shout of 'Coal, coal, one and nine a hundredweight' faded down the street.

That was the first of many years of nights I spent tossing restlessly, napping, waking, unable to settle because of cold or gnawing hunger. Four of us, still dressed in our underwear, were packed somehow into one bed, and Father, Alan and Brian were to manage in the other bed. Mother stayed on the settee with the baby. For a long time I lay and listened to my parents quarrelling with each other, while the baby whimpered and Fiona, her head against my shoulder, chattered inconsequently in her own uneasy sleep, her doll clasped tightly to her. I fell into a doze, from which I was awakened by Mother calling me in the early morning. I was glad to leave the bed, which smelled of urine, put on my gym-slip and blouse and go to her.

It had been decided, she said, that Father should enrol Alan, Fiona, Brian and Tony at an elementary school he had noticed on his way to the corner shop the previous night. I was to stay at home and help with the baby. My loud protest that I would get behind with my schooling was sharply hushed. I was to see the children washed and tidied for school and was to divide the remaining bread and margarine between them for breakfast. All this I did, whilst shivering with cold. Brian and Tony were also shivering and were scared of going to school; Fiona and Alan were frankly relieved at the thought of something normal creeping back into their lives.

A breakfastless Father was gone with them for an hour and came back to report the children safely ensconced. He had put into his pocket, when leaving home, an old-fashioned cut-throat razor, and he now did his best to shave with it, in cold water, without soap. The result was not very good, and his clothing, still wet from yesterday's soaking, looked crumpled and old. He then departed for the employment exchange, a three-mile walk.

Mother, Avril and I sat almost silent in the icy room. Occasionally, we would feed the baby a little of the remaining milk. We warmed it slightly by putting the bottle next to Mother's skin down the front of her dress, and we wrapped the baby in Mother's coat, which had not got much wetted the previous day. I then tucked our two precious blankets round both mother and child. I longed to get out of the fetid room, even if it was only to stand at the front door, but I was too afraid of my mother in her present state to ask permission to do so.

The other children came home for lunch, but there was no lunch, and they departed again for school, cold, hungry and in tears, even brave Alan's lips quivering. Mother, Avril and I, like Father, had neither eaten nor drunk.

The afternoon dragged on and the children returned, except for Fiona.

'Fiona's ill,' explained Alan anxiously. 'A teacher is going to bring her home in a little while, when she feels better.'

I suppose my mother was past caring, for she said nothing, but, to the griping hunger pains in my stomach, was added a tightening pain of apprehension for Fiona, the frailest of us all. I tried, however, to be cheerful while I helped the boys off with their coats and then put them on again immediately, because they said they were so cold.

The front door bell clanged sonorously through the house. I expected to hear the clatter of our landlady coming down the stairs to open it, but there was no sound from the upper regions of the house, so very diffidently I rose and answered it.

At the door, stood an enormously tall man in long, black skirts. In his arms he carried Fiona.

Chapter four

I quailed before the apparition on the doorstep—it reminded me of an outsize bat and my over-stimulated imagination suggested that it might be a vampire; in the chaotic mess that our world had become, anything was possible. The voice that issued from the apparition's bearded face was, however, gentle and melodious, and asked to see my mother.

Nervously, I invited him (it was obviously male, despite the long, black dress) into the hall, and he slid a whey-faced Fiona to the floor, while I went to see Mother. She told me to bring the gentleman into our room, and, for the first time since our arrival, a slight animation was apparent in her face.

He entered, leading Fiona by the hand, and immediately my mother assumed the gracious manner which had, in the past, contributed to her reputation as an accomplished hostess.

'Father!' Her voice was bell-like. 'This is a pleasure! Come in. Do sit down.' She ignored poor Fiona, who came and stood by me, and stared dumbly at our new-found friend.

'Father'? It was beyond me. I had never seen an Anglican priest in high church robes, nor yet a Roman Catholic one, in the small towns in which we had previously lived. I stood, with fingers pressed against my mouth, and wondered what further troubles this visit portended.

He was explaining to Mother that the school was an Anglican Church school. After Fiona had come out of her faint, the headmistress had wormed out of her something of what was happening to us, and had then telephoned him. The advent of four well-dressed, well-behaved children entering a slum school had already caused some stir among the teachers and considerable jeering and cat-calling among the other pupils, so the headmistress had asked him to call upon us. Here he was, he announced gravely, and could he be of help?

As I examined the beautiful, serene face of the young priest, Mother poured out a condensed version of the story of Father's losses. He was a Liverpool man originally, she said, and had come back to his native city in the hope of earning his living there. To me, the well-edited tale still presented a picture of foolishness, extravagance and carelessness.

Now, at last, I knew why we were in Liverpool and what the word 'bankruptcy' really meant to our family. I knew, with terrible clarity, that I would never see my bosom friend, Joan, again, never play with my doll's house, never be the captain of the hockey team or be in the Easter pageant. My little world was swept away.

I looked at Alan, who was standing equally silently by the window. His eyes met mine and we shared the same sense of desolation. Then his golden eyelashes covered his eyes and shone with tears, half-hidden.

'Have you no relations who would help you?' asked the priest.

'I have no relations,' said Mother coldly, 'and my husband's refused to know us at present.'

The priest combed his beard with his fingers, and smiled when Avril tried to reach up to touch it. He took her hand gently and held it, and within thirty seconds she had established herself triumphantly on his knee, from which safe throne she surveyed the rest of the family gleefully.

'There is a great deal of unemployment in Liverpool,' he said. 'I fear your husband may find difficulty in finding work.'

Mother just stared disconsolately at him.

At that moment Father entered, dragging his feet slowly and looking almost as hopeless as Mother. The children ignored him, the exhausted baby slept.

Desperate to fill the silence, I cried gladly, 'Daddy!'

He managed to smile faintly.

Mother introduced him formally to the priest, and he sat down and waited politely to hear why the priest was there. This was explained to him, while he shivered with cold and rubbed his blue hands together to restore the circulation.

Finally, the priest said to him, 'First things first. You must have a fire or your youngest child will die. Probably I can persuade old Wright to bring up a hundredweight of coal. I have some small funds and I will bring some food. After you have eaten perhaps I can advise you a little.'

He put his hand out over the children's heads in a

gesture of blessing, said goodbye, strode out of the room and let himself out of the house.

The boys immediately broke into jubilant conversation with each other at the idea of food, and gradually Father began to relax a little for the same reason, though his face looked pinched and white. He had spent hour upon hour in the employment exchange, being chivvied from one huge queue to another, until he had finally got himself registered for work as a clerk. He was not eligible for unemployment insurance as he had never contributed to that fund, and the employment exchange clerk just laughed when he asked when he might hope to be sent to apply for a job. There were, he said, a hundred men for every job, and my father's age was a grave difficulty—at thirty-eight he was too old to hope seriously for employment.

He had hardly finished telling us of his adventures, when the doorbell rang again. I answered it quickly this time.

A surly voice from beneath a large hump inquired where it should put t' coal, and not to keep 'im waiting cos 'e 'adn't all night to run after folks as 'adn't enough sense to get it in the daytime.

The landlady had shown me where our coal could be stored, and the coalman clomped through the house behind me, scattering slack liberally around him, and heaved the coal expertly over his head, out of the sack and into a broken-down box in an outhouse. Then, still muttering about improvident folks, he stomped back through the passage and departed into the darkness.

I flew in to Mother, and it seemed no time at all before we had a huge fire glowing, with Father's coat and jacket and Edward's nappy steaming in front of it. The already heavy atmosphere of the room was intensified by the cloying stench of these garments drying, but we did not care. We learned then that, when one has to choose between warmth and being half-fed, except in the last extremities of starvation, warmth is the better choice.

An hour later the priest presented himself again, carrying two large boxes and accompanied by a boy carrying two more. The boy dropped his burdens on the step and trotted away. The priest came in, at my shy invitation. He smiled at the sight of the comforted children kneeling by the fire between the drying clothes, and, with Father's aid, he unpacked the boxes.

The table was soon loaded with six loaves of bread, oatmeal, potatoes, sugar, margarine, a tin of baby milk, two bottles of milk, salt, bacon, some tea, a bar of common soap, a pile of torn-up old sheeting (for cleaning, and for the baby, he explained apologetically) and, wonder of wonders, a towel, a big one.

The priest sat down, and called the boys to him, while Father and I made baby formula and porridge, and Alan collected all the dishes he could find. It felt oddly like a Christmas celebration, and even Mother seemed to come a little out of her apathy as she sipped the tea and ate the porridge Father eventually brought to her. I fed the baby while the children stuffed themselves with porridge, bread and margarine and chattered excitedly, Avril's shrill falsetto and Brian's contralto occasionally emerging from the general hubbub. At the priest's insistence, Father and I finally ate, and Father became more his old, lively self.

We boiled another panful of water, and I took Fiona, Brian, Tony and Avril to the bathroom, and washed their hands, faces and knees. They had not had their underclothes off for thirty-six hours and did not smell very sweet, even after my washing efforts, but a quart of water does not go very far in washing four people, and I reasoned that the beds stank so much that they were bound to smell by morning no matter what I did.

Afterwards I took them into the bedroom, tucked their overcoats over them, covered these with a greasy blanket, heard their prayers, and returned to Alan and my parents.

Chapter five

Unemployment was so rampant in Liverpool that the young priest felt it necessary to warn Father that getting work would be a very slow process—he was too kind to say that it would be virtually impossible. He suggested that Father should apply for parish relief.

'What is that?' asked Father.

'Well, it is really the old poor-law relief for the destitute, but it is now administered by the city through the public assistance committee. More help is given by way of allowances rather than by committal to the workhouse.'

Father went white at the mention of the workhouse. I stared in shocked horror at the priest. I had read all of Charles Dickens' books—I knew about workhouses.

'I see,' said Father, his voice not much more than a whisper. 'I suppose I have no alternative.'

The priest asked about our accommodation, and sat, drumming his finger-tips upon his skirt-clad knee, when he was told that our landlady wanted her rooms back for another tenant, at the end of the week.

At last he spoke.

'There are a lot of older houses in the south end of the city. You might find a couple of rooms in one of those. Some of them are still quite respectable. There is also a High Church school in that area, which is a little better than an ordinary board school. However, you might have to pay twopence a week for each child at the school—and that might pose a problem.'

Father said optimistically that he could not imagine such a small amount being a problem, once we got settled.

The priest smiled at him pityingly, opened his mouth to speak and then decided otherwise. We would soon learn.

'Would you like to ask me about anything else?' he inquired.

'No, thank you,' said Mother suddenly. 'You have been most kind.'

I was surprised at her firmness, and then remembered that neither she nor Father had ever had any great respect for the Church. In addition, the priest represented to her the class of people who, she must have felt, had left her in the lurch when she most needed friends. She had accepted this stranger's help because she had to, but her grey eyes were steely, when she politely held out her hand to indicate dismissal.

I could see Father beginning to dither, like Bertie Wooster. He was obviously loath to let the priest go and yet was afraid that, if he said anything, Mother might start another bitter family row.

The priest settled the question by getting up abruptly. There was a hurt expression in the mild eyes. He ignored Mother's hand but inclined his head slightly towards her, as he moved through the crowded room to the door. Alan, Father and I hastened to see him out, with many protestations of gratitude. He bowed gravely, blessed us and, with slow, dignified tread, went down the steps into the darkness.

I closed the door, and stood leaning against the inside of it, while the others went back to the family. I had hoped so much that the young priest would have noticed that there were five children of school age in the family and realized that only four had been enrolled in his school. I had envisaged him instructing Father to send me with the others for lessons the following morning. But he had not noticed. I fought back my disappointment and told myself that I would probably go to school as soon as we were settled in a more permanent home, and then I would be able to play in the fresh air with new friends and perhaps even be top of the class in English once more.

The untold amount of anguish that I could have been saved if the good priest had only counted his little flock is hard to imagine. Undoubtedly, the education committee and its army of attendance officers and inspectors would have enforced my right to schooling had he but observed and reported this discrepancy.

I slunk back into the room.

'A capable man,' Mother was saying to Father, with a look which added 'unlike you'.

Before this subtle barb could be plucked out and shot back, she announced that she would go up to the bathroom. She had, hitherto, managed to use an ancient, cracked chamber-pot found under one of the beds.

Refusing Father's help with a lofty air, but using me and anything else she could to hold on to, she slowly eased her way into the hall and halfway up the narrow staircase. We sat down and rested on the stairs, and then continued. This was her first real effort to walk since her return from hospital, and she came down the stairs by going from step to step on her bottom. In spite of all the calamities she was undergoing, her strong body was healing and all that was required to return her to reasonable physical health was the will to try and strengthen her muscles. Her pretty, pink wool dress was already spoiled where the baby had wetted it, and the journey down the dusty stairs did not improve it.

The following day, she pottered round the room quite a lot, while Father went in search of that mysterious personage, 'The Parish'. The children, including Fiona, went to school and I again stayed at home. Father had made the fire and I managed to heat some water and wash Edward. When the sun came out about mid-morning, on Mother's instructions I gingerly wrapped the baby in one of the blankets.

'Take him outside and walk up and down in the sun with him,' she said.

I was gone in a flash, the startled child whimpering at my sudden movements.

The bliss of being out of the fetid room overwhelmed me, though the street was not much better. The wind, sweeping in from the estuary, was, however, invigorating despite the gas fumes carried on it.

A blank brick wall shielded one side of the street, and from behind it came the shuddering sounds of shunting trains.

The house in which we were staying was one of a row of shabby, jerry-built Edwardian houses, with a grocery store at one end of the block and a public house at the other end. Toddlers with runny noses and sores on their faces scrabbled around in the gutter. An older boy, a piece of jammy bread in one hand, flitted barefoot up the road and called something insolent after me. At the door of the public house, droopy men in shabby raincoats waited for opening time. They stared at me, and I wondered why, but I must have been an unusual sight in my private school uniform, ugly velour hat rammed neatly down on to my forehead, and carrying an almost new baby up and down the pavement. School uniforms would not, in those days, have been seen in such a slummy area. I endured the silent observation with embarrassment.

A sudden diversion brought a number of women to their doors, and in some houses ragged blinds and curtains were hastily drawn.

A funeral procession came slowly down the street, led by a gaunt man in deep black. He was followed by the hearse, a wonderful creation of black and silver, with glass side panels and small, black curtains drawn back to expose the fine wooden coffin. The coffin itself was almost covered by wreath after wreath of gorgeous flowers, including many arum lilies. The four horses which drew the hearse were well matched black carriage-horses and as they paced slowly along they tossed their heads as if to show off the long black plumes fastened to their bridles. They were driven by a coachman draped in a black cloak and wearing a top hat which shone in the sun; his face beneath the shadow of the hat looked suitably lugubrious.

The men outside the public house, with one accord, removed their caps, and the toddlers scampered out of the gutter and took refuge behind me.

The hearse was followed by a carriage in which sat a woman dressed in heavy widow's weeds. She sat well forward, so that all could see her and dabbed her purple face from time to time with a white handkerchief edged with black. Occasionally, she would bow, in a fair imitation of royalty, to one of the onlookers and then put her handkerchief again to her dry eyes. Opposite her, sat two pale, acne-pocked young men in black suits too large for them, looking thoroughly uncomfortable.

The widow's carriage was followed by five other carriages, each filled with black-clad mourners.

'Smith always does 'is funerals very nice,' said a voice behind me, rich with approval.

I glanced back quickly.

Two fat women, garbed in grubby, flowered cotton frocks, their arms tucked into their equally grubby pinafores to keep them a little warm, had come out to see the procession.

''e does. Better'n old Johnson. 'e did her daughter's wedding, too.'

There was a faint chuckle from the first woman. 'She's got more money to spend on 'er 'usband's funeral than she 'ad on the wedding, what with 'is insurance and all.' There was silence for a moment, then the voice continued, 'Ah wonder if 'er Joe will keep on the rag-and-bone business?'

Her companion murmured some reply, but I was too intrigued at the idea of a rag-and-bone man having such a large funeral procession to be interested in them further. Everybody I had seen that morning had looked so poor, and yet one of their number was being laid to rest like a prince. Surely the money such a thing would cost was needed for food.

The sun went in and my spirits drooped as the cortège turned round the corner grocery store and disappeared. Like most children, I was afraid of death and the funeral seemed an ill omen to me.

I turned, and went indoors.

Alan came home at lunch-time with a black eye. A boy had asked him if he carried a marble in his mouth, because he spoke so queerly. Alan had replied that he spoke properly, not like a half-baked savage. The half-baked savage had then blacked his eye for him.

'He's got a black eye, too,' said Alan with some satisfaction as I put a wet piece of cloth over the injured part. 'You're lucky not to have to go to this school—even the girls fight.'

'I'd like to go, just to get out of this horrid house,' I said vehemently. 'And, oh, Alan, I'm so afraid Father won't bother about sending me. You know he has always said that all a woman needed was to be able to read and write, and I can do that.'

'He'll have to send you. Isn't there a law about it?'

'Yes there is.'

'Well, the school inspector will tell him he must.'

I removed the wet cloth from his eye and cooled it again under the tap. 'If he knew I existed, I expect he would,' I agreed. 'But, Alan, I was thinking about it all night and if Father never tells them about me they will never know I am here.'

He looked at me uneasily before closing his eyes again so that I could replace the cloth over the blackened one. After wincing at my ministrations, he said doubtfully, 'Probably when we get a proper house, he'll arrange for you to go.'

'I hope so,' I responded earnestly; but I remembered the funeral and my stomach muscles were clenched with apprehension.

Chapter six

Father returned at lunch-time with food vouchers to last us for two days, while 'The Parish' made inquiries as to the rates of relief paid in the small town from which we came. Apparently, this town would have to reimburse the Liverpool public assistance committee for any relief given to us. It was expected that we would be granted forty-three shillings per week. This sum must cover everything for nine people—rent, food, clothing, heating, lighting, washing, doctor, medicines, haircuts and the thousand and one needs of a growing family.

Mother looked at him disbelievingly.

'It's impossible,' she said, her unpainted face puckered up with surprise. She was used to spending more than that on a hat.

'I can't help it,' Father said helplessly. 'That is what they told me.'

He sat, rubbing his cold hands gently together to restore the circulation, anxiety apparent in every line of him.

'I must obtain a position. But I don't even know anybody whom I could ask about a post. I have never lived in Liverpool long enough to make close friends, as you know.'

I remembered that when Mother wanted a servant she used sometimes to advertise in the newspaper, and I suggested that perhaps other posts were advertised also.

This idea was a revelation to Father and he hailed it with delight.

'By Jove, the girl is right. Look in the newspapers.'

We succeeded in borrowing the landlady's newspaper, after promising faithfully to return it intact.

And so began an endless writing of replies to advertisements on pennyworths of notepaper. Father did not know that firms frequently got seventy to eighty replies to an advertisement for a clerk, and that they just picked a few envelopes at random from the mighty pile, knowing that almost every applicant would be qualified for the post advertised.

That afternoon, Father undertook another long, cold walk, this time to the south end of the city, to look for accommodation. He had no success and returned hungry and dispirited.

Two days later 'The Parish' presented him with thirty-eight shillings, which represented forty-three shillings less five shillings for the food vouchers already supplied.

Only two more days were left of our tenancy of the rooms and our landlady had already reminded us, quite civilly, that she would require the rooms at the end of the week. Mother said, therefore, that she would take the money from 'The Parish' and, with the aid of a taxi, go to the south end of the town to see if she could find us a home.

Father protested that she was not fit for the journey, but she insisted coldly that she could manage and, after instructing me to look after baby Edward and Avril, she sent him to arrange for a taxi.

I was truly relieved to see Mother beginning to take an interest in what was to become of us, but I did not dare to tell her that my throat was ominously sore and I feared that I was getting tonsilitis again, a disease which had always plagued me.

On the advice of the taxi-driver, she alighted in an area of tall, narrow, Victorian houses surrounding a series of squares. In the middle of each square was a communal garden which seemed to be permanently locked.

From house to house, up and down the imposing front steps, she dragged herself, knocking on doors which were cautiously opened by black, white, brown and yellow hands. Nobody would consider a family of seven children.

When she had come almost to the point of giving up, she came to a house where the door-bell actually worked. She could hear the old-fashioned clapper bell pealing in the basement. The door was answered by a tiny old lady in a long black-and-white-striped dress and a black apron. Her white hair was brushed up in Edwardian poufs and she looked very clean.

In reply to Mother's query regarding accommodation, she lifted a finger heavenward and announced piously, 'The Lord will provide!'

Mother blinked and prepared to turn away.

'Wait!' exclaimed the old lady imperiously. 'I will call Mrs Foster. Please step into the hall.'

Mother stepped in, as requested. The house was not nearly as clean as the old lady, and the lofty hall, with its peeling, olive-green wallpaper, its threadbare, dusty rug and strong smell of cooking, did not inspire confidence. An old-fashioned hatrack and an umbrella-stand made from an elephant's foot stood near the door, and behind them, set rigidly against the wall, were three Edwardian dining chairs, their woodwork lustreless and their upholstery torn.

The old lady toddled to the back of the hall and shrieked up the stairs in a strong, Liverpool accent, 'Bissis Fostaire!'

A door upstairs squeaked open and a deeper shriek replied, followed by a heavy tread on the stairs.

'God bless you, my child,' said the old lady to Mother, and vanished into what must once have been the dining-room of the house.

There was the sound of steady panting coming closer down the stairs, and Mrs Foster emerged from the gloom of the staircase.

She probably measured nearly as much round as she did in height, a veritable ball of a woman, clad in folds of black chiffon. Her neck was draped in a series of long bead necklaces, such as were worn in the nineteen-twenties, and as she moved they swayed across her bosom making rhythmical tiny clicks as they hit each other. Her pale-blue eyes had a hard, myopic stare and her double chin wobbled, as she continued to pant after reaching the hall.

Mother repeated her inquiry regarding rooms, then sat down suddenly on one of the hall chairs, and fainted.

She was aroused by the strong odour of smelling

salts proffered by an old gentleman with a tobacco-stained handlebar moustache. She was vaguely aware that she was leaning against the ample bulk of Mrs Foster who was sitting in the next chair, still panting softly, like a lap-dog.

With the aid of the old gentleman and encouragement from Mrs Foster plodding up behind her, she managed to climb a double flight of stairs into what had been the drawing-room of the house, on the first floor.

The room was furnished as a bed-sitting-room. Two Cairn terriers frolicked under the high double bed; in the window stood a large cage occupied by two dismal grey parrots, and near it a cat lay on the linoleum and watched the birds with narrow, lazy eyes. The unmade bed was piled high with old clothes, and a basket table held a perilous pile of dirty dishes, while the shelf underneath it was filled with dusty ladies' magazines. A strong aroma of cats and birds permeated everything.

Mother was assisted to a chair by the cheerfully blazing fire and after a moment's hesitation the old gentleman retired, closing the door quietly after him. Mrs Foster pushed a kettle already standing on the hob round on to the fire.

'You'll feel better when you've had a cup o' tea, luv. Would you like to take off yer hat?'

Mother thankfully took off her hat and leaned back in her chair.

'That was me brother,' remarked Mrs Foster, gesturing towards the closed door. 'He has the old breakfast-room and does for himself. Me grandfather built this house.' She looked round the room proudly. 'Left it to me father, and he left it to me brother and me. We must be almost the only people left round here as owns their own house.'

She turned round and surveyed Mother, weighing her up quite accurately, as it transpired. She observed the fashionable hat, the dirty dress, the beautifully cut tweed coat, the white hands and, finally, the dead, grey face.

'Been real ill, haven't yer, luv?'

'I have, rather.'

'And you want a place for you'n' the kids?'

'And my husband.'

'Oh, I thought mebbe he'd left you.'

'No.'

Mrs Foster silently considered this information while she assembled a tray of fine, rose-patterned crockery from a corner cupboard and made the tea.

She poured Mother a cup of tea, ladling a generous amount of sugar into it, and then sat down herself, stirring her own tea with slow, thoughtful turning of the battered spoon.

'I've got two rooms and an attic at the top of the house,' she said. 'I hadn't had in mind to have kids in them.' She paused and ran her tongue round her ill-fitting, artificial teeth. 'I had three kids there before, but they was little horrors, if you know what I mean. I don't suppose yours will be that bad.'

'They are fairly well-mannered,' Mother assured her hopefully. She sipped her over-sweet tea and its scalding heat began to revive her.

'I got two married couples and two single ladies in

the rooms underneath. The married ones is at work all day, so they won't hear the noise, and the ladies—well, there's plenty like them, if they don't like it.' She put her spoon into the saucer with a decisive smack, her mind made up. 'You can have the rooms for twenty-seven shillings a week—in advance, mind you. There's a gas meter and gaslight in the kitchen–living-room.'

Mother was too thankful at having found a place for us to live in, to realize that the rent was exorbitant for such accommodation.

'Is it furnished?' Mother asked.

'Yes. There's enough furniture—and you can add a bit of your own, no doubt.'

Mother put down her cup.

'I wonder if I may see it?'

'Certainly, if you feel O.K. now.'

Laboriously, Mother climbed thirty-two more stairs; they were covered in ancient linoleum in which the holes threatened to trip her up from time to time.

There was a kitchen–living-room with a small bedroom fireplace. It contained a wooden table, two straight chairs, a cupboard with odds and ends of crockery and a couple of saucepans in it, a rickety, bamboo bookcase filled with dusty books and a horsehair sofa exhibiting its intestines.

The bedroom held a black metal double bed, covered with a lumpy, stained mattress, and an ancient wardrobe with a broken door and no mirror. A further small staircase led to an attic which held another double bed. This bed lacked a leg and one corner was held up by a pile of bricks. Two trunks lay in a corner, and an old door was propped against one wall. A forgotten candlestick lay on the floor by the bed. All the floors had some linoleum on them, with dirty, wooden floor showing through in places, and all the windows were shrouded in lace curtains, grey and ragged with age.

Mother looked around her in despair.

'Nobody'd take seven children nowadays,' puffed Mrs Foster, as they descended the stairs once more.

Mother knew this to be true and, since the accommodation represented at least a roof under which to shelter, she said, 'I appreciate that, and I will take the rooms.'

They went back to Mrs Foster's room, a rent book was carefully made out and Mother paid over a week's rent. She was informed that she could hang clothes out to dry in the tiny, overgrown back garden, but the children could not play there because, to quote Mrs Foster: 'Me brother faces out back and he can't stand noise—he's a professional pianist. He used to play reelly well in a cinema.'

Mother sighed. She must have been sickened by the squalor of the place. She asked how to reach our present rooms by bus and found that a tram went from a nearby corner.

The trams were open at the front and back and the driver in a shabby uniform augmented by a huge scarf round his neck stood exposed to wind and rain, his foot for ever on his clanging bell. The conductor, not quite so well armoured against the elements, heaved young and old on and off, crammed the vehicle with loud admonitions to 'Move farther daan t' back there and make some room for them as comes atter yer', and collected the fares into his leather pouch with jingling efficiency, as he shoved and pushed his way between his close-packed passengers.

As she sat swaying in the noisy vehicle, Mother watched them work and realized that Mrs Foster had not asked if Father was employed or not; we discovered later that she had taken it for granted that he was not.

Darkness had long since fallen when Mother at last staggered into our living-room and collapsed on to the settee.

Chapter seven

Half an hour after moving into our new abode on the following Monday, we began to appreciate some of the difficulties of living there.

Our coal was to be kept in a cupboard by the back door of the basement, where a series of old pantries had been converted for this purpose. This meant that every bucketful had to be carried up sixty-four stairs. We were to share the bathroom on the first floor with eleven other residents, and this meant innumerable trips for me up and down thirty-two stairs, since Brian, Tony and Avril were far too scared of the dark staircase and crypt-like, filthy bathroom to go down alone, and they needed help to manage in such a dirty place. I was getting resigned to disgusting bathrooms—they seemed to be part of the way of life in Liverpool, as I saw it.

The gas for the light in the living-room, and for a gas stove if we had had one to put in, came through a slot meter which ate pennies at an alarming rate. We did not know that such subsidiary meters were installed and set by landlords at the highest rate they thought they could squeeze out of their tenants. The landlords emptied these meters. They had only to pay the gas company the amount calculated on the reading of the main house meter in the basement, and they pocketed quite a substantial profit on this transaction, in addition to their rent. A more worldly-wise person than my mother would have inserted a penny and run the gas, to see how long a penny lasted, before accepting the tenancy.

Father went out and stopped a passing coal-cart, and the man brought in a sack of coal. He then went to buy cigarettes at a tiny corner store. Both he and Mother had been heavy smokers and found their enforced abstinence hard to bear.

We had brought with us on our tram journey a little oatmeal, a few potatoes, sugar and tea. There was still some baby food for Edward, and, since it was late afternoon by the time we arrived and Edward was whimpering, I made a bottle of formula and then some porridge for the other children. Alan had managed to get a smoky fire going, having lugged a handleless bucket full of coal upstairs by hugging it to his chest. His shirt, already dirty from a week's wear, was now streaked with coal dust.

Although my head was throbbing and my throat was very sore, I ate some porridge gratefully.

As there was no hot water in the bathroom, I afterwards heated pans of water on our fire, and, starting with Avril, washed all the children, except Alan, who washed himself. Little Tony, fair and silent like Fiona, felt very hot, too, and I sat him on my knee and got him back into his grubby clothes as fast as possible.

I tucked Alan, Brian and Tony up in the bed in the attic, spreading over them their three overcoats, and left them squabbling with each other regarding the fair distribution of room in the bed.

My weary mother had been resting on the bed in the bedroom, and we now held a hasty debate about where Fiona, Avril and I should sleep, it being tacitly agreed that Mother, still in pain, had to have a bed. After a long argument, Father and I brought down into the bedroom the old door which had been left in the attic. We propped this up at each corner with a pile of long-forgotten Victorian books taken from the bamboo bookcase, and then covered it with crumpled newspaper found in the wardrobe. Avril had a wonderful time chasing the spiders we dislodged from the bookcase when we took the books out. She was delighted that Fiona, she and I were going to share this improbable bed. Father and Edward would share Mother's bed.

Mother got up and went into the living-room, while I put Avril to bed, and when I joined my parents later, they were quietly muttering reproaches at each other through clouds of cigarette smoke. The problem was that we had only three shillings left from our parish relief, and we had to live, somehow, nearly three more days until Thursday afternoon when the benevolent parish would disgorge another forty-three shillings.

As I entered they broke off their recriminations and Father told me to go to bed. I went, thankfully, clinging to Fiona because I felt so dizzy. Fiona, as she took off her shoes preparatory to crawling in beside a soundly sleeping Avril, was crying silently as if her heart was already broken. Avril refused to make room for us when we pushed her gently, and grumbled drowsily that it was her bed. Desperate with the need to lie down, I slapped her legs and, with a howl and an occasional kick at her not-too-loving sisters, she made way.

With nothing over us except our overcoats, and only newspaper under us, it was unbearably cold, and yet at times I felt dreadfully hot.

After a broken night of bad dreams, through which I could hear Edward crying steadily most of the time, I staggered out of bed when Mother called me. I could hardly speak and my throat was swollen from ear to chin.

With eyes still closed she told me in a whisper to call the others, get them ready for school, cut them some bread to eat and make some milkless tea to drink.

Obediently, I built a fire and when I had fanned it with a newspaper into some semblance of heat, I put a pan of water on to it for the tea. Fiona got up from her rustling couch, leaving Avril still slumbering, and without being bidden, went downstairs to wash in the bathroom.

'The Minister's soap is nearly finished,' she reported as she brought the remains of the tablet back to me.

I went upstairs to call the boys and clung to the rickety banister because of the dizziness that enveloped me. The boys were not making their usual rumpus, and I found Alan anxiously surveying a tearful Tony, whose neck was as swollen as mine, while Brian, his small brown face looking wizened and old, was lying miserably on the mattress and saying that he didn't feel well and he wanted to go home.

'I'll tell Mother,' I said, through nearly closed lips. I noticed, in terror, that we all seemed to have very large red spots on us—mine itched abominably.

Mother looked so utterly defeated when I told her about the boys and when she had really looked at me that my heart went out to her. She woke Father, who had been sleeping the deep sleep of exhaustion.

He sat up quickly, looking very quaint in his rumpled outer clothes, and put on his spectacles.

He peered at me in an effort to persuade his slumber-ridden eyes to focus.

'I think it's mumps,' he said incredulously.

'It's my old tonsilitis,' I said in a whisper. 'My ear hurts like it always does when tonsilitis is coming.'

My voice and the room seemed to be receding from me and I burned with heat.

'I think you have mumps as well.'

'Does mumps bring you out in spots?' I asked.

He was scratching absent-mindedly at himself, as I spoke.

'Oh my God!'

He looked at his own arms, and then at my bright red tummy, which I obligingly bared for his inspection.

'Bug bites, I think,' he said slowly. 'Saw them in the army.'

Slow tears welled into Mother's eyes.

'I can't bear it!' she cried out suddenly. 'I can't bear it!' She hammered the mattress with closed fists. 'I can't bear it!' she screamed, her pretty face distorted. 'I can't stand any more.'

She continued to shriek hysterically as we gaped

at her in terrified silence. For me the scene was almost totally unreal, as fever gained on me; yet I knew that one of my parents had nearly reached the end of the amount of suffering she could accept, and it was difficult for me to contain my own screams of sheer fright.

There was the sound of heavy feet on the stairs and a coarse male voice shouted up, 'For Christ's sake, shut up up there!'

In spite of the pain it gave my throat, I began to cry.

'Don't cry, Mummy,' I begged, 'we'll get through somehow.'

Father, ever optimistic like Mr Micawber that something would turn up, bestirred himself and scrambled out of bed.

'Yes, don't cry,' he said kindly. 'I'll tell Mrs Foster about the bugs—she'll probably do something about them.'

Having seen Mrs Foster I doubted this, but I heartily agreed. Anything, I thought, to get that desperate look off Mother's face and stop her screaming.

Slowly, as Father pottered round trying to bring some order to his distraught family, her cries gave way to sobs and she laid her head down on the mattress. She continued to weep, sobbing quietly to herself for hours.

Father trailed down to the basement to fetch some more coal and coaxed the fire into a more cheerful blaze than I had been able to create. Then we all went and stood by it while he took us one by one and looked us over.

Mother wept on, Edward and Avril slept.

In his opinion, Father said with a sigh, Tony and I had mumps. In addition, I undoubtedly had tonsilitis. Everybody was so used to my sporadic bouts of tonsilitis that this latter pronouncement did not bring me any particular sympathy. Rather, it was taken as an example of my usual awkwardness and waywardness of character. As Father said, 'You would! Just at this time.'

It was presumed that Brian was also sickening with mumps.

We three sick children were piled into the attic bed. I hardly knew, by this time, what was happening around me. Apparently, Mother was persuaded to feed Edward, when he woke, and Father fed Fiona and Alan. He then took them to their new school, where he had to part with fourpence for a week's fees.

I am not sure how my parents managed during the next few days, except that, according to Alan, they pawned my overcoat for two shillings in order to be able to buy coal. I remember, between bouts of delirium, seeing my mother crawling about, sometimes literally on her hands and knees, tears streaming down her face, as she struggled to look after Edward; and Fiona bringing me drinks of hot water with a tiny piece of Oxo cube dissolved in it.

The pain in my ears was intolerable, but there was no doctor to paint my throat with glycerine and tannin, no hot-water-bottle or aspirin to ease the searing pain, no drops in my ears to encourage a discharge. The mumps soon decreased, but it was several days before the agony in my ears suddenly diminished. There was a heavy discharge from them on to the bare mattress and my temperature began to go down. I became aware that Brian and Tony were no longer with me, and I called out, my voice seeming muffled and far away to me.

They both came clattering up the attic stairs.

Their faces seemed to have shrunk far more than the vanquished mumps justified. Brian looked more monkeylike than ever, and Tony's blue eyes and the bones of his head seemed grotesquely prominent. They both had large, scarlet spots about their faces and necks.

'It's very quiet,' I whispered. 'Where is everyone?'

'Alan and Fiona are at school. Mummy's in the living-room with the baby. We have to be quiet so she can rest.'

'That is right,' I said, trying to sit up and finding that the room swam around me, so that I was glad to lie down again. I looked imploringly at Brian. 'I'm so cold, Brian. Could you find something more to cover me with?'

He immediately went and fetched his overcoat and put it over my shoulders.

'Where is Daddy?'

'He's gone to see Mr Parish,' volunteered Tony.

I smiled at his name for the public assistance committee.

'Be a darling and bring me my specs,' I commanded him. 'I think I have to stay here a little longer. I still feel a bit hot between the shivers. Gosh, I do smell!'

The sides of my head were sticky with the discharge from my ears, but for the moment I had neither the strength nor the will to do anything about it.

'Tell Daddy I'm better, when he comes,' I said. 'You can play in here if you like.' And I closed my eyes, thankful to be free of pain at last, and fell into a deep sleep while the boys played tag up and down the room. I awoke much later to find Father bending over me, trying to see me by the light of a candle-stub. He felt my head. It was cool.

'Feel better?' he asked.

'Yes.'

'That's my girl.'

'How is Mummy?'

'Much better. She is walking quite well now.'

'Has she stopped crying?' I could not keep a hint of fear out of my voice.

Father looked old and very tired, as he said quietly, 'Yes, she is better now.'

'Can I get up?'

'Yes, I think it would be a good idea. We've got a fire today, so it's warmer in the other room.'

I craved a hot cup of tea and I hoped that if we had a fire to boil the water we might also have a little tea in the cupboard. My legs almost refused to obey me and I clung to Father's arm as I shuffled across the floor, down the attic stairs and into the living-room, where I was greeted rapturously by Fiona and Alan and with a wan smile by my exhausted mother. Avril was sitting on the floor in a corner, her face red and tear-stained, getting over a tantrum.

Chapter eight

Brian and Tony went back to school, two subdued ghosts walking hand in hand for fear of being bullied by the heavily booted older boys in the street.

Mrs Foster, declaring that she had never had a complaint before, produced half a tin of Keating's powder to repel the bugs. It did have some temporary effect, but the pests were coming in from the house next door and only a thorough stoving of both houses would ever have cleared them. We had to learn to live with them, just as we soon had to learn to live with head-lice which the children picked up in school.

I went through each child's clothing before it set off for school, hoping to save them the humiliation of being labelled verminous; they were already cowed enough.

The days dragged by and both Mother and I became stronger, despite our poor diet of white bread, potatoes and tea. Though Mother's physical health was improving, she seemed to withdraw further and further away from us. It was as if she could not bear to face the miserable existence which was our lot. She tried very hard to appear normal and calm, but attacks of hopeless hysteria descended on her without warning and she would rage and weep over some trifle, while whichever child happened to be the cause of the explosion made matters worse by trying to defend himself verbally. We were all still at the age when we believed that grown-ups knew what they were about and had sensible reasons for all that they did, and in consequence we were thrown into real fright each time one of these distressing scenes occurred. The idea that a person's life could be so shattered that they were unable to build anything new was unknown to us. We were young—we hoped for better times in the early future.

I learned to do practically everything for the baby, and when my legs were steady enough I borrowed Mother's overcoat, which though too wide was not too long for me, and took Edward and Avril down to the street for fresh air.

In Victorian times the street had been quite a fashionable one and each house had a flight of steps up to its front door. The steps had heavy iron railings running up either side and round the area bordering the basement of the building, so that no one should fall into these tiny front yards below the level of the street.

Avril, like a squirrel released from a cage, skipped joyfully up and down the pavement, stopping occasionally to peek through the railings and catch a glimpse of someone's basement home. Her pretty blue satin bonnet, though by now rather battered, caused quite a number of favourable comments from women sitting on the steps or standing in groups gossiping. The women were mostly of the labouring class, dressing in dull greys and blacks, some with flowered pinafores and most of them wearing black shawls as protection against the cold wind. Their hair either hung in greasy confusion to their shoulders or was braided and pinned up in fashions I had seen in early Victorian photographs. Their teeth, when they smiled at Edward, were uniformly bad or non-existent. I passed them without speaking as I shyly walked up and down with Edward in my arms.

A Spanish woman was seated on the steps of the next-door house. Her greying hair was done high on her head and held at the back by a fine tortoise-shell comb and she watched my promenade with merry black eyes. Finally, she called me to her.

'Can I see your baby?' she asked in a throaty voice.

Obediently I brought Edward to her and lowered him so that she could see his sleepy face. She made delighted clucking sounds at him.

'You not have pram?' she asked.

'No.'

She looked at me carefully, weighing me up.

'Not your baby?'

'Of course he's my baby. He's my brother.'

My innocence nonplussed her for a moment. Then she laughed and pinched my cheek.

'So! He is little brother.'

'Yes. Mummy's ill,' I volunteered, warmed by her cheerfulness.

'I know. Mrs Foster tell me.'

She put her finger into Edward's hand. He promptly clutched it, and she sighed gustily.

'I got old pram. You have it. My baby big boy now. No more babies for me. You wait.'

She got up and tripped down the area steps and into the basement door under the main front steps, and I waited quietly, rocking Edward in my arms under the approving glances of her neighbours.

The best that could be said about that pram was that it had four wheels. Its lining was torn and grey with dirt; its wheels had no tyres; the ribs of its hood stood out as if it was hungry and its cover had so many cracks in it that it looked like a map of Europe. When it was moved it squeaked steadily in protest. It was, however, to be my constant companion for years and the cover had the virtue that it was firm enough to support an open book, so that I could read as I trudged along.

I was immensely grateful to my new friend and I happily laid the swaddled Edward into his new carriage. Cautiously I pulled it up the front steps of Mrs Foster's house, then up the three double flights of stairs to our room. Bumpety-bump it went on each stair and bumpety-bump went the patient Edward inside it. Mrs Foster's brother, Mr Ferris, infuriated by the regular pounding on the stairs, burst out of his room.

'For God Almighty's sake be quiet!' he shouted up. 'I can't concentrate.'

I did not answer him. I did not care about his practising on his piano. I was triumphant at having found something for Edward to sleep in and to wheel him out in.

Mother was lying down on the bed but, at the sound of the pram's appalling squeak in the room, she sat up.

'Good heavens!' she exclaimed. 'Where did you get that ghastly chariot?'

I explained, as I took Edward out of it.

'We can't put him in a thing like that,' Mother said.

'Why not?' I asked. 'It gives him a place to sleep – you might be able to sleep better, if he wasn't in the same bed as you.'

Mother nodded acceptance, her face mirroring the hopelessness which recent events had made part of her character.

So the Chariot became part of Edward's and my life and squeaked its way painfully through miles and miles of black Liverpool streets. Sometimes I think there must still be two little ghosts and a squeak floating gently through Princes Park because we went there so often.

Chapter nine

Mother still had in the stitches from the major operation which had been performed upon her soon after Edward's birth. I had seen the scarifying gash which ran from above her waist to her pelvis; it was now healed and should really have been examined by a surgeon some time back. We considered getting the stitches out ourselves, but we had no scissors and Father was afraid to risk cutting them with his blunt razor. It was decided, therefore, that next time Father drew our allowance from the public assistance committee, Mother would have to see a doctor, no matter what we had to go without as a result of having to pay his fee.

Two mysterious middle-aged ladies, who went out only in the evening, and two married couples lived on the floor below us. With strict instructions from Father not to speak to either of the single ladies, who were, I was assured, not 'nice', I was dispatched to inquire from one of the married couples the name of a doctor.

A man in mechanic's overalls answered my knock. He was undersized and very thin, his hair slicked back from a long, narrow face. Tired, hazel eyes regarded me kindly.

'What do you want, luv?'

'My father sent me down to ask if you know where we could find a doctor round here.'

'Soombody took ill, luv?' His voice was much more alert.

'No, thank you. Mummy was very ill before we came here and now she must see a doctor – to have her stitches removed.'

'Oh, ay. Just a minute, ducks, I'll ask the wife.'

He left me standing at the open door, while he retreated into the room. I caught a glimpse of a stoutish blonde girl ladling stew out of a saucepan on to plates at a table by the window. The room was crowded with a bed, a stove and living-room furniture, but the general effect was of cosy friendliness. The smell of the stew was unbelievably good and I sniffed appreciatively as I waited.

The girl put down the saucepan and they both came to the door. She wiped her hands on a grubby apron as she looked down at me.

'There's the parish doctor,' she said doubtfully. 'But none of us goes to 'im unless we're dying. Tell yer Dad that Dr Dent around the corner by the grocery shop is proper kind. He wouldn't charge you much—but you'd better take half a crown, in case.'

I thanked her and was just about to turn and run back upstairs, when she put her hand in her pocket and brought out a toffee. ''Ere yer are, luv. Have a toffee.'

I had not tasted a sweet since I had arrived in Liverpool and I accepted the gift delightedly and rushed up the stairs with unseemly exuberance.

‘’is surgery hours are seven to nine,’ she called up after me.

Father normally went to the library in the evening to read the *Liverpool Echo* and write replies to any advertisements which offered office jobs, so I was told to accompany Mother to the doctor’s surgery. Alan would take care of the rest of the family while we were away.

Mother washed herself as best she could with a piece of rag dipped into cold water, and made sure she had no vermin on her. I did the same and also combed my hair; we had only one small pocket comb between us and were always afraid of breaking it, as we could not afford to replace it; consequently, I hardly ever combed my straggling locks. Since my overcoat was still in pawn, I borrowed Fiona’s.

For the first time since she had arrived, Mother made the long trip downstairs. The night was clear and frosty and she paused at the top of the front steps to take a big breath of fresh air; it smelled good after the foul atmosphere of the house. Slowly we proceeded down the steps and down the street, to a cross street of smaller houses and shops. We found the doctor’s front door, which led straight off the street, except for two small steps. A notice on the door invited us to enter. I turned the well-polished brass handle, it gave, and we went in.

We found ourselves in a narrow hall in which ancient brown linoleum gleamed with much polishing under a low-watt light. To our right was a door slightly ajar, marked ‘Waiting-Room’. This proved to be packed with people, many of them Negroes, sitting on chairs ranged round the walls of the room; the centre was occupied by a large Victorian dining-table on which a number of tattered magazines lay in disarray. A gas fire, turned low, stood in front of a black, iron fireplace. On the varnished mantelpiece a marble clock ticked despondently, while on either side of it two cast-iron Greek warriors kept guard.

A whisper of conversation ceased as we entered and all eyes regarded us. I suppose that Mother's pale pink hat caused the interest. While we hesitated, a huge man in an old macintosh got up off his chair and offered it to Mother, who, by this time, was looking very white.

'Thank you,' she said and sat down gratefully.

The man grinned sheepishly, his great red face breaking into a thousand wrinkles, as he stood near us fingering a greasy cap. I stood close to Mother, feeling a little frightened. This was all so different from the chintz-clad sitting-room of our old doctor and the ready welcome of his smart little wife.

Neither of us had any idea how one communicated the fact of one's presence to the doctor. But we soon saw that at the other end of the room was another door and that at the sound of a buzzer people went in and out of it. Presumably the doctor was in the next room. We could not guess how people established when they could go in so we sat and sat until we were the last people in the waiting-room, and the front door was closed and locked by an elderly woman. When the buzzer rang again, Mother rose and went in to see the doctor, and I was left alone.

I got up and went to stand by the gas fire. The

unaccustomed warmth was delicious and wrapped itself around me in a comfortable blanket of heat. I gazed at the iron Greek soldiers on the mantelpiece and smiled at them. My grandmother had such a pair on her kitchen mantelpiece in her beautiful little house on the other side of the Mersey. The tears sprang to my eyes as I remembered it. How long would it be, I wondered, before I had twopence so that I could take the ferry across the Mersey and visit her. My parents never mentioned her and she did not write to me. Probably she did not even know where I was. I wondered if I dare write to her without my parents' permission. Impatiently I wiped away the tears. Paper and stamps cost money, too, you stupid, I told myself.

The doctor was taking a long time over Mother's stitches. Perhaps he would make her quite well. Then she could look after the children and I could go back to school. Perhaps in school there would be a school-teacher who would tell me what steps one had to take to get work when one had finished school.

I had always wanted to be a ballet-dancer and my father had indulged me in this by sending me to a very good teacher when I was about five years old. Just before my seventh birthday, however, a very heavy, old-fashioned wardrobe had unexpectedly fallen over while I was in my parents' bedroom, catching my legs under it. This had resulted in one of my feet being permanently slightly twisted. It was not an unsightly crippling but was sufficient to make any dancing career impossible. During the months I had had to lie with the foot up I had discovered a natural ability for drawing, and this had led to an ambition to design clothes for the theatre.

I gazed into the doctor's miserable gas fire and saw gorgeous imaginary figures in clothes designed by me tripping and leaping across an imaginary stage. I wished I had a pencil and paper to catch and record permanently my pretty dream. If only the doctor would make Mother well, I would study and draw and practise and fill the stage of the Liverpool Empire with such glamour as its old walls had never seen before.

There was a click as the doctor opened his surgery door for Mother and bowed her out, and she smiled her delicate, beguiling smile at him.

He was a dark, intense-looking young man; he was, I later discovered, an ardent communist who tried his best to practise his beliefs in the stinking slum in which we lived. He grinned cheerfully at me and said good night to us both.

'What did he say?' I asked anxiously as I held Mother's arm to steady her, after the doctor's housekeeper had locked the front door behind us.

We walked slowly down the empty street for a little way before Mother answered.

'He said I should have gone to the outpatients department of a hospital.'

'Did he take the stitches out? Did it hurt?'

'Yes, he took them out—it didn't hurt much—he's a surgeon as well as a physician.'

In a trembling voice I asked another question, one with selfish intent. Behind it was my despair at the drudgery I was facing and my hopes that if I was allowed to go to school I might find a way out from being for ever the unpaid, unthanked housekeeper for our poverty-stricken family.

'Will you be all right?' I asked. 'Will you get better?'

'He thinks I will, if I go to work—in the open air.'

'Work?' I was truly astonished.

At my query she looked down at me, but there was no affection, no real interest in her gaze or in her voice as she answered, 'Yes. Work.'

The idea that work could cure someone who had been ill was too difficult for me to understand. I knew nothing of mental illness, except that lunatics were shut up in lunatic asylums, and I had no comprehension of the mental stress under which my poor mother laboured and which the doctor had diagnosed.

'You can't,' I said desperately. 'There is Edward—and Avril—and me—I haven't got my matric yet—I have to go back to school.'

'We shall see,' she said thoughtfully.

My stomach clenched in a deadly nervous pain. In a perceptive flash I saw myself for ever at home, the uneducated daughter retained to help in the house—and there were still some of these when I was a child—grey, uninteresting, the butt of everyone's ill-temper, without money of my own and consequently entirely dependent upon the goodwill of the rest of the family. I saw myself for ever struggling with the care of Edward, with Avril's tantrums and the boys' fights, with Mr Parish's miserable pittance, and I realized that the daughter who did not have to go to school or to work would be the one to be clothed and fed last.

I burst into tears, my hopes shattered.

'Oh no, Mummy!' I wailed. 'I want to go to school! I want to be like other girls!'

'Be quiet,' said Mother sharply. 'You are making an exhibition of yourself.'

I continued to weep—but quietly. Little ladies did not make exhibitions of themselves in public.

'You have to learn that you cannot have everything you want. The family must come first.'

Chapter ten

Immediately we arrived home, I threw a tantrum which left even Avril awed. I stamped, I cried, I shouted that I would go to school. Twelve and a half was too young an age to have to leave. I would not stay at home and look after babies.

My bewildered father, who did not know what the cause of my rage was, shouted at me above the storm to be quiet. Mother shouted back at him. Fiona and Tony, terrified by the noise, wept steadily in a corner, while Alan did his best to placate the various contestants by telling everyone to shut up. Brian took refuge halfway up the attic stairs and watched through the banister. Baby Edward cried for his forgotten bottle. A voice from below yelled up to us, 'Shut that bloody racket, can't yer!'

As my anger gave way to hopeless tears Father gradually picked up the story and said he thought the doctor's idea of Mother's going to work was an excellent one and that it would probably be for only a little while. When I continued to weep passionately, he slapped me across the buttocks and told me to go into the bedroom until I could behave in a civilized manner.

I lay face down on the bed until I could not stand the stench of it any more. The nervous strain under which the children laboured in their cold, hungry, new world was so great that Brian, Tony and Avril had become incontinent at night and Edward had no rubber undersheet to help him, so that the already disgusting beds had become even more so and were invariably wet somewhere on their surface.

Emerging finally in sulky silence and with bloodshot eyes, I found Edward still whimpering disconsolately, but the children were silently getting themselves ready for bed, by taking off their outer clothes. My parents were arguing heatedly about what kind of occupation my Mother could undertake.

Still sniffing, I made a bottle for Edward with the last of the baby food, and, since I was still filled with resentment at my parents, I took him outside and sat down on the top stair of the long flights of gloomy staircase and fed him.

The smell of the overcrowded, verminous house, its filthy, over-used bathroom and the efforts of nine different cooks combined with Edward's rancid odour was almost overpowering, and I put my cheek against his scurvy little head and wept again.

During the next few days my mother went out each afternoon for a walk to strengthen her legs, and then one day she sponged her dress and pressed it with an iron borrowed from Miss Sinford, the benevolent, crazy old lady on the ground floor, wiped her shoes over with a wet cloth, and washed herself down with a rag and cold water. She then made up her face with the last of her make-up and the aid of her handbag mirror, and went out without saying where she was going.

As she went down the stairs, I realized for the first

time how much my mother had changed. She had been considered beautiful and extremely vivacious and had always had a court of young men who called upon her—there were still some gentlemen who lived on private incomes in those days and who had time to call and take tea with a pretty woman and her friends—but now her dress hung loosely on her, her face was haggard and lined, her shining black hair, which had been exquisitely kept by her hairdresser, had grown long and straggling; she had pushed it up under her hat before going out. The polished ovals of her nails were ruined by her having to bite them to shorten them, as we all had to do, because we had no scissors. How much had Father changed, I wondered? And the children? And me?

Avril was howling because she could not go out too, and I decided that I might create a diversion by washing her and washing Edward.

We had a fire that day, a luxury we frequently had to forgo despite the icy February weather, so I went down to the bathroom with our kettle and only saucepan, filled them with water, brought them upstairs and set them on the fire. Carrying Edward on my hip, I took the handleless coal bucket down to the basement area, a stone-lined yard from which steps led up to the back garden. I laid Edward on a counter which must have been part of a butler's pantry in the more palmy days of the house, and washed the coal dust out of the bucket as thoroughly as I could under a tap in the yard.

Watched by a fascinated Avril, who had by now forgotten her desire to go out and had tripped up and downstairs behind me puffing excitedly, I set the bucket in front of the fire, put the warm water in it, stripped a protesting Edward and washed him from head to heel, holding him on my knee as I had seen my nanny hold Avril when she was a baby. This was the first time he had had a complete bath since we had left home and I found that he had numerous bug bites and his little back was sore where the urine had not been properly washed off him; his head was covered with scurf.

I had no change of clothing for him, but I pinned a piece of the rag the priest had given us on him as a rough diaper and laid his blanket over him to keep him warm in the Chariot while I dealt with Avril.

Fortunately, Avril thought it was a wonderful game and submitted to being rubbed all over with a wet cloth. I could not wash her head because I could not think how to do it in a bucket. Dirt was ingrained in her skin and I could not get her completely clean without soap. I had an uneasy feeling that her fine golden hair was verminous and certainly she had scurf around her forehead and along the line of the parting. It seemed, too, as if the hair on the crown of her head was thinner than before. I told her cheerfully, however, that I would wash her vest and knickers after she was in bed.

I sighed as I slicked the water off her in front of the fire, so that she would dry quickly. She, like Mother, had changed. She had been a pudgy child with rosy cheeks; now she looked wan, her ribs showed and her stomach stuck out too much.

While I scrubbed the children, Father was stuck in one of his everlasting queues.

He worked very hard at being unemployed. He spent most of two days a week walking to the employment exchange, standing in a long queue, signing on as being available for work and walking back up the hill which was Leece Street, pausing outside the old Philharmonic Hall to read the concert notices with wistful attention, then on past the black-faced ear, nose and throat hospital and then through an endless maze of decaying Victorian houses to our comfortless eyrie at the top of one of them. He was not so badly off as dock labourers, he told us. They had to sign on for work twice a day.

Another day was spent walking to the offices of the public assistance committee, where could be found Tony's 'Mr Parish'. Here he stood in a long queue again, soaked by rain or frozen in the winter wind, and received his precious forty-three shillings a week. He then walked home. On the other three mornings a week he went to the public library, scanned the advertisements in the newspapers in the reading-room, and wrote replies to those offering work he felt he could do. Then he walked all the way into the centre of the town to deliver his replies to the offices of the *Liverpool Echo* in Victoria Street, because we had no money for stamps—the postage for a letter in those days was three-halfpence.

His shoes wore through at the soles and he stuffed them with cardboard begged from the corner grocery shop, until the holes were so big that the cardboard would not stay in place. Without tools he could not hope to mend them himself, so one week we very nearly starved completely while we paid the shoemaker. He had not had a haircut or a clean shirt for a month, though he had managed to wash himself quite thoroughly. His socks had very little left from the ankle down, and I remember his blue, frozen feet sticking out of them when he removed his soaking wet shoes on his return in the evenings. I think it was rubbing his feet with my hands which truly brought home to me our desperate position and made me accept the fact that I had to stay at home. I would rub until I had the circulation going again and he would whistle under his breath with the pain of it, and each time it happened my heart broke anew.

For a month or more, he never spoke to anyone outside the family, except the city and government clerks who dealt with him and to whom he was just another statistic. One morning, however, the wait at the employment exchange was particularly long and chilly, and the ragged queue of weary men began to mutter rebelliously, and Father was drawn into sympathetic conversation with his fellow sufferers. They were, for the most part, respectable working men many of whose jobs were dependent upon the ships which went in and out of the port of Liverpool in normal times. They were curious about my father, because he spoke like an educated man. They could not imagine that anyone highly educated could be unemployed; they assumed, and Father did not disillusion them, that he had been a senior clerk in one of the shipping companies which had been dispensing with its office staff. They were friendly and, as Father met them again and again, they began to fill him in on how to stay alive under almost impossible circumstances.

He discovered that many of them had wives who went out cleaning private homes or worked in stores to augment their parish relief; though these earnings should have been declared to the public assistance committee, they were not, and they made all the difference between starvation and dying more slowly of malnutrition.

'If you can live long enough, there just might be a job for you one morning,' a leather-faced old warehouseman told him jokingly.

There were agencies in the town, he was told, which would provide the odd pair of shoes or an old blanket for a child. There were regimental funds willing to provide a little help to old soldiers. He gathered other scraps of information, which were revelations to a man who had never had to think twice about the basic necessities of life. An open fire, he was assured, could be kept going almost all day from the refuse of the streets, old shoes, scraps of paper, twigs, wooden boxes, potato peelings; if one was very ill or had a broken bone, the outpatients departments of most of the local hospitals would give some medical care. Pawnbrokers would take almost anything saleable, and one could buy second-hand clothing from them. Junk yards would sometimes yield a much needed pram wheel or a piece for an old bike. One could travel from Liverpool to London by tramcar, if one knew the route, and it was much cheaper than going by train. Some of the men had done it several times in an effort to find work in the more prosperous south-east of the country.

Father thanked them gratefully and came home very thoughtful, marvelling at their sheer resilience and good nature in such adversity.

All of us had colds, including the baby, and lacked even handkerchiefs, though we did our best by using newspaper culled from the greengrocer, who wrapped our small purchases of potatoes in it. Father began to realize that unless help came quickly the younger children would probably die from the first germ that infected them. The death rate in Liverpool, at that time, was one of the highest in the country and the infant mortality rate was correspondingly horrifying. He knew that we were worse off than most of the people who stood in the endless queues with him, since we did not draw the Liverpool level of relief, nor were we eligible for help with clothing which 'Mr Parish' sometimes gave out. No one, in all his conversations, happened to tell him that he was paying three times the rent that most people paid and that this was largely what was crippling us.

By far the greatest proportion of the Liverpool work-force was casual labour, dependent upon the erratic comings and goings of ships in the river, and most men were accustomed to being unemployed from time to time, particularly dock labourers. Their pattern of life reflected this in that they could never make a proper domestic budget, because they never knew from one week to the next what their earnings would be. They spent their earnings and 'made do' in between jobs. My father, being an educated man trained to study economic trends, could never manage to be as philosophical and optimistic as they were. He feared not only for himself but for his children's future.

In those days there were no midday meals or drinks of milk at school to help children along. One good lady who suggested that the skimmed milk thrown down the drain by one of the city's bigger dairies might be given free to children in the elementary schools was soundly snubbed for her socialistic ideas.

Father swallowed what little pride he had left. He sat down at our greasy table and wrote to the headquarters of his old regiment.

Mother came home white with weariness and irritable with frustration, having tried unsuccessfully against about thirty other applicants for a job as a saleswoman.

'They looked like a flock of crows,' she remarked of the applicants. 'They all wore black dresses, stockings and shoes—just little white collars to relieve the dreariness.'

'I thought that was what shop-girls always wore,' replied Father.

'I suppose so,' Mother said. She added, 'And the hours one was expected to work—nine until nine on Saturdays!'

'What wages were they offering?'

'Fifteen shillings a week.'

Father whistled. 'That's not a living wage,' he said.

'They don't care,' replied Mother wearily. 'All the women there were anxious to get the job.'

Chapter eleven

Each day my mother went out to try and get work and spent most of the morning and afternoon in a fruitless round of offices and shops. Before leaving, she would give me a shilling to buy the day's food. This I laid out to the best of my ability on bread, potatoes, rice, tea, sugar, pennyworths of bacon scraps or margarine and, that dire necessity, a pint of milk for Edward, which cost twopence.

At first, Edward used to cry with hunger, but as he grew a little older, he would lie lethargically in the Chariot, making no sound most of the time. The other children also grew apathetic and the smaller ones tried to take bits of bread when I was not looking. We never heard from the school about their progress nor did my father inquire.

One morning my parents went out quite early, before Edward had been fed. After the children had been given a meagre bowl of porridge each and had been sent to school, there was no food left in the house. I was desperate with hunger. And the usual pint of milk would, I knew, not be enough to last Edward for twenty-four hours. However, clutching the shilling, I wrapped Edward up in his stinking blanket, put on my woollen cardigan, my coat being still in pawn, and went downstairs to buy milk from the first passing milkman.

Standing on the doorstep were two pint bottles of milk, presumably delivered for Miss Sinford, the lady with religious mania, and Mrs Hicks, who lived with her unemployed husband in the bowels of the basement. The other tenants patronized a milkman who came later.

I looked at the bottles and then up and down the apparently empty street, hoping that the milkman might still be near by. There was no sign of him, however, and I turned back into the house with the idea of getting out the Chariot and wheeling it round to the dairy to purchase Edward's precious pint.

Edward began to whimper. I looked down longingly at the milk bottles. Then, like a fleeing cat, I tore up the stairs, Edward bobbing up and down in my arms. I laid him down gently in the Chariot, took our two cracked cups, ran down to the bathroom and filled one with water, then ran silently down the rest of the stairs to the front door.

I glanced quickly up and down the street. Everyone was apparently sleeping the long hopeless sleep of the unemployed.

Quickly I took the lids off the bottles, filled the empty cup with a little milk from each bottle, topped the bottles up with water, carefully replaced the lids, shook the bottles gently, and then crept upstairs again with my precious prize.

I managed to make a feed for Edward before the little fire I made from paper flickered out, and I fed him contentedly, knowing that I could make the pint of milk I would buy stretch further for him. I had no qualms of conscience about my theft—I thought only of Edward—and I was mercifully unaware that the policeman on the beat had quietly watched the whole operation.

It was late February, with days of pouring rain interspersed with weak sunshine. The trees and bushes in the locked gardens in the squares were beginning to show a faint swelling of their buds, and, as I wheeled Edward to the tiny local grocery shop and to the greengrocer's each day, I would wonder why the children running in and out of the traffic or playing with cigarette cards on the pavement could not be allowed to play in the gardens. I would stand watching them dully as they cursed and tumbled each other about, their white or black skins equally grey with dirt and dust, their noses dribbling, their bare legs chapped and with septic sores on their knees. Little girls would play endless games of skipping and hopscotch, each with its appropriate song, learned from their elder sisters and passed down from generation to generation.

> 'I am a girl guide dressed i' blue,
> These are the actions I must do.
> Salute to the King, bow to the Queen
> And turn my back to the people.
> Pepper!'

And at the word 'pepper' they would turn the skipping-rope with feverish speed to see how many fast skips they could do before being tripped up. Sometimes, I would wish wistfully that I might be able to join in, but I had always to watch Avril and Edward and I was mortally afraid of something happening to them in this strange world which I did not understand.

Another pleasure was to stand in front of the greengrocer's and contemplate the neat pyramids of oranges, apples, lemons and tomatoes. Mentally, I ate my way through the piles from top to bottom. I lacked the courage and initiative of the little street arabs, who would sometimes snatch a piece of fruit and fly like jets down the narrow back alleys, there to consume it with much ribaldry at the expense of the outraged greengrocer. A cry of 'Bobby' or 'Cop' or 'Flattie' would, however, send them speeding off again, old gym shoes or bare feet thudding over the flagstones like rapidly bouncing rubber balls.

With Edward replete with Miss Sinford's and Mrs Hicks's milk and sleeping quietly in the Chariot, Avril and I went on the usual shopping round. At the greengrocer's I stood and dithered. If I bought rice, I argued with myself, Mother would say that I should have bought potatoes; if potatoes, then she would say rice. I knew I could not win. Mother was getting better and her increasing irritability at my sins was a sign of it.

The policeman on his beat stopped and chucked Edward under his chin. Edward opened his eyes and managed a small smile. I looked up and smiled too, my morning peccadillo completely forgotten.

'Nice baby you've got,' he said, putting his hands behind his back and rocking gently on his heels. He beamed at me from under his helmet. 'What's his name?'

'Edward,' I said. He was a nice-looking young

man, neat and clean, despite the acne spots all over his face.

'And what's your name?'

'Helen,' I replied promptly.

He looked down at the baby again, while the greengrocer peered through the glass of his window, which he had been polishing.

'No Mummy?'

'Yes, she's looking for work. So's Daddy.'

He looked surprised, apparently at my clear English, so different from that of the other children round about. It was better English than he spoke himself.

'Having a hard time? Got any other brothers and sisters?'

'Yes,' I said simply, in answer to the first question. 'We are seven. The others are all at school.'

The wind was getting up and it was beginning to rain. My teeth started to chatter and I wrapped my cardigan closer round me.

The policeman stared at me with calm blue eyes and said, 'Humph.' He adjusted the collar of his cape. I became aware of the interested gaze of the greengrocer, and decided on rice for supper.

'Goodbye,' I said to the policeman and pushed the pram a bit farther along the street and parked it outside the grocery shop, where Avril watched it while I went inside. The policeman, after a moment's hesitation, went into the greengrocer's shop.

The following morning a pint of milk was delivered to the top landing of our staircase. When I ran downstairs to catch the milkman and return the bottle to him, he insisted that it was for Edward and was sent by a friend, and not even Father could make him say any more. For two long intolerable years the milkman stolidly climbed the stairs and deposited a pint of milk on our top step. It probably saved Edward's life.

Many years later, the greengrocer told my mother about the young policeman who had inquired about us from him, and had then gone round to the dairy and ordered a daily pint of milk to be delivered for Edward, and had paid for it out of his own meagre wages.

Chapter twelve

One of the advantages of being very poor is that one has time. Since we had no clothes except those on our backs, there was no pile of washing to be dealt with each Monday. When there is little food, there is little cooking, and since we possessed no bed linen, towels, cleaning materials or tools, most other domestic jobs either were non-existent or could not be carried out. As the weather improved, therefore, I began to take a walk each day, pushing Edward and Avril in the Chariot.

These were, for me, voyages of discovery into a world I had never dreamed of before. I meandered along narrow streets, where the soot-blackened early Victorian houses opened directly upon the pavement. Some of the houses had the flagstone across their front door scrubbed and neatly whitened, with a strip of well-shone brass covering the sill; their painted window-sills were carefully polished and their garish chintz curtains were starched as stiff as the sentries outside Buckingham Palace. Others were like our house: dull windows veiled in grey webs of lace, window-panes missing and filled in with cardboard, old orange-peel and cigarette-ends littering their frontage.

The local pawnbroker's shop, with its dusty sign of three golden balls hanging outside over a wooden table piled high with second-hand clothing, made for me a fascinating treat. I loved to gaze in the windows at the rows of Victorian and Edwardian rings for sale, the war medals, violins, blankets, china ornaments and sailors' lucky gold charms.

The pawnbroker himself was part of the scene, as he stood in his doorway puffing at a cigarette, shirt-sleeves rolled up to show olive-coloured arms, tight black curls receding from his forehead, a magnificent watch-chain with dangling seals swathed across a wrinkled, blue serge waistcoat over a comfortable paunch.

'Come on, me little blue-eyed duck!' he would call to Avril when he saw her, and occasionally he would feel around in his waistcoat pocket with his tobacco-stained fingers to dig out a grubby sweet for her. She loved him and would howl dismally on the days when we did not walk that way. For me, he would have a polite nod and a brief 'Afternoon. Nice day', regardless of whether it rained or shone.

One mild March afternoon, I circled the cathedral and listened to the ring of the stonemasons' tools on its great sandstone walls. It rose like a graceful queen above slums which put Christianity to shame. I stared up the beautiful sweep of steps leading to its entrance, wondering if I dare go in, but I was too afraid. I had not seen myself in a mirror since coming to Liverpool, but I knew I was both dirty and shabby. My hat and shoes had been passed to Fiona, who was obliged to go out to school, whereas I could stay indoors. The shoes had been replaced by a pair of second-hand running shoes with holes in the toes; my head was bare and my hair straggled in an unruly mass down my neck; it was rarely combed and never washed.

Still pushing aimlessly, I wandered along Rodney Street, a lovely street of well-kept Georgian houses, the homes and surgeries of Liverpool's more eminent doctors. A brass plaque on No. 62 informed me that Gladstone was born there. Mr Gladstone was not one of my heroes, so I continued onward enjoying the peace and orderliness of the quiet road.

I turned down Leece Street, past the employment exchange where Father spent so many unhappy hours, past tall, black St Luke's Church and into Bold Street, the most elegant shopping centre in Liverpool. Although there were at least a dozen empty shops up for rent, the atmosphere was one of opulence. I pushed past women in fur coats and pretty hats, who stared at me in disgust, to look in windows which held a single dress or fur or a few discreet bottles of perfume. A delicious odour of roasting coffee permeated the place.

Onward I went, through the packed shopping area of Church Street, where trams, nose to tail, clanged their way amid horsedrawn drays, delivery vans and private cars, and newspaper men shouted to me to 'read all abaat it'. The cry of '*Echo*, *Echo*, *Liverpool Echo*, sir' comes wafting down the years, like the overwhelming scent of vanilla pods, the sound and smell of a great port.

'I know where we'll go,' I said to Avril, who was bouncing up and down in the Chariot pretending it was a horse.

'Where?'

'We'll go down to the Pier Head!'

I knew this part of the town, because I had been shopping in it on many occasions with my grandmother. I pushed the Chariot purposefully up Lord Street to the top of the hill, where Queen Victoria in pigeon-dropped grey stone presided, down the hill, through a district of shipping offices with noble names upon their doors: Cunard, White Star, Union Castle, Pacific & Orient, the fine strands which tied Liverpool to the whole world. Past the end of the Goree Piazzas, an arcade of tiny shops and offices, where out-of-work sailors lounged and spat tobacco and called hopefully after me, under the overhead railway which served to take the dockers to work, and a last wild run across the Pier Head, dodging trams and taxis, to the entrance to the floating dock.

At last I had found it!

The river scintillated in the sunshine; a row of ships was coming in on the tide; a ferry-boat and a pilot-boat tethered to the landing-stage rocked rhythmically; screeching gulls circled overhead and swooped occasionally to snatch food from the river. A cold wind from the sea tore at my cardigan, jostling and buffeting my skinny frame. I put the hood of the Chariot up to shield Avril and Edward from it.

The shore hands were casting off the ferry-boat, and I looked wistfully out across the water at the empty Cammell Laird shipyards in Birkenhead. My eyes followed the shore along to the spires of Wallasey, and mentally I followed the railway with all its dear familiar station names along the coast to West Kirby.

On that railway-line lived Grandma, who was so angry with Father that she never wrote to us. There was a middle-class world, where people could still wash every day in clean bathrooms. The slump had reached some of them, I guessed; but once past Birkenhead, I thought sadly, it could not be half as miserable as Liverpool was. Perhaps, if I could see Grandma and describe to her my mother's terrible suffering and my father's despair, she would forgive them and help them.

I longed to push the Chariot up the ramp of the ferry-boat and escape, run away from our smelly rooms, from hunger and cold, the cold which was raking through me mercilessly now, and from people who looked like the gargoyles on the old cathedrals I had attended in the past.

'The ferry costs twopence,' I reminded myself, as I wrapped Avril and Edward closer in their inadequate piece of blanket, 'and you haven't got twopence.' Furthermore, Grandma, though long since widowed, had been married to a businessman who never failed, and who had come from a long line of ironmasters and merchants who always seemed to have done very well for themselves—she just would not understand.

The way home seemed incredibly long, and I paused at the bottom of Bold Street, to stand for a moment in the warmth of a shop doorway before continuing. A shopwalker behind the glass door frowned at me as I hauled the Chariot close in. The shoppers were thinning out rapidly and I watched them hurrying to their cars, parked at the kerb, or into Central Station. And there she was!

Joan! My own best friend!

She was sauntering down the pavement in her neat school uniform, her mother beside her, presumably here on one of her visits to her grandmother. I had not seen her since leaving my old home and, presumably, she knew nothing of my recent adventures—one day I had attended school with her; the next day I had been whisked away to Liverpool.

I started forward.

'Joan!' I cried, my heart so full of gladness I thought that I would burst with sheer joy. 'Oh, Joan!'

The mother stopped, as did Joan. The smiles which had begun to curve on their lips died half born. Without a word, they both wheeled towards the road, crossed it and disappeared into Central Station.

I stared after them dumbly. They *had* recognized me. I knew they had. Then why had they not stopped and spoken to me?

A gentleman told me irritably to get out of the way and I became aware that the Chariot and I were blocking the pavement. Still dumbfounded, I turned the pram homeward and slowly pushed it up the hill, gazing vacantly before me.

Coming towards me, amid the well-dressed shoppers, was an apparition. A very thin thing draped in an indescribably dirty woollen garment which flapped hopelessly, hair which hung in rat's tails over a wraithlike grey face, thin legs partially encased in black stockings torn at the knees and gaping at the thighs, flapping, broken canvas covering the feet. This thing was attached to another one which rolled drunkenly along on four bent wheels; it had a torn hood through which metal ribs poked rakishly.

I slowed down nervously, and then stared with dawning horror.

I was looking at myself in a dress-shop window.

It was a moment of terrifying revelation and I started to run away from myself, pushing the pram recklessly through groups of irate pedestrians, nearly running down a neatly gaitered bishop. Every instinct demanded that I run away and hide, and for a few minutes my feet were winged. Halfway up the hill, back in the shadow of St Luke's, however, undernourishment had its say, and I sank exhausted on the church steps, while Avril giggled contentedly in the pram after her rapid transit up the street.

I was disgusted with myself. I felt I could have done more. I was old enough to know that I should wash myself; at least cold water was available. And if I could wash garments through for the children, I could have put some of my own through the same water. I realized, with some astonishment, that I had always been told what to do. The lives of all the children had until recently been strictly regulated by a whole heirachy of domestics, some of them very heavy-handed, and a father who had, at times, used a cane with sharp effect. I washed when told to wash, went to school when told to go, however irksome it seemed, got out my playthings when permission was given. Disobedience was a crime and to query or object to adult orders, which were given without any supporting explanation or reason for them, was quite unthinkable. I don't think that I had ever had an original thought until I had been plunged into this queer life in Liverpool, where I had been given the job of looking after my brothers and sisters.

Now, sitting on the blackened stone steps of the soaring Gothic church, I realized that neither Father nor Mother nor Grandmother nor servant was particularly interested in me. With all the bitterness and unreasonableness of a budding teenager, I saw myself as a convenient tool of my parents, my only reason for existence that I could take the care of the children off them.

I fastened the two remaining buttons of my cardigan, got up and wheeled the Chariot slowly up Upper Duke Street, skirting St James Cemetery with some trepidation in the gathering gloom. For the first time, I tried to think constructively, to devise ways in which the family might get out of the morass in which it was floundering; but my experience was too limited and my mind too dulled by lack of use, my body by lack of food, for me to be able to come up with a possible solution. Greater minds than mine were having trouble with the same problem. We were but one family amid millions of others.

I cried openly as I trudged along, my glasses sliding slowly down my nose, the tears making white rivers in my grey face.

When my parents came in that evening, I again brought up the question of my going to school. I was always very nervous when trying to communicate with them and probably I mentioned the subject too diffidently, because when I suggested that I would have to complete my education before I could hope to go to work in the future, Mother simply dismissed me by saying, 'Don't be absurd. Go and put Avril to bed.' Father laughed and added, 'I hope no daughter of mine will ever have to go to work.'

Father's kindly meant remark startled me. Even a young girl like myself knew that times were changing and more and more women were entering the labour force. Lancashire had, in addition, a long tradition of women working, and the only future I could visualize as holding an iota of happiness for myself was one which contained a career.

'But ... ' I began.

'That is enough, Helen. Do as you are told.'

And Helen, being a coward, did as she was told.

Chapter thirteen

With the exception of a weekly visit from an officer of the public assistance committee, which consisted of a quick counting of heads and a few questions snapped at my parents, we had no visitors. I was, therefore, surprised when I arrived home from one of my visits to the Pier Head to find a well-dressed gentleman standing at the door, asking Miss Sinford where he could find my father.

I waved at Alan, who was shepherding the other children along the road, and went up the steps backwards pulling the Chariot up with me. The gentleman retreated a couple of feet from me.

Miss Sinford noted the movement and said promptly, 'Suffer the little children to come unto me and forbid them not. Child, take this gentleman to your father,' and did her usual vanishing trick into her room next to the front door.

The gentleman regarded me with obvious repulsion, but insisted on helping me up the stairs with the Chariot, which meant that Edward sailed up still sleeping and Avril had a wonderful ride.

Father was at home, reading one of the books from the small battered bookcase which formed part of the furniture of the apartment. He immediately offered his chair to the strange gentleman, who sat down reluctantly as he surveyed the smelly room. His rubicund face, plump figure and well-tailored clothes suggested a successful businessman of some kind.

He cleared his throat, rubbed his well-shaven chin, and said hesitantly, 'I—er—we served in the same regiment—you wrote to our commanding officer. I was asked to call on you.'

Hope lit up my father's face.

The gentleman again cleared his throat, as we stood, tense and silent round him.

'I am authorized to make you a grant of five pounds from our regimental fund, if conditions seem to warrant it.'

He looked round again at the empty fireplace and the ragged, gaunt children watching him breathlessly, and sighed heavily.

Father nodded.

'Could you show me your discharge papers?'

'Yes, indeed I can.'

He took an old business envelope from the top of the bookcase and, from among a pile of birth certificates, finally extracted the precious papers, and handed them to our visitor.

The gentleman examined them.

'You were a private?'

'Yes.'

'I thought you were a lieutenant.'

'I was. I got tired of guarding the East Coast, so I resigned my commission and remustered as a private —and was sent to Russia.'

The gentleman looked very impressed. 'Were you? That was no picnic.'

They went on to discuss the Russian campaign for a few minutes, while the children continued to watch in rapt attention. Alan's hands were clenched together as if in supplication.

Five whole pounds! Would he give it?

He smiled and drew out his wallet, and the sound of a tremendous sigh of relief went through the children. Brian shouted 'Hooray' and went bounding round the room, his little monkey face alight as it had not been for weeks. We all laughed hysterically and escorted our bountiful visitor affectionately down the stairs.

Mother came home and was told the good news and it was wonderful to me to see her expression relax and some of the tenseness go out of her.

Alan and I were immediately despatched to buy a vast quantity of fish and chips and peas and milk, and we spent a blissful ten minutes of anticipation, standing in the steam of the fish-and-chip shop among a shabby, hungry crowd, while the fish sizzled in a great vat of boiling fat.

A fat, sharp-eyed little man, who kept a newspaper and tobacco shop near by, heard me give a big order to the shopkeeper.

'Ain't you the kids from No. 12?' he asked.

'Yes,' replied Alan.

'Got a lot of money to throw around tonight, ain't yer?'

'A man from Daddy's regiment gave us five pounds,' said Alan frankly.

The man's eyes gleamed malevolently.

'Eeee! 'e did, did 'e. Well, yer can tell yer Dad

fra' me that I'll be coming over ternight. Yea, ternight!'

The last word came out like a small explosion and was obviously a threat.

Alan whitened visibly, though he answered quite steadily, 'I'll tell Daddy.'

We picked up the two big newspaper parcels handed us by the fish-and-chip merchant, paid for them with a pound note, grabbed our change, and ran down the steps and through the gloomy, gas-lit streets as if pursued by ghosts. We knew instinctively what the newspaper-shop man was. He was a Creditor! Creditors had crowded round Daddy before and caused all our troubles.

'Do you think he'll take our five pounds?' I panted to Alan.

'Not all of it,' said Alan defiantly. 'We'll have finished the fish and chips before he gets to our house. Let's get the milk quickly.'

Not even the colossal row which immediately broke out between my parents when we told them about the Creditor, could dim the pleasure of eating, really eating, once more. My fish and chips and peas were cold by the time I had fed Edward and got the children settled at their meal, but they still tasted like a meal fit for a king.

'Well, where did you think I got the cigarettes from?' asked Father, his teeth deep in fish.

'I never considered the matter,' said Mother haughtily.

I had been so used to seeing my parents smoke, that it had never struck me to question the source of the supply of cigarettes which I had sometimes seen them consume lately.

'How did you imagine you would pay for them?' she inquired.

'I didn't know. I *had* to have a smoke. You smoked them, too!'

Mother began to cry, while Father phlegmatically started to gnaw at another piece of fish.

'I don't know how you persuaded him to trust you,' she sniffed unhappily.

I knew how he had obtained credit. I had already discovered that a good Oxford accent was a much respected asset. A man who spoke as Father did would be trusted by working-class people; they would be sure in their minds that a man who was so well spoken and refined would have the means to pay, no matter how shabby he was.

At that moment there was a knock on the door of the room, and a fearful silence fell upon us all.

Trying not to tremble, I opened the door to reveal an irate member of the working class, our Creditor.

'I want me money,' he said grimly.

'How much?' asked Father, licking his fingers as he got up.

'You know! Thirty-seven and sixpence—and I want it all. Pack o' bloody liars, the lot o' ye,' and he glared around the room.

'Here,' said Father, counting out the money, 'and get out before I throw you out for swearing in front of a lady.'

Quite undaunted, the little man carefully pocketed the money before he moved.

'Lady!' he sneered. 'Ha.'

Father was very neatly made, though by no means tall. His face went red, and he charged straight at the offender, who shot down the first flight of stairs with a nimbleness which would have done credit to a ballet dancer, from which comparatively safe refuge he shook his fist, and then continued downward.

Mother had sat silently through the exchange. Alan and I looked at each other. I could see his visions of plenty to eat for days mixed up with hopes of a new pair of socks slowly fading away. Thirty-seven and sixpence was more than a quarter of the regiment's grant. My own dreams of a broom to sweep with and piles and piles of soap lay shattered.

Fiona, who had not understood anything except the threat of a fight, whimpered and ran to me, and made me take a further step towards growing up.

I put my arms around her and said, with reassuring cheerfulness, 'Daddy still has lots of money left, haven't you, Daddy? We'll be able to have fish and chips again tomorrow, won't we?'

Father had come back into the room and was standing looking worn out in front of the fireplace, but he caught his cue.

'Of course, Fiona, of course we will. Don't worry, little girl. Fish and chips tomorrow.'

Brian suddenly vomited. It seemed to me the worst possible waste of good fish and chips.

Chapter fourteen

Mother went to town on a shopping expedition the following morning, while Edward, Avril and I went to the pawnbroker's to redeem my overcoat.

The pawnbroker hailed his blue-eyed duck with pleasure, when, trembling with apprehension at my unaccustomed task, I entered the dark, back part of his shop, pawn-ticket in hand.

He smiled at us both, his dark face gleaming in the poor light like a portrait by Frans Hals.

'Sit the little girl up on the counter, while I deal with these ladies,' he told me cheerfully.

I lifted Avril on to the high counter.

The counter was divided up into three by means of partitions, so as to give people a little privacy in their transactions, and in the next cubicle were a couple of Irish women in black shawls and white aprons. They had each brought their husband's best suit to pawn, since both men had got ships and gone to sea.

The pawnbroker pulled down his waistcoat over his bursting waistline.

'Now, ladies?'

'Himself sailed last night, and a bloody good riddance to him, I say.'

A bundled-up suit was pushed over the counter.

'Will you get an allotment?' asked the pawnbroker, as he inspected the seams of the jacket for wear.

'Och, for sure. Not much though—himself will see to that.'

'I won't be seeing you for a while then, once that starts to come in.'

'And will it be breaking your heart?' She dug a stout elbow into her friend's ribs, and they both chortled.

'I don't think I'll be able to live without you.'

And so on, bickering about how much the suits were worth—worth more than shiftless husbands, I gathered—until finally they swayed out of the shop, their layers of black skirts giving out an unbelievable stench as they moved.

Mother had given me three shillings, which I handed to the pawnbroker with his receipt for the coat. He gave it to his gangling young assistant, who disappeared up a ladder into the loft. A bundle wrapped in a piece of cloth was tossed down and neatly caught by the pawnbroker.

'There you are. When you bring it back, wrap it in the cloth again,' he said kindly. 'Everything has to be wrapped up in a bundle.' He pushed the tightly wrapped package over the counter to me. 'You should undo it and check it.'

I did this and my hopelessly crushed coat was revealed.

'Would threepence buy an iron?' I asked, emboldened by his amiable manner.

His black eyebrows shot up and his sharp brown eyes looked at me shrewdly, when he heard me speak. He rubbed his chin thoughtfully.

'Not from me,' he replied. 'You might get one from the junk-yard at the back.'

He turned, and shouted up the shute to the store-room above, 'George! Mind shop! I'm going out back a minute.'

George came tumbling down the ladder, and I lifted Avril off the counter, where she had been contentedly kicking her heels and watching the proceedings.

We went out through the back door, and through the pawnbroker's yard. The yard was paved with brick, and neat flower-beds filled with daffodils lined the high walls. A hut next to the back gate presumably held a lavatory. He opened the gate and we crossed the narrow alley separating the two lines of business properties, and went into a yard piled high with rusting iron—all the domestic debris of the neighbourhood, from old bedsteads to hip baths.

'Hey, Joe! Where are ye? Got any old flat irons?'

An aged, hunch-backed gnome emerged from under a lean-to. He peered at us from under a greasy, black cap, with the bright perky look of a blackbird. I had often heard him calling through the streets as he pushed his hand-cart along, 'Any rags, bottles or bones? Any old rags today?' His cry would bring the children rushing to him, armed with jam-jars or rags to trade for a windmill or some other small toy.

'Humph,' he grunted. 'Ah might 'ave.'

He rooted through a collection of old kitchen pails, washboards and dollies lying under an ancient wooden mangle, and finally came up with a small, rusty iron, which he agreed to part with for threepence.

Back in the pawnbroker's shop, I was made to wait while George was instructed to find a piece of sandpaper and rub the iron clean for me.

Gold teeth flashing amid tobacco-stained white ones, the pawnbroker finally presented me with quite a respectable-looking iron.

'There ye are, luv,' he said.

'Thank you very, very much,' I said, and swept out, iron in hand, my coat with its attendant bit of cloth over my arm, and a protesting Avril held firmly by the other hand.

'I want to stay here,' she yelled. 'I like it here.'

I had not forgotten the awful scarecrow I had seen in the Bold Street shop window, however, and I took Edward and her straight home, because I was determined to make a fire with some of the coal the regimental grant had enabled us to buy, heat water and wash myself.

This I did, though I had no soap. I hoped Mother would buy plenty of washing soap, so that I could wash my clothes too. I knew that our family looked far more neglected than many children did.

I had pressed my coat reasonably well by the time Mother came home. She was laden with socks, vests, a real towel, a wash bowl, some cups, saucers and plates, knives and forks, a saucepan, some Aspirin, some cigarettes, and, best of all, some toilet soap and soap powder.

It was Friday, and, when the children came home,

I stripped their clothes off them, put on their overcoats, which they considered a great joke, and washed everything. Soon the room was festooned with steaming garments.

Then I washed the children thoroughly, one by one. They were all emaciated, bug-bitten and shaky on their feet in spite of their two fish-and-chip dinners. Only years later, when I saw pictures of the prisoners released from Belsen, did I fully realize how close we were to dying of starvation, and also what an ordeal it must have been for those children at school to drag themselves there and back and try to pay attention while their bodies gradually wasted.

Nobody in the school seemed to notice the children's suffering. The school nurse found that their hair was verminous, and sent a note to say that we should buy a certain kind of ointment and rub it into their scalps. We had no money for ointment, however, so nothing was done.

No priest of any denomination ever came to see us, though the school was a Church school and a Church of England minister came once or twice to visit Miss Sinford. We knew that we were too dirty and shabby to be welcome in a church, and, except for any religious instruction the children might have received in school, God, like Santa Claus, went out of our lives.

For some time, our only entertainment was to walk the streets and look in shop windows, but gradually the younger ones found ways of amusing themselves. Better weather brought little urchins out to play cricket, with a piece of wood for a bat and a couple of beer bottles for wickets, and my brothers were tolerated in these games. Fiona and Avril learned from Fiona's schoolfriends how to skip and play hopscotch on the pavement in front of the house. They all quickly learned to scream and swear with an unlovely Liverpool accent, though they did not do so in their own home.

I read all the books in the small bookcase in our room. I often read while washing the dishes or feeding the baby and it was then that I discovered that a book laid on the cover of the Chariot could be read while pushing it along the street. I waded through a curious collection of reading matter, including *Hadji Baba of Isphahan*, *Ideal Marriage*, most of Walter Scott's works, a handbook for midwives and several copies of *Moore's Almanac*.

With the last few pennies from the grant from the regiment, Father enrolled himself and Mother in the local branch of the public library, and immediately life seemed filled with untold riches, because I, too, could obtain books on their tickets. The modest little building had a certain elegance—and it was warm. I could not sit in it for hours, as Father did, because I had Edward and Avril always with me and they could not keep quiet for long, but I eagerly snatched books from the shelves and read avidly and haphazardly.

In her shopping list, Mother had included a packet of needles and darning wool and black and white cotton. I now spent most of my evenings darning socks, since nylon socks were not yet on the market, and doing other mending, until the cotton and wool ran out.

The good effect of the regimental grant remained with us, in some degree, for several weeks, though we were still verminous, still had no change of clothing, and were desperate over the need for shoe repairs and, indeed, for new shoes, particularly in the spring rain. We searched the second-hand shops for old running-shoes, anything to cover our feet. Even a few pence spent on such things, however, meant that we could not, at times, have even enough starches to eat. Mother and I found it ever more difficult to drag ourselves up and down the endless stairs; and Father looked like a scarecrow.

Would it ever end, I wondered; and then was seized with childish terror that it might end in death.

Then, in April Mother got a job. She had tried recently for domestic work, but well-to-do housewives did not want a refined woman to scrub their floors; it made them feel uncomfortable. She had also tried all the city shops. But many of them employed, as far as possible, girls under sixteen years of age, and dismissed them on their sixteenth birthday, because at that age they had to pay to the government heavier National Health and unemployment insurance contributions for them. The number of women seeking work was so great that some stores demanded and got girls of matriculation standard to run their lifts and clean their lavatories. Almost all of those who survived their sixteenth birthday in employment, lost their jobs when they were eighteen because at that age, again, the employers' contributions to their insurance went up. Perhaps it was as well that my parents did not know that in Liverpool unemployment was rapidly reaching a peak of 31·5 per cent, one of the highest in the country; they were close enough to suicide as it was.

Mother's employer was a slippery eel of a man who lived near-by. In his kitchen, he mixed that old-fashioned spring remedy, brimstone and treacle, filled ice-cream cartons with it, and sold it door-to-door for threepence and sixpence a pot, according to size. He had done so well that he decided to employ Mother on a commission basis. She would receive a halfpenny on a small pot and a penny on any larger pot she sold.

Unaware of the need for a pedlar's licence, Mother set out hopefully to knock on the front doors of the better class districts, her supply of brimstone and treacle carried in a paper bag.

Since she had a very dignified presence, not many doors were slammed in her face, and at the end of a six-day week she found she had made seven shillings and sixpence and her tram fares. The weather had mercifully been fine and the steady walking had strengthened her muscles. Moreover, a number of kindly housewives had helped her along with cups of tea and biscuits.

It was agreed that her wages must be spent on new shoes for her, so that she could continue to work. I tucked my bare feet under the rickety table. Mother looked really animated for the first time since we had arrived in Liverpool, and took a penny tram-ride to town at our urging, to buy the precious shoes.

Mother's modest success at her first job dimmed considerably any hope I had of ever being able to go to school again; it was as if a jailer had clanged shut yet another prison door between me and freedom. I realized abruptly how deeply I had hoped she would prove a failure at work, so that she would be forced to stay at home and take over from me her normal duties as a mother. I felt wretched and could comfort myself only with the thought that when Father got work I might stand a chance of going to school, since possibly Mother would then feel there was no necessity for her to work.

After she had left for town, I bumped the Chariot slowly down the stairs. Edward who, by now, was trying to sit up, hit his head when I went over a stair more clumsily than usual and started to cry. Avril, who was hungry and tired, joined in.

At the bottom of the stairs, an infuriated Mr Ferris awaited me. His droopy yellow moustache was fluffed out as he blew through it with rage and his eyes bulged like a Pekinese dog's.

'What the hell are you doing, making such a noise?' he shouted.

I stared blankly at him, not knowing how to reply.

'I can't practise with such a racket. I won't stand for it! You'll have to go. Mrs Foster will have to put you out!'

Miss Sinford came through her door, like the old lady on a weather vane.

'Thou shalt not take the Name of the Lord in vain,' she said primly to Mr Ferris. 'I am preparing to go to Communion. Kindly be quiet.'

'I have not taken Him in vain,' roared Mr Ferris, his false teeth threatening to come out, as he nearly spat at her.

Miss Sinford shook a blue-veined fist at him.

'Go back to your piano, sir,' she squeaked. 'And pray for forgiveness for your bad temper.'

I stood between them as they ranted at each other, so filled with fear that I could not move.

He had said: 'You'll have to go! Mrs Foster will have to put you out!'

'Oh no, O Lord,' I prayed. 'Nobody else will ever take us in. We'll have to go to the workhouse. Don't, please don't, let Mrs Foster turn us out.'

Miss Sinford had dived past the Chariot and struck Mr Ferris a sharp blow on the nose, and, like a terrified rabbit, I was suddenly galvanized into trying to escape.

Hastily, I manœuvred the Chariot past the contestants, through the front door and down the worn steps to the street. Fear beat at me, and I ran as fast as the Chariot and its two wailing passengers would allow me to.

I ran blindly through the grey streets and did not stop until my stick-like legs began to fail me and I found myself on Princes Avenue.

The workhouse or Institution, as it had recently been renamed, loomed like a scarifying black shadow over all the destitute of England; even I knew that. And I was ready to die of fear.

Chapter fifteen

Very slowly, I trundled the Chariot down the Avenue. The trees which lined it were in leaf, and each leaf of the privet hedges in the small town gardens in front of the houses looked as if it had been specially polished. On the stone-flagged pavement the puddles from recent rain were drying up under a mild sun. It was mid-afternoon and very quiet. My teeth gradually stopped chattering, and Avril ceased her lament and demanded to be lifted out so that she could walk.

When I picked her up out of the pram she felt remarkably light, even in my wasted arms, and my teeth again began to chatter like castanets, as I looked down at her. She began to toddle along contentedly, however, singing in a rasping little voice 'Little Bo Peep' which we had been practising together.

The warmth of the sun and the peace had its effect. Perhaps, I argued to myself, 'Mr Parish' or even Daddy's regiment would protect us from the ire of Mr Ferris. I stopped in the middle of the pavement and smiled to myself, as I visualized Father's regiment marching down the street, their putteed legs moving in purposeful unison, to rescue us from Mr Ferris.

'Frog's eyes! Frog's eyes!' shouted a rough voice

in my ear, and a couple of big boys made playful snatches at my spectacles.

Avril screamed. I instinctively clutched at the precious spectacles. They laughed, and quickly kicked my shins with their heavy boots. Screaming wildly, they ran on down the Avenue, leaving me quivering with pain and mortification.

'Beasts!' shouted Avril after them, with considerable spirit.

Crying quietly with pain, I walked on into Princes Park and into the rose garden which, though as yet bare of roses, was a pretty place, with a little lake much favoured by ducks and other small water birds.

My legs felt like jelly and I thought I was going to faint, so I sat down on the first bench we could find. At the other end of the seat was an old gentleman. He was shabbily, though respectably, dressed, with a stiff winged collar encircling a thin, turtle-like neck. A heavily moustached, sallow face was framed by a trilby hat set a little to the back of his head. His expression was benign and he had an air of quiet dignity. He was perusing a small, leatherbound book.

Avril came to sit on my knee, and I began to teach her the names of the various kinds of ducks swimming on the lake. The faintness receded and I forgot my bruised shins.

Our peace was soon broken.

'Hey, you there with the pram! Get out o' here! No children allowed in this here garden without an adult.' A uniformed park attendant was waving a stick at us from the rose-garden gate.

Because I did not immediately respond—I was still

unaccustomed to my reduction to the ranks of the under-privileged—he started down the path towards us, his stick raised menacingly.

Without warning, a quiet commanding voice beside me said, 'The children are with me. I am responsible for them.'

The old gentleman had closed his book, and was staring coldly at the attendant.

The parkkeeper lowered his stick and looked disbelievingly at the old gentleman, who gazed back calmly at him, until finally the parkkeeper, his lips curled in a sneer, grunted, 'Humph!' and turned away, to continue his promenade through the park.

In a quiet voice, with an accent that might have been French, the old gentleman asked me, 'And where did you learn to speak English like that, child?'

I blushed guiltily. He must have been listening to Avril and me.

What was wrong with my English? And how does one learn one's own language? I asked myself. I was nonplussed.

Sharp brown eyes, with yellowed whites, appraised my bare feet, greasy gym slip, worn without a blouse, which I had had to lend to Fiona, and knitted cardigan with holes through which my elbows stuck.

Ashamed, I bowed my head so that my face was shielded by a mass of untended hair.

'I . . . er . . . I learned it at home,' I muttered.

'You speak it beautifully,' he said with a gentle smile. 'I have not heard better speech during my many years in Liverpool.' The intonation was definitely foreign.

The bent head shot up. This was the first compliment anyone had ever paid me.

'Do you really think so?' I asked incredulously.

'I do.'

I said impulsively, 'Mummy and Nanny thought it was important to speak well. Neither of them seemed to think that I spoke very well.'

'Nanny?'

I nodded confusedly.

'We don't have a nurse now.'

A watery sniff muffled the much admired accent.

He said dryly, 'I imagine not.'

Avril clambered down off my knee and went on one of her small perambulations. Edward slept. My acquaintance opened his book, as if to continue his reading. Instead, he sat tapping the page with a swollen, chilblained finger.

My eyes were carried to the page by the pointing finger, and I was astonished to see that the print in the book consisted of curly dashes with occasional dots.

He noticed my interest, and smiled at me.

'It is Arabic,' he said.

I was impressed.

'Can you speak it, sir?'

'Of course. My mother was an Arab.'

That accounted for the darker skin, I thought, and I wondered if I dare ask him what brought him to England. How romantic to have a real Arab for a mother! I wondered if she wore a yashmak and transparent trousers, like the princesses in my fairy-tale books.

His eyes were twinkling. Perhaps he was lonely, too, for he said suddenly, 'I speak seven languages and can read four more.'

'How wonderful!' I exclaimed in genuine admiration, remembering my own struggles with the French language.

'Tell me,' he said. 'How is it that—that—' and he waved his hand in a comprehensive gesture, which took in the Chariot with its half-starved baby and Avril's and my deplorable condition.

Hesitating and seeking for words at first, I explained as best I could about bankruptcy and unemployment. Gradually I gained courage and confided in him my despair at not being able to continue at school and my fear of what would become of us.

He listened patiently, occasionally interjecting a question or nodding understandingly.

Finally I trailed to a hopeless stop.

He sat silent for a while, contemplating the lake, his book still open on his knee, his face full of the sad resignation of the very old.

At last, he sighed and said, 'You know, child, it is not what happens to you that matters—it is how you deal with it.'

This was a new idea to me and I pondered on it, as I shyly watched his face.

'You can read?'

'Yes.'

'You go to the library?'

'Yes.'

'Then read! Read everything you can. Read the great historians, the philosophers, especially the German ones, read autobiographies, read novels. One day, you will have the opportunity to make use of the knowledge you will accumulate, and you will be surprised to find that you know much more than those who have had a more formal education.'

He closed his book and put it in his pocket, and then said quite cheerfully, 'Your day will come, child. Your parents are having a difficult time at present and cannot help you.'

He got up from his seat slowly and stiffly and then bowed politely to me.

'I come here every sunny afternoon to commune with nature. Come one day and tell me what you have read.'

The faintness which had threatened me before was making his face dim to me, but I thanked him warmly and promised that I would come. I felt wonderfully comforted.

I sat down again after he had left, to allow my faintness to recede. Then I called Avril and hastened out of the rose garden before the keeper could find us without a guardian.

The way home seemed infinitely long and the momentary peace engendered by the conversation with the old man gradually left me, to be replaced with memories of Dickens's descriptions of workhouses.

Chapter sixteen

When I arrived home, Alan and Fiona were sitting on the bottom step of the imposing flight of steps which led up to the front door of Mrs Foster's house. The evening was drawing on and the lamplighter was going on his rounds, pulling on the gas lights with his long rod as he paused, wobbling on his bicycle, at each lamp-post.

Alan was talking cheerfully to Fiona, who looked white and woebegone, her blue eyes wide and her china-doll features crumpled with fear.

'What's the matter?' I asked in some alarm, as I stopped the Chariot beside them.

Alan peered up at me through his tousled mop of yellow hair.

'Fiona's scared, and I'm telling her that there is nothing to be scared about,' he said stoutly.

Trying not to show that I was frightened, I lifted Avril out of the Chariot with elaborate casualness and clucked encouragingly at Edward, who smiled at me angelically.

I sat down beside Alan.

'What *is* the matter?'

Fiona answered through trembling lips.

'Mrs Foster is shouting at Mother, and Mother is shouting at Father—and—and it's an awful noise.

'And I want to go home to Nanny!' And she began to cry.

'Be quiet!' I snapped at her, and she was immediately reduced to cowed silence.

I turned to Alan.

'Has Mr Ferris complained?'

Alan looked puzzled.

'Mr Ferris? You mean about the noise we make?'

'Yes.'

'Oh no.' Alan chuckled suddenly and began to play an imaginary piano with gusto. 'He makes too much noise himself. He just shouts at us because it makes him feel better.' He tossed back his hair, exactly as Mr Ferris did, and finished his piano piece with a mighty boom on the bottom notes, 'Boom-tiddly-boom—boo-om—boom!'

I wished that I had Alan's cool common sense. In one sentence he had calmed my fears. But not Fiona's apparently. Tears were running down her cheeks like raindrops.

'What has happened, then?'

Alan sobered.

'Daddy didn't pay the rent. He spent the money on cigarettes, and Mrs Foster is as cross as two sticks. And Mother is crossest of all, because she helped to smoke the cigarettes without thinking of where they came from. And—well, you know Mother.'

I did know Mother. Even in her most halcyon days, her temper had been something to avoid at all costs. Now, sick, bewildered, hungry and despairing, her bouts of temper bordered on insanity. She was terrifying in her rages, more terrifying in her subsequent withdrawn silences.

I licked my lips and voiced my dread in a whisper, so as not to frighten Avril, who was sitting on the pavement playing with two matchsticks and a piece of orange-peel. Alan and Fiona bent their heads close to mine.

'Do you think she'll turn us out into the street—Mrs Foster, I mean?'

'No idea,' replied Alan phlegmatically. 'Fiona and I just opened the door when we came back from school, and understood what the trouble was inside a minute. So we just left them to it—and came down here.'

'Where are Brian and Tony?'

Alan sighed. 'They bounced right into the room. Now they'll be expected to take sides—and Brian will have nightmares—and probably be sick after tea.'

I nodded silent agreement: Poor Brian, sensitive to every nuance of every word spoken to him, would be reduced to incoherence by such an episode.

'Have we got bread for tea?' asked Fiona.

'A little,' I said.

'Shall we ever have butter again?'

'Of course,' said Alan.

Avril toddled up to us.

'I like jam as well as butter,' she announced. 'I want jam for tea.'

I suppressed an irrational desire to slap Avril, and we sat quietly watching seamen crowding into the hall of a house opposite to ours. In this house lived an assortment of middle-aged women, who were a great mystery to me. They were much better dressed than their neighbours, though they never seemed to go out to work. And they had lots of visitors—all men.

I watched the rolling gait of the men lounging up the steps. Many of them were already drunk. They shouted raucously to each other and laughed at remarks of which I did not get the import.

One of the single ladies who lived on the same floor as Mrs Foster, came down our steps and paused by us. She looked across the road and then regarded us uneasily.

'Dawn't yer think ye'd better go in, luv?' she asked.

I looked up at her dully. She seemed magnificent to me with her veiled, flowered hat and flashing diamanté earrings. Her silver evening shoes and rayon stockings were close to me, however, and she did not smell very nice.

Uneasily, I turned my head away.

'We can't,' I said.

'Daddy and Mummy are cross,' announced Avril, rising from the pavement and dusting down her little backside.

The lady bit her scarlet lower lip, as she considered this, and then said in confidential tones to me, 'Eee, luv, ah think you had better get inside. Over there is going to be ruddy noisy—and rough to the likes o' you. There's four ships in.'

Though none of us knew what she meant, we rose reluctantly and Alan helped me pull the Chariot up the steps.

I appreciated that she had tried to be kind to us,

and I thanked her, as she started to walk with swaying hips to the bus stop at the corner.

'That's all right, luv,' she said cheerfully, and she hitched her mangy fox fur up round her chin and called to Avril, 'Now, run along, luv.'

'She's pretty kind, isn't she?' I remarked to Alan, as we jointly heaved the Chariot up the stairs to the top of the house, from whence the sounds of battle still proceeded.

'Yes,' said Alan. But he did not sound convinced, though he added, 'She gave me a sweet the other day.'

Just as we were about to tackle the last flight of stairs, we heard Mrs Foster's heavy tread coming down. We cringed together on the landing as, without a word, she passed us, her black georgette draperies floating around her. Behind her she left a mixed odour of cats and birds.

Dead silence greeted us as we entered our room. My parents occupied the two kitchen chairs which the room boasted. Their mouths were clamped shut, and only my mother's fast breathing told of the earlier strife. Brian was biting his nails feverishly, as he stood watching them. Tony was calmly playing with a pebble on the table, pretending it was a train: he muttered 'chuff-chuff-chuff' to himself as he ran it into a station. He looked up as we entered, his large intelligent eyes sad with a sadness unnatural in one so young.

'Hello, Helen,' he said, his voice sounding loud in the prevailing quietness. 'What about some tea—it's late.'

I did not know what to do about my parents, so I ignored them and answered him.

'Yes, dear. Just let me unload.'

From around Edward's feet in the pram, I exhumed a mass of small pieces of rubbish, which I had gleaned during my walk, and laid them in the hearth. There were empty match-boxes, cigarette cartons—which did not usually burn very well—bits of stick, twigs and paper of every description, and a whole tattered copy of the *Liverpool Echo*.

I raked through the cold ashes in the grate and salvaged a few cinders. Would I have enough fuel to boil some water, I wondered anxiously.

Alan kindly volunteered to run down to the bathroom and fetch a pan of water, and Fiona, without being asked, took Edward on her knee. She gasped as his wet napkin damped her gym slip and bare legs, but she did not complain. And all the time my parents sat in silence, almost prostrated by their quarrels.

It was nearly dark by the time the water was persuaded to boil and the tea was made. I cut a dry, white loaf into eight pieces of roughly equal size, and gave each of my parents a piece of it with a cup of the smoky tea, which had, of course, no milk or sugar in it. I gave a little tea to each child in whatever receptacles I could muster, with a piece of bread.

'Can I dip?' asked Tony. 'The crust is too hard to bite.'

I looked at my mother, who ignored the question and stared moodily into her teacup.

My father picked up his cup, and said suddenly, 'You may.'

Thankfully, Tony and Brian plunged their bread into their tea.

'The bread is so stale it's second-hand,' remarked Tony.

Brian giggled and snorted helplessly into his jam-jar of tea. 'I've got a second-hand teacup to match,' he gurgled, a note of hysteria in his voice.

'I want some jam,' shouted Avril.

'Be quiet, Avril,' said Fiona, who had given a little of her bread to Edward to suck on. 'You know there is no jam.'

'Not even any second-hand jam?' the younger girl demanded with mock indignation.

My father began to laugh, at first a small wry chuckle in his throat and, then, gaining momentum, one of his old hearty laughs. I joined in, and soon the whole family was laughing hysterically, the noise pealing along the cobwebbed ceiling and down the stairs to the floor below, where the other tenants, hearing us, must have believed us to be mad.

Only Mother, wrapped in pain, fatigue and semi-starvation, sat silently staring at her cup of tea, her piece of bread in her hand.

Chapter seventeen

We crept through the spring and summer, cursing wet days, rejoicing in warm, dry ones, ignoring petty ailments and hunger, since we could do nothing about either.

Several of the children had sores which took a long time to heal. These were sometimes caused by normal cuts and abrasions, acquired while playing, going septic; and sometimes from their scratching at their vermin-ridden bodies. We nearly all suffered from toothache from time to time, and Mother's teeth began to loosen. Brian suffered torture from gum-boils. His first teeth had been good but he had several large cavities in his second ones, caused, perhaps, by the large amount of white bread in his diet. His wizened face would swell up and he would cry hour after hour, until finally the abscess would burst and the pain would be reduced. On one occasion his weeping was heard as far away as the basement of the house; and Mrs Hicks, prodded by her out-of-work, bricklayer husband, made the long journey up the stairs, to inquire what was the matter.

'He's got a bad tooth,' I explained. 'He can't go to school today, because it hurts too much.'

'Well, poor luv!' she exclaimed, her double chin, with its little crown of spiky hairs, wobbling sympathetically. 'Na, then, I got some oil of cloves.

Come daanstairs with me, luv,' she called to Brian, who was hovering nervously in the background. 'Ah got somethin' as will help yer. Come on, na.'

Brian allowed himself to be beguiled downstairs, where he spent the afternoon lying on Mrs Hicks's horsehair sofa in front of her blazing fire, having hot cloths put on his cheeks and quantities of bitter oil of cloves dabbed into his cavities.

Nobody had ever made such a fuss of him, and, despite the pain and the foul taste of oil of cloves, he loved it. He loved also the warmth, the cosiness and the old tin teapot keeping its contents warm on the hob.

Mr Hicks called him a brave lad, and, when he was feeling better, and was ready to return to our cold, clammy apartment, Mrs Hicks invited him to come down again on a day when his teeth were not hurting, and have a cup of tea and a homemade scone with them.

He came back full of glee, in spite of his swollen face, and remained Mr and Mrs Hicks's devoted friend and message-runner for years.

The Hickses had so little, and yet they managed to make their dark basement so cosy. Mrs Hicks must have been an excellent housekeeper and, unlike many of her neighbours, she understood the nutritional value of many cheap foods like herrings and lentils, and she pointed out to me that brown bread was better than white. My mother, like many middle-class English people at that time, knew very little about the need for a well-balanced diet.

Another good cook was the Spanish lady who had given us the Chariot. I found she had a Spanish husband, who was a warehouseman in one of the fruit warehouses near the Fruit Exchange, and he kept her well supplied with oranges, apples and other delicacies in season. He was, she confided to me as we sat on the steps in the sun, a man of choleric temper and colossal jealousy. But, ah me, what a man!

I smiled sympathetically, and bounced Edward up and down on my knee, to his great delight.

She pulled her black, knitted shawl tightly round her shoulders, and looked at me coquettishly.

'You not understand yet, I think. But you learn.'

'I expect so,' I replied guardedly, not at all sure what I would learn but sensing it would be something interesting.

She cooed in Spanish to Edward.

He could crawl a little now, but he was not a pretty baby. His head, which looked too big, was covered with scurf, and his stomach stuck out grotesquely. His smile, however, was sweet as he responded to the Spanish words.

'My last boy, Peter, he go to school with your Tony. Say your Tony very clever—can read well and do his arithmetic.'

This was news to me, there being no contact between home and school. My father, eternally busy at being unemployed, had given no consideration to his children's progress. My mother, after the brimstone and treacle season came to an end, about the end of May, kept trying unsuccessfully for other work, and long walks to see prospective employers took up much of her time. She was now well, in the sense that she had recovered from Edward's birth and her subsequent major operation, but she was nearly starving and was still walking the razor's edge between mental health and nervous breakdown. She was a mere wreckage of the lovely woman she had been a short eighteen months previously.

The Spanish lady was speaking again.

'What your Dadda work at?'

'He is registered as a bookkeeper–clerk.'

I felt reticent. I did not want to tell our story to anyone who asked, and I parried all further questions.

Frequently, I walked down the avenue to Princes Park and, seated on the sun-warmed bench in the rose garden, had long conversations with the old gentleman who had defended us against the parkkeeper.

'I was never rich,' he once volunteered in his precise English. 'I have always worked as an interpreter —and I still do sometimes interpret for Arab and Chinese seamen in the magistrate's court.'

'Were you born in China, sir?' I ventured.

'No. I was born in Lebanon. My father was a German and, as I think I told you once, Mother was an Arab. So I had three languages—German, Arabic and French, which is widely spoken in Lebanon. Father was an engineer by profession and I had the chance to learn Chinese and English while he was working in Singapore, then Spanish in Mexico and Portuguese in Brazil. I taught myself Italian.' He paused for breath, and then went on, 'Now I study Greek and Hebrew, so that I can study the Scriptures in more detail.'

I was awed by such a catalogue of learning.

'You must have been able to live quite comfortably,' I hazarded.

'I had sufficient. But, you must know, child, that scholarship does not often bring one money—one can earn, yes—but it is the enrichment of the mind rather than of the pocket which it gives.' He laughed softly. 'I was rich in friends, a good wife, three sons ... ' His voice broke, and he stopped.

'Do your boys live with you?' I inquired, wondering that he had not mentioned them before.

He looked at me absently.

'My boys—my wonderful boys—all died in the war. My dear wife followed them three years ago. Soon I shall join them.' He snapped his little book shut as if to show how suddenly he would finish.

I was ashamed at having pried into his affairs. Adult suffering had a way of springing upon one from unexpected sources, and I had yet to learn how heavy a burden the adult world carried at times.

'I'm truly sorry to have been so impertinent,' I mumbled.

I hoped passionately that he would not die. He was the only clean, civilized person I knew in Liverpool; and he was as wise as my grandmother, who lived so far away, a whole twopence away, in the Wirral. That my parents were civilized did not occur to me. They always seemed to be so far away from me.

The old gentleman shook his depression away, realized I was distressed and comforted me.

'When you are eighty-one years old, you look forward to being once more with your loved ones,' he said.

We sat quietly together. I tended to agree with him that death was something to look forward to.

'Do you believe in God—and Heaven?' I asked timidly.

'Yes, indeed,' he said. 'My mother was a Mohamedan and my father was a Lutheran, and neither impressed a religion upon me. They both explained their beliefs to me, but they made me study and search for God.'

'We are Church of England,' I said. 'That is . . .' I hesitated. 'That is, when we are clean and rich we are Church of England. I suppose at present we are nothing.' I laughed a little guiltily. 'I have never been inside a church in Liverpool. When we were at home, the minister called from time to time—but he does not do so here. I suppose we are too wicked.'

He sat contemplating the placid lake for a minute, and then asked, 'Has nobody from your Church been to see you?'

'Yes. When we first came, a very kind priest in a long black robe brought us some food. He was very nice. I do not think our present house is in his parish.'

'You should go to your parish church.'

'We could not,' I replied emphatically. 'We are so dirty—we can't afford soap.'

He nodded understandingly.

I added, 'I do not know what we did to deserve it all.'

He smiled gently.

'God tries us all, child. Pray to Him for help. He will hear you.'

I thanked him, and got up heavily from the bench. There was no hope in me.

All the way home, however, I prayed silently in the well-known words of the Anglican prayer-book, in the belief that there is no harm in trying.

Chapter eighteen

One of the penalties frequently paid for being poor is that of being cut off from the rest of the world. The normal means of communication such as newspapers, radio and letters cost money. Some of our neighbours had radios, and they clung to them no matter what else they had to part with. It was their main source of both entertainment and news, as long as they had a penny to put into the electric meter or could afford to get the wet batteries recharged. These families could hear the first rumbling of the Nazi movement in Germany and Mussolini's fiery speeches, and of strikes and riots in Spain, the prelude to the Spanish Civil War. Nearer home, there was the crisis of the resignation of the Labour Government.

My father read several national newspapers and the *Liverpool Echo* whenever he went to the library. My mother, also, would skim through the *Echo* during a quick visit to the library, when she would jot down on a piece of paper details of jobs advertised. They were, however, the exception; most people around us found reading a laborious effort and there was a fair sprinkling among the older inhabitants who could neither read nor write.

The newspaper room in the library seemed to be the preserve of adults, who did not like a dirty raga-muffin with a baby on her hip, pushing in front of them. In consequence, I knew more about Walsingham and Lord Burghley, Queen Elizabeth I's ministers, than I did about George V's Ramsay MacDonald.

I knew nobody of my own age and was cut off from all forms of play. Some girls of about fourteen years of age lived in the vicinity. They were tough, brassy lasses, who regarded themselves as adults and worked all day in factories or shops. Each girl had a best friend who was known as her mate and together they went to the cinema or to dances, where they danced together; if a boy asked one of them for a dance she circled the floor with him in silence, her face exhibiting about as much expression as the back of a tram. Every Friday evening they solemnly washed and set each other's hair, and on Sundays, dressed in their best, they would walk together in the streets, regarding hopeful males with joint disdain. This was a matriarchal society where ferocious grandmothers and nagging mothers reigned supreme and men seemed to have hardly a toehold in the home, and these young girls were already aware of this.

They were cheap labour and at the age of sixteen they would often be unemployed, like their elder sisters, but in the meantime they were frequently the most affluent members of their household, with money to spend in Woolworth's on cosmetics and rhinestone jewellery. I envied them their neat, black, work dresses and, even more, their best Sunday coats and hats and high-heeled shoes. They never spoke to me, except sometimes to jeer at my rags. At such times my glasses would mist over with tears, and I would whisk Avril and the Chariot round a corner, before the children could realize what was happening.

The local boys bullied both Avril and me, just as they did a subnormal boy who lived in the next street and a little Negress, the daughter of a medical student, who lived round the corner. None of us was human by the standards of these lads—we looked different—and we ranked with dogs and cats, to be teased and mishandled if caught.

Our family received no letters. It was as if everybody we had known before that first day in Liverpool had dropped dead. My parents always hoped for letters in reply to the endless applications for work which they wrote, but nothing arrived. Occasionally, my mother would write to an old acquaintance to beg for financial help in our predicament; there was no response.

I longed passionately to go to school, to have some small communion with a more ordered world where I might find some spark of hope of a better life through learning. I continued to pray that, since my brothers and sisters attended a Church school, the priest would one day call upon us and would discover my existence; I was sure he could make my parents send me to his school. But the Church knew us not, and I was thrown back upon my library books and what I could remember from the past.

Unlike many children, I had always enjoyed going to church. The major festivals of the year were to me wonderful theatrical productions, and my introduction to the works of many great composers had been through hearing their music pouring forth from a well-played organ on such occasions. Some of the churches I had attended were hundreds of years old and had priceless paintings, tapestries, vestments, carvings in stone and wood, magnificent brasswork and gold ornaments, a wealth of beauty on which the myopic eyes of a small girl could feast when the sermon became boring.

The beauty of the language of King James's Version of the Bible and of the Church of England Prayer-Book and the rich poetry of the hymn-book were not lost upon me, and enriched my knowledge of the English tongue.

Now, when mental stimulus was most required and religious comfort desperately needed, these things were gone from us. I believed that God was not just angry with us—he was simply furious.

Apart from being exposed to the scholarship and intellectual wealth of the Church of England, I was fortunate in having well-educated parents. They were extremely modern in their day and surrounded themselves with friends who discussed at length ideas and concepts of the times as well as more mundane matters.

As the eldest child, I was sometimes allowed to leave the nursery and sit with my elders in the drawing-room. Bearing in mind the hissed instructions of Nanny to 'hold my hush', I would sit, like a sleepy owl, on a stool by the white marble fireplace, admiring Mother's collection of Georgian silver which winked at me in the firelight from an antique sideboard.

The drawing-room always seemed to be full of well-tailored gentlemen, some of them economists and bankers, others wealthy merchants; and a younger group clustered round my mother talking witty nonsense to her. I did not always understand what was discussed—I was too young. I soon became aware of the world and its problems, however, as seen through the eyes of the upper middle class. There was a place called the Stock Market inhabited by bulls and bears; and there were far-away countries, like India and China, where men made fortunes. There were terrifying food shortages called famines when men died in the streets; there were wonderful farms, full of sheep, in Australia, and others equally full of wheat in Canada. There were ships to be built, railways to sell and venturesome investments to be made in car, radio and electric-light-bulb firms.

The world was a wonderful, exciting place, and I longed to grow up and be part of it.

Nobody mentioned the kind of world in which I now lived. Perhaps my father's friends did not know of its existence, or, if they did, preferred to forget it. And where were my father's friends?

I kneeled on the floor by the window of our top-floor eyrie and looked down at the unemployed men playing one of their endless games of ollies, a form of marbles. I remembered how Joan had ignored me when I had met her. I supposed that Father's friends had done the same.

So much for friendship.

One form of communication which was very rare in such streets as I looked down upon was telephoning.

The public telephone was beginning to make its appearance; but even that assumed that the public had friends or businesses with telephones, to whom they wished to speak. In my new world, families still sent one of the family with either a written or verbal message.

Father had always been interested in French history, particularly the reign of Louis XIV, and I had been with him on a number of interesting trips to museums to see new acquisitions of jewellery, clothing or furniture of this period. It occurred to me, one day, that Avril and I could go to the museum together, so I pushed the little girl and Edward in the Chariot all the way to the city and then across it to William Brown Street. I pulled the Chariot up and down three huge flights of steps until I found the right building, and was just struggling to get the pram through a recalcitrant door when a voice boomed, 'Where are you going with that thing?'

A very large commissionaire stood behind me.

'I'm going to the museum,' I replied nervously.

'Not with that you're not.'

His remark was clear enough, but there was a hint of puzzlement in the tone of his voice when he made it.

I looked sadly down at Avril. I was afraid to leave the Chariot outside, in case some urchin thought it was abandoned and took it to play with.

I looked up at the commissionaire and was prepared to do battle.

He must have seen the malignant gleam in my eye, because he said sharply, 'Now you just take that thing back to where you found it, and don't let me find you loitering round here again.'

Loitering was something one could be arrested for, I knew, so I swallowed the bitter words that came to mind, and silently turned and bounced the Chariot back down the steps so fast that I cannonaded into an elderly, distinguished-looking gentleman coming up.

'Oh, I beg your pardon, sir,' I said, horrified at having struck such a gentle, scholarly type of person. 'I hope I haven't hurt you badly.'

'Not at all. My briefcase took the blow,' he replied kindly, as he stared in surprise at Avril and me. His lips parted, as if to ask me something, but I had been so humiliated by the commissionaire that I felt I was going to cry, and I hastened onward across the street to St George's Hall. Once there, I looked back.

The gentleman was standing at the door of the museum still staring curiously at me.

I giggled suddenly through my tears. An Oxford accent coming from a bundle of rags and bones like me must have really puzzled him. It had not, however, impressed the commissionaire and gained me entry to the museum.

So much for public cultural emporia.

Chapter nineteen

Summertime had always meant to me a period of waving green wheat slowly turning yellow, a time for walks along a meadow-bordered river where buttercups waited to be threaded into chains, a time to lie under a plum-tree and read to my heart's content, a time to play at theatres and dressing-up with my friend, Joan, while the walnuts ripened overhead.

Liverpool summers are not like that. In the nineteen-thirties not much was understood about pollution; and on days when it did not rain the acrid smoke was enough to obscure the sun until a harsh, Atlantic wind temporarily lifted the veil. On hot days the alleyways and garbage cans stank, despite the ministrations of an army of dustmen who not only laboriously cleared the garbage but also washed down the alleys themselves. There were still a lot of horses in Liverpool and where there are horses there are always myriads of flies to carry dysentery. Our milkman kept his cows in a shippen at the back of his dairy, but fortunately in summer for part of the time they grazed outside the city, and took their quota of flies with them.

Hens and pigeons were common in back yards. Men kept fighting-cocks, though this was illegal, and many were the bloody battles in the long summer evenings on which men wagered a large portion of their public assistance money.

Much of this the younger children were able to accept as a way of life as they slowly forgot their earlier life, though Tony once said to me earnestly as I bathed a grazed knee he had acquired while playing rounders in the street, 'I don't like the kind of life we live, Helen, and when I grow big I shall change it.'

'I hope you will,' I replied equally gravely. 'You've got brains and you could get a scholarship to a better school—and that would get you out of it.'

'Why don't you go to school, Helen?'

The tears, never far from my myopic eyes, sprang up. I bent my head so that he could not see them. 'Mother needs me at home, dear.'

'How will you get out of it then?'

'I really don't know.' I made myself sound cheerful, as I carefully dried the small wound because wounds seemed to go septic so fast. 'When Daddy gets a job, things will change a lot.'

He stood up and stretched his thin little body. 'Perhaps you will marry a prince,' he suggested hopefully.

'Perhaps,' I agreed, though I knew that girls as ugly as I who also wore spectacles did not stand a chance of matrimony; my mother had always indicated that such was the case and I think I had already been written off as a future maiden aunt. This did not stop me, however, from dreaming for the rest of the afternoon that I married the beautiful, humane and exciting Edward, Prince of Wales.

Tony and Brian also had a dream world of their own. They rarely quarrelled and, with Fiona, they played highly imaginative games in which they sailed the world—Brian always fell overboard and was rescued by Tony—or drove trains and cars which had innumerable comic accidents.

Playing in the open, even if the air was polluted, made them more hungry and it was impossible to satisfy them. If we were to cook anything, we still had to buy coal, so that summer expenses were much the same as winter ones.

We approached our second winter in Liverpool with undisguised dread. We had commenced the first bitter January there with one set of good winter clothing apiece and two blankets. Now, not one of us had a whole garment or a pair of shoes without holes in them. Indeed, four of us were reduced to ragged running-shoes or nothing at all on our feet.

My father was a pitiful sight even in comparison with the ragged crew who lined up with him for public assistance. His elbows stuck through the sleeves of what had once been a tweed jacket and his knees were equally naked. He had no socks and there was very little left of his shirt. He used to thread the remains of his old school tie through the torn collar and knot it, in the mistaken belief that nobody would notice the bare chest underneath it. His underwear had, like that of the rest of the family, worn out, its life shortened by inadequate laundering. His chest was red from being chapped by the wind; but he suffered most from pain in his hands.

Both hands had been badly frost-bitten during his

military service in Russia, and, on the hospital ship which brought him home, the surgeons had debated whether or not they should be amputated. The wonderful care he received, however, saved him from this; but intensely cold weather turned them white, and I used to sit and massage them to revive the circulation. It was then that they became most painful.

One freezing November day, urged on by two shipping clerks shivering with him in one of the endless queues in which he spent most of his life, he applied to the relieving officer of the public assistance committee for help to buy a pair of shoes and a pair of gloves.

Clothing, he was told tartly, was given in kind and stamped with the initials of the public assistance committee, so that it could not be sold or pawned.

'I don't mind what it is stamped with,' replied Father humbly, 'as long as it lessens the pain in my hands.'

His case file was sent for and examined.

'You are not eligible for help with clothing,' was the verdict. 'You do not come under the jurisdiction of Liverpool.'

The same old problem. We were not from Liverpool. Our rate of public assistance was that given in the small town from which we came, and the sum was collected from that town by Liverpool. We got none of the little extras such as money for winter coal or for Christmas which Liverpool struggled to give its less fortunate citizens, nor were we eligible for clothing.

'What shall I do?' my father cried, in despair.

'Try one of the voluntary agencies.'

So Father got the run-around as it was sometimes called. He was sent from agency to agency. And they all said they could not help, because he was drawing public assistance and could get boots from that committee. In vain, he explained that the town from which we had come did not give clothing and we were ineligible for help from Liverpool.

One agency offered second-hand boots at a very reduced price, but any price was too high for us to pay. We had once spent three shillings in a second-hand clothes shop in an effort to make my mother presentable again, feeling that she had the better chance of employment, and had had to reduce our meagre food intake to a dangerous level, in consequence. If it had not been for our kind policeman's pint of milk, Edward would have surely died that week.

Then Mother suddenly got a job 'on commission only'. She was to sell radios from door to door.

Up and down the better-class streets she tramped, knocking at each door and trying to beguile reluctant housewives into agreeing to a demonstration of the radio in their homes. On the third day, she did find a woman willing to listen to her, and it was agreed that the radio would be brought that night for her husband to see.

The demonstration radio, meanwhile, was delivered to the door of our house by a supervisor, and was taken in by Miss Sinford, the most presentable of all the inhabitants.

'Helen!' she shrieked up the stairs to me. 'Come and remove this wicked temptation from the hall!'

I ran down the stairs with Edward on my hip.

Miss Sinford pointed an accusing finger at a cardboard box and a wet battery beside it. The box was clearly marked that it contained a radio, and I guessed that it had been delivered in connection with Mother's new job.

'Thank you, Miss Sinford.'

I sat Edward down on the grubby hall runner, and Miss Sinford withdrew with one of her loudest sniffs of disapproval. Avril had followed me down, and I left her to mind Edward while I puffed my way upstairs again with the radio. I made a second journey for the wet battery and carried it up so fast that I splashed some of the acid on my bare legs, burning them painfully.

A third journey was made to retrieve Edward and Avril.

Still panting from the journeys up and down, I read the instructions on the outside of the box to Avril, and then very carefully unpacked the radio and put it on the table. I plugged in the wet and dry batteries and nervously turned one of the knobs. The shining newness of it awed us both.

Suddenly the room was filled with the sweet sound of violins.

Avril climbed up on to one of the chairs and put her head close to the speaker and Edward smiled and sucked his thumb. I stood in ecstasy while the music swept round me.

We spent a blissful afternoon listening to a faraway

world where people spoke as we did and music was part of life.

My parents were extremely angry when they came home and found the radio unpacked and working.

'It does not belong to us,' said my mother furiously. 'You know quite well that you are not to touch anything which does not belong to you.'

'I haven't harmed it,' I said defiantly.

'No, she has not,' interrupted Avril aggressively. 'And I heard a nice lady say "happy birthday" and "hello, twins" on Children's Hour and I liked it.'

'Well,' said Father, turning it off firmly. 'Don't touch it again.'

Mother said, 'I have to demonstrate it tonight, to Mr and Mrs Smithers, and I don't know how to do it.'

'You just put these plugs in here, like Helen did, and you turn that knob there,' instructed Avril, stabbing the appropriate plugs and knob with a grubby finger. 'And it goes.'

She looked up at my mother with hard blue eyes, as if daring her to say she was not right.

Father smiled.

'She is right, you know. That is all you have to do.' He looked worried. 'I suppose the supervisor will move the thing to the Smithers' house for you in his car?'

'Heavens, no. I have to take it myself.'

'But you can't carry that weight,' we said in chorus.

'Besides,' I added, sadly surveying the burning marks on my grey legs, 'the acid from the wet battery can splash and burn your stockings.'

We all knew that without stockings Mother was not suitably dressed for work, and we had all observed that even if she was not much interested in us, she was more alive, more aware of things going on around her, when looking for work.

Silence fell upon the family. The radio and its batteries were really too awkward for anyone to carry any distance.

Tony, who had been playing one of his endless games of puffer-trains with a dead cinder from the fireplace, looked up, as he shunted his imaginary train into an imaginary siding, and said quietly, 'Put it in the Chariot and wheel it round to the lady's house.'

We all burst out laughing, and I snatched Edward out of the pram.

'Try it for size,' I invited.

Very carefully, the radio was put back into its box and lowered into the stinking pram. The batteries followed. It all fitted in.

A gentle sigh of relief went through the family.

We ate a hasty meal of boiled potatoes, which tasted strongly of the smoke from an old shoe I had picked up in the street and brought home for fuel. Then, since it was dark, the whole family went in procession behind Father, who carefully wheeled the Chariot with its unusual contents. I clutched Edward to me and brought up the rear.

Down the street under the light of the gas-lamps we marched, past the brothels, past the garish lights and conversational roar of the local pub, past the boys lounging at the street corners, who watched the weird procession speculatively, out of the slum which was our world, into quieter streets of neat terrace housing.

At a corner, out of sight of the home of Mother's customer, we unloaded the radio and set it down on the pavement. We whispered conspiratorially together, trying to decide how to get it to the house concerned, without the customer seeing any of us except Mother.

Father finally decided that he would make the first sortie and carry the batteries to the front step of the customer's house which led straight on to the pavement; there was no front yard or garden to be negotiated.

We watched with excited anticipation as he glided ghostlike down the empty street, quickly deposited the batteries, and continued on down the street, round the block and back to us, so that he actually passed the house only once. Then Alan and Mother together carried the radio itself to the house, and put it down on the step. Mother stood by it, while Alan fled down the street, taking the same course as Father had.

Mother was out of sight of all of us, but we heard the peal of the old-fashioned front door bell when she rang it; and the sounds of the door opening and shutting and of strong Lancashire voices came to us clearly through the frosty air.

Brian and Tony started an excited conversation. Father hushed them immediately. He was standing tense, listening like a hound.

My arms were aching with Edward's weight, so I put him into the pram. Avril complained that she was cold and I put her in with him and rubbed her legs which were mottled like an old woman's from exposure.

Coatless, hatless and hungry, we were all shivering by the time we heard the sound of the door opening again and cheerful voices bidding Mother 'good night'.

She was coming slowly towards us. In the gaslight, her face had a look of stupefied wonderment, as if she had just experienced a religious revelation of some kind.

The policeman on the beat was coming slowly towards us, trying the doors of each shop which faced the road on which we stood; and Father, ever fearful of being arrested for vagrancy, moved us slowly to meet Mother.

'I sold it—that very one—they wanted the demonstration model. They signed the hire purchase agreement and gave me the deposit there and then. And they gave me tea and cake.' Her voice quivered, as she mentioned the last item.

'Really?' exclaimed Father, unable to believe that in Depression-bound Liverpool anybody could afford to buy anything. 'Are you sure?'

'Yes,' she whispered, sudden pride in her voice.

'What will you get for it? Your commission?'

'Thirty shillings.'

'We shall have to tell the public assistance committee. The little bit you earned selling treacle was not worth worrying about. We shall have to declare thirty shillings—and they will just cut it off our allowance.' Father's voice was tired and old.

'Are you mad?' cried Mother with an unexpected burst of spirit.

'No, of course not. But it is not honest not to tell them.'

'We will not tell them,' said Mother savagely. 'They'd let us die. They don't care. Why should we bother about what is honest and what is not?' The bitter question sounded all the more so because it was expressed in her beautiful contralto voice, a voice almost identical to Brian's.

Father had his arms crossed over his chest and his hands tucked into his armpits to keep them warm. He said in a broken voice, 'I must have some gloves. I can't bear the pain in my hands any more.'

'And I must have lots of fish and chips,' shouted Avril unexpectedly. 'Lots of lovely fish and chips.'

Fiona clutched my arm.

'Helen, I feel awfully odd.' Her face was ashen.

I caught her as she fainted. She was the quietest, most uncomplaining of us all and, as I held her frail little frame in my arms and looked down at her closed eyes with lashes like Michaelmas daisies, it seemed as if Death was breathing down the back of my neck.

'Fish and chips,' roared Avril again, quite unperturbed by her sister's collapse.

Chapter twenty

Mother never sold another radio. It did teach her, however, that she might be able to sell things. Even her dismissal a week later because of her lack of sales did not deter her, and a little while later she got a temporary job in a store demonstrating baby baths. The store was gloriously warm, and she spent her days bathing a doll and extolling the virtues of rubber baths to expectant mothers who came to buy layettes in the baby-wear department. An arduous week's bathing netted her ten shillings in commission, which she spent on shoes and stockings for herself, necessities if she was to continue to try for work.

Christmas loomed near. I did not mention it to Avril or Edward. The other children whispered to each other about it. None of them was in the Christmas play the school was producing and it was clear that none of them had any hope of our being able to celebrate the birth of Christ.

On Christmas Eve, we were all seated in our living-room. The only light was a shaft of moonlight across the floor. We had a small stub of candle and a couple of matches to be used in emergency and these lay ready on the mantelpiece. Outside the church bells were ringing for Christmas services, and across the road in the mysterious house doors slammed occasionally and rowdy voices rose and fell upon the still air.

I had just decided that Edward, Avril and Tony should go to bed, when Mrs Foster's genteel bass could be heard in the lower hall.

'A parcel has come for the top floor. Please come and collect it!'

We were all immediately galvanized into action, except Mother, who continued to sit with her head leaning against the window-frame staring out of the window. We clattered like an army down the myriad of stairs into the hallway, which was dimly lit by a single gas jet.

'Wow!' exclaimed Tony.

It was a very large parcel, addressed to Father, and it took the combined strength of Father, Alan and me to carry it up to our top-floor rooms.

We placed it reverently on the dirty table, and, with shaking hands, Father fumbled with the knots of twine, trying to open it. Finally, he gave up, and we tore at the brown paper and the corrugated cardboard box underneath, frantically trying to find the contents.

We clawed at straw and the infuriating string, and suddenly a golden orange rolled out, sailed slowly across the table and fell with a juicy plonk on to the floor.

An *orange*! An exquisitely perfumed, golden fruit was sitting right in the middle of our floor.

We all gaped at it, and then renewed our frenzied opening up of the package, while Edward crawled across to look at the strange object which had fallen off the table.

We disinterred a turkey of proportions generous enough to have pleased a king, a large plum pudding in a bowl, a bag of potatoes, more oranges, and a box of sweets. Sweets! We were nearly hysterical with excitement.

We had heard of these Christmas parcels, though we had not expected to be the recipients of one; there had been considerable controversy about them in the columns of the *Liverpool Echo*. Many people held that it was ridiculous to help the poor only at Christmas, that the money spent could be put to better uses throughout the year. Whoever made up the parcel for us, however, would have been amply rewarded by the ecstasy with which we received it. It was too much for me, and I burst into tears.

All this time, Mother had continued to sit with her head against the window-frame, though she had shown some interest at first. Suddenly she began to laugh in a high-pitched, wild fashion.

We were silenced immediately. My father was trembling visibly, as he looked at her. Was this the breakdown he had been fearing?

'How are we going to cook it?' she screamed between gusts of laughter. 'With no fire, no oven, no nothing!'

'Be quiet!' Father said firmly, trying to keep a grip on the situation.

Edward and Avril began to cry. Brian stood, an orange in his hand, as if turned to stone. Fiona, clutching the tattered remains of her doll, moved closer to Alan, who put his arm protectively round her shoulder. The darkness of the room made the whole scene macabre and unreal.

Tony, who had been about to open the box of sweets, said, 'Listen!'

Through Mother's wild laughter could be heard the sound of a heavy tread on the top staircase leading to our landing.

'Mrs Foster,' muttered Brian, his voice full of dread. 'Have we paid our rent?'

Avril stopped crying and listened: 'Mr Parish,' she suggested.

The thought of the public assistance committee's visitor discovering that we had a secret hoard of turkey and oranges and deducting its value from our miserable weekly pittance made me frantic, and I ran to the door with the idea of stopping his entering.

I was too late.

A knock sounded on our door.

Mother was still giggling to herself and Father seemed unable to move.

I will be brave. I will be polite, I told myself, and opened the door.

A huge, joint sigh of relief nearly blew the visitor back down the stairs.

'Ah come,' said the visitor, peering round in the gloom, 'to wish yer all a Happy Christmas from Mr Hicks and meself.'

'Mrs Hicks!' exclaimed Brian, and flew to his dear friend from the basement. She caught him in her one free arm.

'Well, now me little peacock! How's our Brian?'

Father came out of his trance and led her through the darkness to our second chair. She sat down and carefully arranged her skirts over it like Queen Victoria about to be photographed.

Mother was quietened by this unexpected visitor and regarded her with silent dislike. Mother, as far as possible, never spoke to anyone in the house, except Mrs Foster, and regarded all our neighbours with abhorrence. Her chilling stare did nothing to cool Mrs Hicks's exuberance. She carefully laid a paper shopping-bag on the floor in front of her, and one by one she brought out a little package for each child and for Father. Lastly, she brought one out for Mother.

'Here yer are, luv. Happy Christmas to yez.'

Mother just stared.

'Come on, luv. It won't always be like this. Maybe the New Year'll bring some luck to yez.'

I could see my mother fighting to make a tremendous effort, and, at last, in a little, panting voice, she said, 'Thank you, Mrs Hicks. You are very kind. I heartily reciprocate your good wishes.' She took the parcel and laid it in her lap.

Mrs Hicks was obviously nonplussed by the word 'reciprocate' but she beamed at Mother in a maternally approving way, and said, 'Na, that's better. You'll soon be well, luv.'

'Helen, can we open them? Please!' Fiona had forgotten her earlier fright and was entranced at having a present.

I looked at Father and he said, 'Yes, of course.'

We all tore at the crumpled, old tissue paper of our parcels.

Mrs Hicks had knitted each of us a pair of gloves and each pair had a distinguishing Fair Isle pattern in a contrasting colour worked into it.

'So as you will know whose is which,' she explained. 'Ah made 'em outta a couple of old pullovers ah bought at Maurrie's.'

I looked at her with wonderment. Such an enterprising idea had never occurred to me. The idea was better than the Christmas present itself, for I could knit. Grandma had taught me. Mrs Hicks was brilliant! Bits of old hand-knitted sweaters and cardigans, too holey to be sold as complete garments, could be bought from old Maurrie at the second-hand clothing store for as little as two for a penny. I could buy some, unravel them and knit, just as old Mrs Hicks had done. Edward could have a warm sweater. I forgot my earlier tears in the splendour of this new idea.

Mrs Hicks meantime had grown accustomed to the darkness and spotted the turkey on the table.

'Got a Christmas parcel, have yer? Proper nice, ain't it?'

Father agreed that it was proper nice. Mother stared emptily at the naked bird.

'There is one difficulty,' said Father.

Mrs Hicks looked puzzled.

'We haven't got an oven to cook it in,' and he added rather apologetically, 'or a knife to cut it up small enough to stew on our fireplace.'

'We haven't even got a fire,' said Alan.

'Oh aye,' responded Mrs Hicks. 'Now that's a bit of a difficulty, aint it?' She ran her red hands up and down her ample thighs while she considered the matter.

'Tell yer what. Ah'll be cooking me own turkey on the morning, but there's a good fire going downstairs now. If I turn it to the oven you could cook yours now. It would be cooked afore midnight, when we goes to bed.'

'Oh, Mrs Hicks!' I burst out. 'That would be marvellous.'

Father looked dimly hopeful.

'Would you mind?' he asked.

She laughed at him. 'Not a bit. You could put some potatoes round it, to bake, and you'd have a reet good meal.' She looked at our dead fireplace, and added, 'You can put the pudding at the back o' me fire at the same time. Most o' the heat's only going up t' chimney right now.'

Mother said suddenly, 'Thank you, Mrs Hicks.' I thought for a horrid minute that she was going to follow it with 'But we do not require your assistance'. She controlled herself, however, when the whole family, sensing this, turned on her in frozen, silent rage.

While the children sucked the oranges, Father and I took the bird, the pudding and the potatoes downstairs.

Mrs Hicks put it into a baking-tin which was thick with the encrustations of twenty-five years of cooking, and larded it with a bit of bacon fat. Then, guided by her instructions, Father laid it in the ancient oven to the side of the kitchen fire. Some potatoes followed and the heavy, iron door was swung shut, Mrs Hicks having carefully checked that the cat, who apparently slept there normally, was not inside behind the turkey. Mr Hicks grinned all over his little, ferrety face and promised to sit and watch that it did not burn and to add water as needed to the blackened saucepan into which the pudding was subsequently lowered.

'One of yez come down in three hours' time,' commanded Mrs Hicks, poking up the fire with a large iron poker. 'Ah reckon it'll be done by then. You could wrap it in a blanket and it'll keep a bit warm till tomorrer.'

Joy gave strength to our weakened legs and we ran all the way up the stairs, to sink, half fainting, upon the floor when we got to the top.

Nobody could bear to be put to bed, so we sat around in the dim light from the moon and the street, until the closing of the nearby public house told us it was ten o' clock. After that we took it in turns to count up to sixty, so as to make a rough estimate of thirty minutes more, at the end of which Alan and I bolted down to the basement.

We knocked and entered the vast cavern which had been the kitchen when the house was built. Our bare feet pattered on the old brick tiles as we crossed to the fireplace in response to Mr Hicks's invitation to come and get warm. He was just lifting the pudding saucepan from the hob. His wife took it from him and carried it across to the sandstone sink in the corner. With a skilful twist she got the pudding out without scalding herself, and set it on the bare wooden table, which I noticed with surprise was scrubbed almost pure white. She spread a newspaper on another corner and went to the oven to get the turkey.

Immediately she unlatched the heavy door a heavenly aroma flooded the room, drowning out the usual odours of damp, pine disinfectant and unwashed winter clothes. Saliva ran from my mouth and I hastily brushed it away.

'Ah think it's cooked,' she said, twisting one of the bird's legs with expert fingers. 'Are yer goin' to carry it oop like it is?'

We had few plates and none big enough to hold a turkey, so I said that we would carry it up in the meat-tin and bring the receptacle back in the morning, early enough for her to cook her own Christmas dinner in it. I did not tell her that I could not bear, in any case, to part with a single drop of the fat in the pan.

She agreed to this cheerfully, wrapped up the baked potatoes in a newspaper, then told us to wait a moment, while she rummaged in the back of her dusty kitchen dresser.

'Here yer are,' she said triumphantly. 'Here's a bit o' candle to light you up them stairs.'

She lit the small candle stub she had found and presented it to Alan, gave me two crumpled sheets of newspaper so that I would not burn my hands while carrying the hot meat-tin, and sent us upstairs again.

'Gosh, the pudding feels lovely and hot,' exclaimed Alan, as he staggered up with the paper parcels of pudding and potatoes.

The family, except for Mother, was gathered to

greet us on the top landing, and a great oooh sounded at the sight of the turkey, as we mounted the last flight.

'I'll wrap it in the newspaper I carried it with,' I said firmly. 'Perhaps it will keep it a little warm till tomorrow.'

I could see Father's Adam's apple bob in the candlelight, as he swallowed; and hope died on the children's faces.

Avril kicked my shin to draw my attention to her.

'I want to eat mine now,' she said determinedly.

Tony's eyes looked enormous in his death's head face.

Again the saliva gathered in my mouth, but I said, 'It's not Christmas until tomorrow.'

'To hell with Christmas,' said Alan bitterly.

An hour later, there was only a white skeleton left, scraped clean by small clawing hands and teeth. Even Mother came alive, after devouring nearly a whole leg with the gulping enthusiasm of an ex-prisoner of war. We ate the baked potatoes, skin and all, we ate the sweets and pudding, every scrap.

We slept.

Chapter twenty-one

Malnutrition, when much prolonged, causes a terrible apathy, an inability to concentrate or think constructively, and that winter was so grim that my mind was closed to the intense suffering of my parents. A child's world is a small one and given a reasonable round of home and school, his life is fairly full. Our little ones suffered unbelievably, however, as they dragged themselves to and from school through snow and rain. Even brave Alan cried when the great chilblains on his heels burst and went septic, and it seemed as if the clothes of all of them were permanently wet; good fires are a necessity in a climate as rainy as Lancashire's. In my parents' case, however, they suffered not only all that we did but also from social deprivation; they starved mentally as well as physically.

To me, the suffering of Fiona and baby Edward was the more scarifying, because it was silent. Fiona never complained as the others did; she sat quiet and terrified in a kind of mental burrow like a fox that has been savaged by hounds and must be quiet lest they find him again; only when she was playing with Brian and Tony did a happier little girl emerge. And I loved her so much that it filled me with grief to be unable to comfort her—she was past comforting. Edward, who could now crawl rapidly and occasionally stood up, was making valiant efforts to speak. He seemed to have a natural serenity, but when he cried (which he rarely did), it was with terrible deep sobs that came slowly, not at all like Avril's ferocious bellows when she was thwarted in any way.

Until hunger made him fall into lethargy, my father tried to pick the brains of other men who stood with him in the endless queues. He tried to find out how they stayed alive and how they hoped to get a job. But, finally, it took all his strength to get to the labour exchange or to the offices of the public assistance committee and stand, without fainting, until he received a curt 'nothing today' from the former and forty-three shillings each Thursday from the latter.

We always had colds. Old copies of the *Liverpool Echo* were collected from anywhere we could find them and torn up for use as handkerchiefs. The paper was then used to make a fire in the tiny bedroom fireplace in our living-room.

The acid which I had spilled on my leg from the battery of the radio caused a burn which went septic, and the sore showed signs of spreading. Old Miss Sinford noticed the mark on my leg as I went upstairs one day and commanded that I come into her room to have it examined. She sat me down on a wooden chair placed on a piece of newspaper and, having put on a pair of gold-rimmed spectacles, she took a good look at it.

'I'll poultice it for you,' she decided. 'You should have kept it cleaner.'

The fact that I was seated in the middle of a newspaper indicated that she knew how dirty our family was, so I just smiled weakly.

She found a clean piece of white cloth, put it in an old sugar basin and poured over it boiling water from the kettle on the hob. She then wrung it out and slapped it on to the sore, scalding the surrounding flesh until I clutched Edward too hard and he cried out. She hurled texts about Good Samaritans at me, as she worked with trembly ancient fingers, and then ordered me down to her room the next morning for a repeat performance.

Her room was spotless, filled with crochet work which she had done herself. In the window on a wickerwork table stood a large aspidistra in a plum-coloured china pot, and I gathered that an aspidistra was a lot of work, as she felt the need to dust it daily. She cooked at the fireplace, which was larger than ours, her room having been the dining-room of the original home.

It was from her that I learned that the house opposite, which was visited by so many seamen, was a House of Sin and that the women who lived in it were harlots. 'Harlot' was a word which occurred in the Bible, so I ventured to ask her what it meant.

She blinked at me through her spectacles, as if realizing for the first time how young and innocent I was. Then she pointed a bony finger at me and said sharply, 'Girls should not ask such questions.' Her voice became shrill. 'It is not a word I should have used. It is a word you must not use. Out! I must pray!'

She seized me by the shoulder, turned me about and pushed me into the hall.

Bewildered, I took myself back upstairs and left my leg to heal by itself, which it eventually did.

Next time I went to the library, I looked up the offending word. It really sounded very wicked indeed, and I was most impressed.

Fiona came home from school one day, in tears. She said she had a pain in her back and chest. I felt her forehead. It was burning with heat. Helplessly, I looked at her and we were both terribly afraid.

When Father came home from the library, I told him about Fiona. I had laid her on the bed and, to keep her warm, had covered her with what few odds and ends of blanket and garments I could find.

We went to look at her and found that she had tossed aside her wrappings and was muttering feverishly, her mouselike hands clenching and unclenching.

Father clamped his mouth tight. His breath came in small gasps and perspiration glistened on his forehead.

Alan came softly up to us.

'Don't you think we had better send for the doctor, Daddy?' he asked.

'I haven't any money to pay him,' was the despairing response.

'We could tell him that.' Alan's lips trembled. Like all of us, he loved Fiona. 'He might come anyway.'

I said, 'We have nothing to lose by asking. Is Fiona very ill, Daddy?'

'Yes,' he replied. 'I can see that she is very ill indeed—I am not sure what it is, though.'

I leaned over Fiona and whispered that we would get a doctor for her and she would soon be better.

'I'll go and ask,' said Alan in his bravest voice, sticking his chest out and trying to look strong.

'Yes, do so. I think Helen and I had better stay here. I haven't any paper on which to write a letter. You will have to explain to him yourself. Tell him about the pain and the temperature.'

Tony, Brian and Avril tiptoed into the room and went silently out again.

Alan plunged out into the February wind once more. Terrified of facing whoever would answer the doctor's door but even more terrified about Fiona's illness, he seized the doctor's brass knocker and banged it.

The door was answered by a neatly dressed older woman.

'The doctor's out,' she said before Alan could open his mouth.

'It's my sister,' said Alan. 'She's awfully ill and we haven't any money to pay the doctor. But, please, will he come?'

The boy's evident fear made the woman soften her tone.

'Well,' she said, 'step in, lad. I am not sure that the doctor can come. He's very busy.'

Alan, shivering, stepped into the linoleumed hall. Under the faint light of a very low wattage electric light bulb, the lady surveyed him.

She sighed at what she saw, and took down a

notebook from beside a telephone on the hall wall. 'Tell me your name and address and I'll ask him. Now then.'

Alan told her, and explained the symptoms of the illness as best he could.

'Now mind,' said his questioner as she shut the notebook. 'I don't know whether the doctor can come. I'll have to ask him. If he does come, it will be after surgery, about half past nine.'

The hours dragged by. We took it in turns to sit by Fiona. She would not take the tea we offered her. I wetted our only towel which was, as usual, very dirty, and wiped her face and hands with cold water. This seemed to console her a little. Occasionally, she was racked by coughing.

Mother came home and stared dumbly at her second daughter. It was as if she could not let any more troubles in upon herself; she seemed numbed, unable to accept any more. Her unkempt hair had escaped from her hat and hung in straggling oily tails down to her shoulders. Her hands were swollen with chilblains, in spite of Mrs Hicks's gloves, and she stood awkwardly, because the heels of her shoes were worn down so badly that she walked almost as if she was bandy-legged.

'We must keep her covered,' she said at last.

It was difficult to see in the reflected light from the street lamp, and Father said worriedly, 'I don't know how the doctor is going to be able to see to examine her—if he comes.'

'Couldn't we borrow a shilling to put in the electric meter?' I asked.

'Brian went down and tried the couple below; they didn't have one. I can't ask Mrs Foster—we still owe her a week's rent—and I can't ask Mrs Hicks because I haven't yet paid her back the last shilling I borrowed.'

This was the first intimation I had had of his borrowing from the other tenants; it accounted for a general coldness towards us recently.

Without a watch it was difficult to tell the time, but both house and street were quiet when the front door bell rang. Hopefully, Brian pounded down the stairs to open the door.

A firm voice said, 'We can't afford to fall down this black pit—I'll put my flashlight on.'

Brian laughed shrilly and called, 'Daddy, Daddy, Helen! The doctor has come!'

The bedroom door opened and the light of a torch blinded me momentarily. The doctor must have had long experience of the straits of poverty to carry such a powerful torch.

'Come in, come in,' said Father, his voice filled with relief.

I stood up respectfully as the doctor put down his bag.

'Now, what have we here?' he asked as he got out his stethoscope, and then took Fiona's wrist in long, capable fingers.

Father explained the symptoms and I nearly stopped breathing as the doctor listened to his patient's labouring lungs and frequent coughing.

'Pleurisy, I think,' he said. 'She must have hospital treatment immediately. I will go and telephone the

Children's Sanatorium, and arrange for an ambulance.'

Father whispered, 'It isn't tuberculosis, is it?' In those days, tuberculosis was still a major killer.

'I doubt it. The hospital will take X-rays.' He stood looking down at Fiona's face by the light of the torch. 'Does she have a mother?'

'Yes,' Father replied. 'You kindly took some stitches out for her after an abdominal operation some time ago.'

'Oh, did I,' he said absently, and then rather more alertly, 'Yes, I remember. How is she?'

Father looked uneasily at me, and then plunged in. 'Her physical health has improved—as far as it can in our circumstances.' He paused, and then added, 'She isn't herself, though.'

The doctor nodded understandingly. He did not offer any more help. He would deal with our emergency; he could not do more. He had to treat first those patients who could pay. In the torchlight I could see the frayed cuffs of his overcoat and I guessed that he had very little himself.

The doctor asked to see Mother, who had been up in the attic room dealing with Tony. Tony had had a nightmare and had woken up screaming.

When she came, he instructed her to get Fiona ready for hospital.

Mother said in a flat tone of voice, 'There is nothing to do. She must go as she is. She has no other garments than those she has on—and I cannot wash her in cold water in her present state.'

So Fiona went to a huge hospital on the farther

outskirts of the city, without benefit of bath, toothbrush or nightgown, and my poor, crushed mother suffered the indignity of seeing her almost unconscious child stripped of her clothes and plunged into a disinfecting bath, her head rolling on her neck as the probationers washed her crawling hair. The tattered clothes were rolled into a bundle and handed to Mother, with the curt information that she could wait.

Mother was used to waiting—she spent her days in office and shop waiting-rooms as she applied for job after job with hordes of other applicants. Finally, about three in the morning a night nurse remembered that she was still there and told her she could go.

'I want to know what is the matter with the child and I want to see her, now she is in bed.'

'You will have to come on visiting days. Your doctor will be informed regarding her illness, and he will tell you.'

My mother lifted her hand to slap this inhuman automaton, but she was afraid of what might happen to Fiona if she made a fuss of any kind, so she turned slowly into the long, brown corridor to the front door.

She had come to the hospital with Fiona in the ambulance. Nobody had considered how she was to get home again. Outside was the dark and bitter cold of a February night.

She paused on the step, shaken by the knowledge that the only way to get home was to walk the seven miles to our part of the city. She was not even sure of the route.

The city was completely quiet and, emboldened by this, she set out, following the tram lines which glimmered in the gaslight. The freezing wind cut into her and, after a couple of miles, she was so cold that she was staggering in a ragged line along the pavement.

A dim light at a corner attracted her attention. It was a telephone box, and she quickened her step and sought refuge inside it.

Paralysed with cold, she stood there looking dully at the receiver on its hook, the telephone book hanging below it, and at two buttons marked 'A' and 'B'. Idly, she read the instructions for making a call.

'Insert two pennies. When the telephone is answered press Button A. If no reply, press button B for the return of the twopence.'

Return of the twopence!

She hopefully pressed Button B.

Nothing happened, so, after a few minutes, she started again on her long hike homewards. An early tram rumbled past her, its lights flashing as it pitched and tossed its way along the lines.

When she reached the next public telephone box, she entered it and, without much hope, pressed Button B, and was immediately rewarded by the happy rattle of two falling pennies. She snatched them up and took the next tram home.

Father and I had waited up for her and were frantic with anxiety. Our anxiety turned to fury when we heard of the discourteous treatment she had received, and we did our best to comfort her before managing to get her to go to bed.

Our visits to the sanatorium were strictly regulated by whether we could find a telephone box where someone had forgotten to press Button B for the return of their twopence—and it was remarkable how many we found.

Though Fiona's illness was long and our public assistance was reduced by the amount given for her maintenance, we were not altogether sorry. She was at least fed in hospital—great hunks of bread and margarine, bowls of sugarless porridge, meat stews, boiled puddings and steamed fish. Patients were expected to augment the hospital's food by supplying their own sugar, jam, cake and fruit. We had nothing to bring Fiona. The diet was, however, so much better than she had received for many a month that, once the pleurisy was drained, she began to look much stronger.

She was sorely troubled by bugs in the hospital bed. Father complained, and was told roughly that she must have brought them in with her.

'She was stripped and bathed when she came in,' he said. 'Perhaps the bed could be stoved.'

A ferocious female, who looked as if she had been put through a starch solution with her uniform, said cruelly, 'Of course, it will be stoved—after your child is discharged.'

Father's expression, after that remark, was like that in the painting of Christ crucified which hung over my grandmother's bed. He bowed his head and turned silently away.

A slightly plumper waif of a child was returned to us six weeks later. There was no ambulance this time and she found the long tram ride a sore trial. She came home to again face hunger and cold with us.

'The spring is coming,' we comforted her.

The studied rudeness with which every member of the family was faced whenever dealing with officialdom, as personified by the public assistance committee, by the labour exchanges, by the voluntary agencies working in the city, was a revelation to us. We began to understand, as never before, the great gulf between rich and poor, between middle class and labour. It considerably improved our manners towards our less fortunate neighbours.

When I grew up, I told myself, I would do some kind of work which would improve this situation and make it possible for people to be helped without at the same time humiliating them.

When I grew up!

But I was growing up. Even in my pinched body, changes were taking place which indicated that soon I would be a young woman. A ghastly, ugly, uneducated wreck of a young woman but still a woman.

As I sat on the doorstep in the weak April sunshine, Edward on my knee, I wondered what would become of me. Other girls went to school and then to work, but for me life had stopped in one place on my first day in Liverpool. The other children were getting at least a basic education; Alan talked hopefully of Tony and Brian being able to win scholarships to grammar school; he himself was too old to sit the examination, but he worked hard at school and read a lot afterwards. At fourteen, he could leave school and he hoped to get a job 'with a future'. Fiona, I thought, would sooner or later marry well—she was so pretty; I did not consider how, in this wilderness of slum, she would manage to do that.

Avril, throwing her weight about both physically and verbally, amongst a number of small girls from neighbouring houses, was tough enough to take care of herself, and Edward, watching the world go by from the safe refuge of my lap, was young enough not to have to worry.

Without an education, I saw myself being kept at home until my parents died and then becoming some bad-tempered old lady's companion–help, subject always to the whims and fancies of others. I knew I was far too plain ever to hope for marriage.

I laid my cheek on little Edward's scurvy head and decided that such a life was not worth living.

Chapter twenty-two

Encouraged by the friendly old gentleman on the park bench, I continued to read. When I explained to him that I ought to be in school, he said firmly and wisely that it was my parents' responsibility. He pointed out that, in studying by myself, I was following in the footsteps of many great Lancastrians, who, though doomed to poverty because they were weavers and caught up in the industrial revolution, found means to study and outshine their better-educated contemporaries. He cited the examples of John Butterworth, the mathematician from Haggate, who never earned more than fifteen shillings a week and learned to read and write at the age of twenty. Such was his love of learning that he became one of the finest geometricians of his day; and James Crowther and Richard Buxton, the Manchester botanists, both self-taught, both always poor, both famous.

I sighed. There was no help there. I wanted to eat and be warm every day of my life.

Avril and I had discovered one beautifully warm spot in Liverpool, although it was rather a long way from home. Sefton Park had a fine glass palm-house, which was kept at tropical temperatures to encourage the growth of the palms and similar plants inside. Avril, Edward and I used to go into it often and crawl under the great creepers to get warm, emerging later with our bottoms covered with earth, damper but warmer.

Once we were discovered by two earnest young men carrying notebooks and pencils. They were wreathed around with long scarves in the colours of the university, and when they found us they were at first puzzled and then amused.

Avril and I stared at them like a pair of scared rabbits.

'Hide and seek?' one young man inquired.

I nodded assent, and, like fellow conspirators, they rearranged the foliage over us and tiptoed away. A gardener on another occasion was not so kind.

'We don't want no dirty ragamuffins in here,' he shouted, and sent us packing.

Crestfallen, we stalked out of the glass house with what dignity we could muster, and I pushed the Chariot homeward, passing through a working-class shopping street on the way.

Halfway up the street, I came to a large, red brick building surrounded by a matching brick wall. It was an elementary school, silent and deserted because it was Saturday. I was about to pass it without much interest, when the remains of a poster flapping in the wind caught my attention. It announced the opening of evening school the previous September. Courses in commercial arithmetic, bookkeeping, English, shorthand and several other subjects were offered.

I stopped.

I had never heard of evening school and I could hardly believe that one could go to school outside the normal hours. I could have skipped for joy.

I wondered if one could enroll at times other than September. Perhaps there would be someone on the premises who could tell me about it. I wheeled the Chariot through the gate leading to the school yard and was hesitantly moving round the building searching for a door, when a hoarse voice shouted, 'What the hell do you think you're doing?'

The voice came from an upper window, where a bald man in shirt sleeves, holding a duster he had apparently been shaking, was looking down at me. His expression was hostile, and I wilted.

'I—I was looking for someone to ask about evening school,' I stuttered.

My questioner looked pained.

'There's not likely to be night school on Saturday afternoon, now is there? You'll have to come on Monday night.' And he started to lower the window.

I did not move. I wanted to ask what time I should come.

He threw the window up again impatiently.

'Now get outta here! We don't want the likes of you hanging around. Get out!'

I got out, and stood in the street quivering with mortification.

Avril, looking like a pocket-sized thundercloud, stamped her foot and said, 'Nasty old man! I don't like him.'

I laughed a little weakly, and looked again at the poster. It said the classes were from 7.30 p.m. to 9.30 p.m.

My mind made up, I went home determined not to be put off by nasty old men.

Father was sitting by the empty fireplace, reading *War and Peace*. Without preamble, I mentioned the evening school to him.

He hardly seemed to hear me, and I busied myself making a bit of fire to boil a panful of water for tea.

'Daddy?' I queried again.

At last he said, 'You cannot go to evening school.'

'But, Daddy, why not?' I protested. 'Fiona and you could watch Avril, and I could put Edward to bed before I went. Tony and Brian will go to bed whenever you or Mother tell them.'

His face was wooden, though at the same time sad.

'If you go to evening school, my dear, it will be necessary to state your age and other details. You are not yet fourteen and the school inspectors would order you back to day school.'

'Well, I can't see why I can't go to either day school or evening school,' I said with all the irritating belligerence of a thirteen-year-old. 'Why can't Mother look after Edward and Avril, while I go to school? She's much better now.'

'Mother still isn't fit, you know that. She is doing her very best.' He stopped. The marriage had been far from happy; yet they had stayed together and his anxiety about Mother was based on genuine respect for her. 'Your mother is just able to manage if she goes out into the fresh air or works among adults,' he continued. 'I don't know what might happen to her if she was confined with a whining baby.'

'He doesn't whine,' I exclaimed angrily. 'And I nearly go mad trying to make this beastly fire and buy us enough to eat, and . . . and . . .' I burst into loud crying.

That was the beginning of a tremendous family row, in which everyone joined.

Alan tried to soothe me. 'You could go back to school when Edward's bigger,' he said hopefully.

'Once I am fourteen the school won't take me back,' I screamed in an abandonment of rage.

'Stop making an exhibition of yourself,' said Father. 'When I get a job, you will be able to go to finishing school.'

I looked at him scornfully. French finishing schools were expensive and seemed far removed from the realities of life in Liverpool.

Fiona began to cry. 'Don't be cross with Helen, Daddy.'

'Oh, shut up, Fiona,' I snarled.

'I want my tea,' demanded Avril.

I slapped her.

She immediately began to bellow like a lovesick moose.

This brought Tony hotly to her defence and a smart rebuke to me from Father.

Into the uproar came Mother, weary and hungry.

'What *is* the matter?' she asked, putting down her battered handbag.

'Helen wants to go to evening school and I have told her that it is impractical, because the school inspectors would pick her up as being young enough for day school.'

'Well, why can't I go to day school?'

Mother's lips began to tremble. 'You are needed at home, dear.'

'No, I am not. You can very well look after the children.'

'I have to go to work. The doctor recommended it. And I am the most likely one to get work.'

'I don't believe it,' I said. Thirteen-year-olds can be very cruel.

'The general welfare of the family demands that you stay home.'

'I won't!'

Mother suddenly started to cry hysterically, shrieking that it was too much and I was a hard-hearted, thankless daughter.

'I have nothing to be thankful for,' I retorted bitterly.

'Helen, Helen, don't!' Fiona whispered, her eyes wide and terrified, as she clutched my arm. Alan, from across the room, implored me silently.

The fight went out of me. I turned to Fiona and let her lead me back to our newspaper bed. There, crouched together with my head on her shoulder, I wept myself to exhaustion. I had lost my Waterloo.

By mid-May, Fiona seemed well enough to go back to school. She was by nature placid to the point of apathy, and her gentle pliability made her popular at school. At home, she received no attention and, without playthings, she began to get bored and to ask to be allowed to return to the more lively world of school. My parents had not mentioned school to her. They went out on their various rounds of employment agencies, libraries, etc., and seemed to have forgotten her. I, therefore, prepared her for school one morning as best I could.

At the last moment she balked.

'I feel shy,' she said, standing uneasily in the dark hall and rubbing one foot against the other. 'And I haven't got twopence for the fee. Alan should have waited for me.'

Impatiently I thrust twopence into her hand from the daily shilling I received to buy food. But still she would not move and stood biting her nails and staring anxiously through the glass door at the busy street.

'Come with me,' she demanded.

In a home as empty as ours, there was little for me to do, so I put Edward and Avril into the Chariot and together we walked the four blocks to school.

The school was a fine, stone building, matching architecturally the adjoining church and presbytery. A high, iron railing surrounded the playground, and we paused by the gate to see if we could find one of Fiona's playmates, so that she would not feel so lonely when going into school.

A pretty lady teacher came hurrying towards the gate. When she saw Fiona she smiled at her through the veil of her smart, little hat.

'Good morning, Fiona. I am glad to see you back. Are you feeling quite well again now? Alan told me that you were in hospital.'

She ran her eyes over Fiona's thin, underclothed body and returned Fiona's angelic, worshipping smile. Then she looked at me in a puzzled fashion. A question trembled on her lips.

Fiona had been brought up properly and she

immediately said politely, 'Miss Brough, may I introduce my elder sister, Helen, and this is Avril and this is my baby brother, Edward.'

Miss Brough's brow cleared.

She said, 'How do you do.'

I murmured, 'Very well, thank you.'

'I don't remember you going through our school, my dear,' she remarked to me. 'You must have left before I came—I have only been here three years.' She chucked Edward under the chin with a finger clothed in good brown leather. Then she looked at me again, more sharply. 'But that is not possible—you are quite young.' She laughed. 'You must have gone to school somewhere else.'

My tongue clove to the roof of my mouth and I could not answer.

Fiona said brightly, 'She used to go to our old school. She has never been to school in Liverpool.'

'Haven't you, my dear?'

'No, Miss Brough.'

I was nearly tongue-tied with fear of what my parents would say if they found out about this conversation.

She was looking at me keenly now, and must have seen the stark fright in my eyes. She pursed her delicately painted lips, and said, 'Well, never mind. Fiona, hurry up or you will be late.'

The school bell began to ring and she smiled reassuringly at me and said, 'Goodbye. Goodbye, Avril and Edward.'

'Goodbye,' I muttered through clenched teeth.

My legs were shaking so much that I could not

start the pram. I watched her disappear through the school's ornately carved doorway before, at last, I could make my feet move.

I said nothing to my parents.

A week later a school attendance officer called upon my parents while I was out. How they evaded being prosecuted and sent to prison for my long truancy I will never know. Perhaps their calm authoritative manners made even school attendance officers quail. My immediate attendance was, however, ordered.

I faced two outraged parents every day for the next six weeks until my fourteenth birthday. The day after that, I was back home again looking after Edward.

I had never been to an elementary school, and I found myself far ahead of the other children in the class in everything except mathematics. It was, however, bliss to hold a pencil in my unaccustomed fingers and to try my wits against the work put before me.

This school had a new and enthusiastic drawing-master. He had to teach children who, for the most part, hardly knew that artists created pictures, and he had only pencils, paper and pastel crayons with which to work, but at my first lesson he did his utmost to explain perspective to the disinterested class.

'Any questions?' he asked.

While the rest of the class stared at him glumly, I put up my hand.

'Could you explain why medieval pictures often look so alive and real though they have no perspective?' I asked hopefully.

The class turned round in a body and stared at me

open mouthed. The teacher's Adam's apple bobbed up and down as he sought to reply to me.

Finally, he answered me briefly and then set the class the task of drawing a picture of mountains and roads.

He came and sat on the bench beside me and examined my work. He looked carefully at the little picture and suggested a technical method of improving the texture of the shading in it, while I sat in frozen silence beside him afraid that I would smell abominable to him.

'I should like you to draw me one or two more, as homework,' he said at last. 'You can sketch anything which takes your fancy. I want to see what you can do.'

Breathless with excitement, I said I would like to do the drawings but I had neither paper nor pencils.

He smiled and said calmly, 'I can provide you with them.'

I sat on the steps for several evenings, Edward crawling at my feet, while I sketched the life of the street and a picture of Avril, who was hugely flattered at having a drawing made of her.

A week or two later, the drawing-master expressed his approval of my work and produced a small examination paper for me to work my way through. The paper, with my drawings, vanished into officialdom.

'There is a scholarship available at the City School of Art,' he explained kindly to me, 'and I have put you in for it.'

I was happy. For the first time in two years I played

with other girls, and I was being taught, though in a rough-and-ready manner. Nobody wanted to sit by me because I was so disgustingly dirty, even by the low standards prevalent in the neighbourhood, but in the open school yard I played tag and skipped until my limited strength gave out.

My fourteenth birthday passed, and my parents put an end to my little holiday. I wept and raged, but to no purpose. I was wanted at home, and Father thankfully turned over Avril and Edward to me again.

Although I had played with other girls at school, I had found nothing in common with them. They had a hearty vulgarity of speech and manner which made me recoil from them and, to them, a girl who spoke as if she had ollies in her mouth was very suspect. A small group of girls who were better behaved and came from better homes regarded me with undisguised horror.

I was back where I had started from, pushing Edward's Chariot to and from the shops or the park, and without any hope of bettering myself.

During the summer holidays, I took all the children to the parks to play, and sat wistfully amongst stout mothers in black shawls, watching my little charges play just as they did. The children accepted me as just another 'Mum' and I was too shy to ask if I could play too.

September saw the children back at school again. I watched them go with envy. Now I was over fourteen I could not hope for further education.

Chapter twenty-three

Alan and I sat huddled together on the front step. The October evening was cold and clammy; yet we were reluctant to go into the stuffy house. The gas-lamps' light gleamed softly on the damp pavement and women hurried by, their black shawls held tightly round them, their children whining at their heels. Three young men lolled against the iron railings of the corner house; their noisy laughter mingled with that from the public house on the corner opposite to them. Maurrie, the second-hand clothes man, shuffled by with a sack on his back.

An Irish woman plodded stolidly up the street. Near us, she stepped out into the middle of the street and turned, to take up a belligerent stance facing the front steps of the house opposite.

She was a scarifying-looking person, hugely fat with legs like wool-clad pillars. Her hair was parted across her head from ear to ear and the back part had been plaited and made into a neat bun; the front hair had been parted again down the middle and plaited forwards, the resulting braids being draped down either side of her face and under her ears, to be fastened at the back. The result was outlandishly fierce-looking to anyone unaccustomed to the Victorian hair-styles of some Liverpool Irish women. She smoothed down her white apron over her black skirt, wrapped her black, crocheted shawl around her and folded her enormous arms. Then, gathering her breath until her purple cheeks stood out like balloons, she opened her mouth and screamed.

'Yer pack o' bloody whores!' she yelled at the house Miss Sinford called The House of Sin. 'I'll show yer! Taking a decent woman's hoosband.'

A crowd materialized from nowhere.

'Go it, Ma!' shouted one of the young men from the corner.

There was a flutter of sniggering laughter from the crowd and a murmur of encouragement.

A frail-looking, middle-aged woman, her bare legs thick with varicose veins and her feet shoved into ancient carpet slippers, was unwise enough to open the door and appear on the steps before her.

'You'd better stop that,' she shouted, 'or I'll call a copper.'

This produced such a description of the moral habits of the local constabulary that even the young men in the crowd were impressed. The Irish have a vivid way of expressing themselves, and the shawl woman was no exception. She lifted a fist as stout as a leg of mutton and shook it at the prostitute.

'Yer harlot, yer!' She finished up, and spat accurately at the feet of the Lady of Sin.

Alan giggled behind his hand and whispered, 'Has the lady on the steps taken the other lady's husband from her?'

'Yes,' I said under my breath.

'I'm not surprised. I imagine he ran away from her—she looks as fierce as a tiger.'

I looked at the woman on the steps. She was quite old, her face haggard under its paint. Her hair was dyed a startling red, and diamanté earrings hung from each ear. I was mystified as to where her charm lay. I had read most of Emile Zola's works and now understood the occupation of the ladies opposite. But Zola's heroines were beautiful, and I had always gathered from the conversation of grown-ups that, unless one was beautiful, one did not stand a chance of even a husband, never mind a queue of men such as these ladies commanded.

The woman on the steps drew back towards her front door. She glanced uneasily up and down the street. Several possible clients, hands in pockets, were wandering a trifle unsteadily towards the crowd.

She became anxious to placate, and whined, 'Ah dawn't know who yer hoosband is. Ah dawn't even knaw who yer mean. Na go home,' she wheedled, 'and stop making an exhibition of yerself.'

This infuriated the Irish woman so much that she went up the steps like a tank and punched the small woman in the face.

In a moment, clutched together, they were rolling down the steps and on to the pavement, clawing at each other's eyes, using teeth and knees to inflict as much damage as possible.

The crowd surged forward, roaring approval, and shouting encouragement to whichever participant they favoured.

Three very large dock labourers, who had been standing uneasily watching the exchange, raised their voices against the general hubbub.

'Na, Ma, come on,' they cajoled the Irish woman. 'This is too much. Come on, na. Break it oop!'

But Ma, shawlless and nearly blouseless by now, was too busy holding off the red-haired cat she had provoked to take anybody's advice. Alan and I watched, open-mouthed, through the shifting legs of the crowd.

Suddenly, a little spurt of blood showed on the shawl woman's face, and the crowd hushed.

A male voice said sharply, 'Ee, that's not fair. Get off, you.'

A boot was sharply applied to the prostitute's bottom and she let go immediately, whipped to her feet and whirled on her new assailant.

He backed away from her warily.

'Na, you just take that blade out from under yer thumb-nail, yer lousy bitch.'

The shawl woman heaved herself to her feet, panting. She wiped her face with the back of her hand. When she saw blood on it, she screamed in mixed rage and terror.

'I'll get yer for this!' she shrieked, at the same time putting a little distance between herself and her opponent.

Two of the dockers jumped the prostitute suddenly from behind, caught her arm and twisted it behind her back. While one held her, the other extracted a piece of razor blade from under one of her long nails and held it up for the crowd to see.

There was a threatening murmur.

'Let me go,' she shouted, her voice full of fear.

The men released her and she ran up the steps, her

carpet slippers, still on her feet, flapping as they hit the stone.

We became aware of another heated altercation on the edge of the crowd. The pub had closed and its patrons were coming home, among them a huge, bull-necked man who was bellowing, 'Ah'll teach 'er to make a row in t' street, ah will!'

His friends pulled anxiously at his shabby jacket sleeve and murmured, 'Na, then, Bill. Na, then.'

With a sigh of delightful anticipation, the crowd opened to make way for the bull-necked man, while the prostitute vanished into the House of Sin and the sound of a bolt being shot on the inside of the door came clearly across the street.

The bull-necked man charged through the expectant crowd, undoing his trouser belt as he came. His seamed face was red with rage and the muscles and veins of his neck bulged above the neckband of his union shirt. With a smart pull, he whipped his belt out and, swinging it by its buckle, he advanced on the shawl woman, who came towards him, her shawl again draped across her back, but her huge bosom almost bare. She threw back her shoulders to exhibit her ample charm and swayed her hips seductively. Blood still trickled down her cheek but she smiled slyly at the newcomer.

'Na, then, our Mary Ann. What yer think yer doing? I won't stand for it, d' yer hear me!'

She stuck her chin in the air and spat an epithet at him.

Infuriated, he shot out a huge red fist, tore at her bun, took a firm hold on the tumbling plaits and twisted her by her hair till her back was towards him. Then, lifting his belt he brought it down hard on her buttocks. She screamed, and her shawl fell off again, revealing her fat, naked shoulders already scratched in the fight. A second time the belt whistled through the air and a red welt appeared across the buxom shoulders.

I started up with a cry of horror, but one of the women who lived in our house pushed me sharply down on to the step again.

'Let him be,' she hissed. 'She loves it.'

'Loves it?' I hissed back. 'But she's being hurt!' And I winced as the belt cracked down again, and the woman screamed.

The crowd was silent now, tense with the same tenseness of dogs sitting in front of a house where there is a bitch in heat. I felt sick.

The woman from our house said kindly, 'You go inside and leave the likes of them to themselves.'

Alan and I, both frightened, ran into the hall of our house, from which vantage point we continued to watch.

Beating her steadily, while the shawl woman alternately screamed and cursed, the man was gradually dragging the woman through the crowd and over the cross-road to a smaller house than ours farther down the street, where apparently they lived. He flung her against the closed door and she stood with her back against it, sobbing wildly. The man threw himself against her, and the crowd whooped.

'Go it, Bill,' they shouted.

Bill reached behind his wife and turned the door

knob of his home, put his hand on the woman's naked breast and pushed her, so that she seemed to fly backwards into the narrow hall. He followed, and slammed the door after him.

Regretfully, the crowd slowly broke up and departed. Alan and I, both shaking with nervous tension, went slowly up to our apartment.

Fiona was sitting by the window having watched the same scene from a better vantage point. She had evidently been much impressed by the prostitute.

'Wasn't it exciting, Helen? Wasn't the little woman opposite brave to fight that big, fat shawl woman? What were they fighting about?'

'I am not sure,' I said untruthfully.

Fiona said, 'You should draw a picture of it, Helen.'

I laughed.

'I don't think Mummy or Daddy would like me to draw pictures of things like that. Come along, I think you had better go to bed.'

Alan was wandering about the dark room and he came, finally, and stood by us, hands in pockets, looking down at the street which was now practically empty, except for one or two jolly-looking sailors rolling unsteadily up the steps of the House of Sin.

'Why didn't you go to art school, Helen?' Alan asked unexpectedly.

I turned and asked in surprise, 'Art school? What do you mean?'

The response was truly brotherly.

'Art school, stupid. What do you think I meant?

You know, when you got the scholarship. I always meant to ask you, but there never seems to be much peace for conversations.'

'Scholarship? I have never won a scholarship, you know that.'

'Heavens, you are dumb! Don't you remember—you sat for it when you got caught and had to go back to school.'

Alan looked at me as if I had lost my reason.

'Oh, that. I didn't get it. I never heard anything about it, after Mr Piper entered my name for it.'

'But—but—' stammered Alan, 'Mr Browning—the headmaster—asked me only the other day how you were getting on, and I meant to ask you what happened. If you got it, why didn't you go to art school? It would have been wonderful for you.'

The episode in the street had left me rather trembly and I sat down suddenly as a horrible suspicion went through my head.

Had I indeed won the scholarship? If I had, my parents would have been informed of it. Had they refused it on my behalf? They were perfectly entitled to do so—schooling was not compulsory after the age of fourteen.

This idea was so repulsive to me that at first I could not accept it. Surely, my parents would realize that it was a wonderful opportunity for me. Surely, they would have my interests at heart. It must be a mistake—I could not have won.

Yet if Alan's headmaster said I had won, won I had. He would not forget that one of the few scholarships available at that time had been awarded to his school.

'If I won,' I said through clenched teeth, 'I was never told about it.'

'How queer,' said Alan, and Fiona's enormous eyes widened even farther as she, too, considered the matter. 'You'd better ask Mummy or Daddy.'

Such a rush of pain went through my skimpy body that I wrapped my arms around myself and leaned my head nearly down to my knees. In little gasps, I said, 'I don't think I want to ask them. I don't think I can bear to.'

'I'll ask,' said Alan stoutly. 'I'm not afraid.'

'Oh no, Alan,' I said. 'You will only be told that it's none of your business—and the whole family will be upset.'

He knew I was right and was silent.

I was almost certain in my mind that my parents had just not told me because my attendance at school for a prolonged period would have compounded their difficulties; they would have lost their baby-sitter and housekeeper—and they would have had to pay a substitute.

I rocked myself backwards and forwards, as my touching belief that my parents, even if they had not much love for me, would do their best for me, and that they had always done so, died. I was in agony. The research into the ruthless exploitation of the eldest child was still far in the future, and there was no explanation to console my childish despair.

Two bony pairs of arms were quietly wrapped around me, and two young heads came close to mine.

'Never mind, Helen. Please don't cry. What's a silly old scholarship, anyway? You got it. You're clever. You'll get another one some day.'

I did not cry. I could not.

Gently, I told Alan to go to bed.

I pushed Fiona quietly towards our pile of newspapers laid on top of the old door; the papers had an irritating habit of spreading themselves on to the floor as well. I laid myself down on them, facing the wall, and pulled my knees up tight like a baby in the womb. If I took little breaths and lay perfectly still, perhaps the pain inside me would go away.

I slept little, but felt calmer in the morning. The children were dispatched to school. Mother went out. Father hurriedly prepared to go down to the labour exchange. As he struggled to neaten himself, I asked him diffidently, 'Did you ever hear anything about the art scholarship I sat for?'

He looked at me abstractedly. 'Art scholarship?'

'Yes. You remember—the one I sat for while I was at school—just before my birthday.'

He was quiet for a moment and sat staring at his shoelace which had broken.

'Yes,' he said at last. 'We did hear something about it. It couldn't be awarded to you.'

'But did I win?' I asked in a whisper.

'You did. However, when we said that you were born in Cheshire, we were told that you were ineligible and should never have been entered for it. Cheshire comes under a different education committee.'

'Why didn't you tell me about it?'

'There seemed no point—children get upset about these things.'

I nodded. I could not speak because my teeth were chattering so much from the nervous effort I had made to ask about the scholarship.

I hugged Edward to me, while he seized his battered trilby hat and departed. I could hear the loose sole on one of his shoes flipping on each step.

All that morning, I thought about the scholarship. Pressed against the glass-topped biscuit tins in the tiny grocery store, the rancid smell of the bacon-cutting machine enveloping me, I had a long wait in the tiny shop while the grocery woman measured out single ounces of tea, sugar and margarine, climbed her ladder to reach down tins of condensed milk and had long arguments with several desperate women trying to extend their credit with her.

By the time it was my turn to be served with the twopennyworth of rice I wanted, I had come to the conclusion that I must accept my father's explanation, despite the fact that the school had known my place of birth.

Chapter twenty-four

Dully, sulkily, I continued to look after the children through the winter, trying to dry their rags when they came in rain-soaked, trying to buy with pennies enough food for nine, living in a world where handkerchiefs, toilet-paper, hot water and soap ranked as unobtainable luxuries. Fortunately, the stomach can become accustomed to very little food, and the children did not now cry very often that they were hungry, as long as they had bread and potatoes.

In an effort to make sales and increase their profits, even the more reputable local shopkeepers now cut margarine into quarter pounds, though it cost only fourpence to buy a whole pound, and opened pots of jam to sell at a penny a tablespoonful—bring your own cup. One tiny corner shop, presided over by a skinny harridan whose hands never seemed to have been washed, would make up a pennyworth of almost anything that could be divided up. This resulted in a very high price per pound—but if one has only a penny one has little choice in the matter.

A learned professor published a detailed menu showing that a full-grown man could eat well on four shillings a week but it was of no help to me. Four shillings per week per head to spend on food would have represented to us an unattainable height of luxurious living.

In the city council, a stout, outspoken Labour couple tore into the mayor, aldermen and councillors with bitter tongues on behalf of the unemployed, the homeless and the aged. Mr and Mrs Braddock—our Bessie, as Mrs Braddock was known to many—started a lifelong battle on behalf of the poor of Liverpool. On the docks, the Communists made inroads among the despised and ill-treated dock labourers, the results of which are still apparent in the labour unrest rampant in the docks of Liverpool forty years later.

City health officials looked in despair at horrifying infant mortality rates and at a general death rate nearly the highest in the country. Nobody, of course, died of starvation—only of malnutrition.

The Roman Catholic Church and the Church of England continued to build themselves a cathedral apiece and solicited donations.

My parents at about this time seemed to have given up all hope of any real future and struggled on from one day to the next, too dulled by hunger and privation to plan how they might get out of the morass they were in.

My father tended to sit silently indoors now, only going to the labour exchange and the public assistance committee, because he was more ragged than the most poverty-stricken tramp I ever encountered. My mother still made valiant efforts to keep her appearance reasonable so that she could apply to shops and offices for work.

One sunny Sunday in March, however, Father decided he could stand the rank atmosphere of the house no more and he and Brian went for a walk in the town, which was fairly deserted on Sundays. Father always feared being arrested for vagrancy, but he hoped police would be few and far between on this day of rest.

Two hours later, a petrified Brian came rushing up the stairs and into our living-room, where I was rocking Edward to sleep in his Chariot. He buried his face in my shoulder.

'Daddy's been arrested,' he cried.

I jumped up in alarm and Edward cried out as the rocking ceased.

'Oh, Heavens! Whatever did he do?'

Brian continued to sob in my arms in sheer fright.

'Tell me, Brian. What did he do? Did he steal some cigarettes?'

I felt Brian nod negatively.

'Well, he must have done *something*!'

'He didn't do anything.'

I knelt down and hugged Brian close.

'Well, tell me what happened. Come on, love, tell me.'

Brian's sobs reduced to sniffs and with all the maddening long-windedness of children, he said, 'Well, we walked down into the town and we looked in Cooper's and MacSymon's windows at all the lovely food—they had peaches in brandy in Cooper's. And then we looked in the furniture stores and Daddy showed me a jade idol in Bunney's, at the corner of Whitechapel. Then we walked up Lord Street—opposite Frisby Dykes—and looked at the tailors' shops in North John Street.'

'Yes, yes,' I said impatiently.

'Well, then Daddy wanted to look at the gentlemen's shops in the arcade in Cook Street—and it was at the corner of Cook Street that we saw this strange man.'

'What kind of a strange man?'

'Well, he was big and nicely dressed with lovely polished boots. Daddy said he was a plain-clothes policeman—and we were both a bit scared—but Daddy said to keep on walking as if there was nothing wrong.' Brian wiped his nose on the cuff of his jersey. 'So we did—and we looked at all the pipes and tobacco and suits and things and this man started to walk up behind us.'

'What did you do?'

'We started to walk faster and faster and when we got to Castle Street and turned the corner, we ran like anything and the man ran after us. Daddy pushed me into a doorway by a pillar and told me to stay there, and he went on running. When the policeman had passed me by, I peeped out—and the policeman had his hand on Daddy's shoulder like they do in books.' Brian burst into tears again. 'So I doubled back down Cook Street and came home.' he wailed.

'Never mind, Brian. I am sure Daddy will be all right. It is probably a mistake. We'll tell Mummy about it. You just wait here a minute.'

Mother was taking a little nap in the bedroom and I was very afraid that if I woke her with Brian's story she would have one of her periodic outbursts of temper, or perhaps have hysterics; but she sat on the edge of the old mattress while she considered it, and then said quite sensibly, 'I don't think we can do anything except wait. We don't know which police station he is in. I expect they will let us know what he is charged with.'

Her calmness calmed Brian and me, and he went off to play with Tony, while I went back to my book. I could not read, however. I realized suddenly how much officialdom Father coped with on our behalf. Without him, we were defenceless against those who would put us in the workhouse.

I began to shake with fear, fear for my father and terror at the inhumanity of the workhouse.

Chapter twenty-five

Edward had been put to bed, and Mother and I sat on our two chairs staring out of the window, united by our worry over Father. Occasionally, there was a steady clang-clang and flashes of electricity from behind the houses opposite as tram cars a couple of streets away swayed around a corner. The irate 'whip-whip-whip' of a naval vessel making its way upriver competed with the noise of the trams, and, in the far distance, the shunting yard at Edge Hill lent a background of clanking to the other sounds. No cars passed—the district was too poor for anything more ambitious than a horsedrawn milk cart. A boy came by on a bicycle and two giggling girls paused to gossip under the gaslight outside.

A car drew up outside our house so quietly that we were at first unaware of its presence. Someone got out.

'Good night, and—thank you very much.'

It was Father. His voice was unmistakable.

We jumped up as the front door slammed in the distance. We could hear Father's laborious step on the stairs. He was whistling 'It's a long way to Tipperary'.

Never had the old tune sounded so welcome. If he could whistle, things were not that bad. We ran to the top of the stairs, six small grey ghosts and one adult, and peered over the banisters.

'Hello, children. Is Brian safely home?'

'Yes,' we chorused. 'What happened to you?'

Father emerged from the darkness of the stairwell. He was smiling broadly and his step was jaunty.

'It's a long story. Come in and I'll tell you.'

He even smiled at his wife, I noticed, and I could see in the small light from the street the sudden, unreasoned hope spring in Mother's eyes when she saw Father's cheerful expression.

'Come in. I have lots to tell you, and you are all old enough to hear it.'

He led us, like the Pied Piper, into the living-room.

'Tell us,' we implored, hunger, filth, misery forgotten.

Father made the most of his moment. He settled himself in a chair and took Avril on his knee. He was still beaming.

He cleared his throat.

'I expect Brian told you about our walk.'

'Yes,' we said impatiently.

'What happened when the policeman caught you?' asked Brian.

'He wanted to see my tie.'

'Your tie?' exclaimed Mother.

'Yes, my old All Saints tie. I thought he was mad, but I was afraid to do anything else but pull it out and show it to him.'

Avril shoved herself around on Father's lap and pulled out the sad remains of his old school tie. It looked the same as usual.

'When he saw it, he opened his own overcoat at the neck, and he was wearing the same tie—I mean a nice, new version of it.'

Alan whistled.

'He asked me how I came to be down and out.

'"It is a long story," I told him. Suddenly, my legs began to give under me—we had walked a very long way, you know, and I get faint very easily these days. He saw that I was feeling ill, and said it didn't matter.

'"Come and sit in the car for a few minutes," he said. "I have to wait for a colleague who has business in this building here."

'I was thankful to get into the car and sit down. Almost immediately his colleague came and was surprised to find me in the car—I suppose he thought the man on the beat would normally deal with vagrants like me. However, my friend of the tie put the car into gear and said that we were going to go to the police canteen.

'"Don't get the wind up," he said to me. "I think you can do with a meal."

'I felt too weak to care what happened to me, but a meal sounded a wonderful idea. So away we went to the police station and through to the canteen.' He paused reminiscently, and then went on, 'He stood me a full meal—stew and steamed pudding.'

'Delicious,' we murmured enviously.

'And when I had finished, he gave me a cigarette, and he seemed such a decent sort that I told him about everything that happened to us.

'He did not interrupt me once—and his friend sat

and watched me. At the end they looked at each other —and mulled over what I had said.

'He asked me quite a lot about our school, and then said he remembered me. He left All Saints the year after I was sent there, but he recollected that blow on the head I got from a cricket ball; it caused a good deal of consternation because I took a long time to come round and they were not able to get a doctor for some time.'

'Childhood episodes do stick in one's mind,' said Mother.

I looked at her in surprise. It had never occurred to me that she understood the world of children or that she had been a child herself. Nanny was the person who understood children.

Father continued, 'He said he thought he could get me a job with the City.'

'Really?' queried Mother, frank disbelief in her voice.

'Yes. I told him that I had made every endeavour to obtain employment—but now I was so shabby it was impossible. I said frankly that the rags he saw me in were all I had, that I had not even soap to wash myself with.

'And do you know what he said then? It was most unexpected.'

'No?' we breathed.

'He said the school would undoubtedly outfit me from their benevolent fund—I used to subscribe to that, you know, but I never thought of it in connection with myself. He is going to write tonight to ask for immediate help. Meantime, he is going to talk to the City about me.'

'How wonderful,' Alan cried.

'Yes, it is,' said Mother.

Fiona began to cry slowly; they were tears of relief. Her illness had left her with practically no stamina, but she rarely complained and, I believe, most of the family hardly realized she existed.

She was a great contrast to her lively, noisy younger sister, who now said unsympathetically, 'Oh, shut up, Fiona. You're supposed to be glad, not sad!' And cuddling up to Father, she inquired, 'Shall we be able to have a roast joint?'

We all laughed, and afterwards, we sat up late while we discussed every detail of this miraculous encounter. Even Mother was quite excited and animated about it.

The days dragged by, however, and nothing happened. Father stood in his queues; Mother got two days' work, looking after a special photography display in a store which found that cameras were a slow-moving item amid the general penury in the city. We ate fish and chips one night as a result of this windfall, and Mother was able to buy some stockings, makeup, etc., so that she could look more respectable and, therefore, more employable. We always despaired about our lack of simple articles, like scissors, combs, hair grips, things one takes for granted in a normal home.

At last, when we had given up standing on the front steps waiting for the postman and the spring had again gone out of Father's step, the plain-clothes man called in person. He was let in by Miss Sinford, who fortunately did not connect him with the police, and he clumped up to our evil-smelling den.

Father was out.

Mother received him with her usual grace and sat down on one chair, while he, in response to her invitation, lowered himself cautiously on to the other. Most of the children were at school; Avril, Edward and I, however, stood in a group and stared goggle-eyed at our saviour.

All Saints School, the visitor said with a friendly grin, had made a grant sufficient to outfit Father completely, provided he shopped carefully. He stopped, his beefy face showing some concern. 'Er—the school has asked me to administer the grant—and—er—I hate to say this—they want me to go with your husband to shop. Now, I don't mind in the least—but I hope he won't be offended.'

'I am sure he won't,' said Mother with unusual briskness. 'However, you will appreciate that he is in no state to go out with you—or enter a decent shop.' Her voice broke, and she looked as if she was going to weep. She recovered herself, however, and said as she studied her chapped, unmanicured hands, 'Do you think the grant committee would mind giving enough money first to buy some soap for a bath—and a haircut?'

The plain-clothes man leaned forward and patted her hand.

'I am sure that would be all right. I do understand—you know, in my job I see a lot of things.' He thought for a moment, and then added, 'The public swimming-baths have also places where you can take a full bath—I think it costs sixpence—and they provide soap and towels, as well.'

I marvelled that a man whose life had obviously been comfortable, should understand that it was likely we had no towels.

'Oh, how lovely,' I said impetuously, only to be silenced by an icy look from Mother.

I could hear Father dragging himself slowly up our endless staircase, and, picking up Edward, I ran to meet him and whispered about the visitor.

When Father entered, the man rose courteously and held out his hand. Father clasped it. I doubt if anyone had felt that his hand was worth shaking since our arrival in Liverpool.

Father's fatigue fell away from him. It was arranged that the policeman would buy some underwear and bring it to us. He also said gently that, if Father would accept them, he could bring a pair of flannels and an old tweed jacket from his own home, so that Father could go into a store without embarrassment to choose a suit and raincoat.

It was obvious that Father felt his humiliation very deeply. His face was sadder than I had ever seen it. He appreciated, however, the great kindness of this police officer on whom he had no other call than that they had attended the same public school, and he thanked him gratefully for his thoughtfulness.

'I have tentatively arranged for you to see this man in the Municipal Buildings at ten o'clock next Friday morning,' said our friend, standing up and handing Father a slip of paper.

Father nodded, took the slip of paper and carefully laid it on the dusty mantelpiece.

'I don't know how I am going to repay you for all this,' he said.

'Don't mention it,' said the plain-clothes man cheerfully. 'Very glad to be able to help—put it down to the old school tie!'

The underwear, trousers, jacket and a shirt arrived in a brown paper parcel, addressed to Father and left on our landing. When I asked our incorrigible old lookout, Miss Sinford, who had delivered the parcel, she insisted that nobody had called at the house that day. I can only imagine that someone like the milkman, who still brought Edward his pint of milk, must have been asked to bring them in, so as to avoid a police car being yet again stationed outside the house. Miss Sinford would not have counted the milkman as being a person; like the postman, the public assistance visitor and the poor, he was always with us.

Armed with five shillings given him for the purpose, Father went to the public baths and found that, indeed, a spotlessly clean bath, towels and soap, not to speak of hot water, were all his for the sum of sixpence. Apparently, he spent so much time in the bath that the attendant threatened to charge him another sixpence or empty the bath if Father did not come out.

He dressed himself in his clean clothes, rolled up his rags into a bundle, except for his broken-down shoes, which he had, perforce, to retain, dumped the bundle into a litter-bin outside the baths, and went for a shave and a haircut.

When he came home, I hardly knew him. Although the jacket and pants were too large for him and his shoes were a mess, he had an aura of respectability about him that did more for our spirits than anything heretofore.

There was still some money left from the five shillings, and Father sent Alan and Fiona to buy fish and chips and peas and a packet of cigarettes. I hoped that All Saints School did not learn, by some extraordinary means, that we had spent two and sixpence of their money on food instead of on outfitting Father, and, even worse, sixpence on cigarettes.

The detective picked Father up two days later, and they went together to buy a good ready-made suit, another shirt, a raincoat and a pair of shoes.

It seemed to Alan and me that we had got our Father back from the dead, because he now looked to us as he had done before we came to Liverpool, except that he had shrunk considerably.

Without any difficulty, Father got the clerical post for which he was interviewed—the detective was apparently sufficient reference. He was infinitely better educated and more widely experienced in the business world than the type of clerk the City was normally able to command, and, except when it came to running his own affairs, had a clear and analytical mind.

Though the post was a temporary one, he soon discovered that many of his colleagues had been 'temporary' for ten years or more—it saved the impoverished City from having to provide pensions for them.

He served the city of his birth faithfully and well. Later, he became part of its permanent staff, and, when his department was taken over by the Government as part of the new National Health scheme, he became a civil servant and gradually worked his way upwards. He was never very well-to-do again; on the other hand, he was never again reduced to penury, and he managed to enjoy the latter part of his life in a modest way.

Chapter twenty-six

It seemed reasonable to assume that Father's going to work would make a considerable difference to our standard of living and, consequently, to my own life. The hope that had sustained me through all our bad times had been pinned on this one point. Now, at last, perhaps I would be allowed to go to evening school or take some kind of work and Mother would take her rightful place at home. Life, however, went on exactly as before as far as Edward and I were concerned.

There was no more money to spend on food than there had been before. Wages were so low in Liverpool that Father did not earn much more than he had received when unemployed; the difference was swallowed up in tram fares, lunches and cigarettes—and, of course, the need to keep himself clean and tidy.

Childish hopes waxed again when Mother began to get more regular employment; she was proving to be an excellent saleswoman and was recommended by one employer to another for moving specially difficult merchandise. If she must work, I argued, she might soon earn enough to employ a girl to look after Edward and so release me. In her case also, however, she had first to meet her expenses and then extend her wardrobe so that she looked decent enough to continue work.

Father's being employed sparked a desire in my parents to find a better place in which to live. It had been hopeless even to consider this while he was unemployed—no landlord was prepared to rent a house to an unemployed man with seven children. A city clerk was a different matter, and they finally obtained a neat-looking terrace house with three bedrooms, a sitting-room and a living-room. It had no bathroom, and the water-closet was at the far end of a soot-begrimed back yard. Cooking was done on an old-fashioned coal range in the living-room. It was unfurnished and the rent was seventeen shillings a week. It was a great improvement upon our present accommodation, though not to be compared with the home we had abandoned to our creditors. The relief from climbing stairs was tremendous and, of course, we would save ten shillings a week in rent.

Moving was not difficult as we had almost nothing to move, and suddenly it seemed as if we needed everything much more than we had done before—I suppose it was because we had a whole house to ourselves.

There are always sharks willing to oblige the foolish. In their eagerness to become once more established, my parents bought a set of drawing-room furniture and curtains for the whole house on hire purchase. A hint that we needed beds met with a sharp rebuke. An iniquitous system of 'cheques' enabled them to purchase bedding, crockery and kitchen tools, all of which we badly needed. The cheques, however, were peddled by finance companies and consisted of a permit to buy a given amount of goods from a limited list of stores at greatly inflated prices. Repayment and interest were collected in weekly instalments by the companies' agents. The goods rarely lasted until they were paid for and the rate of interest was high. This type of indebtedness was very prevalent in Liverpool.

This plunge into debt meant that Mother had to work, whether she wished to or not, and I had to care for the children. My little faint hope which had lighted my way through so much was doused, and dark clouds of melancholy gathered round me and were made worse by indifferent health. I watched as the heavy weekly payments drained away money urgently needed for clothing and food. Sufficient did trickle down to buy new running-shoes for the older children; but Edward and Avril had the Chariot to ride in and I did not have to go anywhere except to the shops.

Avril started school in September and Alan would be leaving it at Christmas, a poignant reminder that everybody was making a little progress except me. Would Edward and I always be chained together? Would our needs always be at the bottom of the family's list? Would I always be hungry?

My despair was abysmal. I felt I had no one to turn to for comfort or help. Even hours of weeping as I went about my household tasks failed to relieve the depression which engulfed me.

My father had spent some time talking with Alan about what he would do when he finished school, and it had been agreed that he would try for a job as office boy in a firm where there was a certain amount of training given and where he might sit professionally set examinations. Amongst other openings, this gave him a choice of estate agencies, banking and shipping firms. A bright fourteen-year-old could do better than his forty-year-old father, as far as choice of jobs was concerned.

Nobody asked me what I would like to do. My role in life had been silently decided for me. It was obvious that my parents had no intention of allowing me to be anything but an unpaid, unrespected housekeeper. With all the passion of a fifteen-year-old, I decided that such a life was not worth living.

A foggy September day saw Edward being pushed in the Chariot along the gently heaving Georges Landing-Stage. The Birkenhead ferry was slowly leaving the stage and vanishing into the misty river. The shore hands were coiling up their ropes ready for the next ferry-boat. Upon the invisible river invisible ferries clanged their bells and were answered by freighters sounding their foghorns. Behind me, the lights of the Royal Liver and Cunard buildings barely penetrated the unseasonable gloom. At one end of the landing-stage a pilot-boat had just returned from beyond the bar, after collecting the pilot from an outgoing ship. At the other end a group of customs officers chatted, their raincoats gleaming with moisture. No passengers were waiting for the ferries.

Carefully, I tucked the cover round the sleeping Edward and made sure that the hood protected him from the slight wind which occasionally lifted the fog. I hoped someone kind would find him and take him home and love him. I propped the pram against a post so that it could not roll into the water, and left it.

Very slowly, I approached the chain fence that stopped pedestrians from falling off the edge of the landing-stage. When I felt its cold links against my shins, I paused. Some three feet still separated me from the swirling water, invisible for the moment because of the mist.

I stepped over the fence and took a couple of paces more. I could see the water now. Everyone in Liverpool knew that if anybody fell into the water at the end of the landing-stage the tremendous undertow would suck them right under the stage to certain death. It would not take long.

I was shivering violently, nauseated by the thought of the oily water and the choking death which seemed to be the only available way of committing suicide. At the same time I could not bear the thought of turning back into a life which was unendurable to me.

I took a large breath preparatory to jumping.

A huge paw clamped suddenly down on my shoulders and a voice behind me said, 'And phwhat in the Name o' God do you think you're doing?'

The sudden interruption was so terrifying that my knees buckled under me, and another huge hand grasped the back of my dress, and I was yanked bodily back over the fence.

Supported only by the iron grip on my shoulder, I found myself looking at the middle fastenings of a sailor's waterproofs. I followed the line of the fastenings upwards with my eyes and found myself looking into the rubicund face of the pilot who had just landed. The water dripping off the peak of his cap did not obscure the concern in his eyes.

I could not answer. I was fainting.

'Mother of Heaven, you gave me a fright,' he said sharply.

I must have fainted completely, because the next thing I remember was being in a little canteen and having hot tea forced between my lips by a careworn woman in grubby white.

'Och, you'll be all right now,' she said in a rich Irish voice. 'Sure, and you frightened the Captain out of his wits.'

I put my head down on the tea-stained table by me until the world ceased whirling round me. I felt dreadfully cold and so tired that all I could think about was sleep.

After a minute or two, I straightened up. My rescuer said heartily, 'Well, now, you'll be all right. And don't you step over that chain again, young lady, or you'll fall right in.' He turned to the hovering waitress, put his hand in his trouser pocket, took out a coin and gave it to her. 'Here's for the tea. I've no doubt the gel will be all right in a minute or two. I have to report to the office.'

He looked down at me, his face beaming.

'Goodbye, young lady.'

'Goodbye,' I said, 'and thank you.'

I drank the rest of the tea gratefully and, at the urging of the waitress, sat for about ten minutes to rest. Gradually, my numbed brain began to work once more. I knew I could not screw up enough courage to go out into the fog and try to jump again; yet I could not stay long where I was.

I suddenly remembered Edward.

It seemed that I would have to go home, because there was nowhere else to go.

Slowly I got up, thanked the waitress and, with many protestations that I was now quite well, I went to collect the Chariot. Edward was sitting up and whimpering.

The children were home when I arrived, slowly dragging the Chariot after me.

'You haven't got tea ready,' said Avril indignantly, 'and Alan can't find a knife to cut the bread.'

Chapter twenty-seven

Very few people who try to commit suicide really want to kill themselves; their attempt is a last hysterical cry for help. When willing hands are outstretched to aid them and some effort is made to alter the circumstances that drove them to such despair, they will try again to cope with life. I was no exception; two people had been very kind to me and I was extremely touched by the fact. On my return home, the necessity of dealing with the children's needs steadied me and Fiona's loving help with these tasks comforted me. I clung to her when we went to bed and drew some strength from the touch of her frail body and from her gentle spirit. By morning, something of my normal common sense had returned.

The day was as bright and clear as its predecessor had been foggy and damp. The family dispersed to school and to work, Avril going proudly to school holding Fiona's hand. Edward and I were left to contemplate a bare house, except for our shiny new drawing-room, which I dusted very carefully from time to time. The few dishes were soon washed, what beds and substitutes for beds we had were soon tidied and the fire allowed to go out until evening. Though still very exhausted, my spirits rose a little as Edward and I went out to buy food.

Outside the elementary school a fresh poster announced the opening of evening schools that day for the winter session. I contemplated it with a feeling of hopelessness. It would certainly be inconvenient to my parents if I was out in the evening—they would almost certainly veto any such idea.

The hopelessness gave way to a slow burning anger, and then to determination. I would try once more to go to school. Perhaps if Father and Mother were faced with a *fait accompli*, they would give in. I therefore took Fiona and Alan into my confidence at tea-time, and they agreed to help with Edward and Avril while I was away and to cover up for me if my parents noticed my absence.

When both parents went out to the library, I slipped away to the school and joined a crowd of youngsters moving slowly through the entrance.

A young teacher asked me, as I stood uncertainly in the hall, what courses I wanted to take.

I was aghast. I had no idea what courses to take. All I wanted was to continue my education from where I had left off nearly three years earlier.

'I am not sure,' I managed to mutter. 'I know I need to learn arithmetic.'

She pointed to an open doorway farther down the hall.

'Try bookkeeping,' she said kindly, as she turned to attend to another lost youngster.

I did not know what bookkeeping was, but I was so scared of the shifting, staring young people crowding round me, some of whom sniggered when they looked at me, that I bolted down the corridor and turned thankfully into a classroom holding about a dozen boys and girls and a young lady teacher.

The classroom, with its walls of frosted glass and varnished wood, had enough desks, made to accommodate two pupils each, to swallow about fifty children; four electric lights hanging from the ceiling failed to illuminate it adequately; the bare wooden floor was grey from years of tramping boots. Facing the pupils' desks was a high, single desk for the teacher and near it stood a blackboard on an easel. The air smelled of chalk dust and damp woollens. A dingy, uninspiring room it was, but it was made more lively by the buzz of conversation among the pupils.

As I came through the door, the teacher looked up, and a pall of silence fell upon the gathering. The mouths of the neatly clad, well-scrubbed young people fell open. Then a well-curled blonde began to giggle. She hastily stuffed her handkerchief into her mouth, while a derisive grin spread through the class.

The dim electric lights became blurred, as tears of realization welled up. I must have been a horrible sight, with hair draggling round my shoulders, its greasiness combed through with my fingers; septic acne sores all over my face; hands with dirty, broken nails, sticking out from an ancient cardigan with huge holes in its elbows, no blouse, and a gym slip shiny with accumulated grime. Red blotches of bug bites were clearly visible on my naked legs and thighs, our new house being equally as verminous as our old one, and my toes stuck out of the holes in the laceless gym shoes on my feet.

I fought back my tears. I was made of better stuff than the children before me. My family had been fighting England's battles while theirs were still serfs fit only to keep pigs. I would show them.

Lifting my ugly hooked nose into the air I stared calmly back at them. Gradually, the grins were replaced by uneasy looks and they began self-consciously to talk to each other again.

There ought to be a special medal for understanding teachers. I do not know what prompted the small, perfumed occupant of the teacher's podium to come down from her perch, put her arm around my shoulders, regardless of the fact that I was obviously verminous, and say sweetly, 'Do you want to take bookkeeping, too, my dear?'

She was taken aback visibly when I answered her in my clearest English—she must have expected a strong Liverpool accent.

'I had hoped to learn arithmetic, ma'am. Do you teach it?'

She recovered herself and guided me to an unoccupied double desk at the front of the class, as she replied.

'No. This school has only commercial courses—it is assumed that you will have done the necessary arithmetic already in day-school.'

The other children were again staring at me, and she turned to them and said sharply, 'Please fill in the forms I have given to you. I will take them in in a few minutes.' She turned back to me. 'Now,' she said, 'what kind of arithmetic do you want to learn?'

I explained my lack of algebra, that my academic training had come to an end at a chapter called 'Compound Interest', and that was as much as I knew.

She sat casually on the desk in front of me and looked me over thoughtfully.

'When did you leave school?' she asked.

I explained about leaving school when I was twelve and the subsequent glorious six weeks I had enjoyed just before my fourteenth birthday, and about Edward and Avril and the family.

'I see,' she said, drawing her pale blue cardigan more tightly around her. 'Do you want to train for any particular occupation?'

An occupation seemed so far away, so unattainable, that I said hastily, 'I have not thought of anything special—except that I would like to be able to help the hungry, unemployed people round me.'

She smiled at this and suggested, after some consideration, that I should take the standard commercial course, in which she taught bookkeeping. In addition, she would guide me through a basic course in arithmetic and algebra, which I could do as part of my homework.

'If you take the commercial course, it will form a basis for several different ways of earning a living,' she said practically.

I agreed because it seemed that I had no choice and, at least, she had opened a tiny door of hope for me. Yesterday there had been no hope; today there was a faint gleam.

She lent me her pen and I filled in the form she gave me, while the other members of the class handed theirs in, had them checked and were told to report back two nights later to commence their instruction.

When the classroom had emptied, I went to the teacher's desk and handed in my form.

'Fine,' she said cheerfully. 'Now, that will be half a crown; and here is a list of books you will need. They will cost about ten and sixpence.'

I was stunned. My tiny hope door slammed shut. I managed to gasp out, 'I did not know there was a fee for evening school—I thought it was like elementary day-school—provided by the city—so—so I haven't brought any money.'

The amounts were so small; but they might just as well have been hundreds of pounds, because I did not have them.

The teacher was collecting her papers, and she replied, without looking up, 'Well, never mind. Ask your mother to give you the fee for next time—and you can get the books from any bookshop sometime during the week. Now, be here on Thursday at 7.30, remember.'

'Yes, ma'am,' I said heavily. 'Good night—and thank you.'

I turned and marched out.

As soon as I was outside the school, I rushed to a corner behind a buttress of the building where the street lamps' rays did not penetrate, and, putting my face against the damp, red bricks of the wall, I cried hopelessly and helplessly until not another tear would come. I cried from the frightful pent-up tension of yesterday and the disappointment and humiliation of today. I cried because I was drifting helplessly on a sea of life for which I had not been prepared and which I did not understand. I cried for the perfect peace and safe refuge of my grandmother's house by the sea. I cried because I could not cross the Mersey to reach the green fields and wild seashores I loved.

Frozen and exhausted, I stuffed my blue hands into my cardigan pockets and turned towards home.

I took two steps and stopped. In my pocket was a hard little card. Mother's library card!

Books! Perhaps the library had the books I needed. If they had, I could keep on reborrowing them, I argued. If it was not yet nine o'clock, I could run to the library and look.

I tore through the streets, taking shortcuts through every alleyway I could, regardless of danger. Dogs barked and cats and rats scampered away at the sound of my thudding feet.

I squeezed into the library's muggy warmth five minutes before closing-time, the list of books clutched in one hand.

Feverishly, I sought through the index. Had they got them? Had they?

They had.

A few minutes later, I emerged, equipped with text-books.

At home I poured out my adventures to Alan and Fiona. It was a long time since I had had such a conversation with any of the family, and they were jubilant about the enrolment and the books. Alan offered to lend me his pen each evening.

'If you don't remind them, perhaps they'll forget that you owe them half a crown,' he said hopefully, in reference to the school fee.

'They will have to,' I said woodenly, 'because I am going to school, no matter what happens.'

Brave words, but I still needed at least one notebook, and, as I put the family to bed, I worried more about obtaining twopence to buy a notebook than I worried about the half-crown.

On Wednesday, I found a piece of comb in a gutter and painfully attacked my tangled mop of hair with it. Mother had a tiny pocket-comb, which of a necessity she had kept for herself, because she could not make herself neat for work if the precious object was broken. Father was fortunately almost bald. The children went uncombed and, mostly, unwashed, until more regular work enabled Mother to buy a strong comb for use by the family.

If ever I became rich, I told myself savagely, I would help to provide a basic kit for the more unfortunate of this world. It would consist of a large bar of kitchen soap, a pile of old white cloth, a pile of newspapers (newspapers can be made into beds, handkerchiefs, toilet-paper, warm padding under thin garments, draught excluders, makeshift window-pane replacements, firing, and a thousand other uses), some razor blades, for beards and nails, and a comb. One has to be without such small amenities to appreciate their worth.

My appearance was not much improved when I again presented myself at school, quailing at the thought of not being able to pay the fee.

The bookkeeping teacher was as kind as before and, after she had given the class some work to do, she brought over to me a small arithmetic text-book, told me to take it home, read the instructions in the first chapter and see if I could work my way through the problems based on them. She promised to mark the work for me.

Several children had no notebooks, so she provided some paper both for their work and mine. I soon became absorbed in the struggle to make my sluggish brain work, and forgot the silent distaste with which my fellow students were treating me.

Halfway through the evening, the class was taken over by a thin, energetic teacher who was to instruct us in English grammar. She proved equally as friendly and as helpful as the bookkeeping teacher.

Evening school has a long tradition in Lancashire and all over the city classrooms were crowded with young people desirous of improving their education. Again I was following in the footsteps of the humble weavers about whom my old gentleman in the park had told me.

It was Fiona who, accidentally, let fall one evening the information to my parents that I had gone to evening school.

They were rightly angry that I had taken such action without consulting them and both stormed at me about it.

It would have brought more wrath down upon my head if I had defended myself by saying that I had long since concluded that consultation was waste of time, so I just stated firmly, 'I have been going to evening school and I'm going to continue going.' I had nothing to lose but my chains.

'Where did you get the money from?' asked Mother suddenly, her voice full of suspicion.

I had to own up that I owed the Liverpool education committee two shillings and sixpence—and, worse still, I needed two shillings more for book-keeping books and other notebooks.

This led to further recrimination, and, with unusual impudence, I asked, 'Would you prefer that I stole it rather than owed it?'

Such insolence was so unlike me, that it brought my parents up short.

Mother said quietly, in a tone more normal than anything she had used since we had arrived in Liverpool, 'No, we would not. Probably we shall manage to find the money somehow.'

This sudden reasonableness frightened me more than if she had had hysterics. I had become so used to her being ill and being unable to pay normal attention to us, that I had forgotten that new hope had recently entered her life and was helping her to get better quite rapidly. Once I had got over the shock and stopped staring at her, round-eyed and fearful, I was piteously grateful.

The following Tuesday evening, hair neatly combed into a bun held with a piece of string, and wearing Fiona's cardigan, which was reasonably clean, I ran through the dank September evening to school. Hot in the palm of my hand was a half-crown, the most important coin I was ever to possess. I was to spend seven years in evening schools and I managed in each subsequent year to win a small scholarship, which covered the increasing fees and my books, as I advanced through the system; so that I did not cost my parents anything more.

The electric lights had already been turned on in the school and a great shaft of light blazed out across the pavement from the main doorway. It was early and no one else was entering. I looked up the stone steps, hollowed out by hundreds of feet, through the hall and up the staircase to the second floor.

The welcoming doorway was my hoping door; the worn stone steps my ladder to the stars. Kind hands, earnest people, were there to help me up them.

I bared my yellow teeth in a smile of pure happiness, charged across the threshold and galloped up the stairs.